GEORGE A. PROCTOR is a member of the Faculty of Music at the University of Western Ontario, where he teaches in the Department of Music History.

Canadian music has come of age in the twentieth century. The number of composers of serious music has grown remarkably, particularly in the last thirty-five years, and Canadian compositions are now performed worldwide. Yet listeners are not always familiar with the names or the music of composers such as Barbara Pentland, Claude Champagne, Serge Garant, and Harry Somers, in part because commentaries are rare and recordings and scores are often difficult to find. This book discusses, in historical sequence, selected works of approximately 125 representative composers, combining detailed descriptions of their works with valuable summaries of stylistic trends. Canadian musical activity is studied in relation to developments in the music of the Western world. In addition, influences from jazz, folk, and popular music are identified, and there is a welcome attempt to integrate musical developments with those in literature, painting, and the arts in general.

This book is the first practical guide to Canadian classical music of the twentieth century; it includes extensive lists of scores and recordings, arranged chronologically by performance medium. It is the best available introduction to modern Canadian music – a book every listener will want to own.

Creative activity lags behind performance
but it is in the long run the most important manifestation
of musical life.

Sir Ernest MacMillan, quoted in *Massey Report,* 1951

UNIVERSITY OF TORONTO PRESS

Toronto Buffalo London

GEORGE A. PROCTOR

Canadian Music of the Twentieth Century

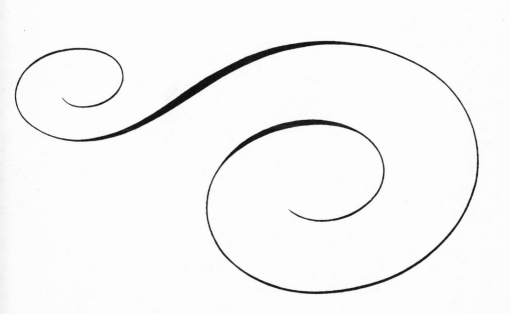

© University of Toronto Press 1980
Toronto Buffalo London
Printed in Canada
ISBN 0-8020-5419-6

Canadian Cataloguing in Publication Data

Proctor, George A., 1931-

Canadian music of the twentieth century

Bibliography: p.
Includes index.
ISBN 0-8020-5419-6
1. Music, Canadian – History and criticism.
2. Music – History and criticism – 20th century.
I. Title.
ML205.5.P76   780'.971   c80-094169-1

To my parents, *in memoriam*

Contents

Preface

This book is a study of Canadian music in the twentieth century. It is not a history of musical activity, even though such activity has increased greatly during the course of this century. Neither is it a documentary of the lives of Canadian composers, fascinating though these may be. It is, rather, an introduction to the music itself, the varied products of musical creation by many individual composers. While the book has grown out of the university classroom and seminar, I hope that it will also be of use to students of other ages and levels of interest.

The book is restricted to what is normally called concert, classical, or 'serious music' (no one term is completely satisfactory). Popular, jazz, folk, and rock music are not included, except indirectly, largely because they have their own promotional and critical avenues and are constantly before the public in some form or other. Although many groups and individuals have been promoting Canadian concert music for some time, it has yet to receive the depth of understanding and informed appreciation which it deserves. The first aim of this book, then, is to help to bring about such an understanding between the composer and his audience and to bridge the sizeable gap which at present exists between the producer and the consumer of Canadian music.

It is only in the last thirty-five years that extended musical compositions have been created in any quantity in Canada. Nevertheless, at the present time there is a great wealth of Canadian musical literature waiting to be explored, performed, experienced, understood, and appreciated. Books on contemporary Western music published outside Canada have almost totally ignored Canadian music. One of the most recent and comprehensive of these made reference to Canadian music in a single sentence! It was not until the *Dictionary of Contemporary Music*, edited by John Vinton, appeared in 1974, with articles on thirty-four Canadian composers as well as an extensive article on composition in Canada, that Canadian musical composition was recognized internationally.

The picture on the domestic scene has been slightly better, largely through the indefatigable efforts of the Canadian Music Centre (in Toronto, and, more recently, also in Montreal) and the Canadian Broadcasting Corporation. Noteworthy are two recent products of the Canadian Music Centre and the Centre de musique canadienne: *Contemporary Canadian Composers*, edited by Keith MacMillan and John Beckwith (1975), and *Compositeurs canadiens contemporains*, edited by Louise Laplante (1977). The French volume, which supplies more up-to-date information and includes 160 composers, is an expansion of the earlier English version of 144 composers. Both editions give biographical details, lists of works, and some discussion of individual works and influences. Nevertheless, it is fair to say that only a small percentage of Canadians, let alone foreigners, have heard of Claude Champagne, Serge Garant, Jean Papineau-Couture, John Weinzweig, Harry Somers, R. Murray Schafer, or Barbara Pentland – to name a few of Canada's important composers. And even fewer are familiar with their compositions, at least to the degree that they are familiar with the paintings of, say, Lawren Harris or Jean-Paul Riopelle, or the novels of Robertson Davies or Gabrielle Roy, or the poems of Irving Layton or E.J. Pratt. Music has special problems in that it depends on a performer, live or recorded, who in turn is dependent on some form of printed score. It is particularly the dearth of live or recorded performances as well as of printed scores which has made communication between the contemporary composer and the listening public tenuous at best. Although the situation is still far from ideal, it has improved as a result of the CBC's Canadian Collection of recordings and the subsidization of Canadian music publishers and performing groups by the Canada Council, provincial arts councils, universities, and the CBC. It is no longer true that sufficient materials are not available for the serious study of Canadian music.

However, one of the main problems in any systematic study of Canadian music is the scattered nature of the materials that do exist. It is not always easy to track down the source of a score, a recording, or a critical discussion of a particular work. The second main aim of this book is, therefore, to bring together the sources of scores and recordings. At the end of each chapter lists of scores and recordings of selected works are presented according to performance medium (that is, piano music, orchestral music, and so on). While every attempt has been made to discuss works which are readily available in score or recording, if not both, many works, particularly those which have been published or recorded, are included in these lists even though they are not discussed in the body of the text. Thus the book can serve not only as an introduction to Canadian music but also as a tool for further study.

A few words of practical advice about acquiring these materials would seem to be in order. To obtain a printed score the reader is advised to approach, first, a music dealer and, secondly, the publisher of the item (for the names and addresses of publishers see the Abbreviations, p xv, or the various Canadian Music Centre catalogues). Manuscript scores may be borrowed, free of charge and for a reasonable time period, from any of the offices of the Canadian Music Centre. To purchase a recording listed as 'RCI' the reader should order directly from CBC Merchandizing, Box 500, Station A, Toronto, Ontario M5W 1E6, or from Droits dérivés, Société Radio-Canada, CP 6000, Montréal, Québec H3C 3A8. Recordings have a tendency to come and go in the Canadian Collection catalogues, but most of the RCI discs above no. 203 are available and at reasonable cost. CBC SM recordings are available only from CBC Merchandizing in Toronto. It is important to know that the three Canadian Music Centre offices also sell these recordings, including some which are not available from the CBC or Radio-Canada. The few commercial recordings which have been made may be bought through record-dealers. New recording enterprises such as Music Gallery Editions (30 St Patrick Street, Toronto) and McGill University Records (555 Sherbrooke Street West, Montreal) offer mail-order subscriptions. Scores and recordings which are not available for purchase or are out of print may be consulted at any of the libraries of the Canadian Music Centre (1263 Bay Street, Toronto, Ontario M5R 2C1; 1259, rue Berri, bureau 300, Montréal, Québec H2L 4C7; and 2007 West 4th avenue, Suite 3, Vancouver, BC V6J 1N3). Out-of-print scores and manuscripts of the pre-1940 period are likely to be found in the National Library of Canada, Music Division, Ottawa. The reader may also find it helpful to consult Lynne Jarman, editor, *Canadian Music: A Selected Checklist, 1950–73/La Musique canadienne: une liste sélective, 1950–73*; G. Creelman, E. Cooke, and G. King, editors, *Canadian Music Scores and Recordings: A Classified Catalogue*; any of the catalogues of the Canadian Music Centre; and my own *Sources in Canadian Music: A Bibliography of Bibliographies*, second edition.

In this book selected works of representative composers are discussed by genre and related to general stylistic trends in Western music. In addition, the direct or indirect influences of other aspects of Canadiana – folk songs, jazz, popular music, paintings, literary works, political events, and geography – are discussed and brought into focus where appropriate. A chronological order has been followed, and every attempt has been made to avoid the excesses of categorization which may arise when one tries to view musical works in relation to general patterns and influences. The definition of 'Canadian composer' is generally that of the Canadian Music Centre; it includes practising composers who are Canadian citizens or others who have been resident in Canada for at least five years. Canadian-born composers who have become naturalized citizens of other countries and whose professional careers have taken place outside of Canada, such as Colin McPhee, Henry Brant, Alan Detweiler, and Neil McKay, are not included.

While it goes without saying that it has not been possible to include all worthwhile works, I have attempted to convey to the reader the very real excitement which awaits the person who opens his or her ears, mind, and heart to the riches of our music in this century. In the course of writing this book I have been mindful of an editorial written by Clarence Britten in the first issue of the *Canadian Journal of Music* (May 1914): Mr Britten noted that he wished his fledgling journal to be 'neither too erudite for the general, nor too popular for the professional, nor too dull for anybody.'

Acknowledgments

The author wishes to thank all those who have helped to make this book possible: the composers themselves, whose creative efforts sparked the need for such a book; the composers who generously supplied information or gave permission to use copyrighted materials; the publishers who gave permission to use copyrighted materials; Mount Allison University and the University of Western Ontario for library support and leaves granted; the Canada Council for a Research Fellowship in 1972–3 and a Leave Fellowship in 1978–9; the Marjorie Young Bell Fund, Mount Allison University; the J.B. Smallman Research Fund of the University of Western Ontario; the Canadian Music Centre in Toronto; the numerous students whose interest and enthusiasm kept the project alive, particularly graduate students David Boothroyd, Jack Eby, Terence Ford, and Martin Waltz who assisted in the compiling of the appendix, and Jenni Beale who assisted in the preparation of the index; Joan A. Bulger of University of Toronto Press whose keen editorial supervision helped immeasurably in the final stages; and my wife, Nancy, my son, Andrew, and my daughter, Martha, who patiently watched and waited.

   This book has been published with the help of a grant from the Canadian Federation for the Humanities, using funds provided by the Social Sciences and Humanities Research Council of Canada, and a grant to University of Toronto Press from the Andrew W. Mellon Foundation.

London, Ontario March 1980

Abbreviations

PUBLISHERS

Abingdon
Abingdon Press
c/o G.R. Welch Company Ltd
310 Judson Street
Toronto (Etobicoke), Ontario M8Z 5T6

AMP
Associated Music Publishers Inc
(a division of G. Schirmer Inc)
866 Third Avenue
New York, New York 10022, USA

Anglo-Can
Anglo-Canadian (defunct)

Archambault
Ed Archambault Inc
500 est, rue Ste-Catherine
Montréal, Québec H2L 2C6

Avant
Avant Music
c/o Western International Music
2859 Holt Avenue
Los Angeles, California 90034, USA

Barger & Barclay
Barger & Barclay
1325 Orange Isle
Fort Lauderdale, Florida 33315, USA

Berandol   Berandol Music Limited
11 St Joseph Street
Toronto, Ontario M4Y 1J8

Berandol Musicache   Berandol Musicache
(a basic music library on microfiche)
c/o Berandol Music Limited
11 St Joseph Street
Toronto, Ontario M4Y 1J8

Billaudot   Editions Gérard Billaudot
a/s Editions M.-R. Braun
14, rue l'Echiquier
Paris 10e, France

BMI Can   BMI Canada Limited (changed to P.R.O. Canada Limited in
July 1977)
Publishing division sold to Berandol Music Limited in 1969.
Works listed as published by BMI Can are available from
Berandol.

Bonart   Publications Bonart
a/s Michel Perrault
831, avenue Rockland
Montréal, Québec H2V 2Z9

Boosey   Boosey and Hawkes (Canada) Ltd
279 Yorkland Blvd
Willowdale, Ontario M2J 1S7

Boston   Boston Music Company
116 Boylston Street
Boston, Massachusetts 02116, USA

Bosworth   Bosworth & Company, Ltd
14–18 Heddon Street
London W1R 8DP, England

Caveat   Caveat Music Publishers Limited
198 Davenport Road
Toronto, Ontario M5R 1J2

Chanteclair   Chanteclair Music Limited
29 Birch Avenue
Toronto, Ontario M4V 1E2

Chappell (L)   Chappell & Company Limited
                    50 New Bond Street
                    London W1, England

CMC   Canadian Music Centre
                    1263 Bay Street
                    Toronto, Ontario M5R 2C1
                    and
                    Centre de musique canadienne
                    1259, rue Berri, bureau 300
                    Montréal, Québec H2L 4C7

CMC ms film   Canadian Music Centre
                    Microfilms of Unpublished Canadian Music (1969–70)
                    1263 Bay Street
                    Toronto, Ontario M5R 2C1

Composer's Press   Anerca Music
                    35 St Andrew's Gardens
                    Toronto, Ontario M4W 2C9

Concordia   Concordia Publishing House
                    3558 South Jefferson Avenue
                    Saint Louis, Missouri 63118, USA

Ditson   Oliver Ditson Co
                    Presser Place
                    Bryn Mawr, Pennsylvania 19010, USA

Durand   Editions Durand & Cie
                    4 Place de la Madeleine
                    Paris 8e, France

Editions musicales Editions musicales transatlantiques
                    14 avenue Hoche
                    Paris 8, France

Elkin   Elkin & Co Ltd
                    Borough Green
                    Sevenoaks, Kent TN15 8DT, England

Excello   Montreal Brass Quintet Series
                    145 Graham Blvd
                    Town of Mount Royal
                    Montréal, Québec H3P 2C3

Fischer

Carl Fischer Inc
62 Cooper Square
New York, New York 10003, USA

G. Schirmer

G. Schirmer Inc
866 Third Avenue
New York, New York 10022, USA

Gray

H.W. Gray Company Inc
159 East 49th Street
New York, New York 10017, USA

GVT

Gordon V. Thompson Limited
29 Birch Avenue
Toronto, Ontario M4V 1E2

Harmuse

Harmuse Publications
PO Box 670
Oakville, Ontario L6J 5C2

Harris

Frederick Harris Music Company Ltd
PO Box 670
Oakville, Ontario L6J 5C2

Hérelle

Hérelle (defunct)

Huron

Huron Press
PO Box 3083
London, Ontario N6A 4J4

International

International Music Sales
648a Yonge Street
Toronto, Ontario M4Y 2A6

Jaymar

Jaymar Music Limited
PO Box 3083
London, Ontario N6A 4J4

Jobert

Société des editions Jobert (Paris)
c/o Theodore Presser Company
(sole representative USA and Canada)
Presser Place
Bryn Mawr, Pennsylvania 19010, USA

Jost

Jost & Sander, Leipzig (defunct)

Joubert

Joubert & Cie
25 rue d'Hauteville
Paris 10, France

Kerby

E.C. Kerby Limited
198 Davenport Road
Toronto, Ontario M5R 1J2

Leeds

Leeds Music (Canada)
(a division of MCA Canada Limited)
2450 Victoria Park Avenue
Willowdale, Ontario M2J 4A2

Marseg

Marseg Limited
18 Farmstead Road
Willowdale, Ontario M2L 2G2

McKee

Peter McKee Music Company Limited
3 Regina Street North
Waterloo, Ontario N2J 4A5

Morawetz

Private publication by Oskar Morawetz
59 Duncannon Drive
Toronto, Ontario M5P 2M3

NatLibOtt

Music Division
National Library of Canada
395 Wellington Street
Ottawa, Ontario K1A 0N4

Nordheimer

A & S Nordheimer Ltd (defunct)

Novello

Novello and Company Ltd
Borough Green
Sevenoaks, Kent TN15 8DT, England

Okra

Okra Music Corporation
177 East 87th Street
New York, New York 10028, USA

Oxford

Oxford University Press
Music Department
Ely House
37 Dover Street
London W1X 4AH England

Parnasse	Parnasse musical (agent: Berandol Music Limited) 11 St Joseph Street Toronto, Ontario M4Y 1J8
Peer	Peer-Southern Organization (Canada) Limited 4 New Street, Suite 107 Toronto, Ontario M5R 1P6
Peters	C.F. Peters Corporation 373 Park Avenue South New York, New York 10016, USA
Preissler	Joseph Preissler 8 München 2, West Germany
Presser	Theodore Presser Company Bryn Mawr, Pennsylvania 19010, USA
Ricordi	G. Ricordi & Company (Canada) Limited 497 Eglinton Avenue West Toronto, Ontario M5N 1A7
Roberton	Roberton Publications The Windmill Wendover Aylesbury, Buckinghamshire HP22 6JJ, England
Salabert	Editions Francis Salabert 22, rue Chauchat Paris, France 75009
Schmidt	A.P. Schmidt (defunct)
S.E.L.	S.E.L. Engravers and Publishers 2 Totteridge Road Islington, Ontario M9A 1Z1
Sifton	I.A. Sifton (defunct)
Summit	Summit Music Limited 497 Eglinton Avenue West Toronto, Ontario M5N 1A7

Tenuto

Tenuto Publications
(sole selling agent: Theodore Presser Company)
Bryn Mawr, Pennsylvania 19010, USA

Third Stream

Third Stream Music, Inc
200 West 57th Street
New York, New York, USA

Universal

Universal Edition (London), Ltd
2/3 Fareham Street
London W1, England
(Canadian agent: Berandol Music Limited)

Universal (Can)

Universal Edition (Canada) Limited
11 St Joseph Street
Toronto, Ontario M4Y 1J8

Waterloo

Waterloo Music Company Limited
3 Regina Street North
Waterloo, Ontario N2J 4A5

Western

Western Music Company Ltd
c/o Leslie Music Supply
PO Box 471
Oakville, Ontario L6J 5A8

Whaley-Royce

Whaley, Royce & Co Limited
(now Algord Music Limited)
372a Yonge Street
Toronto, Ontario M5B 1S6

World Library

World Library of Sacred Music
1846 Westwood Avenue
Cincinnati, Ohio 45214, USA

RECORDING COMPANIES

Acadia

Acadia Records
4422 avenue Kent
Montréal, Québec H3S 1N6

Audat

World Records
484 Waterloo Court
Oshawa, Ontario L1H 3X1

Bar   Baroque Records of Canada Limited
11432 Tardivel Street
Montréal, Québec H3M 2L2

Boot   Boot Records Limited
1343 Matheson Blvd West
Mississauga, Ontario L4W 1R1

Cap   Capitol Records of Canada Limited
635 Queen Street East
Toronto, Ontario M4M 1G4

CAPAC   CAPAC Musical Portrait
Composers, Authors and Publishers Association of Canada, Limited
1240 Bay Street
Toronto, Ontario M5R 2C2

CAPAC-CAB   Composers, Authors, and Publishers Association of Canada
and the Canadian Association of Broadcasters
1240 Bay Street
Toronto, Ontario M5R 2C2

CBC SM   Canadian Broadcasting Corporation
English Services Division
PO Box 500, Station A
Toronto, Ontario M5W 1E6

CCM   Waterloo Music Company Limited, Distributor
3 Regina Street North
Waterloo, Ontario N2J 4A5

CGA   Marie Curie Sklodowska Women's Club
Box 278
Mississauga, Ontario L5A 3A1

CH   Concert Hall
La Guide internationale du disque
22, rue de Cocherel
27029 Evreux, France

CMC tape   Reference Library
Canadian Music Centre
1263 Bay Street
Toronto, Ontario M5R 2C1

	and Centre de musique canadienne 1259, rue Berri, bureau 300 Montréal, Québec H2L 4C7
Col	Columbia Records of Canada 1121 Leslie Street Don Mills, Ontario M3C 2J9
Conc	Concordia Records Concordia College Moorhead, Minnesota 56560, USA
Cornell	Cornell University Wind Ensemble Music Department Cornell University Ithaca, New York 14850, USA
CRI	Composers Recording Inc 170 West 74th Street New York, New York 10023, USA
CTL	Canadian Talent Library 2 St Clair Avenue West Toronto, Ontario M4V 1L9
Decca	Decca Records (a division of MCA Inc) 445 Park Avenue New York, New York 10022, USA
DGG	Polydor/Deutsche Gramophon 6000 Côte de liesse St Laurent, Québec H4T 1E3
Dom	Dominion (Canada) c/o Canadian Music Sales Corporation Limited 58 Advance Road Toronto, Ontario M8Z 2T8
Folkways	Folkways/Scholastic 906 Sylvan Avenue Englewood Cliffs, New Jersey 07632, USA

Golden Crest   Golden Crest Records Inc
220 Broadway
Huntington Station
New York, New York 11746, USA

Hallmark   Hallmark (defunct)

HMV   *see* RCA

JMC   Jeunesses musicales du Canada
430 ouest, boulevard St-Joseph
Montréal, Québec H2V 2P6

Latvian   Latvian Heritage Foundation
Boston, Massachusetts, USA

Lethbridge   Lethbridge Symphony Association
PO Box 1101
Lethbridge, Alberta T1J 4A2

London   London Records of Canada (1967) Limited
1630 Midland Avenue
Scarborough, Ontario M1P 3C5

Louisville   The Louisville Orchestra
211 Brown Building
321 West Broadway
Louisville, Kentucky 40202, USA

Madrigal   Madrigal Records
1385 Montpellier
Montréal (Saint-Laurent), Québec H4L 4R4

Master   Master Recordings
PO Box 5186, Terminal A
Toronto, Ontario M5W 1E4

McGill   McGill University Records
555 Sherbrooke Street West
Montréal, Québec H3A 1E3

Mel   Melbourne Records of Canada Limited
(distributed by Waterloo Music Company Limited)
3 Regina Street North
Waterloo, Ontario N2J 4A5

Merc   Mercury Record Corporation
c/o Phonogram Inc
1 IBM Plaza
Chicago, Illinois 60611, USA

MHIC   Berandol Music Limited
11 St Joseph Sreet
Toronto, Ontario M4Y 1J8

Musican   MusicCanada discs
(joint project of RCI and CAPAC)
RCI Transcription Service
CP 6000
Montréal, Québec H3C 3A8

Music Gallery   Music Gallery Editions
30 St Patrick Street
Toronto, Ontario M5T 1V1

Odeon   Penco Recording Company
428 Wood Street
New Bedford, Massachusetts 02745, USA

Odyssey   *see* Columbia Records of Canada

Philips   Philips Records
c/o Phonogram Inc
1 IBM Plaza
Chicago, Illinois 60611, USA

Poly   *see* DGG

RCA   Radio Corporation of America (Canada) Limited
101 Duncan Mill Road
Don Mills, Ontario M3B 1Z3

RCA-CCS   Radio Corporation of America (Canada) and Radio Canada
International: Canadian Centennial Series
CP 6000
Montréal, Québec H3C 3A8

RCI   Radio Canada International
(formerly CBC International Service)
CP 6000
Montréal, Québec H3C 3A8

RCI *ACM*   Radio Canada International
                       Anthology of Canadian Music
                       CP 6000
                       Montréal, Québec H3C 3A8

Select   Select Records
                       500 est, rue Ste-Catherine
                       Montréal, Québec H2L 2C6

Sim   St Simon's Church
                       40 Howard Street
                       Toronto, Ontario M4X 1J7

SNE   Société nouvelle d'enregistrement
                       10175, rue Meunier
                       Montréal, Québec H3L 2Z2

SR   St Mark's Cathedral
                       Minneapolis, Minnesota, USA

ST   All Saints' Cathedral, Edmonton, Alberta

TBC   TBC Recording Limited
                       1262 Don Mills Road
                       Toronto (Don Mills), Ontario M3B 2W7

Vogt   *see* Latvian

CANADIAN MUSIC OF THE TWENTIETH CENTURY

CHAPTER ONE

1900 to 1920
The Colonial Period

While I wish to pipe Canadian tunes, ... what I fear will always be: that they are sung to an English ground bass.
    Pearl McCarthy, *Leo Smith, A Biographical Sketch* (1956)

There was a remarkable amount of musical activity in Canada at the turn of the century, particularly in the larger centres such as Toronto and Montreal. Helmut Kallmann's *History of Music in Canada 1534–1914* reveals that the quantity of music-making and teaching which took place prior to World War I was impressive, even by later standards. Documenting this activity are the many journals of the time which were devoted to music: *Winnipeg Town Topics* (1898–1913), the *Canadian Music Trades Journal* (1900–32), *The Conservatory Bi-Monthly* (1902–13), *Musical Canada* (1906–33), *Le Montréal qui chante* (1908–19), and *The Canadian Journal of Music* (1914–19). The thriving state of the music industry, particularly in the making of pianos and the printing of sheet music, is evidence of the fact that music played an important part in daily community and family life.

In the area of original musical composition some composers' works numbered in the hundreds; many of these were published. Most works were either songs with piano accompaniment or short character pieces for solo piano. Music at this time was one of the favourite parlour activities, and such songs and piano pieces provided many hours of happy entertainment for performers and listeners alike, hours which in later years were spent in the movie house or in front of the television screen. The reason behind the remarkable quantity of music publishing was simply that in this period it made money, since musical scores of the type described were extremely marketable. So also were pianos: there were approximately thirty piano manufacturers in Canada prior to 1914, compared with fewer than half a dozen sixty years later.

Musical composition was, and still is in most cases, invariably tied to some other professional activity. Most often during the first four decades of the century the composer was a teacher of piano, organ, voice, and theory in a private studio during the week and an organist and choirmaster on the weekends. W.O. Forsyth, a prominent Toronto musician, lamented the fact that musicians were so busy earning a living by teaching and performing that they had little time left for creative work.[1] In 1915 Forsyth listed eighteen composers who were very active in the early part of the century, but, typically, he failed to mention two of the most prominent French-Canadian composers, Alexis Contant and Guillaume Couture.

Another gauge of musical activity in the early 1900s is the number of music conservatories which flourished, sometimes amidst bitter quarrelling and institutional rivalry. In Toronto alone there were at least seven conservatories. Original composition did not have priority in the curricula of the conservatories, even though some prominent musicians, notably Luigi von Kunits, the first conductor of the Toronto Symphony (1923–31), stressed that the education of a well-rounded musician should include studies in music history and composition as well as performance skills on an instrument.[2] The critic Augustus Bridle asked 'Is Canada Musical?' in the 25 October 1913 issue of the *Canadian Courier*, and answered, with a degree of self-righteous pride, that 'there is at present, and will be for a long time to come, a huge wave of musical development all over this country comparable to the best known in any country, and on a basis of population superior to any.'

Many critics over the course of the century have attempted to explain why Canadians are generally ignorant of the creative products of their composers. One of the first of these was John Daniel Logan, a perceptive if rather verbose critic and the author of *Aesthetic Criticism in Canada* (1917). Logan gives three reasons for this state of affairs: music's abstract nature in comparison with the other expressive arts; the restriction of Canadian works to small, popular forms and occasional pieces; and the fact that Canadian conservatories had imitated Canadian universities by not including Canadian studies in their curricula. Stating the more commonly held view that Canada was obsessed with utilitarianism and the Puritan work ethic which regarded works of art as somehow frivolous or the products of the devil, Harry C. Perrin, then director of the McGill Conservatorium, made a plea in 1911[3] to the universities to study music as a literature as well as to establish a unified examination system which would create and maintain performance standards in music throughout the country. Like many writers and educators of his time Perrin was more concerned with musical re-creation (performance) than creation (original composition).

Much of what was composed in Canada between 1900 and 1920 shows the influence of the countries of origin of the composers, or of their ancestors, namely, England and France. We have already noted that Leo Smith, who came to

Canada from England in 1910, commented that he feared his 'Canadian tunes' would always be 'sung to an English ground bass.'[4] Some of Smith's fellow-countrymen felt less guilty about the lack of a Canadian quality in their works. Charles A.E. Harriss, the first director of the McGill Conservatorium, organized a Canada-wide group of music festivals, an important criterion of which was that all works performed must be by British composers! For the most part French-speaking composers such as Alexis Contant and Guillaume Couture followed the models of Franck, d'Indy, and Gounod. Unfortunately there was not much exchange between French-speaking and English-speaking composers. For example, one Montreal composer who came from England as a young man admitted in later life that he had met a prominent French-Canadian composer who lived in the same city only once or twice in the twenty-five years he was resident in the city.

Musical nationalism of the sort found in Bohemia, Russia, and Norway (e.g. Dvořák, Mussorgsky, and Grieg respectively) in the late nineteenth century did not appear in Canada prior to the 1920s, and even then the results were not particularly significant. In the early years Canadian music had a tendency to retain stylistic traits long after the latter had gone out of fashion in their country of origin. It was some time before the innovations of Debussy, Schönberg, Ives, and others at the beginning of the century had any large-scale effect on musical composition in Canada.

Of the songs and piano character pieces that formed the bulk of Canadian music for the period 1900–20 very few were extended in length and most were written for a particular person or occasion. As Kallmann notes, there is no evidence of any symphonies or concerti being written by Canadians and performed in Canada before World War I.[5] The major works composed were cantatas and oratorios, such as *Caïn* (1905) by Alexis Contant, *Jean le Précurseur* (1911) and *Messe de Requiem* (1906) by Guillaume Couture, and *Coronation Mass Edward VII* (1902) and *The Crowning of the King* (1911) by Charles A.E. Harriss. Chamber music formed a small but significant part of the creative effort of Canadian musicians (e.g. the *String Quartet in C Minor* (1914–21) by Ernest MacMillan, the *Sonata No. 1 in E Minor* (1916) for violin and piano by Healey Willan, and the *Trio No. 1* (1907) for violin, cello, and piano by Contant.

PIANO MUSIC

The piano repertoire of this period falls exclusively within the realm of the nineteenth-century character piece. In Canada at the turn of the century symphony orchestras and chamber music groups were either non-existent or just coming into being,[6] opera was an expensive luxury few communities could afford, and choral music was almost exclusively of the sacred variety; thus, it was natural that composers turned to the writing of short pieces for the piano, aptly described as 'songs-without-words.'[7] There was no dearth of musical activity in Canada to foster this type of music for, as Kallmann points out, 'it was a rare day when the living-room piano stood silent.'[8]

The best-known composers of character pieces were Gena Branscombe, W.O. Forsyth, Charles A.E. Harriss, Clarence Lucas, and Rodolphe Mathieu, who followed the pattern of Alexis Contant in *La Lyre enchantée* (1875) in modelling their works after Chopin, Schumann, and Liszt. Most of their works now lie forgotten in the National Library in Ottawa (which has by far the largest single collection of such character pieces). Typical are Branscombe's *Chansonette*, *Impromptu*, and *Valse-Caprice*, all simple and well-constructed works which use some of the chromatic vocabulary of the late nineteenth century. Forsyth was one of the most prolific composers in this genre, but his works are generally shallow in content and conservative in style. A typical work, *At Parting*, follows the pattern of a simple, sentimental melody with chromatic bravura sections interspersed throughout, the latter designed to exercise the fingers and impress the listener. His *In the Twilight* (*Im Dämmerlicht*), Op. 31, No. 1 falls prey to excessive repetition, while *Two Pieces for Pianoforte*, Op. 50 ('In the Vale of Shadowland' and 'Southern Love Song') and *Prelude and Fugue*, Op. 25 (1897) show more imagination and serious constructive effort. Many of the character pieces for piano written by Canadian composers in this period are overly sentimental and seem to have been manufactured for the commercial market. One would have to place them in the third-rate category to which the *Harvard Dictionary of Music* assigns much of the character-piece repertoire.[9] After 1900 there is not much evidence of the naive and picturesque humour of earlier examples, such as Lucas's *The Spectre Bridegroom*, Op. 11, No. 2 (1888), where, in true romantic fashion, the work begins in the dramatic key of C minor but eventually finds its way to a happy ending in C major.

One of the more interesting works of the period was written by a young French-Canadian composer who was to have an important influence during the course of the century. Claude Champagne's *Prélude et filigrane* (1918) gave an early indication that Canadian composers were not entirely unaware of recent European developments. Under the influence of Alfred Laliberté, Champagne was introduced to the music of Scriabin prior to his departure for Paris in 1921. Champagne's combination of augmented fourths, minor ninths and seconds, and non-functional chord progressions to create an atmosphere of mysticism in this work may be traced to Scriabin. Such stylistic features were uncommon in Canadian music at this time.

SOLO SONG

Many of the solo songs written in this period were, like the character pieces for piano, sentimental pieces designed for the salon. Literally hundreds of them were composed for an eager market, and a large percentage reached publication. The main composers were Gena Branscombe (who left Canada for New York at the time of her marriage to John Ferguson Tenney in 1910), Alexis Contant, W.O. Forsyth, Albert Ham, Charles A.E. Harriss, Geoffrey O'Hara, and Leo Smith. Comments made by contemporary critics give an indication of the degree of conservatism in musical taste in Canada at this time. In the *Canadian Courier* of 4 October 1913 Katherine Hale described Branscombe's works in this genre as having 'a hint of the bizarre, the too unusual in the swift progressions, the strange turns, the much-embroidered harmonies.' Another critic, Clarence Britten, said in the *Canadian Journal of Music* for 25 June 1914 that her songs are 'futuristic in their imagery' and contain 'footloose progressions and a contempt for resolution.' At a later time Augustus Bridle described Smith's songs as 'characteristically modern in style, sometimes highly dramatic.'[10] For the most part Canadian critics and musicians were not in sympathy with, or even aware of, the revolution which was taking place in musical style in other parts of the Western world.

There are, however, interesting aspects to the Canadian song repertoire of this period aside from stylistic considerations. Prior to World War I many of the songs were composed to German texts with German titles, for example, *Frühlingsabend* (before 1900) by Forsyth and *Auf Nimmerwiedersehen* (published 1906) by Ham. Canadian composers were susceptible to the Anglo-Saxon idea that a foreign name added prestige to a work and ensured its wider acceptance. (In a similar way opera singers adopted Italianate names; for example, the noted Canadian tenor Edward Johnson used as his stage name Eduardo di Giovanni.) Another aspect of song literature in the second decade of the century was the great number of patriotic songs which were inspired by and served an important function in World War I: Ham's *Jack Canuck, Canadians We Stand,* and *The Call of Empire,* published in 1910, 1914, and 1917 respectively, are three such songs. In the days before radio and television the contemporary song was sometimes used for commercial advertisements as well: *Nukol Sparks* or *The Burning Love Song,* published in 1919 by Jules Brazil, was circulated, free of charge, to advertise the wares of the Nukol Fuel Company of Toronto. It is interesting to note that Brazil was the only advertised teacher of musical composition in Toronto at this time. His advertisement in the August 1915 issue of *Musical Canada* refers to him as a teacher of composition, transposing, and arranging, and states that he provided 'an immediate service.'

Most of the songs of this period are in strophic or modified strophic form. All are homophonic in texture without much counterpoint between the voice and its accompaniment. Most make frequent use of nineteenth-century chromatic harmony with the inevitable German-sixth and diminished-seventh chords. The English Canadian song of this period was influenced by the composers of Victorian England, who for their part had been brought up in the Germanic tradition. Composers from French Canada, on the other hand, followed the sentimental side of French music, as represented by Gounod and Dubois, with the exception of the young Rodolphe Mathieu, whose *Les Yeux noirs* (1911) shows the influence of Debussy.

CHORAL MUSIC

Sacred choral works comprise most of the large-scale *œuvres* of this period. Since nearly all the composers depended upon their activity as church organists to make a living, it was natural for them to channel their major creative efforts in this direction when a special occasion presented itself. Such occasions were not frequent, but the works which resulted are noteworthy.

The Canadian composer-organist-teacher-conductor was generally too busy meeting the daily requirements of life for composition to occupy a large proportion of his time and energy. At least that was the viewpoint of the musician.[11] On the other hand Bridle attributed this state of affairs to the fact that 'we have no absolute simon-pure composers because we have no Bohemianism.'[12] Furthermore, Bridle felt that the explanation was not solely a lack of time and money but the fact that Canadian musicians lacked the imagination to write musical works of sizeable dimension.

In sacred choral music the bulk of the repertoire was in the form of the anthem in English Canada and the mass and motet in French Canada. Branscombe, H.A. Fricker, Ham, Harriss, Lucas, and a newcomer to Canada by the name of Healey Willan were the major contributors of anthems, although it would be safe to say that most organists and choirmasters of the day tried their hand at composing in this genre. English stylistic influence was strong. *O, Give Thanks Unto the Lord* by Ham, who was organist and choirmaster of St James Cathedral in Toronto from 1897 to 1933, is typical of the Victorian church anthem with its homophonic texture and liberal use of diminished-seventh chords, German sixths, and chromatic non-harmonic tones.

Contant and Couture were the major contributors of masses and motets in French Canada. In spite of Pope Pius x's *Motu proprio* of 1903, which attempted to discourage the writing of church music in a theatrical style (including the use of instruments other than organ), both of these composers wrote sacred works of large dimension. Contant composed an oratorio, *Caïn* (1905), and three large-scale masses. His *Messe no 3ᵉ pour soli, chœur et orchestre* (1903) called for two flutes, three trombones, timpani, strings, harp, and organ. The choral parts were for male voices only (TTB). It is not surprising that the composer was rebuked for the cost of this extravaganza and that the inaugural performance was cancelled because of the prohibitive expense, although the first performance did take place later in 1903.[13] Contant admitted that the influence of Gounod was strong, saying that the general public wanted an essentially simple and sentimental style rather than what he termed the hard, modern sonorities.[14] In *Caïn*, which was eighteen months in the making, a large orchestra was also used. Although there are a few contrapuntal sections in this work (such as the fugal second section of the over-ture), for the most part polyphonic interest is lacking. The size of the work is impressive, but the orchestration is very much like a transcription of an organ work.

A less prolific but more influential composer was Couture, whose *Jean le Précurseur* was actually published in Paris in 1914, although it was not performed in public until 1923, eight years after the death of the composer. It is in the style of Couture's teacher, Théodore Dubois, whose music, like that of Gounod, was characterized by chromatic harmonies and sentimental melodies. Contrapuntal elements derived from the *stile antico* of the Roman church style were used sparingly.[15] One critic claimed in 1951 that *Jean le Précurseur* is 'la plus belle œuvre que le Canada ait produite.'[16] Couture's *Messe de Requiem* (1906) was scored originally for soli, chorus, and organ, but the composer revised it and provided an orchestration in 1913. This effective work was performed at Couture's own funeral in 1915.

English organist-composer-impressario Charles A.E. Harriss was, besides being the first director of the McGill Conservatorium (1904–7), organist and choirmaster in various churches in Ottawa and Montreal from 1882 until his death in 1929. His large works include the *Coronation Mass Edward VII* (1902), composed for the first cycle of musical festivals in Canada devoted to British compositions (1903), and *The Crowning of the King*, written for the coronation of George V in 1911. Both works call for soli, chorus, and orchestra, and the musical style is that of the English cathedral at the turn-of-the-century. It is not surprising that Dr Harriss, a tireless promoter of British music throughout the Empire, was referred to as 'the Napoleon of Imperial Music'[17] when one considers his texts, such as these lines from *The Crowning of the King*:

> Arise! arise! Imperial hearts, Arise!
> Sing paeans to the Mighty, the All-wise,
> And shout for George, our great Imperial King!

No discussion of sacred choral music in Canada in this century would be complete without reference to the man who was, and is, probably better known outside Canada than within, Healey Willan. Willan exerted a tremendous influence in the field of sacred choral music throughout the English-speaking world and was only the second Canadian to receive the Lambeth doctoral degree (1956) awarded by the archbishop of Canterbury for service to church music (the first was Harriss). When he came to Canada from England in 1913 at the age of 33, Willan brought with him a sense of reverence for the historical continuity of the music of the church. He had come under the influence of the Oxford movement, which sought to restore the spirit of mysticism of the pre-Reformation church.

Originally organist and choirmaster at a large and prestigious low Anglican church, St Paul's on Bloor Street in Toronto, Willan moved to a much smaller, high Anglican church, St Mary Magdalene, in 1921. From this post, which he held until his death in 1968, he put into practice his ideals for church music, which included plainchant in the vernacular, as well as a type of unaccompanied choral polyphony which was a stylistic blend of sixteenth-century counterpoint with nineteenth-century harmony. He became an acknowledged master of the setting of words to music in this idiom. The services which he led as precentor were aesthetically as well as spiritually rewarding for all who attended.

Willan's early works consist mainly of part-songs, settings of the Anglican liturgy, anthems with organ accompaniment, and single works for organ.[18] His *Christmas Song of the 14th Century*, 'Now, O Zion Gladly Raise Songs of Triumph' (published 1915), is a simple yet effective arrangement of the traditional melody *Resonet in laudibus* (this is the same melody which Brahms used in the second of two songs for contralto and viola obbligato entitled *Geistliches Wiegenlied*, Op. 91 [1884]). From the outset of his career Willan displayed great sensitivity to the text in his settings, while at the same time he clothed his arrangements in a quality of counterpoint which was not common in Canadian music of this period.

The large-scale concert anthem *An Apostrophe to the Heavenly Hosts* (1921), written for the Toronto Mendelssohn Choir, represents a high point in Willan's style to that time. The work is for unaccompanied double chorus plus two mystic, or echo, choirs. The text is based upon the liturgy of the Eastern church, and Willan, appropriately, draws his musical style from Mussorgsky, Rachmaninof, and Gretchaninof. The harmonies are modal and the chords progress much of the time by parallel movement. It was this feature which no doubt led Bridle to call Willan's choral works 'modern.'[19] Willan's choral style was firmly established by the 1920s, and he was not to depart from it appreciably over the course of the next half-century. Nor was he to compose other large-scale concert anthems after this one. The final section of *An Apostrophe* includes a simple unison setting of the chorale 'Lasst uns erfreuen,' known to English singers as 'Ye Watchers and Ye Holy Ones.' The anthem ends with a brilliant antiphonal display.

Secular choral music of consequence is rare in this period. Most works fall in the realm of patriotic music and almost all are insignificant musically. Ham's *Canada*, subtitled 'God and Our Land' (published 1906), was a typical part-song setting for SATB or TTBB. Based on a text by W.A. Fraser and dedicated to the people of Canada, it is in a simple, homophonic style. Ham's choral ballad for mixed voices and orchestra *Hope of the Ages* (published 1903) is more adventurous in scope but no more successful in achievement.

Harriss was a more ambitious composer than Ham in the secular as well as the sacred field. His symphonic-choric idyll *Pan* (1904), which was performed at the Musical Festival of the Empire in Toronto in 1911 along with Elgar's *Dream of*

Gerontius (1900), uses modality to achieve an archaic flavour much like Willan's in his sacred music.

Ernest MacMillan (later Sir Ernest) composed *Ode – 'England'* while he was detained in a German concentration camp during World War I. The work is a setting for soprano, baritone, chorus, and orchestra of the Swinburne poem 'England: An Ode' (1893). Accepted as MacMillan's thesis for the MUS.DOC. degree at Oxford University (1918), it is a large-scale work. The text is appropriately nationalistic ('Hope, faith, and remembrance of glory that found but in England her throne and shrine'), and MacMillan set it in the style of a composer whom he admired a great deal, Sir Edward Elgar. It is interesting to note that Elgar's *The Spirit of England* for soprano and tenor soli, chorus, and orchestra was composed at about the same time (1916) and received its first performance in the Albert Hall on 24 November 1917. MacMillan's *Ode – 'England'* received its première on 17 March 1921 in Sheffield, England, under Henry Coward and was later revived for the opening of the MacMillan Theatre at the University of Toronto in 1962.

ORCHESTRAL MUSIC

Orchestral music is a minor part of the output of composers in this period. There were no long-established professional orchestras to play such works, and consequently there was little opportunity for composers to learn at first hand how to write for a large instrumental ensemble. Contant and Couture each composed works for orchestra; Couture's *Rêverie*, Op. 2 (1875) actually predates the period under discussion. Scored for two flutes, two oboes, two clarinets, two bassoons, four horns, harp, timpani, and strings, this work is written in the same sentimental style as Couture's character pieces for piano.

The most prolific composer of orchestral music was Clarence Lucas, an itinerant musician who at various times held conducting posts in Hamilton, Ontario (Philharmonic Society), and London, England (Westminster Orchestral Society). Undoubtedly spurred on by these associations, he wrote a number of orchestral works, including one symphony, two symphonic poems, and overtures to *Othello, As You Like It,* and *Macbeth.*[20] *As You Like It* (1899), the only orchestral work of Lucas's which has been recorded, is reminiscent of the style of Edward German – tuneful and diatonic but overly repetitious and sequential.

The younger French-Canadian composers showed most promise in the field of orchestral music. Claude Champagne's early symphonic poem *Hercule et Omphale* (1918) so impressed Alfred Laliberté that he gave Champagne financial and moral support to enable him to further his studies in Paris from 1921 to 1928. This youthful work follows the Lisztian plan of representing two opposing ideas (virility and strength versus femininity and charm) by two contrasting musical themes, with charm, in this case, emerging as the winner. Two works featuring solo material, Georges-Emile Tanguay's *Romance* (1915) for violin, harp, and orchestra and Rodolphe Mathieu's *Un Peu d'ombre* (1913) for voice and orchestra, are also noteworthy, the former following the traditional pattern of the nineteenth-century French school and the latter the more adventurous style of Debussy.[21]

CHAMBER MUSIC

There were few works for chamber ensembles written in the early part of the century. One might think that the greater economy of means would have lent itself to more compositional activity in this field, but this was not the case. Kallmann notes that chamber music groups, professional as well as amateur, did exist, but Canadian composers did not produce many new compositions for them. The few exceptions are works by composers already discussed above: Contant, Couture, MacMillan, and Willan.

The *Trio No. 1* (1907) for violin, cello, and piano by Contant is one of the more significant Canadian chamber music scores of the period. Although its last two movements do not stand up to the promise of the first because of an overuse of sequence, it is a work which possesses considerable charm. The treatment of the violin and the cello in a romantically lyrical fashion shows the strong influence of Fauré. It is a pity that Contant did not follow this trio with other works in the genre. Couture had composed his *Quatuor fugue*, Op. 3 during his student days in Paris (around 1875), but he did not follow it with any chamber works in his maturity. Willan made various starts on a string quartet but he never completed any of them. The adagio movement of the unfinished quartet in E minor was begun in 1903–5, completed in 1930, and rewritten for string orchestra in 1959. It calls to mind the *Siegfried Idyll* (1870) of Wagner, a composer whom Willan admired a great deal and whose work served as the model for Willan's opera *Deirdre*.

The most significant string quartet composed by a Canadian in this period was the *String Quartet in C Minor* by MacMillan (1914–18; rev 1921). The first and second movements were written in Nürnberg, Germany, where the 21-year-old MacMillan had gone after attending the Wagner festival at Bayreuth. Movements three and four were continued in the confines of the Ruhleben prison camp where MacMillan was detained during the course of World War I. The entire quartet was revised and completed in 1921. The work shows a close affinity to the motivic development and predilection for parallel thirds and sixths of Brahms and the continuous melody and chromatic harmony of Wagner, and these elements are combined with the angular melody and imperial tone which were characteristic of Elgar. It is another coincidence that Elgar completed his own string quartet in 1918 (we have noted above that MacMillan was composing his *Ode – England* at the same time as Elgar was writing *The Spirit of England*). MacMillan no doubt became familiar with much of Elgar's work during his studies in Edinburgh (1905–11) and developed a close affinity for the English composer's music during that time. The MacMillan quartet is unquestionably a work of promise and worthy of the recognition which it has recently received on the international scene (it was recorded by the Amadeus Quartet in 1967). For the cause of Canadian music it is a pity that Sir Ernest's conducting and administrative career left so little time for composition.

The two violin and piano sonatas by Healey Willan are also noteworthy. The *Sonata No. 1 in E Minor* is dated February 1916 and *Sonata No. 2 in E Major* was completed before March 1921. Both works are clearly derivative, but of two different styles. The first sonata is constructed along the lines of Franck's *Sonata for Violin and Piano* (1886). The first movement is in clearly marked sections indicating sonata-allegro form; there are two distinguishable subjects, the second being derived from the first and often combined with it. Much of the development is concerned with canonic interplay between the violin and piano, a device reminiscent of Franck. Harmonically the first movement is tonal, but there are times when this is obscure. Unity is often achieved through ostinato figures or repetition of chord types, rather than through traditional functional progressions. The result is typical of much of the progressive music of the turn of the century which, while attempting to say something fresh and new, does so through an expansion of tonality rather than an abandonment of it. The recall of material from the first movement in the second is again reminiscent of Franck. The last movement has hints of the *Sonata in C Minor* (1886–7) by Grieg, a work of the same vintage as Franck's sonata. Willan's final movement is in an ABACABA-plus-coda structure, the classic rondo form. The regularity of the six-eight metre is mitigated by hemiola at appropriate points. Thematically the B and C sections provide a subtle reminder of the first and second movements, but Willan does not employ cyclicism to the same extent as Franck. In this work Willan is much more a composer of his time than he was to be henceforth.

The second violin and piano sonata is the result of a conscious effort to write a work in the style of the baroque period, particularly that of Handel. Willan felt that much of what was being written in the early part of the twentieth century was anti-music and that earlier styles had not exhausted their usefulness. This sonata has remained a standard work in the repertoire of the student violinist in Canada because of its sound construction, singable melodies, and approachable technical problems. Texturally thick, it is doubly anachronistic in that it follows a nineteenth-century approach to baroque style.

ORGAN MUSIC

It is fitting to close this first chapter with a discussion of one of the most highly acclaimed works written in Canada during the first two decades of the century. This is Willan's *Introduction, Passacaglia and Fugue*, which was completed on 31 July

EXAMPLE 1-1   Healey Willan, *Introduction, Passacaglia and Fugue* (1916), beginning of passacaglia

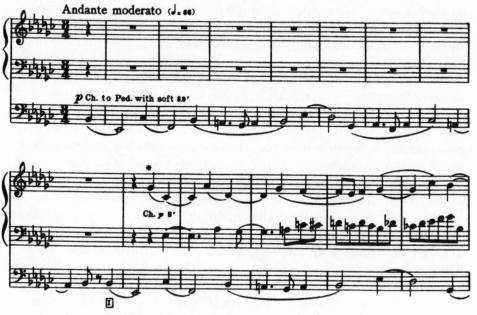

Copyright © 1919 by G. Schirmer, Inc. Used by permission

1916 and performed by the composer on 30 November of the same year. It is dedicated to Walter G. Alcock, then assistant organist of Westminster Abbey and organist for the coronations of three British sovereigns, Edward VII, George V, and George VI. Joseph Bonnet (1884–1944), the eminent French organist and editor, proclaimed this work to be the greatest of its type since Bach. Even though this may be regarded as an exaggeration, the work merits the international recognition which it has received.

Besides its more famous predecessor by Bach, the *Passacaglia in C Minor,* BWV 582, Willan's work had a more immediate model in the *Introduction, Passacaglia and Fugue* in E minor by Max Reger. Composed just a few years before Willan's (Berlin, c 1913), the Reger work was performed one summer in Convocation Hall at the University of Toronto. Godfrey Ridout, one of Willan's most illustrious students, relates that, 'Dalton Baker remarked that such a work could only have been produced by a Germanic philosophical mind. Healey's only comment was: "To Hell with it." By the time he had reached home he had worked out a theme, and each weekend while riding the radial trolley between Toronto and Jackson's Point where he had established his family in a summer cottage, he wrote two variations, one each way.'[22]

A comparison between the Reger and Willan works points up interesting similarities and differences. The introductions are similar in length and in their descending chromatic bass lines, but the Reger is almost twice as long in the passacaglia and fugue sections. Each passacaglia subject involves leaps of fourths and fifths, but Reger's is more chromatic and more disguised tonally. The fugues are in greater contrast with regard to thematic material and texture, the Reger being quite Mozartean in character while the Willan is more Handelean. In spite of his attempt to emulate the German style, Willan's *Introduction, Passacaglia and Fugue* is very much in the texturally heavy and murky idiom of English organ music of the Victorian era (see example 1-1).

SELECTED WORKS

composer	title	score	recording
PIANO MUSIC			
Branscombe, Gena	*Chansonette*	Whaley-Royce, 1903	
	Impromptu	Whaley-Royce, 1903	
	Valse-Caprice	Whaley-Royce, 1903	
Champagne, Claude	*Prélude et filigrane* (1918)	BMI Can, 1960	RCI 397
Forsyth, W.O.	*At Parting*, Op. 42, No. 3	Presser, 1917	
	Song of the Silver Night, Op. 34, No. 2	Whaley-Royce, 1914	
	In the Twilight (Im Dämmerlicht), Op. 31, No. 1	Nordheimer, 1907	
	Two Pieces for Pianoforte Op. 50, No. 2	Elkin, 1922	
Mathieu, Rodolphe	*Trois préludes* (1912–15)	Hérelle, 1921	
Tanguay, Georges-Emile	*Pavane* (1914)	Ditson, 1914	RCI 252
SOLO SONG			
Branscombe, Gena	*A Dirge* [Tennyson]	Whaley-Royce, 1903	
	Happiness – Glück [Eichendorff]	Schmidt, 1911	

composer	title	score	recording
Brazil, Jules	*Nukol Sparks* or *The Burning Love Song*	Anglo-Can, 1919	
Contant, Alexis	*Clos ta paupière*	Archambault, 1925	
	Récueil de chants réligieux	Archambault, n.d.	
Forsyth, W.O.	*Frühlingsabend*, Op. 16, No. 2	Jost, n.d.	
	Two Songs for Medium Voice, Op. 39	Fischer, 1915	
	Love's Tribute, Op. 35	Nordheimer, 1914	
Ham, Albert	*The Call of Empire* [T.H. Litster]	Anglo-Can, 1917	
	Canadians We Stand [I.A. Sifton]	Sifton, 1914	
	Auf Nimmerwiedersehen	Nordheimer, 1906	
(arr)	*Jack Canuck* [words and melody by Ravenor Bullen]	Whaley-Royce, 1910	
	O Perfect Love	Whaley-Royce, 1902	
Mathieu, Rodolphe	*Les Yeux noirs* (1911) [J.-E. Marsoin]	ms	
Smith, Leo	*My Mother Sea* [Swinburne]	G. Schirmer, 1914	
	O Oranges, Sweet Oranges	G. Schirmer, 1914	

CHORAL MUSIC

composer	title	score	recording
Contant, Alexis	**Caïn* (1905)	ms	
	*Les Deux âmes (1909)	ms	
	*Messe no. 3 (1903) [orchestrated 1913]	ms	
Couture, Guillaume	**Jean le Précurseur* (1911)	Joubert, 1914	
	*Messe de Requiem (1906) [orchestrated 1913]	ms	
Ham, Albert	*Canada* [W.A. Fraser]	Whaley-Royce, 1906	
	O, Give Thanks Unto the Lord	Anglo-Can, 1898	
	Hope of the Ages [J. Greenleaf Whittier]	Nordheimer, 1903	
Harriss, Charles, A.E.	**Coronation Mass Edward VII* (1902)	Boosey, 1903	
	*Pan (1904)	ms	
	*The Crowning of the King	Novello, 1911	

*Denotes large-scale work for chorus, [soli], and orchestra

composer	title	score	recording
Lucas, Clarence	*God of Our Fathers* [Agnes Grote Copeland]	Anglo-Can, 1911	
MacMillan, Ernest	*Ode – 'England'* (1918) [Swinburne]	Novello, 1918	
Willan, Healey	*An Apostrophe to the Heavenly Hosts* (1921)	Harris, 1936, 1952	RCI 207; RCA LSC3054
	Christmas Song of the 14th Century	Gray, 1915	RCI 207; Cap ST 6248

ORCHESTRAL MUSIC

composer	title	score	recording
Champagne, Claude	*Hercule et Omphale* (1918)	Berandol	
Lucas, Clarence	*Overture, 'As You Like It',* Op. 35 (1899)		RCI 233; Cap ST 6261
Mathieu, Rodolphe	*Un Peu d'ombre* (1913), soprano and orchestra [Pierre Newton]	CMS ms	
Tanguay, Georges-Emile	*Romance* (1915), violin and orchestra	ms	

CHAMBER MUSIC

composer	title	score	recording
Contant, Alexis	*Trio No. 1* (1907)	ms	RCI 229; RCA-CCS 1023
MacMillan, Ernest	*String Quartet in C Minor* (1914–18; rev 1921)	CMC ms film 2/21	RCI 236; DGG SLPM 139900
Willan, Healey	*Sonata No. 1 in E Minor* (1916), violin and piano	BMI Can, 1955	RCI 124
	Sonata No. 2 in E Major (1921), violin and piano	Bosworth, 1923	RCI 243

ORGAN MUSIC

composer	title	score	recording
Willan, Healey	*Introduction, Passacaglia and Fugue* (1916)	G. Schirmer, 1919	Odeon CSD 1550; Philips 6587 001

CHAPTER TWO

1921 to 1940
Early Nationalism

On dit couramment que la musique est un langage; il serait plus juste de dire que dans la musique il y a plusieurs langues.
    Rodolphe Mathieu, *Parlons musique* (1932)

Since the time of Confederation much has been written about the question of Canadian identity. Whether there is one or should be one, and, if so, how it can be described, has been the subject of much debate. Amidst great diversity of opinion, which is as varied as the geographical regions of the country, it is generally agreed that artistic endeavours not only reflect national identity but greatly influence its existence. Poetry was the first of the arts to present a distinctively Canadian view of things, a perspective which was recognized both inside and outside the country. Charles G.D. Roberts in *Orion and Other Poems* (1880), Bliss Carman in *Low Tide on Grande Pré* (1893), Duncan Campbell Scott in *The Magic House* (1893), and Archibald Lampman in *Among the Millet* (1888) established themselves as poets who were not only in command of their craft but whose works had a particularly Canadian flavour. At the same time Louis Fréchette in his grand epic poem *La Légende d'un peuple* (1887) illuminated the French-Canadian *esprit*, as did Emile Nelligan in his symbolist sonnet *Le Vaisseau d'or* (1896–9) and his poetic manifesto *La Romance du vin* (1899). In the 1910s and 1920s the painters of the Group of Seven, including A.Y. Jackson, Lawren Harris, and J.E.H. MacDonald, achieved notable results by turning from romantic pictorialism to a lean depiction of what was for them the essence of Canada–Quebec villages, the Canadian Shield, and the Rocky Mountains. Although their work later came to symbolize the ideal of nationalism in Canadian art, it was at first regarded as too modern and too far removed from reality. Both Emily Carr on the west coast and Marc-Aurèle Fortin in Quebec also fostered the new nationalism in Canadian art.

In Canada music, which generally tends to lag behind the other arts in following new trends, was slow to adopt identifiable nationalistic elements. It was not until the 1920s, and then only in a modest way, that Canadian composers began to incorporate in their work distinctly national materials (i.e. folk songs and dances), as Vaughan Williams and Bartók had done in the early years of the century. However, most Canadian composers agreed with Léo-Pol Morin who maintained in 1928 that a work need not quote or use folk music directly in order to be distinctively Canadian.[1] Rodolphe Mathieu expressed a similar view in 1932: 'le véritable nationalisme en art consiste, non pas à chanter l'âme nationale, mais à la laisser chanter sur tous les sujets.'[2] Sir Ernest MacMillan also summed up the prevailing attitude in 1936: 'we cannot by taking thought produce a national music; all we can do is to create an atmosphere in which strong musical personalities can express themselves creatively and naturally.'[3]

Nevertheless, in the 1920s some attempts were made to create musical works which drew their material and inspiration directly from Canadian life. One of the most active promoters of musical nationalism was not a musician but an anthropologist and folklorist, C. Marius Barbeau, who was associated with the National Museum of Canada in Ottawa (now the National Museum of Man) throughout his long career. Barbeau was particularly interested in French-Canadian folk music and folklore as well as the artistic creations of the west-coast Indians. Even as late as 1961, when the International Folk Music Society met in Quebec City, Barbeau acted as an intermediary in trying to get Canadian composers to use some of the vast quantities of Canadian folk music which he and others had so arduously collected. Earlier attempts in this direction centred on the two festivals of Canadian folk arts held in Quebec City in 1927 and 1928 under the joint auspices of the National Museum of Canada and the Canadian Pacific Railway. Barbeau's colleague in these enterprises was John Murray Gibbon, publicity agent for the CPR from 1913 to 1945. Many prominent musicians of the day were brought together for the purpose of celebrating Canadian folk arts. Healey Willan, Ernest MacMillan, Alfred E. Whitehead, Alfred Laliberté, Leo Smith, Claude Champagne, Henri Gagnon, Hector Gratton, Achille Fortier, and the internationally recognized Hart House String Quartet (Géza de Kresz and Harry Adaskin, violins, Milton Blackstone, viola, Boris Hambourg, cello) all contributed in some fashion to the Quebec festivals (John Langley substituted for de Kresz in 1928).

Most of the works which resulted directly or indirectly from the Quebec festivals were settings for voice and piano or choral arrangements which used Canadian folk songs as their basis. A few examples of ballad operas also appeared. Ernest Gagnon's *Chansons populaires du Canada* and Barbeau and Edward Sapir's *Folk Songs of French Canada* were the first works to bring French-Canadian folk songs to the attention of the musical world, but they consisted only of transcriptions of and commentary on the songs as they had been passed down orally from generation to generation (many of them dated back to the early colonization in the seventeenth century). These transcriptions did not meet performance conventions of the twentieth century, which required full accompaniments in addition to the melody line and text of the original song. Barbeau was active in prodding composers into providing such accompaniments so that the songs would become more widely used.

Vingt-et-une chansons canadiennes/Twenty-one French-Canadian Folk Songs, edited by Ernest MacMillan, was one of the volumes of settings for voice and piano which grew out of the Barbeau-inspired folk-song movement of the 1920s. The settings by Achille Fortier (5), Alfred Laliberté (1), Ernest MacMillan (9), Leo Smith (2), and Oscar O'Brien (4) are generally simple, although the MacMillan accompaniments have more pianistic flourishes than the others. The arrangers attempt to capture the modal flavour of many of the melodies but succumb at times to an inappropriate use of chromatic harmony. Moreover, the thick texture of many of the piano accompaniments tends to interfere with the simple, narrative style of the original songs.

The first choral arrangements of Canadian folk songs appeared at about the same time. The Boston Music Company even published the prize-winning arrangements from the 1928 Quebec festival, four by Alfred E. Whitehead and four by Ernest MacMillan. Whitehead's arrangements are for mixed voices (a cappella) and employ a thick and heavy texture reminiscent of Brahms's arrangements of folk songs. MacMillan's arrangements for men's voices show more imagination, especially his *Blanche comme la neige*, which is through-composed and considerably more extended than most choral arrangements of folk songs. Both sets of arrangements have English translations by John Murray Gibbon, underlining the fact that one of the main purposes of the Quebec festivals and the subsequent publications was to make the great wealth of French-Canadian folk song available to English-speaking North America.

The ballad opera as a genre dates back to 1728 and *The Beggar's Opera* (libretto by John Gay and musical arrangements of ballad tunes by Johann Pepusch).[4] Expressing as it did a middle-class revolt against the stylized Italian opera which had dominated the musical scene in England since before Handel's arrival in 1710, the ballad opera consisted of popular songs (anonymous ballads or arias by known composers), dance tunes, and spoken dialogue in the vernacular. This genre was ideally suited to the purposes of the Quebec festivals, which were trying to reach as wide an audience as possible and to promote the folk arts of French Canada. Works in this genre also appeared in other countries in the 1920s, notably *Hugh the Drover* (1924) by Vaughan Williams and *Die Dreigroschenoper* (1928; *The Three-penny Opera*, 1933) by Kurt Weill.

Three ballad operas were produced at the Quebec festival of 1928, all with libretti by Louvigny de Montigny (1876–1955). The most successful was Healey Willan's *L'Ordre de bon temps* (Oakville: F. Harris, 1928), which was based on the story of the celebrations at the first permanent settlement in what was to become Canada (Port-Royal, 1605), where music was performed in a cultivated social setting for the first time. The principal characters are Marc Lescarbot, Samuel de Champlain, and Jean de Biencourt. Willan, who had prepared an arrangement of *The Beggar's Opera* in 1927 for use in the Hart House Theatre at the University of Toronto, created a work which maintains contrapuntal interest at the same time as it adheres to the simplicity of the folk songs, many of which date from the time of the story. *L'Ordre de bon temps* is ideally suited for school or amateur production because of its happy combination of music, drama, the French and English languages, and national history.

Another work connected with the Quebec festivals is Champagne's *Suite canadienne* (1927) for chorus and orchestra, which won first prize at the Quebec festival of 1928 and is probably the first Canadian orchestral score to receive international recognition. It is based on four French-Canadian folk songs: 'C'est pinson avec cendrouille,' 'Nous étions trois capitaines,' 'Et moi je m'en passe,' and 'Le Fils du roi s'en va chassant.' Approximately eight minutes in length, this well-constructed work employs a modal approach in modern dress, a style which is not surprising in view of the fact that Champagne spent most of the 1920s in the centre of neoclassicism, Paris. Whether based on folk material or not, his relatively few works are characterized by a strong lyrical sense, clarity of texture, and a sure contrapuntal technique.

The presence of the Hart House String Quartet (founded in Toronto in 1924 by the late Honourable Vincent Massey) at the Quebec festivals of 1927 and 1928 prompted several attempts to incorporate Canadian folk material into chamber music, particularly the string quartet. Alfred Laliberté, Leo Smith, and Ernest MacMillan each wrote what they modestly termed 'sketches' for string quartet. Most significant of these is MacMillan's *Two Sketches for String Quartet* (1927), which is based on two folk songs, 'Notre Seigneur en pauvre' (Our Lord in Beggar's Guise) and 'A Saint-Malo.' MacMillan's treatment shows considerable contrapuntal skill but at the same time allows the expressivity of the songs to show through. An optional double bass part makes the work available for performance by a string orchestra.

In spite of this flurry of nationalistic creativity which centred on the Quebec festivals Barbeau was not satisfied. He noted in 1929 that 'folk songs, to mean something really vital in the art of a nation, must lead to larger forms.'[5] No Canadian composers took up this challenge immediately, and only one, Claude Champagne, did eventually achieve a degree of success, but even his nationalistic works in the larger forms came after 1940. Barbeau later remarked despondently: 'to some observers at the time it seemed that Canada's own music was born and would soon be coming into its own. Perhaps we were too optimistic.'[6]

PIANO MUSIC

The composition of character pieces for piano continued to be a preoccupation of Canadian composers until World War II. W.O. Forsyth added to his long list of pieces such works as *The Stream in the Hills,* Op. 66 (1934), a perpetual-motion piece, and *Prelude,* Op. 59, No. 2 (1929), a technically demanding work with poetic, expressive qualities. Leo Smith's *Three Pieces* (1937), despite their attractive titles, 'The Song Sparrow,' 'Schumannesque,' and 'From an Old Note-book,' possess little musical interest.

Prior to 1940 there are few Canadian works in the larger forms such as the sonata, symphony, or string quartet. One exception in the category of keyboard music is the *Sonate pour piano* (1927) by Rodolphe Mathieu. In contrast to the sensuous and colouristic approach of Claude Champagne in his *Prélude et filigrane* (1918), this sonata shows the constructive tendencies of Franck and d'Indy. Intensely chromatic and at times overly sequential, this one-movement work is a remnant of late-nineteenth-century romanticism.

In the years immediately preceding 1939, while there were soundings of war in Europe, there was also the beginning of a revolution in Canadian music. Several young composers emerged who were much more in tune with the twentieth-century musical developments associated with Bartók, Hindemith, Schönberg, and Stravinsky than were their elders. After Barbara Pentland returned from studies at the Juilliard School, John Weinzweig from the Eastman School, and Jean Papineau-Couture from the New England Conservatory and the Longy School in Boston in the late 1930s and early 1940s, Canadian music took on new directions. Although it was several years before the efforts of these young composers were to be fully realized, the seeds were sown which were to bring Canada into the mainstream of musical composition for the first time in the century.

Pentland's *Rhapsody* (1939) for piano is typical of these new tendencies. Showing the influence of Paul Hindemith, whose style she emulated during her years at the Juilliard School (1936–9), this work combines a strong interest in dissonant counterpoint with free rhapsody, a characteristic style which has remained with Pentland throughout her career. More prophetic in terms of later developments, however, is another work of the same year, John Weinzweig's *Suite for Piano, No. 1* (1939). This is the first work written by a Canadian composer to utilize the twelve-tone system of Arnold Schönberg, albeit in a much modified form. In three movements, labelled 'Waltzling,' 'Dirgeling,' and 'Themes with Variables,' this work uses the tone row as a source of motivic material within traditional neoclassic forms, such as ABA and theme and variations. The result is a work of wit and humour which sounds more like the neoclassicism of Stravinsky and Bartók than the dodecaphonism of Schönberg. In 'Waltzling' Weinzweig uses a nine-note row as the basis of a melodic and rhythmic ostinato within an overall ABA structure. The original statement of the row indicates a preference for the interval of the minor third and minor sixth in the tail-end of its formation. This, along with Weinzweig's tendency towards motivic repetition, mollifies the harsh effect of the twelve-tone technique. Nevertheless, this work and others which followed were rejected not only by a large majority of the listening public, but by many of

Weinzweig's colleagues as well. He spoke out in defence of the composer of new music, but to little avail: 'the modern composer has taken great care to organize his material for its realization by the performer and its communication to the listener, and yet the listener fails to respond! The fault lies in the lack of aural experience.'[7] Weinzweig to this day is chagrined that 'the concert-hall has become a museum where the so-called "classics" are perpetuated to the exclusion of contemporary music.'[8]

SOLO SONG

Fewer songs were written in this period than between 1900 and 1920, perhaps as a result of the introduction of the radio as a device of home entertainment. Gena Branscombe, who lived in New York after 1910, continued to identify with Canadian themes, as her *Our Canada, From Sea to Sea* composed for the royal tour of 1939 exemplifies. Healey Willan also contributed to the repertoire of patriotic song literature with *A Song of Canada* (1930) and *We Sing A Song to Canada* (1939).

Some of the most significant solo songs in this period are those arranged from the repertoire of French-Canadian folklore at about the time of the Quebec festivals of 1927 and 1928. In addition, Ernest MacMillan made settings of west-coast Indian songs collected by Barbeau, and he accompanied Barbeau on one of his trips to the Nass River in British Columbia in search of indigenous material.[9] The outcome of this collaboration was *Three Indian Songs of the West Coast* (1928), with texts in both Nass River dialect and English. Leo Smith also made settings of native songs, but the trend towards using such materials did not continue because of the inappropriateness of the piano, problems associated with the equal-tempered scale, and the difficulty of setting monodic songs of native peoples to nineteenth-century harmonies. Composers quickly realized that to clothe the products of an indigenous, oral tradition in the dress of Western European classical music added nothing to the original songs and even detracted from their inherent beauty.

There are some examples of art songs by Canadian composers in this period but few large-scale works such as song cycles. The one composer who specialized in song-writing was Smith, whose works in this genre are reminiscent of the simplicity and heartfelt fervour of the songs of Grieg. Smith set texts by Canadian poet Duncan Campbell Scott in his *Three Songs* (1930). He also wrote settings for poems of the English romantic school, such as Swinburne's 'Only the Song of a Secret Bird.' Similarly MacMillan composed *Sonnet* (1928), a setting of Elizabeth Barrett Browning's 'If Thou Must Love Me.' Willan published two song albums in 1925 and 1926 which included settings of Keats's 'Sonnet – To Sleep' and W.B. Yeats's 'The Lake Isle of Innisfree.' In French-speaking Canada there were also only a few art songs composed at this time; *Ressemblances* (1937) by J.J. Gagnier, one-time musical director of the CBC, is a typical example composed in a late-nineteenth-century style. *Saisons canadiennes* (before 1927), with both text and music by Rodolphe Mathieu, is a more successful work in the same vein and the only work of the entire period which might properly be termed a song cycle.

CHORAL MUSIC

A considerable amount of choral music was composed and published during this period. Most works were church anthems written in response to particular needs in particular situations. The English-born and English-trained composers who dominated the musical scene, such as Healey Willan, Alfred E. Whitehead, H. Hugh Bancroft, and W.H. Anderson, found it difficult at times to keep up with publishers' demands for choral music.[10] Unfortunately this state of affairs resulted in many works of a workmanlike but uninspired nature.

Willan was by far the most successful composer in this genre, and his best anthems were accepted and used in churches throughout the English-speaking world. In response to the weekly needs of St Mary Magdalene's Willan composed eight of his fourteen missae brevi from 1921 to 1940, as well as twenty-six of his forty liturgical motets. Most of the works were published in the United States and achieved wide popularity there. A typical example of the missae brevi is No. 4 (1934), which is based upon the Christmas sequence 'Corde natus ex parentis' (Divinum mysterium), known in English as 'Of the Father's Love Begotten.' Each of the three sections (Kyrie, Sanctus, Agnus Dei – the Gloria and Credo being omitted in the missa brevis) contains the original melody in whole or in part and the general atmosphere is one of gentleness before the crib of the Christ child. The mode is major (Ionian), but the use of the fifteenth-century device of faburden, together with modal cadences, gives the setting an antique flavour. The horizontal texture resembles renaissance polyphony but the vertical sonorities employ richer chords of a later period, thus giving the whole a hybrid but nevertheless austere character.

It is, however, in the motets that Willan achieved his greatest success. His ability to capture the essence of each word and line of text as it pertained to the particular part of the ecclesiastical year and to add to its expression through music places him in the front rank of composers for the church in the twentieth century. *Rise Up, My Love, My Fair One* (1929), *Fair in Face* (1928), *I Beheld Her, Beautiful as a Dove* (1928), *Behold the Tabernacle of God* (1933), and *Hodie Christus natus es* (1935) were all written between 1928 and 1935. Each is cast in an essentially simple setting in which contrapuntal skill is always in evidence as is the sensitive relationship between text and music. The sonorous quality of the vocal part-writing contributes greatly to the feeling of awe and reverence which these motets generate.

Few composers matched Willan in quantity and none in quality. Whitehead, who was organist and choirmaster at Christ Church Cathedral (Anglican) in Montreal from 1922 to 1947 saw approximately four hundred of his choral works published; most of them were sacred in nature and composed between 1920 and 1940. Well-constructed in the late-nineteenth-century English-cathedral style, Whitehead's works give the impression of being mass-produced and lack the imaginative or poetic qualities which characterize the works of Willan. The best of Whitehead's choral works, such as *Ye Choirs of New Jerusalem* (1933) for SATB and organ and *Magnificat* and *Nunc dimittis* (1933) for double choir and organ, are worthy of retention in the repertoire. Both were favourites of the composer's.

Major works for chorus, soli, and orchestra, either sacred or secular, are almost non-existent in this period. Successors to Alexis Contant and Guillaume Couture in French-speaking Canada did not follow them with large-scale masses or oratorios. In English Canada Willan and MacMillan each wrote a Te Deum and Willan composed *A Coronation Ode* for King George VI and Queen Elizabeth (1936). These works range in length from four to ten minutes, make use of double choir and orchestra, and employ antiphonal techniques of the English school of Stanford and Parry. Works of larger dimension did not appear until after the end of World War II.

ORCHESTRAL MUSIC

Considering the amount of musical activity in the major cities, including the establishment of professional orchestras in Toronto in 1923 and in Montreal in 1934, it is surprising that there are not more original works for orchestra. The first extant work of symphonic proportions to be composed in Canada did appear, however, in this inter-war period: Willan's *Symphony No. 1 in D Minor* (1936). Obviously modelled after the symphony of the same key by another church musician, Franck, the melodies tend to revolve chromatically around a central tone. Combined with this feature is a predilection for a faburden-like use of thirds and sixths in the English manner (particularly in the second and third movements) and a triumphant, imperial-sounding second subject in the third movement which is reminiscent of Elgar's *Pomp and Circumstance* marches (1901–30). The symphony has never been accepted into the repertoire of Canadian orchestras, possibly because of its outdated rhetoric and great length.

Most of the other orchestral works of the period are either suites or overtures, usually varying in length from six to twelve minutes. If a Canadian work was to be performed at all, it almost certainly would be placed in the warm-up position at the beginning of a concert where works beyond ten minutes' duration were not favoured. Claude Champagne's *Berceuse* (1933), Hector Gratton's *Légende* (1937), Rodolphe Mathieu's orchestration of an earlier piano work, *Trois préludes* (1930?), Godfrey Ridout's *Festal Overture* (1939), Leo Smith's *A Summer Idyll* (n.d.), and Ernest MacMillan's *Overture* (1924) are works of this type; some of them are still performed from time to time. Champagne's *Suite canadienne* (1927) and Rodolphe Mathieu's *Harmonie du soir* (1924) employ SATB chorus and solo voice, respectively, in addition to the orchestra but neither is an extended composition. All of the works mentioned belong stylistically more to the nineteenth than to the twentieth century.

CHAMBER MUSIC

As with orchestral music, the chamber music repertoire of this period is small, modest in scope, and unrepresentative of the newer trends in twentieth-century composition. The works which come closest to a twentieth-century style are by Rodolphe Mathieu, who was by far the most prolific and stylistically adventurous composer of chamber music in this period. His *Pièce pour quatuor à cordes* (1920), *Trio pour violon, violoncelle et piano* (1921), *Douze monologues pour violon seul* (before 1924), *Sonate pour violon et piano* (1928), and *Deux poèmes pour chant et quatuor à cordes* (1928) are in a post-Wagnerian idiom which approaches that of Schönberg's *Verklärte Nacht* (1899). These works were, unfortunately, not readily accepted in Canada in the 1920s and 1930s, and Mathieu, discouraged by the lack of public and professional interest in his music, devoted most of his energies after 1930 to teaching and the promotion of the career of his son André, a child-prodigy, pianist, and composer.[12]

The *Two Sketches for String Quartet* (1927) and *Six bergerettes du bas Canada* (1928) for solo voices and instruments by MacMillan are attractive works incorporating Canadian folk material, but neither lives up to the promise indicated by his earlier *String Quartet in C Minor* (1914–18; rev 1921). Laliberté's arrangements of Eskimo and Indian melodies for string quartet (1927), Hector Gratton's four *Danses canadiennes* (1927–35), Smith's *Tambourin* (1930) and *Trochaios* (1930), and Champagne's *Danse villageoise* (1929) for violin and piano are all musical miniatures which fall short of what Barbeau had hoped for in the way of extended compositions based on Canadian folk music. The *Danse villageoise*, which subsequently appeared in arrangements for string quartet (c 1936), string orchestra (before 1947), and full orchestra (after 1954), has been one of the most popular of these pieces. It successfully captures the spirit of the French-Canadian country dance much in the same way that the paintings of Cornelius Krieghoff portray French-Canadian social activities. Andrée Desautels, a Montreal critic, calls attention to the fact that the 'two elements which are blended in the work seem to symbolize the composer's French and Irish background.'[13] Champagne extracts motives from the main melody and uses them as accompaniment figures. Such economy of means was typical of him (see example 2-1).

An attempt was made in Toronto in 1936 to establish a chamber music society which would promote Canadian composition. Originally named the Willan Society in honour of the composer and as a protest by the Conservatory Residence Alumnae Association against the recent abolition of Willan's post of assistant principal of the Toronto Conservatory of Music, the society held a contest for the

EXAMPLE 2-1   Claude Champagne, *Danse villageoise* (1929), violin and piano version, mm 20–5

best Canadian composition. The *Suite No. 1 in D* (1935) for violin and piano by Patricia Blomfield Holt was declared the first-prize winner. At the request of Dr Willan the name of the society was changed to the Vogt Society (in honour of a former principal of the Conservatory, Augustus Vogt) and still later it became the Society for Contemporary Music. The difficulty of agreeing upon a name was symptomatic of other problems, and the amount of new chamber music produced as a result of the society's efforts was small.

Chamber music in Canada was very conservative at this time. For example, Arnold Walter's *Trio* (1940) for violin, cello, and piano, which was written in a Brahmsian style, was awarded the Performing Rights' Society prize in 1943. Even the works of the younger generation of composers as represented by Pentland's *Quartet for Piano and Strings* (1939) and Weinzweig's *String Quartet No. 1* (1937) had not yet broken away from nineteenth-century romanticism. This situation was about to change, however, with the move towards neoclassicism after 1940.

ORGAN MUSIC

The small number of works for organ written in this period is surprising in view of the fact that a large proportion of the professional musicians in the country were church organists. Even Willan's works for organ were few in number, the greater part of his creative efforts being directed towards liturgical choral music. Willan did begin at this time what was to become a series of organ preludes on chorale melodies or hymn tunes, such as the *Chorale Prelude No. 1* (1926) on 'Puer nobis nascitur' and the *Chorale Prelude No. 2* (1928) on 'Andernach'; these are essentially simple pieces of a functional nature, often using the device of faburden. Further chorale preludes by Willan did not appear in print until 1950. The only other organ work by Willan written between 1921 and 1940 is the *Elegy* (1933) which was composed 'in memory of a great artist, a valued friend, and a fellow-student, Lynnwood Farnam.'[14] (Farnam was a prominent Canadian organist who studied at the Royal College of Music in London, and who held posts in Montreal, Boston, and New York; he died at the early age of forty-five.)

Whitehead contributed a few organ pieces, including *Prelude on 'Winchester Old'* (published 1937), a Christmas pastorale, and *Prelude on a Theme by Orlando Gibbons* (published 1940), based upon Gibbons's *Song* I. Both are written in a conservative, tonal style. Other English-born and English-trained organist-composers who contributed similarly to the small repertory of organ music were W.H. Anderson, H. Hugh Bancroft, Vernon Barford, and Douglas Clarke. Montreal organist Arthur Letondal composed a few small-scale works, such as *Prélude grave* and *Offertoire*, in a simple, sentimental style.

The mantle of leadership in Canadian music, which had been in the hands of the organist-choirmaster-composer for over one hundred years, however, was soon to pass to younger men and women who sought to emulate the musical thought and practice of composers such as Bartók, Hindemith, Stravinsky, Schönberg, Berg, Webern, and Ives. This confrontation, which has parallels in the other arts, will be explored in the next chapter.

SELECTED WORKS

composer	title	score	recording
PIANO MUSIC			
Blackburn, Maurice	*Cinq digitales* (1940)	Nos. 2, 5 Harris, 1955	RCI 397 (no. 5)
Forsyth, W.O.	*The Light of the Summer Stars*, Op. 58, No. 2	Nordheimer, 1927	
	Prelude, Op. 59, No. 2	Anglo-Can, 1929	
	The Stream in the Hills, Op. 66	Harris, 1934	
Mathieu, Rodolphe	*Sonate* (1926–7)	CMC ms	RCI 123
Pentland, Barbara	*Rhapsody* (1939)	CMC ms film 12/32	
Smith, Leo	*Three Pieces*	Harris, 1937	
Weinzweig, John	*Suite for Piano No. 1* (1939)	'Waltzling' Harris, 1955; CMC ms film 8/36	
SOLO SONG			
Branscombe, Gena	*Our Canada, From Sea to Sea* [A. Stringer]	GVT, 1939	

composer	title	score	recording
Gagnier, J.-J.	*Ressemblances* (*Romance*) [Sully Prudhomme]	Parnasse, 1937	
MacMillan, Ernest	*Sonnet* [Elizabeth Barrett Browning]	Harris, 1928	
(arr)	*Three Indian Songs of the West Coast*	Harris, 1928	
(ed)	*Vingt-et-une chansons canadiennes/Twenty-one French-Canadian Folk Songs*	Harris, 1928	
Mathieu, Rodolphe	*Saisons canadiennes* (before 1927) [Rodolphe Mathieu]		RCI 365
Smith, Leo	*Three Songs* [Duncan Campbell Scott]	Harris, 1930	
Willan, Healey	*The Lake Isle of Innisfree* [W.B. Yeats]	Harris, 1926	CBC SM 144
	Sonnet – 'To Sleep' [J. Keats]	Harris, 1925	CBC SM 144
	A Song of Canada [H.C. Fricker]	Harris, 1930	
	We Sing a Song to Canada [F. Harris]	Harris, 1939	

CHORAL MUSIC

composer	title	score	recording
Champagne, Claude	*Ave Maria* (1924)	BMI Can, 1954	RCI 206
Fricker, H.A.	*Sleep, Holy Babe*	Whaley-Royce, 1921	RCI 166
MacMillan, Ernest	*The King Shall Rejoice in Thy Strength*	Harris, 1935	
	Te Deum laudamus (1936)	CMC ms film 2/25	CMC tape 548
	Blanche comme la neige (1928; rev 1958)	Boston, 1928; GVT, 1968	RCI 339
Whitehead, Alfred E.	*Alleluia! Sing to Jesus*	Schmidt, 1934	
	Magnificat and *Nunc dimittis*	Fischer, 1933	
	Ye Choirs of New Jerusalem	Schmidt, 1933	
Willan, Healey	*A Coronation Ode*	Harris, 1936	
	Behold the Tabernacle of God (1933)	Fischer, 1934	RCI 207; Cap ST 6248
	Fair in Face (1928)	Oxford, 1928	Cap ST 6248
	Here Are We in Bethlehem (1929)	Oxford, 1930	Cap ST 6248; RCI 207

composer	title	score	recording
	Hodie Christus natus es (1935)	Fischer, 1935	Cap sᴛ 6248; Conc ᴄᴅʟᴘ 4; Sim ᴛ55562-3
	I Beheld Her, Beautiful as a Dove (1928)	Oxford, 1928	ʀᴄɪ 207; Cap sᴛ 6248
	Missa brevis No. 4	Fischer, 1934	ʀᴄɪ 207; ᴄʙᴄ sᴍ 314; Cap sᴛ 6248
	Rise Up, My Love, My Fair One (1929)	Oxford, 1929	Sim ᴛ55562; Cap sᴛ 6248
	Te Deum laudamus (1937)	Harris, 1938	
	The Three Kings (1928)	Oxford, 1928	ʀᴄɪ 207; Cap sᴛ 6248
	Tyrle, Tyrlow (1928)	Harris, 1928	ʀᴄɪ 207; Cap sᴛ 6248

ORCHESTRAL MUSIC

composer	title	score	recording
Champagne, Claude	*Berceuse* (1933)	ᴄᴍᴄ ms film 15/8	ᴄᴍᴄ tape 132
	Suite canadienne (1927)	Durand, 1929	ʀᴄɪ Album 1
Gratton, Hector	*Légende* (1937)	ᴄᴍᴄ ms film 23/9	
MacMillan, Ernest	*Overture* (1924)	ᴄᴍᴄ ms film 2/20	
	Two Sketches for String Orchestra (1927)	Oxford, 1928	Col ᴍs 6962; ʀᴄɪ 238
Mathieu, Rodolphe	*Trois préludes* (orchestrated, 1930?)	ms	
	Harmonie du soir (1924), voice, violin, orchestra	ᴄᴍᴄ ms	
Ridout, Godfrey	*Festal Overture* (1939)	ᴄᴍᴄ ms film 15/35	ᴄᴍᴄ tape 11
Smith, Leo	*A Summer Idyll* (n.d.)	ms	ʀᴄɪ 233; Cap sᴛ 6261; *Musican* rec. 1
Willan, Healey	*Symphony No. 1 in D Minor* (1936)	ᴄᴍᴄ ms	

CHAMBER MUSIC

composer	title	score	recording
Champagne, Claude	*Danse villageoise* (1929), violin, piano	ʙᴍɪ Can, 1949	Acadia 3000ᴄʙ
Gratton, Hector	*Quatrième danse canadienne* (1935), violin, piano	ʙᴍɪ Can, 1952	ʀᴄɪ 136

composer	title	score	recording
Holt, Patricia Blomfield	*Suite No. 1 in D* (1935)	GVT, 1943 (incomplete)	
MacMillan, Ernest	*Two Sketches for String Quartet* (1927)	Oxford, 1928	DGG SLPM 139900
	Six bergerettes du bas Canada (1928), solo voices and instruments	Oxford, 1935	CBC SM 204
Mathieu, Rodolphe	*Pièce pour quatuor à cordes* (1920)	ms	
	Deux poèmes pour chant et quatuor à cordes (1928)	CMC ms	CMC tape
	Sonate pour violon et piano (1928)	ms	
	Douze monologues pour violon seul (before 1924)	ms	RCI 243 nos. 5, 6, 8
	Trio pour violon, violoncelle et piano (1921)	CMC ms	
Pentland, Barbara	*Quartet for Piano and Strings* (1939)	ms	
Smith, Leo	*Tambourin*, violin and piano	Harris, 1930	
	Trochaios, violin and piano	Harris, 1930	
Walter, Arnold	*Trio* (1940)	CMC ms	CMC tape 446
Weinzweig, John	*String Quartet No. 1* (1937)	ms	

ORGAN MUSIC

Letondal, Arthur	*Prélude grave*	Archambault, 1924	
	Offertoire	Archambault, 1925	
Whitehead, Alfred E.	*Prelude on a Theme by Orlando Gibbons*	Gray, 1940	
	Prelude on 'Winchester Old'	Gray, 1937	
Willan, Healey	*Chorale Prelude No. 1* ('Puer nobis nascitur')	Oxford, 1926	
	Chorale Prelude No. 2 ('Andernach')	Oxford, 1928; Western, 1953	Col ML 6198
	Elegy (1933)	Gray, 1947	

BALLAD OPERA

Willan, Healey	*L'Ordre de bon temps* (1928)	Harris, 1928	

CHAPTER THREE

1941 to 1951
A New Beginning

In all other aspects of human activity, including the visual and literary arts, we are very much concerned with the present. It is utterly illogical that in music we should dwell almost entirely in the past.

　John Weinzweig, *Canadian Review of Music and Art* (June 1942)

The early 1940s found Canada in the midst of war and all the attendant reordering of national priorities. As World War I had led the country into increased political independence, culminating in the Statute of Westminster (1931), World War II gave additional impetus to Canadian nationalism, this time leading to developments in the various fields of artistic endeavour. Canadian artists began to experiment with new techniques associated with the assorted 'isms' of the early part of the the century – impressionism, expressionism, cubism, surrealism. It seemed to take the despair of the Depression and the devastation of World War II to shake many Canadians into the realization that the means of expression of the nineteenth century were not appropriate for the twentieth. A few Canadian painters moved away from purely representational art into more abstract realms: Bertram Brooker in the late twenties, Lawren Harris after 1933, Fritz Brandtner after 1936, Paul-Emile Borduas and Fernand Leduc after 1942, and Alfred Pellan when he returned to Canada in 1940 after being exposed to surrealism in Paris. In literature it was not until the 1950s that works embodying the 'stream-of-consciousness' techniques of the expressionist school (Joyce, Kafka) were used: A.M. Klein's *The Second Scroll* (1951), Ethel Wilson's *Swamp Angel* (1954), and the poems of Earle Birney show this influence. Elford Cox, influenced by the work of Henry Moore, experimented with abstraction in sculpture as early as 1939, but the development in this area was 'sporadic and inconclusive.'[1] Drama and architecture were primarily conservative and representational until the 1950s.

Norman McLaren's work in experimental film at the National Film Board after 1941 was one of the few areas in the arts in which Canada led the way on the international scene (e.g. the series *Chants populaires*, 1943–6).

The *Report* (1951) of the Royal Commission on National Development in the Arts, Letters, and Sciences, known as the *Massey Report* after the chairman of the commission, the Honourable Vincent Massey, gave credence to the view that Canada was lagging behind in the arts and that substantial government support was required in order to catch up. The formation of the Canada Council in 1957 as a result of the *Massey Report* had, and continues to have, an incalculable effect on the stimulation of creative activity in the arts, especially the new and experimental. Slightly earlier in the province of Quebec the manifesto *Refus global* (1948), which was proclaimed by the abstract painter Borduas and some artistic associates, opened up the way for new forms of expression by speaking out against the stifling atmosphere which pervaded artistic life in French Canada at that time. Unfortunately, it also led to Borduas's dismissal from his teaching position in Montreal and his self-imposed exile in New York and Paris until his death in 1960. The document has since become the beacon in Quebec for total freedom of expression in art.[2]

By the outbreak of World War II very little of the music of the major twentieth-century figures was known to the Canadian concert-going public. While it is true that Schönberg's *String Quartet No. 1*, Op. 7 (1904–5) was performed by the Academy Quartet in Toronto in 1915,[3] it is equally true that as late as 1946 the conductor of the Toronto Symphony Orchestra felt compelled to speak from the podium and urge the audience to approach the performance of Sibelius's *Fourth Symphony* (1911) with an open mind and 'in a spirit of tolerance for the new and experimental.'[4] A few of the older French-Canadian composers had studied in Paris (Claude Champagne, 1921–9; Rodolphe Mathieu, 1920–7), but the most recent styles by which they were affected were those of Scriabin, Debussy, and early Schönberg.

As we noted in chapter 2, it was when the next generation of composers (e.g. Barbara Pentland, John Weinzweig, Jean Papineau-Couture) came home after foreign study in the late 1930s and early 1940s that things began to change. These composers returned to Canada with a missionary zeal to introduce twentieth-century music to Canadian audiences and to win acceptance for music created in the idioms of their own time. Results were slow in coming, not just because of audience resistance, but also because of open antagonism on the part of many of their conservative colleagues. Healey Willan, the internationally respected composer of church music, was not sympathetic to the new directions which musical style had taken in the twentieth century and believed quite strongly that 'if you tear up anything by the roots, it is bound to die!'[5] His influence on young and formative minds at the University of Toronto, where he was professor of music, was considerable. On the other hand the younger composers, such as Weinzweig, were beginning to speak out, and during the 1940s the controversy erupted on a number of occasions. In 1943 Pentland said that, 'while there's life, there's experiment. Without the element of looking forward, music would stagnate and die.'[6] In a subsequent article Pentland voiced the bitterness that many of the younger composers felt: 'the long dependence on a "mother" country has allowed our resources of native talent to be stifled or exported ... before our time music development was largely in the hands of imported English organists, who, however sound academically, had no creative contribution to make of any general value ... larger works of serious intent are apt to remain piled on the Great Canadian Shelf.'[7]

Furthermore, some composers were concerned not only with the use of new stylistic idioms but also with the addition of a nationalistic, a particularly Canadian, flavour to their works. Composers were, as they still are, divided on whether this is a desirable or even a possible feature. The majority seemed to agree with Papineau-Couture that nationalism is not so important as getting the public to accept contemporary idioms in music and thereby provide an audience for the Canadian composer's works.[8]

It was not until the early 1950s that several events swung the balance in favour of the younger generation of composers. Healey Willan and Leo Smith retired as professors of music at the University of Toronto in 1950; John Weinzweig was appointed to the same institution as a teacher of composition in 1952; Barbara Pentland was appointed to the staff at the University of British Columbia in 1949, as was Murray Adaskin to the University of Saskatchewan in 1952, Istvan Anhalt to McGill University in 1949, and Jean Papineau-Couture to the Université de Montréal in 1951. The CBC International Service, which began in 1947, and the CBC Symphony (1952–64) encouraged composers by providing an outlet and a vehicle for the performance of their works. The composers themselves banded together under the leadership of Weinzweig in 1951 and formed the Canadian League of Composers, which sponsored a number of concerts in the 1950s in Toronto and Montreal. Finally, governmental recommendation (*Massey Report*) was ultimately translated into governmental action (Canada Council). The increased number and the improved quality of Canadian works from this point on are evidence of the fact that Canadian composers quickly met the new opportunities which opened up to them.

PIANO MUSIC

The number of keyboard works composed in this period increased dramatically. Approximately forty works for piano are (or were at one time) available in printed score and recording, compared with the same number of printed scores and only half a dozen recorded works for the entire period 1900–40. Even more significant is the serious and extended nature of the works themselves. Sonatas,

suites, fantasias, and variations were written in place of the character and salon
pieces which had predominated before. The craft displayed by Canadian composers in their works for piano indicate that they had not only absorbed and
understood the various twentieth-century styles but that they were capable of
saying something fresh and new within them.

The majority of the works are in what might be termed a neoclassic idiom, but
within this stylistic framework there is considerable variety. Many of the composers extracted one or two stylistic features from the baroque or classical periods
and combined them with twentieth-century melodic, rhythmic, and harmonic
elements. For example, a parody of the Mozart-type sonata may be found in Violet
Archer's *Sonatina No. 2* (1946), of the Bach two-part invention in Alexander
Brott's *Sacrilège* (1941), and of Couperin's *stile galant* in Gilles Tremblay's *Trois
Huit* (1950). Other composers, rather than creating satirical returns to the past,
followed the general principles of classical restraint, clarity, balance, and objectiv-
ity in their music. The tonal harmony of the eighteenth and nineteenth centuries
was replaced by unity achieved through consistent use of rhythmic, melodic, and
intervallic patterns. A case in point is John Beckwith's *The Music Room* (1951),
which uses the E-flat minor sonority in a non-functional manner, clearly establishing it as the central chord or tonality. Further unity is achieved through a
consistent use of parallel sixths and thirds as well as fourths in the melody. The
result is a work of interest and freshness which also has coherence. Similarly the
Etude en si bémol (1944–5) and *Mouvement perpétuel* (1943) of Jean Papineau-
Couture employ toccata-like textures, frequent polytonality, and rhythmic ostinati which are reminiscent of Stravinsky's neoclassicism in the 1920s. Another
work by Papineau-Couture, *Suite* (1943), is an eclectic piece which shows discerni-
ble traits of Copland (quartal harmony in the opening 'Prelude'), Hindemith
(contrapuntal texture in 'Bagatelle No. 1'), Bartók (rhapsodic, folk-like elements
in 'Aria'), as well as Stravinsky (perpetual motion in 'Rondo'). In the *Suite* the
twelve-tone technique is not to be found, even though, as example 3-1 illustrates,
eleven of the twelve tones of the chromatic scale are used in the first two measures.

John Weinzweig's piano works of this period also exhibit neoclassic tendencies. While his *Suite for Piano No. 2* ('Conversation Piece,' 'Berceuse,' 'Toccata
Dance'; 1950) and his *Sonata* (1950) employ the twelve-tone technique in a free
manner, the sound is more akin to Bartók and Stravinsky of the 1920s than
Schönberg, Berg, or Webern. Showing a distinct preference for ternary form,
both works are characterized by ostinato figures and the expansion of short
rhythmic and melodic motives which are often pungent and witty in nature. Minor
seconds, major sevenths, and irregular metres (2+2+2+3) are favoured. The total
effect is surprisingly tonal, in a non-functional sense.

Barbara Pentland's *Studies in Line* (1941) and Harry Somers's *12 × 12* (1951)
are examples of works which give evidence of a strong interest in counterpoint,
the art of which is the quintessence of classicism. The Pentland work is especially

EXAMPLE 3-1   Jean Papineau-Couture, 'Rondo' from *Suite pour piano* (1943)

© Copyright 1959 BMI Canada Limited. Copyright assigned 1969 to Berandol Music Limited. Used by permission

interesting for the graphic illustrations which accompany each study, since abstract (i.e. non-objective) art was just beginning to be accepted in Canadian art circles. Although the musical lines are not a literal representation of the graphics (or vice versa), the illustrations do give a general indication of the melodic flow. This work is also noteworthy in that, uncompromising as Pentland is in her approach to her own music, she was one of the first Canadians to recognize the importance of working with young children in a creative way and providing for them materials using contemporary idioms. It has become fashionable to do so in Canadian music education since the mid-1960s, but Pentland was involved in such work at the University Settlement music school in Toronto in the early 1940s. *Studies in Line* is one of several works in which Pentland combines didactic and musical purposes, as in Bartók's *Mikrokosmos* (1926–39).

Somers's set of twelve fugues for piano under the title *12 × 12* similarly shows the influence of another major didactic work of the twentieth century, the *Ludus tonalis* (1943) of Paul Hindemith. Unlike Hindemith, however, Somers uses the twelve-tone technique. With the tone rows stated in a linear manner, these sombre fugues represent Somers's strictest use of the twelve-tone technique to date. As the beginning of Fugue No. 1 indicates, the lines are mostly smooth in contour, with tones or motives sometimes being repeated. Dissonance increases as one voice is piled upon the other. The widely spaced voicing, typical of Somers's keyboard works at this time, is also in evidence (see example 3-2). The other eleven fugues are similarly constructed, but each avoids the characteristic melodic intervals of the Schönberg twelve-tone system, notably the augmented fourths and diminished octaves.

EXAMPLE 3-2   Harry Somers, *12 × 12* (1951), Fugue No. 1 (in the composer's hand)

Although character pieces for the piano in the nineteenth-century style were still being written in this period, some of the more adventurous composers were turning out character pieces with a distinctly contemporary flavour. *Strangeness of Heart* (1942) by Somers and *Dirge* (1948) by Pentland are two such examples. The former is the first acknowledged work by Somers, who was then only seventeen years old and admittedly under the influence of Debussy. It is evocative also of certain works of Scriabin. Equally sombre in mood is Pentland's *Dirge*, which shows the influence of two contrasting composers with whom Pentland came into contact in the 1940s, Copland and Schönberg (Pentland studied with Copland in 1941 and 1942 and came under the spell of Schönberg's music at the MacDowell Colony in 1947).

It is especially noteworthy that Canadian composers now dared to venture into the realm of extended abstract works in greater numbers than heretofore. In addition to Weinzweig, whose sonata is mentioned above, Somers wrote four piano sonatas (1945, 1946, 1950, 1950), Pentland two (1945, 1947), and Jean Coulthard one (1948). *Sonata No. 3* (1950) by Somers was written while the composer was a student of Milhaud's in Paris. It is a large-scale work in the virtuoso tradition of the nineteenth century and has a certain rugged quality which is typical of much of Somers's work. To quote the composer: 'today it sounds to me like music related to Prokofief and Hindemith, though I didn't realize it at the time.'[9] The first movement does indeed recall Prokofief, with its march-like rhythm, its use of the whole range of the keyboard, and its employment of a clearly defined sonata-allegro structure. It has a super-charged dramatic quality which is very much a part of Somers's best works. The second movement, on the other hand, with its cumulative introduction and fugue, is more akin to Hindemith, while the third, the Scherzo, shows the satirical vein of Prokofief. The last movement returns to strong, driving rhythms.

Although neoclassicism absorbed the attention of the majority of Canadian composers for the piano at this time, other trends or 'isms' had their representatives. Oskar Morawetz stands out as the main exponent of late romanticism. His penchant for chromatic wanderings, long developments, and virtuoso display link him with Franck and Reger on the one hand and Liszt and Rachmaninof on the other. While his *Scherzo* (1947) is a straightforward work à la Shostakovich, both his *Fantasy in D Minor* (1948) and his *Fantasy on a Hebrew Theme* (1951) are extended works in which romantic rhetoric comes into full play.

Some of the younger French-Canadian composers led the way in the 1950s towards a style in piano-writing which was to treat the instrument as a vehicle for the creation of new sounds. Furthermore, novel sounds became ends in themselves rather than merely the material for motivic constructions. Tremblay's *Trois Huit* (1950), one of his early works, follows very much the beacons of Debussy and Messiaen in this regard. The trio section of *Trois Huit* (which is written for piano or harpsichord with many of the *stile galant* features of the eighteenth century) makes use of the tone-cluster technique, thus creating a sonorous and evocative effect. Tremblay, together with his colleagues François Morel and Serge Garant, may be credited with introducing the concept of sound for sound's sake into Canadian music in the 1950s, a concept which has been associated with avant-garde movements in music in this century.

ORCHESTRAL MUSIC

There was also a considerable increase in the quantity of orchestral music written in this period. Stimulated by greater musical activity as a result of the war effort (army and navy shows, etc) and an ever-increasing use of original music at the CBC during and after the war, more musicians turned to the composition of music than ever before. Many young composers ventured abroad to study, but many more availed themselves of the increasing opportunities at home. Veterans' allowances after 1945 afforded opportunities previously unknown. The orchestral medium held a natural fascination, and the compositional styles chosen by Canadian composers consisted of a blend of the various 'isms' popular in Europe and the United States at the time. Many orchestral works were programmatic in that they had some extra-musical association, such as a painting or natural scene, as a point of departure; others were abstract and followed either neoclassic or late romantic tendencies.

Programmatic works

In Canada nationalistic awareness first found expression through the Confederation poets in the 1880s and 1890s. Later the Group of Seven painters gave expression to a deep, nationalistic feeling by depicting their country in all its stark and natural simplicity. As we noted in chapter 2, some Canadian composers did attempt to translate this nationalistic spirit into musical form in the 1920s, but it was not until 1945 and after that extended works of any consequence were achieved. Even then the trend did not survive the waning of nationalism in the arts after World War II.

Canadian composers did produce some important programmatic works utilizing specific Canadian elements between 1941 and 1951. The most important of these is the *Symphonie gaspésienne* (1945) by Claude Champagne, a one-movement work which evokes the majesty and loneliness of the Gaspé peninsula as well as the 'melancholy of its people.'[10] Champagne achieves this feeling of vastness in time and space by repeating a drone-like bass figure for the first four and one-half minutes of the nineteen-minute work. The next section (Allegretto) describes in sound the physical aspects of the landscape, including a softly ringing church bell. This section is followed by a pastoral interlude, a restatement of the main thematic material, and a coda of large dimension. The style shows some influence of the impressionism of Debussy and Ravel, while the mood is closely akin to many of the paintings of the Group of Seven of the previous generation (e.g. J.E.H. MacDonald's *Solemn Land* [1921] and A.Y. Jackson's *Terre sauvage* [1913]).[11]

Other programmatic orchestral works with a nationalistic flavour include *Concordia* (1946) by Alexander Brott, which is based on Montreal's coat-of-arms, 'Concordia Salus'; *Journey* (1945) by J.J. Gagnier, which is an adaptation of west-coast Indian (Tsimsyan) material; *Coucher de soleil* (1947) by Hector Gratton; *Edge of the World* (1946) and *Red Ear of Corn* (1949) by John Weinzweig; and *North Country* (1948) by Harry Somers. Of these the most significant are the works by Somers and Weinzweig. According to Somers, the only programmatic element in his work is the theme itself; however the composer notwithstanding, the first of the four movements of *North Country* does evoke a pictorial image of stark beauty. The second movement is light and satirical, and the third sombre and introspective. The fourth is inconclusive, perhaps symbolizing the questioning Canadian attitude.

The two works by Weinzweig are early examples of compositions which employ characteristic phrases and rhythms of Canada's folklore without quoting specific material. The *Edge of the World* is based indirectly on Eskimo songs and dances, and the *Red Ear of Corn*, a ballet score, on Indian as well as French-Canadian material. The former work is an adaptation, in the form of a tone poem, of music composed for a series of historical-documentary radio dramas on the Canadian north, commissioned by the CBC. The work is in arch form, proceeding from a mood of stillness to an outburst of primitive fury and ending as it began in a mood of calm. The *Red Ear of Corn* suite shows a strong influence of Copland, whose ballets *Billy the Kid* (1938), *Rodeo* (1942), and *Appalachian Spring* (1944) provided the model for Weinzweig and others who were trying to reach the audiences of the day by utilizing national elements in a new and fresh way. This approach also served Weinzweig and others well in the composition of music for radio and film.

Some of the orchestral works of the period may be regarded as programmatic but not nationalistic. In this group are Weinzweig's *Interlude in an Artist's Life* (1943), which was written prior to the composer's sojourn in the RCAF; *Esquisse* (1946–7) by François Morel, and *Kaleidoscope* (1947–8) and *Pantomime* (1948–9) by Pierre Mercure. Morel's *Esquisse* is an early work which shows obvious influences of the impressionistic techniques of Debussy; the creation of moods and colours are achieved through chord-planing and the like. It also introduces some of the spice and satire of Milhaud and Stravinsky through its use of polychords in parallel motion. Mercure's two works likewise call to mind the two main influences of French music in the first half of the century: impressionism and neo-classicism. *Kaleidoscope*, as the name suggests, depicts constantly changing symmetrical colours and patterns. Motor rhythms, ostinato figures, lyrical melodies spiced with polychords, changing metres, and off-beat accents are all combined to create a panorama of colour while maintaining clarity of texture. *Pantomime* has many of the same characteristics; in addition, *post facto*, this work 'has been choreographed to suggest a sleeping figure, first awakening, then playing, expressing the joy of living and finally returning to peace.'[12] The symmetrical form of the story follows naturally from the structure of the music, both at the micro and macro levels. The intervals and motives which are germinal to the piece reflect the composer's concern for balance and symmetry (see example 3-3).

Abstract works

Canadian composers of this period were equally concerned in their orchestral works with music which was abstract (i.e. simply a design in sound). Recognizing

EXAMPLE 3-3   Pierre Mercure, *Pantomime* (1949), beginning

N.B. La 3e flûte et le cor anglais sont facultatifs.

that within any abstract piece there are not only elements of design (classical features) but also elements of expressiveness (romantic features), this discussion will consider first those works in which classical elements predominate, and secondly those in which romantic elements are strongest.

Neoclassicism in twentieth-century music has emphasized the principles of clarity of texture, emotional restraint, balance, and proportion, as well as the use of specific forms or techniques of the pre-romantic period. Violet Archer's adoption of the baroque passacaglia form (*Fanfare and Passacaglia*, 1948–9), Papineau-Couture's use of the concerto (*Concerto pour violon et orchestre*, 1951–2), the concerto grosso (1943; rev 1955), and the symphony (*Symphonie no. 1 en do majeur*, 1948; rev 1956), Somers's suite (*Suite for Harp and Chamber Orchestra*, 1949), scherzo (*Scherzo for Strings*, 1947), and symphony (1951), and Weinzweig's divertimenti (1945–6, 1948) are all, in varying degrees, representative of that trend in twentieth-century composition which stresses a return to the essence of classicism in reaction against the excesses of nineteenth-century romanticism. In following this trend, particularly from 1945 to 1960, Canadian composers had as their models some of the major musical figures of the century, such as Hindemith, Stravinsky, Prokofief, and Bartók.

Archer's passacaglia theme in *Fanfare and Passacaglia* consists of a six-measure chromatic phrase which is well-balanced in contour, uses intervals of the minor third, perfect fourth, and perfect fifth, and makes a dramatic leap of a minor seventh at the end of the phrase. The theme is stated fifteen times, mostly in the bass but sometimes in an upper voice, at a different pitch level, or with rhythmic variation. The *Fanfare*, which was composed after the *Passacaglia*, is linked with it through the consistent use of perfect fourths and fifths. Whereas the *Passacaglia* shows definite Hindemith influences (Archer studied with Hindemith from 1948 to 1950), the *Fanfare* calls to mind Copland's *Fanfare for the Common Man* (1942).

The three Papineau-Couture works show influences of Stravinsky, Ernest Bloch, Quincy Porter, and Nadia Boulanger, each of whom exerted a significant effect on Papineau-Couture's work at this time. The *Concerto Grosso* (1943; rev 1955) is characterized by the *concertante* idea of answering back and forth, the baroque spinning-out technique, Stravinsky-type motor rhythms, and polychords made up of simultaneously sounding triads a third apart. Clarity of texture is also a feature, as it is in the symphony and the violin concerto. The *Concerto pour violon*, generally more dissonant than the other works, emphasizes the augmented octave and major seventh which are first stated in the opening motive of the solo violin. It also features a grouping of tones by tetrachords, a favourite device of Papineau-Couture. Each work retains a tonal centre by revolving around a central tone or chord in a non-functional manner.

Although at this time Weinzweig often gravitated towards the more romantic side of twentieth-century composition, his *Divertimenti Nos. 1 and 2* illustrate that clarity of texture and classical construction are also two of his trademarks. The

EXAMPLE 3-4   John Weinzweig, *Divertimento No. 1* (1945–6), beginning

Piano reduction by HAROLD PERRY

playful nature of each of these works is a dominating feature. Widely recognized as the first Canadian consistently to use the twelve-tone technique, Weinzweig shows here his typical use of the row as a means of motivic invention rather than as a thoroughgoing technique of organization. Frequent repetitions of row material take place. The opening three-note motive in the accompaniment is never far from the surface and is the dominating rhythmic and melodic force in this piece (see example 3-4). As in the Papineau-Couture works, through the use of repetition one tone is usually predominant in each section of the piece, and thus there is a feeling of tonality – A in the first movement, B and E in the second, and E in the third. The result is a work which has charm and approachability even though it has its roots in the twelve-tone technique.

Although a student of Weinzweig Somers exhibits a thoroughly individual style which is a blend of classical and romantic characteristics. His works of this period emphasize neobaroque and neoclassic forms, yet these are always subservient to an overall dramatic thrust. The *Scherzo for Strings* (1947), which combines the elements of motivic development, imaginative sonorities, and dramatic rise and fall, calls to mind the music of Bartók. In the *Suite for Harp and Chamber Orchestra* (1949), one of Somers's most notable achievements predating his period of study in Paris (1949–50), one sees the combination of a variety of styles. The first movement evolves from a series of motives in the woodwinds punctuated by the harp; frequent planing in the harp gives an impressionistic effect. The second movement, as Somers points out in his analysis, is

> A gentle satire on neo-classicism, that style of writing which attempts to return to Mozart, Gluck, Pergolesi and 'bring them back alive.' Throughout, the woodwinds endeavour to maintain the charm and dignity worthy of the more respectable members of musical society, but the harp refuses to co-operate and play its traditional role, but instead parodies the dignitaries in an impudent and even vulgar manner – strictly a non-conformist.[13]

Both music and analysis exhibit a strong characteristic of Somers's which is to lampoon the type of formality which takes itself too seriously. The third movement is based upon a tone row which is stated by the cello and, in inverted form, by the harp. However, the treatment is not strict, and Somers himself does not regard the movement as twelve-tone or serial. The fourth movement serves as a summing-up and allows the harp to display 'a wide variety of colour and technical ability.'[14]

A stricter use of the twelve-tone technique can be found in Somers's *Symphony No. 1* (1951), which he began in Paris but did not complete until his return to Canada. In one long movement (twenty-eight minutes) with several separate but connected sections, this symphony represents one of the high points achieved in this form by a Canadian composer. It draws heavily upon the accumulated techniques of the first half of the century and adds to it Somers's own personal, dramatic touch. The work was completed in the same year in which Somers wrote the *12 × 12* series of twelve twelve-tone fugues for piano. In the symphony the row, together with its variants, is stated linearly by the violins in unison after a six-bar prologue which is itself based upon the row. The opening melody may be considered snake-like with its emphasis on major and minor seconds. After a lengthy fugal exposition the second section, entitled 'Allegretto Scherzando,' follows. Here the row breaks off into motives with frequent repetitions in the same manner as in Weinzweig's divertimenti. This is followed by a third section, 'Lento' and 'Lento (Development),' which is followed by a lengthy 'Allegro.' The symphony concludes with an 'Epilogue (Lento)' which contains a pointillistic statement of the row, followed by a retrograde version of measures 6–16 (solo violin this time); it ends with a simultaneous statement of the row in the original and retrograde forms. The dramatic arch is thus completed, the work ending as it began.

Several orchestral works in the nineteenth-century romantic tradition were written in this period by composers of the older generation, Claude Champagne, Healey Willan, and Georges-Emile Tanguay, as well as two of their more conservative students, Maurice Blackburn and Godfrey Ridout. The piano concerti by Willan (1944) and Champagne (1948–50) and the *Concertino* (1948) by Blackburn are all in the romantic style. Keys are clearly indicated, harmonic vocabulary is of the nineteenth century, established forms are followed, and singable melodies predominate. Clearly derived from Tchaikovsky and Rachmaninof, these works represent an unabashed late blooming of romanticism. Willan openly admitted that Tchaikovsky was his model. 'You could not have a better,' said Willan.[15]

Tanguay's *Lied* (1947) is a short work for strings which employs a late nineteenth-century chromatic style. In four-part texture with long flowing lines, it contains more evidence of contrapuntal art than many other Canadian short pieces of this period. Romantic also in mood, but more akin to twentieth-century conservatives such as Holst and Barber, is the work entitled *Two Etudes* (1946) by Godfrey Ridout. This is a well-constructed work which is rooted in the chromatic tonality of the nineteenth century. Ridout, like his mentor Willan, does not apologize for his conservative tendencies.

The *Symphony No. 2 in C Minor* (1948) by Willan is also from another time. The first sketches of the work date from 1936, when Willan completed his first symphony, but the finishing touches were not applied until 1948; it did not receive its first performance until 1950. The work is forty-one minutes long. Containing elements of Elgar, Wagner, Franck, and Tchaikovsky, this symphony has a touch of the grandeur, warmth of expression, and religious mysticism of another late-romantic composer, Bruckner. Although not as impressive from the technical standpoint as his opera *Deirdre* (1945; rev 1965), Willan's second symphony, even if it is overly imbued with romantic rhetoric, stands as a monument to the composer's mastery of his harmonic and contrapuntal craft.

CHAMBER MUSIC

Chamber music in this decade generally follows the three traditional groupings of instruments – solo string and piano, string quartet, and woodwind quintet or quartet. The musical style, as well as the combinations of instruments, indicates the neoclassical proclivity of most Canadian composers at this time. The much greater number of large-scale chamber music works is also noteworthy.

From the eighteenth century onward the string quartet has been one of the most challenging and rewarding, if not the most popular, avenues of musical expression. It was natural that Canadian composers in a neoclassical frame of mind should compose several works for this medium. Violet Archer, Alexander Brott, Lorne Betts, Claude Champagne, Jean Coulthard, Harry Freedman, Graham George, Barbara Pentland, Harry Somers, Robert Turner, and John Weinzweig all composed string quartets between 1941 and 1951, some more than one. The styles of these works are true to the individual composers but at the same time they have some features in common.

The quartets of Archer (No. 2, 1949) and Turner (No. 1, 1949) are distinctly classical in format and texture; those of Coulthard (No. 1, 1948) and George (1951) are more in the romantic mould. Betts's two quartets (1950, 1951) are severe works employing the twelve-tone technique, whereas those of Brott (*Critic's Corner*, 1950; string quartet and percussion) and Freedman (1949) are lighter and more playful, in the nature of divertimenti. Somers's quartets (Nos. 1 and 2, 1943, 1950) written when the composer was a student of Weinzweig and Milhaud respectively, illustrate once again this composer's gift for making a strong dramatic statement within a formal framework. The rugged rhythms, contrapuntal tightness, and exploitation of unusual sound effects, as well as a strong sense of dramatic timing, are characteristics which have remained with Somers throughout his career. The Pentland (No. 1, 1944) and Weinzweig (No. 2, 1946) quartets are similarly dramatic in nature. In the works of Somers, Pentland, and Weinzweig the influence of Bela Bartók's six quartets (1908–9, 1915–17, 1927, 1928, 1934, 1939), which were just coming to be known in Canada, is unmistakable.

While most of these quartets were written at relatively early stages in the careers of the composers, the quartet (1951) by Claude Champagne was written when he was sixty and near the end of his career. Harmonically more dissonant than his other works, it features skilful contrapuntal writing and shows the influence of Debussy and Bartók. This quartet, along with the orchestral piece *Altitude* (1959), is one of Champagne's most important works.

The favourite medium for chamber music composed between 1941 and 1951 was, however, solo stringed instrument and piano, usually violin and piano. This combination presented fewer difficulties in the matter of gaining a public performance; at least one violin and piano team went out of its way to promote Canadian music. In the 1940s and 1950s the husband-and-wife duo of Harry Adaskin, violin, and Frances Marr, piano, presented several first performances of Canadian works.

A few of these works employ folk music elements (François Brassard, *Suite villageoise*, 1948; Hector Gratton, *Chanson écossaise*, 1940); some are written in a nineteenth-century romantic idiom (Keith Bissell, *Ballade*, 1947; Oskar Morawetz, *Duo*, 1946; Jean Coulthard, *Sonata for Cello and Piano*, 1947; Jean Vallerand, *Sonate pour violon et piano*, 1950); some include use of the twelve-tone technique (John Weinzweig, *Sonata for Violin and Piano*, 1941; *Sonata 'Israel'*, 1949); the majority follow neobaroque or neoclassic formal procedures. One such example is Jean Papineau-Couture's *Aria* (1946) for solo violin which follows a simple ABA plus codetta structure, emphasizing the interval of the fourth (melodically and harmonically) in the A section, with the B section consisting of a melody and accompaniment in the manner of a Bach slow movement from an unaccompanied sonata or partita. Harmonic intervals of the minor second and major seventh are frequent, thus giving the music a dissonant quality.

Polytonality, a favourite device of neoclassic composers, is used by Murray Adaskin in his *Canzona and Rondo* (1949). The simultaneous sounding of A major and B minor chords at the beginning creates a tonal ambiguity which is characteristic of Milhaud, with whom Adaskin was studying at the time. Polytonality is also a feature of Somers's *Rhapsody for Violin and Piano* (1948) and Pentland's *Sonata for Violin and Piano* (1946).

One of the most significant works is John Weinzweig's *Sonata for Violin and Piano* (1941). In one movement, this sonata, which is unified through the use of a twelve-tone row, follows the romantic side of the dodecaphonic school, as exemplified in the works of Berg. It was, in fact, Weinzweig's acquaintance with Berg's *Lyric Suite* (1926) in the late 1930s which precipitated his initial involvement with the twelve-tone technique.[16]

Chamber music which uses the piano with several stringed instruments is exceptional in this period. The *Quintette pour piano et quatuor à cordes* (1942) of Rodolphe Mathieu, written in a lighter and more sentimental style than his previous works, is one exception and stands as the only significant work from the disillusioned Mathieu after his *Deux poemes* (1928).

Two chamber music works which combine solo voice and instruments are of interest. They are *Eglogues* (1942) by Papineau-Couture and *The Great Lakes Suite* (1949) by John Beckwith. *Eglogues*, for contralto, flute, and piano is based on three pastoral poems by Pierre Baillargeon – 'Printemps,' 'Regards,' and 'L'Ombre.' It displays a combination of classical clarity and impressionistic colour which suggests the music of Ravel. The score, published in the periodical *Amerique française* (1943), contains a sketch by artist Jacques de Tonnancour, a delightful inclusion which, unfortunately, has not become a tradition in the publication of Canadian music. The Beckwith work, on a text by James Reaney, is scored for soprano, baritone, clarinet, cello, and piano. Light in texture and satirical in the treatment of its theme, it captures the local colour of the various regions of the Great Lakes.

An example of a chamber work for brass is *Fantasy in the Form of a Passacaglia* (1951) by Archer. Composed for the North Texas State College Brass Ensemble, it displays stylistic similarities to Archer's *Fanfare and Passacaglia* (1948–9) discussed above. In contrast, Pentland in *Octet for Winds* (1948) breaks away from her earlier style and begins to show the influence of the twelve-tone school for the first time.

SONG

Art-song composition also increased in quantity and quality after 1940, and several song cycles or related groups of songs appeared. Texts were mainly lyrical

EXAMPLE 3-5   John Beckwith, *Five Lyrics of the T'ang Dynasty* (1947), no. 2, 'The Limpid River,' beginning

rather than narrative and dwelt on the traditional themes of love, sadness, longing, and contemplation. The works of a variety of poets were used by Canadian composers, but the preference was clearly for those of the twentieth century, such as Guillaume Apollinaire, James Joyce, Francis Jammes, Paul Eluard, e.e. cummings, Ezra Pound, Patrice de la Tour du Pin, and Canadians Anne Marriott, Anne Wilkinson, James Reaney, Colleen Thibaudeau Reaney, E.J. Pratt, and Paul G. Hiebert. A few works employ texts from Canada's native peoples, such as Jean Coulthard's *Two Songs of the Haida Indians* (1942) and Kenneth Peacock's *Songs of the Cedar* (1950). Most of the song settings are cast in either a nineteenth-century romantic or a twentieth-century neoclassical mould. Two of the most prominent romantic composers are Oskar Morawetz and Godfrey Ridout, whose songs have been widely accepted into the repertoire of contemporary singers.

The neoclassical works include Archer's *Three Biblical Songs* (1950) and Beckwith's *Five Lyrics of the T'ang Dynasty* (1947); in both cases melodic and rhythmic repetition are prominent and provide a sense of unity. In the Beckwith songs the interval of the fourth is featured both melodically and harmonically. In the first song, 'The Staircase of Jade,' an ostinato figure is made out of a vertical piling up of perfect fourths. Similarly, the prominence of the interval of the perfect fifth in the second song, 'The Limpid River,' acts as a unifying element while giving the work an oriental quality (see example 3-5). Jean Coulthard also uses parallel fifths to capture the essence of native poetry in her *Two Songs of the Haida Indians*. In addition, folk-like melodies and romantic expressiveness find their way into these songs, features no doubt derived from one of her teachers, Vaughan Williams.

Other works for solo voice are worthy of special note. Serge Garant's *Concerts sur terre* (1951), a setting of five poems by the contemporary French poet Patrice de la Tour du Pin, shows that combination of the old and new which is characteristic of one of Garant's teachers, Messiaen. Major sevenths are prominent melodically and harmonically, as well as parallel augmented fourths. The emphasis is on imaginative sonorities rather than involved constructions, and the total effect is more akin to Debussy than the post-Webern school which Garant emulated in later works. Papineau-Couture's *Quatrains* (1947) on texts by Francis Jammes illustrate again the strong neoclassical character of this composer's work. Tonal in nature, these songs bring to mind, by their combination of romantic feeling and clarity of texture, the songs of Poulenc. The *Cycle-Eluard* (1949) of Clermont Pépin also shows the influence of Poulenc, that most prolific of contemporary French song writers.

Weinzweig's *Of Time, Rain and the World* (1947) achieves a balance between rhapsodic and motivically structured sections. The interval of the major seventh in song 2, 'Rain,' and an eleven-note tone row in song 3, 'The World,' are developed as motives. This process is typical of Weinzweig, who frequently employs a tone row as a source of motivic material. Although he was the first Canadian composer to use the twelve-tone technique, Weinzweig avoids strict serialist procedures.

One of the most original Canadian song composers in this period is Somers, as his *Three Songs* (1946) and *A Bunch of Rowan* (1947) illustrate. Somers displays a vivid imagination, a strong dramatic flair, and a tendency to use unconventional structures or means, features which have helped to label him as one of the most individualistic of Canadian composers. The use of polytonality at the beginning of *A Bunch of Rowan*, where he spices the basic sonority of D minor with A major, is one such example. As it turns out when the voice enters, both the D minor triad and the note C-sharp are central to the melody. His practice is similar in his *Three Songs*: he uses tertian, quartal, and tone-cluster harmonies at various points in the first song, 'Look Down Fair Moon'; a dazzling accompaniment featuring augmented seconds, diminished fourths, and augmented fourths in the second song, 'After the Dazzle of Day'; and consistent use of the major seventh in the last song, 'A Clear Midnight.' With Somers the means used invariably support the dramatic import of the text.

One of the most prolific of Canadian song composers at this time was Lorne Betts. Betts made a total of nineteen settings of poems by Joyce as well as five by Pound during the years 1949–52. He also composed the *Prelude for Spring* (1951) for mezzo-soprano, baritone, flute, harp, and string quartet on a text by the Canadian poet Dorothy Livesay. In general, these songs, which show the influence of Britten, are more conservative in style than Betts's string quartets of the same period.

CHORAL MUSIC

Choral works of this period belong to one of three general categories: church anthems and liturgical works, folk-song arrangements, and sacred or secular cantatas. The largest number of works continued to be of the first category. Arrangements of Canadian as well as other folk songs did not increase greatly until the 1950s and 1960s, when there was a considerable increase in school music and a renewed national awareness of Canadian cultural resources. Extended works involving orchestral as well as choral resources are limited in number.

The church anthem is one of the few areas in which the Canadian composer has been reasonably assured of publication. The nature of the amateur church choir dictates that these works be relatively simple, short, and in a familiar musical idiom (i.e. the Victorian church anthem). As a result most of the anthems do follow such a pattern, and even some of the most mediocre have been published. Within their stylistic limitations some of the works are effective and convincing and have been readily accepted into the repertoire of church choirs. Healey Willan, who in his anthems successfully melded sixteenth-century polyphonic devices with nineteenth-century harmonic vocabulary, continued to be pre-eminent in this field. His anthems *Hosanna to the Living Lord* (1950) and *Rise, Crowned with Light* (1950) for SATB and organ are representative examples. His use of the chorale melody 'Von Himmel Hoch' in the former and the psalm tune 'Old 124th' in the latter also illustrates his propensity to use familiar tunes as a point of departure. In the 1940s Willan continued to be very much involved in the composition of music for the Anglo-Catholic liturgy and in the promotion of the use of plainchant in English. His *Missae brevi* IX and X belong to this period. In 1950 he founded the Gregorian Association of Toronto, of which he became musical director. All in all his career was marked by a steadfastness of purpose towards the maintenance of a type of sacred music which he believed to be consistent with the aims of the 'high' or Anglo-Catholic church.

Although they are few in number, extended works for chorus and instruments offer some interest. Lorne Betts's *David* (1949) and *Joe Harris 1913–42* (1950) and Jean Coulthard's *Quebec May* (1948) are settings of works by Earle Birney, himself one of the earliest exponents of new directions in Canadian poetry. *David* (1942), a long and intensely dramatic narrative poem in the tradition of Pratt, tells of two men on a mountain-climbing expedition. The story is told in the first person, and the reader becomes convinced that it is autobiographical as the rugged, mountainous terrain and the struggles of the men are vividly described. In his setting Betts chose a modified twelve-tone scheme, emphasizing the interval of the perfect fourth, an interval which has traditionally been associated with the out-of-doors. The general mood is severe. A narrator ties the story together while a chorus reflects on the action. In *Joe Harris 1913–42* Betts takes another Birney narrative poem, this one concerned with and growing out of the poet's experiences in Europe during World War II. Sections of the Requiem Mass (in English), which are interspersed throughout, give the reader a presentiment of the impending tragedy. The musical style is not as severe as that of *David*.

In contrast to Betts's settings of two long narrative poems, Coulthard's *Quebec May* is based on a short, lyric poem by Birney which captures the freshness and spirit of springtime in Quebec. As in Birney's others works there is a down-to-earth feeling in this poem; but Coulthard captures the lyricism better than the earthiness in her setting.

Violet Archer's *The Bell* (1949), which the composer subtitles 'a devotion for mixed voices and orchestra,' is based upon the sermons and devotions of John Donne. The musical realization is romantic in nature, and the serious-minded text is set to a combination of Hindemith-like counterpoint and post-romantic harmony reminiscent of the American composers Howard Hanson and Randall Thompson.

OPERA

The years 1941 to 1951 marked the beginning of the presentation of opera in Canada on a sustained basis. The Opera Guild of Montreal was formed in 1941 by Pauline Donalda and has produced an annual opera ever since. Donalda was a Montreal-born opera singer who won international acclaim in London, Paris, and New York before she returned to Montreal to teach. Later in the 1940s singers such as Pierrette Alarie and Leopold Simoneau emerged as soloists in the world's opera houses following advanced study in the United States. Of more consequence to the long-range development of Canadian opera was the establishment of the Royal Conservatory of Toronto's Opera School in 1946. Many singers who went on to win international acclaim, such as Jon Vickers and Teresa Stratas, received their initial operatic training there. The CBC Opera Company (1948) grew out of this school as did, eventually, the Canadian Opera Company (1959). It was natural that the early efforts in opera concentrated on the staples of the repertoire in order to attract the largest audiences and help keep the inevitable deficits to a minimum. A few radio operas predated the establishment of the Opera School (Willan's *Transit Through Fire*, 1942; *Deirdre of the Sorrows*, 1943–5; both with libretti by John Coulter), but the composition of original Canadian operas for the stage did not come into being until the 1950s.

ORGAN MUSIC

As one may gather from the large proportion of published organ works of this period, the demand for organ music was fairly brisk, at least in comparison with works in other genres. It is obvious that the pieces themselves were written for the church organist with limited background and limited technical ability as well as for the congregation which was invariably conservative in its musical tastes. Much of the considerable quantity of organ music composed by Healey Willan during this time was also simple and functional in nature. Willan, like his colleagues, was more interested in meeting an immediate need than in writing large concert works on the principle of art for art's sake.

Stylistically, most of the organ works are in a nineteenth-century idiom.

Willan's chorale prelude 'Urbs Hierusalem beata' from his *Five Preludes on Plain-chant Melodies* (1951) shows elements of Reger, while George Coutts's *Prelude and Fugue in E Minor* hearkens back to Mendelssohn. Violet Archer, on the other hand, in her short chorale prelude 'Dominus regit me' (1948; rev 1960), writes in the neoclassic idiom of Hindemith.

The English-trained organist-composer dominated musical life in Canada up to the mid-century. But this situation was in the process of changing as composers with interests in orchestral and chamber music genres were appointed to music faculties in the universities. Furthermore, composers of diverse backgrounds, such as István Anhalt, Talivaldis Kenins, and Udo Kasemets, who had immigrated to Canada after World War II, contributed greatly to the widening of the musical base. The rich variety of music which ensued will be the subject of discussion in the chapters which follow.

SELECTED WORKS

composer	title	score	recording
PIANO MUSIC			
Archer, Violet	*Sonatina No. 2* (1946)	Boosey, 1948	RCI 132
Beckwith, John	*Four Conceits* (1945–8)	CMC ms film 7/18	RCI 228; RCA CCS-1022
	*The Music Room (1951)	Harris, 1955	RCI 134
Betts, Lorne	**Suite for Piano* (1950)	No. 3 Harris, 1955; CMC ms film 19/40	
Brassard, François	*Oratoire à la croisse des chemins* (1946)	BMI Can, 1953	RCI 134
Brott, Alexander	**Suite* (1941)	'Sacrilège' Harris, 1955	
Champagne, Claude	*Quadrilha Brasiliera* (1942)	BMI Can, 1960	RCI 242, 397
Coulthard, Jean	*Four Etudes* (1945)	BMI Can, 1952, 1954	Bar BC 2837
	Sonata (1947–8)	BMI Can, 1953	RCI 289
	Theme & Variations (1951)	CMC ms film 5/56	RCI 289
Dela, Maurice	*Hommage* (1948)	BMI Can, 1950	
Duchow, Marvin	*Chant intime* (1947)	BMI Can, 1950	RCI 134
Fiala, George	*Dix Postludes* (1947; rev 1968)	Waterloo, 1969	CCM 1, 2
	Sonatina (1947)	BMI Can, 1960	

* In *14 Piano Pieces by Canadian Composers* (Oakville: F. Harris 1955)

composer	title	score	recording
Fleming, Robert	*Sonatina* (1941–2)	Oxford, 1943	
Freedman, Harry	**Piano Suite* (1950)	No. 4 Harris, 1955	
Matton, Roger	*Trois préludes* (1947–9)	CMC ms	RCI 135
Morawetz, Oskar	*Fantasy in D Minor* (1948)	CMC ms film 14/23	RCI 120; Col 32110045/46
	Fantasy on a Hebrew Theme (1951)	CMC ms film 14/24	RCI 133
	Scherzo (1947)	Boosey, 1958	RCI 121; CBC SM 118
Morel, Francois	*Ronde enfantine* (1949)	BMI Can, 1953	RCI 135
Papineau-Couture, Jean	*Etude en si bémol* (1944–5)	Peer, 1959	RCI 135; RCI ACM; CBC SM 114
	Deux valses (1944)	Harris, 1955	RCI 397; RCI ACM
	Mouvement perpetuel (1943)	BMI Can, 1949	RCI 134; RCI ACM
	Suite (1943)	BMI Can, 1959	RCI 251; RCI ACM Melb. SMLP 4023
Pentland, Barbara	*Dirge* (1948)	BMI Can, 1961	
	Studies in Line (1941)	BMI Can, 1949	RCI 134
Pépin, Clermont	*Suite pour piano* (1951; rev 1955)	Leeds, 1973	Nos. 1, 2 RCI 135; No. 3 RCI 228; RCI ACM
	Trois petites études (1940–7)	Western, 1948	RCI 132; RCI ACM
Somers, Harry	*Sonata No. 3* (1950)	Berandol, 1979	RCI 251; RCI 450-2
	Testament of Youth (1945)	Berandol, 1979	RCI 450-2
	Sonata No. 2 (1946)	Berandol, 1980	RCI 450-2
	Strangeness of Heart (1942)	BMI Can, 1947	RCI 132
	Sonata No. 4 (1950)	Berandol, 1980	RCI 450-2
	12 × 12 (1951)	BMI Can, 1959	RCI 450-2
Tremblay, Gilles	*Trois huit* (1950)	CMC ms film 13/28	RCI 132
Weinzweig, John	*Sonata* (1950)	CMC ms film 8/35	CMC SM 162
	Suite No. 2 (1950)	Oxford, 1956	'Berceuse' – CBC SM 99

ORCHESTRAL MUSIC

Archer, Violet	*Fanfare and Passacaglia* (1948–9)	BMI Can, 1964	RCI 130
Blackburn, Maurice	*Concertino en do majeur pour piano et instruments à vent* (1948)	CMC study score	CMC tape 2

* In *14 Piano Pieces by Canadian Composers* (Oakville: F. Harris 1955)

composer	title	score	recording
Brott, Alexander	*Concordia* (1946)	CMC ms film 3/6	CMC tape 381
	Concerto for Violin and Chamber Orchestra (1950)	CMC ms film 3/16	CBC SM 291
Champagne, Claude	*Concerto for Piano and Orchestra* (1948–50)	CMC ms film 15/10	CBC tape
	Danse villageoise (before 1947)	BMI Can, 1961	CTL S5030
	Images du Canada français (1943)	ms (NatLibOtt)	RCI 152
	Symphonie gaspésienne (1945)	CMC ms	RCI 216; RCA CCS-1010
Coulthard, Jean	*Overture 'Song to the Sea'* (1942)	CMC ms film 4/44	CBC SM 215
Freedman, Harry	*Nocturne* (1949)	CMC ms film 6/1	RCI ACM
Gagnier, J.J.	*Journey* (1945)		RCI 233
Gratton, Hector	*Coucher de soleil* (1947)	CMC ms film 23/10	CMC tape 5
Matton, Roger	*Danse brésilienne* (1946)	ms	RCI 442
Mercure, Pierre	*Kaleidoscope* (1947–8)	Ricordi, 1960	CBC SM 132
	Pantomime (1949)	Ricordi, 1971	CMC tape 393
Morel, François	*Esquisse* (1946–7)	BMI Can, 1964	RCI 129; CBC SM 332
Papineau-Couture, Jean	*Concerto Grosso* (1943; rev 1955	CMC ms film 11/21	RCI 156; RCI ACM
	Concerto pour violon et orchestre de chambre (1951–2)	BMI Can, 1960	CMC tape
	Symphonie no. 1 en do majeur (1948; rev 1956)	CMC ms film 11/22	CMC tape
Rathburn, Eldon	*Images of Childhood* (1950)	CMC ms film 26/35	CBC SM 119
Ridout, Godfrey	*Two Etudes* (1946)	Chappell (L), 1960	CAPAC-CAB tape 6
Somers, Harry	*North Country* (1948)	BMI Can, 1960	RCI 154
	Scherzo for Strings (1947)	AMP, 1948	RCI 238
	Suite for Harp and Chamber Orchestra (1949)	BMI Can, 1959	Col ML 5685
	Symphony No. 1 (1951)	CMC ms film 31/3	CMC tape
Tanguay, Georges-Emile	*Lied* (1947)	CMC ms	CMC tape
Weinzweig, John	*Divertimento No. 1* (1945–6), flute and orchestra	Boosey, 1950 (flute and piano)	Dom s-69006; RCI ACM 1; CAPAC-CAB tape 10; *Musican* rec. 10

composer	title	score	recording
	Divertimento No. 2 (1948), oboe and orchestra	Boosey, 1951 (oboe and piano)	RCI ACM 1; *Musican* rec. 8
	Edge of the World (1946)	Leeds, 1967	CBC SM 163; CMC tape 144A
	Interlude in an Artist's Life (1943)	Leeds, 1961	RCI ACM 1
	Red Ear of Corn (1949)	CMC ms film 8/20	Col MS 6763; CBC SM 345; CMC tape 346; CAPAC-CAB tape 2
Willan, Healey	*Concerto in C Minor* (1944)	BMI Can, 1960	CBC SM 205
	Overture to an Unwritten Comedy (1951)	Berandol, 1974	CMC SM 143
	Royce Hall Suite (1949), symphonic band	AMP, 1952	Cornell
	Symphony No. 2 (1948)	CMC ms film 2/29	CBC SM 133

CHAMBER MUSIC

composer	title	score	recording
Adaskin, Murray	*Canzona and Rondo* (1949), violin and piano	CMC ms film 1/13	RCI 221; RCA CCS-1015
	Sonata (1946), violin and piano	CMC ms film 1/12	CBC SM 211
Archer, Violet	*Divertimento* (1949)	CMC ms film 16/9	RCI 192
	String Quartet No. 2 (1948–9)	CMC ms film 16/8	
	Fantasy in the Form of a Passacaglia (1951), brass instruments	CMC ms film 7/13	
Beckwith, John	*Five Pieces for Flute Duet* (1951)	BMI Can, 1962	
	The Great Lakes Suite (1949)	CMC ms film 7/13	
Betts, Lorne	*String Quartet No. 1* (1950)	CMC ms film 19/19	
	String Quartet No. 2 (1951)	CMC ms film 19/20	
Bissell, Keith	*Ballade* (1947), violin and piano	BMI Can, 1950	
Brassard, François	*Suite villageoise* (1948)	CMC ms film 21/1	
Brott, Alexander	*Critic's Corner* (1950)	CMC ms film 3/21	CMC tape 570
Champagne, Claude	*String Quartet* (1951)	Berandol, 1974	RCI 143

composer	title	score	recording
Coulthard, Jean	*Sonata for Cello and Piano* (1947)	Novello, 1968	Col ML-5942; CBC SM 305
	String Quartet No. 1 (1948)	CMC ms film 5/8	
Fiala, George	*Musique de chambre pour cinq instruments à vent* (1948)	CMC ms film 29/9	CBC SM 196
Freedman, Harry	*Five Pieces for String Quartet* (1949)	CMC ms film 6/14	RCI ACM
Gayfer, James	*Suite for Woodwind Quintette* (1947)	Boosey, 1950	
George, Graham	*Quartet for Strings* (1951)	CMC ms film 29/21	
Gratton, Hector	*Chanson écossaise* (1940)	Berandol, 1957	
Johnston, Richard	*Suite for Bassoon and Piano* (1946)	CMC ms	Mel SMLP 4032
Kenins, Talivaldis	*Septet* (1949)	CMC ms film 9/8	CBC SM 135
Mathieu, Rodolphe	*Quintette pour piano et quatuor à cordes* (1942)	CMC ms	RCI 123
Morawetz, Oskar	*Duo for Violin and Piano* (1946)	Ricordi, 1961	RCI 124; RCI 244; CBC SM 135
Papineau-Couture, Jean	*Aria* (1946), violin solo	BMI Can, 1966	RCI 245; Bar BC 1851/2851; RCI ACM
	Eglogues (1942)	*Amérique française*, 1943	Hallmark RS-6; Allied ARCLP-4
	Sonate en sol (1944; rev 1953), violin and piano	CMC ms film 11/35	RCI 438; RCI ACM
Pentland, Barbara	*Sonata for Violin and Piano* (1946)	CMC ms film 12/16	
	Octet for Winds (1948)	CMC ms film 12/17	
	String Quartet No. 1 (1944)	CMC ms film 12/15	RCI 141; Col MS 6364
	Vista (1945), violin and piano	BMI Can, 1951	
Somers, Harry	*Rhapsody for Violin and Piano* (1948)	CMC ms film 31/9	RCI 244
	String Quartet No. 1 (1943)	Marseg, 1977	
	String Quartet No. 2 (1950)	Marseg, 1977	CBC SM 263
Turner, Robert	*String Quartet No. 1* (1949)	CMC ms film 13/7	
Vallerand, Jean	*Sonate pour violon et piano* (1950)	CMC ms film 6/23	
Weinzweig, John	*Intermissions* (1943), flute and oboe	Peer, 1964	
	Sonata 'Israel' (1949), cello and piano	CMC ms film 8/28	RCI 209; RCI ACM 1

composer	title	score	recording
	String Quartet No. 2 (1946)	CMC ms film 8/27	Col MS 6364
	Sonata for Violin and Piano (1949)	Oxford, 1953	CBC SM 276

S O N G (for voice and piano unless otherwise indicated)

composer	title	score	recording
Adaskin, Murray	*Epitaph* (1948) [Guillaume Apollinaire]	CMC ms film 1/27	
Anderson, W.H.	*Song of Mary*	Western, 1948	
Archer, Violet	*Three Biblical Songs* (1950)	CMC ms film 16/40	
	April Weather (1950) [Amy Bissett England]	CMC ms film 16/42	
Beckwith, John	*Five Lyrics of the T'ang Dynasty* (1947) [trans Witter Brynner]	BMI Can, 1949	RCI 148
	The Formal Garden of the Heart (1950) [Colleen Thibaudeau]	CMC ms film 7/14	
	Four Songs (1950) [e.e. cummings]	CMC ms film 7/15	CMC tape 18
Betts, Lorne	*Five Songs* (1950) [James Joyce]	CMC ms film 19/34	CMC tape 18
	Six Songs (1951) [James Joyce]	CMC ms film 19/33	
	Five Songs for High Voice and String Orchestra (1949) [Ezra Pound]	CMC ms film 19/30	
	Three Songs (1949) [James Joyce]	CMC ms film 19/29	
	Prelude for Spring (1951), mezzo-soprano, baritone, flute, harp, and string quartet [Dorothy Livesay]	CMC ms film 19/32	
Coulthard, Jean	*Two Songs of the Haida Indians* (1942)	CMC ms film 5/30	
Dela, Maurice	*Ronde* (1949) [Victor Hugo]	CMC ms film 21/29 (voice and chamber orchestra); BMI Can, 1951 (voice and piano)	
	Spleen [Paul Verlaine]	BMI Can, 1950	
Fleming, Robert	*The Oxen* [Thomas Hardy]	Oxford, 1945	

composer	title	score	recording
Garant, Serge	*Concerts sur terre* (1951) [Patrice de la Tour du Pin]	CMC ms film 7/33	RCI 201; RCI ACM 2
Holt, Patricia Blomfield	*Songs of My Country* (1950), baritone and instruments [Wilfred Campbell, Susanna Moodie, Marjorie Pickthall]	Harris, 1966	
MacMillan, Ernest (arr)	*Ballads of B.C.* (1947) [edited John Murray Gibbon]	GVT, 1947	
MacNutt, Walter	*Atque Vale* [Robert Nathan]	BMI Can, 1950	
	Two Songs of William Blake	BMI Can, 1949	
Mercure, Pierre	*Colloque* [Paul Valéry]	BMI Can, 1950	Master MA-275
Morawetz, Oskar	*Elegy* (1947) [Anne Wilkinson]	Leeds, 1961	RCI 121
	The Grenadier (1950) [A.E. Housman]	Leeds, 1962	RCI 121; CBC SM 42
	Land of Dreams (1949) [William Blake]	GVT, 1953	
	Mad Song (1947) [William Blake]	Leeds, 1962	RCI 121
	Piping Down the Valleys (1947)	GVT, 1953	
	To the Ottawa River (1950) [Archibald Lampman]	Leeds, 1962	RCI 121
	The Chimney Sweep (1947) [William Blake]	Leeds, 1961	RCL 121
Naylor, Bernard	*A Child's Carol*	Western, 1948	
	Dreams of the Sea	Western, 1950	
Papineau-Couture, Jean	*Quatrains* (1947) [Francis Jammes]	CMC ms film 11/45	RCI 148; RCI ACM
Peacock, Kenneth	*Songs of the Cedar* (1950), voice and instruments [adapted from West Coast Indian texts by Constance Lindsay Skinner ca 1915]	CMC ms film 26/4	
Pentland, Barbara	*Song Cycle* (1942–5) [Anne Marriott]	CMC ms film 12/30	RCI 20
Pépin, Clermont	*Cycle-Eluard* (1949)	CMC ms	RCI 148; RCI ACM
Ridout, Godfrey	*What Star Is This?* (1941) (hymn 'Quae stella sole pulchrior')	Oxford, 1942	

composer	title	score	recording
Somers, Harry	*A Bunch of Rowan* (1947) [Diana Skala]	BMI Can, 1948	
	Three Songs (1946) [Walt Whitman]	CMC ms film 31/14	
Weinzweig, John	*Dance of the Massadah* (1951) [Jewish chant]	CMC ms film 8/33	Master MA-275
	Of Time, Rain and the World	CMC ms film 8/32	RCI ACM 1

CHORAL MUSIC

composer	title	score	recording
Anderson, W.H.	*Five Introits and Vespers*	Western, 1947	
	Give Ear to My Words, O Lord	Western, 1944	
Archer, Violet	*The Bell* (1949)	CMC ms film 16/20	
	Landscapes (1950)	CMC ms film 16/2	CBC SM 274
Bancroft, H. Hugh	*The Temple of God*	Oxford, 1942	
Betts, Lorne	*David* (1949)	CMC ms film 19/25	
	Joe Harris 1913–42 (1950)	CMC ms film 19/26	
Cadoret, Charlotte (Saint-Jean de Sacre Cœur, [Sœur])	*Messe à Notre Dame* (1950)	BMI Can, 1951	
Coulthard, Jean	*Quebec May* (1948)	Waterloo, 1976	
France, William	*Lord of All Power and Might*	Harris, 1947	
George, Graham	*Ride On! Ride On!*	Gray, 1941	
	Unto Us a Son is Given	Oxford, 1945	
Karam, Frederick	*Praise to the Lord*	BMI Can, 1949	
MacMillan, Ernest	*A Song of Deliverance*	Oxford, 1945	
Morawetz, Oskar	*Keep Us Free*	GVT, 1950	
Naylor, Bernard	*The Ascension*	Western, 1950	
	The Crown of Thorns	Western, 1950	
	Easter Sequence	Western, 1950	
Turner, Robert	*Two Choral Pieces*	CMC ms film 13/20	RCI 206
Whitehead, Alfred E.	*Of These I Sing*	Oxford, 1941	
Willan, Healey	*Blessed Art Thou, O Lord* (1951)	Oxford, 1951	
	Hosanna to the Living Lord (1950)	Concordia, 1950	
	Missa brevis IX [St Michael]	Gray, 1947	
	Missa brevis X [St Mary Magdalen) (1948)	Gray, 1949	

composer	title	score	recording
	Le Navire de Bayonne	Harris, 1952	
	On May Morning	BMI Can, 1950	
	Rise, Crowned with Light (1950)	Concordia, 1950	
	To Daffodils	BMI Can, 1952	
	The Trumpet Call	Oxford, 1941	
	Welcome Yule	BMI Can, 1949	
	Deirdre of the Sorrows (1943–5; rev 1962–5)	Berandol, 1972 (vocal score)	
	Brébeuf (1943) (a pageant)	CMC ms film 2/32	TBC 112868
	Transit Through Fire (1942)	CMC ms 2/28	

ORGAN MUSIC

composer	title	score	recording
Archer, Violet	*Chorale Prelude* 'Dominum regit me' (1948; rev 1960)	CMC ms film 16/51	
	Sonatina (1944)	GVT, 1971	
Bancroft, H. Hugh	*Pastorale*	Oxford, 1943	CMC tape
Coutts, George	*Prelude and Fugue in E Minor*	BMI Can, 1952	CMC tape
Crawford, Thomas J.	*In a Great Cathedral*	Western, 1951	
France, William	*Second Suite for Organ*	BMI Can, 1952	CMC tape
Karam, Frederick	*The Modal Trumpet*	BMI Can, 1949	SR-101568
Willan, Healey	*Five Preludes on Plainchant Melodies*	Oxford, 1951	Nos. 4, 5 Col ML 6198
	Six Chorale Preludes, Set I (1950)	Concordia, 1950	Nos. 3, 4 Col ML 6198
	Six Chorale Preludes, Set II (1950–1)	Concordia, 1951	Nos. 1, 2 Col ML 6198

CHAPTER FOUR

The 1950s
Neoclassicism at Its Height

Place à la magie!
Place aux mystères objectifs!
Place à l'amour!
Place aux nécessités!
    Paul-Emile Borduas, 'Refus global' (1948)

Some momentous developments took place in Canadian music in the 1950s. The early years saw the formation of the Canadian League of Composers (1951) and the CBC Symphony Orchestra (1952–64), while the end of the decade witnessed the establishment of the Canadian Music Centre (1959). In between were a number of concerts of Canadian music, mainly in Toronto and Montreal, as well as several commissions, premières, and performances of Canadian music by the CBC. This was the period when many composers out of necessity became impresarios, sometimes at the expense of their own creative work.

'On the evening of 3 February 1951 a number of composers [actually only Samuel Dolin, Harry Somers, and John Weinzweig] gathered in the Toronto home of John Weinzweig to try and tackle some of their common worries.'[1] So writes Helmut Kallmann of the initial meeting which led to the formation of the Canadian League of Composers. Kallmann, who became official historian of the group, relates that 'before they parted that night they had decided the time was ripe to band together in collective action to defend their mutual interests, as composers had done in many other countries.'[2] The formation of the league 'was really a phenomenon of a dawning of a new era in Canadian culture.'[3] Like the members of the Group of Seven over thirty years before in Canadian art, the composers came together not for the purpose of achieving a uniform or national style but rather as brothers (and, before long, sisters) to proclaim a common cause.

Concert Hall
The Royal Conservatory of Music of Toronto

CBC   WEDNESDAY   NIGHT

May 16, 1951

8.30 - 10.00 p.m.
Trans-Canada Network

A   p r o g r a m m e   o f   m u s i c   b y

John   Weinzweig

p r e s e n t e d   b y   t h e
Royal   Conservatory   of   Music   of   Toronto
Canadian   Broadcasting   Corporation
Canadian   League   of   Composers

SOLOISTS

MURRAY ADASKIN	GORDON DAY
LEO BARKIN	REGINALD GODDEN
PERRY BAUMAN	FRANCES JAMES
GEORGE BROUGH	ISAAC MAMOTT

STRING ORCHESTRA — ETTORE MAZZOLENI, conductor
Violins: Hyman Goodman, Isidor Desser, Frank Fuseo, Berul Sugarman, Harold Sumberg, Grant Milligan, Goldie Bell, Steve Staryk.
Violas: Robert Warburton, Jack Neilson, Stanley Solomon.
Cello: Philip Spivak, Rowland Pack.   Bass: Reg Wood.

They wished to tell other Canadians and the world that they were determined to be listened to and taken seriously. By the end of the first decade the membership of the league had grown to forty and included four women. During this period the main function of the group was the presentation of concerts of Canadian music; approximately thirty such programmes took place between 1951 and 1960.

The first concert, held under the joint auspices of the league, the CBC, and the

$\mathcal{P}$rogramme

SONATA FOR VIOLIN AND PIANO

Murray Adaskin and George Brough

"ISRAEL", SONATA FOR VIOLONCELLO AND PIANO
Slow and sustained
Allegro maestoso: Allegro piu mosso

Isaac Mamott and Leo Barkin

THREE SONGS: "OF TIME AND THE WORLD"
Time
Rain
The World

Frances James and George Brough

PIANO SONATA
Allegro scorrevole
Andante quasi allegretto
Con moto giocoso

Reginald Godden

i n t e r m i s s i o n

DIVERTIMENTO NO. 2 FOR OBOE AND STRING ORCHESTRA
Marcato
Slow, expressive
Energetic

Perry Bauman

"INTERLUDE IN AN ARTIST'S LIFE", FOR STRING ORCHESTRA

DIVERTIMENTO NO. 1 FOR FLUTE AND STRING ORCHESTRA
Fast and playful
Slow
Fast

Gordon Day

ETTORE MAZZOLENI, *conductor*

Royal Conservatory of Music of Toronto, consisted of a programme of music by John Weinzweig, the first president of the league. The concert took place on 16 May 1951 and featured the composer's sonatas and divertimenti of the period 1941 to 1950. The *art* critic of the *Toronto Globe and Mail* reviewed the concert favourably and reported that 'an audience of musically informed people showed its feeling that the occasion was important by turning out in full force and being strictly on time in arriving.'[4] The *music* critic of the same newspaper attended the annual concert of the Toronto schools that evening and reported on that event in the same edition of the newspaper! Although reviews of subsequent concerts indicated more interest in Canadian music on the part of the press, it is clear that new music by Canadian composers was considered to be on the periphery of the general concert scene.

The CBC also assumed an active role in the encouragement of Canadian musical composition in this period. The formation of the CBC Symphony by Geoffrey Waddington, after he assumed the position of director of music for the government-owned radio network in 1952, provided a necessary spark for the writing of works for full orchestra. Waddington was very sympathetic towards new Canadian music. In a few cases works were commissioned by the CBC and then broadcast and recorded for its International Service (later known as Radio Canada International), thus giving Canadian orchestral composers a hearing beyond the borders of Canada.

Canadian composers were much less successful in having their works published and commercially recorded. Even though the 1950s marked one of the most active periods of publication of Canadian musical scores, notably through the efforts of BMI Canada Limited, only a fraction of the music written reached printed form. The picture regarding commercial recording of Canadian works was also exceedingly dismal in the 1950s, the period which saw full acceptance of the long-playing disc. In a survey conducted in 1956 only two recordings of Canadian music were available: *Eglogues* by Jean Papineau-Couture and assorted choral works by Healey Willan.[5] Both were on the Hallmark label, a Canadian company which was established for the promotion of Canadian music and talent and which, unfortunately, did not survive the decade.

Undoubtedly one of the most important events for Canadian music and the Canadian composer was the establishment in 1959 of the Canadian Music Centre in Toronto. It was founded by the Canadian Music Council at the instigation of the Canadian League of Composers. It is presently funded by the Canada Council, the Composers', Authors' and Publishers' Association of Canada, Ltd (CAPAC), the Performing Rights Organization of Canada Limited (P.R.O. Canada Limited), the Province of Ontario Council for the Arts, and the Ministry for Cultural Affairs of the Province of Quebec. Since 1973 there has been an Associate Centre in Montreal, and in October 1977 a second Associate Centre opened its doors in Vancouver, BC. The purpose of the centre is to serve as a promotional body which sends scores and parts, free of charge, to individuals or ensemble groups in most countries of the world, as well as at home. It maintains a reference and circulating library of Canadian music scores; the collection numbered close to seven thousand in 1976, and is increasing at a rate of between two and three hundred titles per year. The centre also serves as a reference library of Canadian music recordings, its shelves containing over two thousand tape recordings of Canadian works as well as all the discs of Canadian music which have been produced by the CBC,

Radio Canada International, and commercial companies. From time to time the centre initiates various undertakings designed to increase professional and public interest in the works of Canadian composers; for example, the John Adaskin Project, which was begun in 1962–3 and since 1973 has continued in collaboration with the Canadian Music Educators' Association (CMEA), was designed to encourage the Canadian composer to write works in a contemporary idiom suitable for use in the elementary and secondary schools. The effectiveness of the centre has been largely due to its dedicated and highly efficient staff members, particularly Norma Dickson and Henry Mutsaers in Toronto, and its four chief executives – Jean-Marie Beaudet, 1959–62, John Adaskin, 1962–4, Keith MacMillan, 1964–77, and John P.L. Roberts, 1977– . Louis Laplante has been in charge of the Associate Centre in Montreal since its inception. It would be an understatement to say that without the Canadian Music Centre the plight of the Canadian composer would be a sorry one indeed!

The culmination of this decade of activity in Canadian music came with the International Conference of Composers which took place at Stratford, Ontario, on 7–14 August 1960, under the joint auspices of the Canadian League of Composers and the Stratford Festival. This event, which more than any other to date won recognition for the Canadian composer on the international scene, will be discussed in detail in the next chapter.

PIANO MUSIC

The piano music of this period presents a picture of increasing contrast and complexity. While some composers continued to work in nineteenth-century idioms (Maurice Dela, Séverin Moisse, Oskar Morawetz, Frederick Karam, Lucien Lafortune), and some in conservative twentieth-century styles (Jean Coulthard, Talivaldis Kenins), others ventured forth into the style of Schönberg (István Anhalt) or the complex idioms of the post-Webern school (Serge Garant, Otto Joachim, Barbara Pentland, Gilles Tremblay). For the first time Canadian composers incorporated the styles of the avant garde in Western Europe.

'In its doleful, understated way, this is one of the finest piano works of its period.'[6] Thus pianist Glenn Gould describes Anhalt's *Fantasia* (1954), a subtle, yet warm and romantic work in the expressionistic idiom of Schönberg. Based upon a free manipulation of the tone row (including constant fragmentation and transposition), the *Fantasia* makes frequent reference to the 'front end' and 'back end' of the row, both of which outline the major and minor third. At the same time the texture, while not thick in a chordal sense, is extremely active contrapuntally, with sometimes as many as four separate melodic strands going on simultaneously. The work evolves in a stream-of-consciousness fashion, making frequent use of repetition within each section, but, as in a renaissance fantasia, it gives no sign of a return to such material once it has been treated exhaustively.

If the smooth-flowing lines of densely polyphonic texture in Anhalt's *Fantasia*

EXAMPLE 4-1   François Morel, *Deux études de sonorité*, 'Etude No. 2' (1954), ending

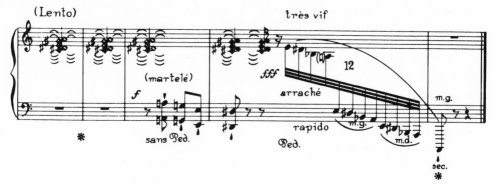

show influences of Schönberg, the pointillism of Tremblay's *Phases* (1956) and *Réseaux* (1958), Joachim's *L'Eclosion* (1954), Garant's *Variations pour piano* (1954), and Pentland's *Toccata* (1958) illustrate the influence of Schönberg's pupil Webern, the posthumous leader of the musical avant garde in the post-World War II era. One can also see and hear in the works of Garant, Tremblay, and the young Bruce Mather the influence of their teacher Messiaen, an equally potent force in the search for new sounds and forms in the 1950s and 1960s. Garant's *Variations*, Tremblay's *Phases* and *Réseaux*, and Mather's *Like Snow* (1960) and *Smaragdin* (1960), a short film score, illustrate that combination of Germanic constructivism and French colouristic elements which typify the music of their more famous colleagues on the international scene, Karlheinz Stockhausen and Pierre Boulez. Although organized in great detail, this music focuses on the imaginative treatment of sound colour. François Morel's *Deux études de sonorité* (1952–4) is similarly colour-oriented. Its style is reminiscent of the impressionism and evocative manner of both Debussy and Messiaen. At certain points the score employs four staves for the one player, thus indicating a modification of existing notational practices to accommodate new sound ideas. The second étude is in contrast to the first with its Milhaud-like passage work and saucy rhythms; it returns to the evocative mood at the end through the use of piano harmonics (see example 4-1).

In Joachim's *L'Eclosion* there is literally a hatching, opening up, or breaking forth of the twelve-tone row, as the title indicates.[7] At the same time this too is a piece which explores new sound effects by using extreme registers of the instrument, special pedal effects, and piano harmonics. The tone row and its various permutations are stated clearly in *L'Eclosion*, as is typical in Joachim's twelve-tone works. This is not true, however, of Pentland's *Toccata*. In the *Toccata* the tone row is not given in its original form in a neat package at the beginning of the work, but rather it is disguised among perpetual variations. Unity is achieved through the

EXAMPLE 4-2   Barbara Pentland, *Toccata* (1958), p 3

repetition of rhythmic patterns, melodic motives, and textures rather than through row manipulation (see example 4-2).

Harry Somers's *Piano Sonata No. 5* (1957), his last work in this genre to date, and Oskar Morawetz's *Fantasy, Elegy and Toccata* (1956) are also significant keyboard works of the period. The first movement of Somers's sonata is in a toccata-like style characterized by short, ejaculatory motives which build to a dramatic climax in cumulative fashion. The second movement (*lento*) features a series of chain suspensions. The third, and last, movement consists of a scherzando and fugue in which a twelve-note row and its inversion form the fugue subject. There is also some recalling of material from the first two movements in the third. Morawetz's *Fantasy, Elegy and Toccata*, on the other hand, is a display piece in the nineteenth-century tradition. Its chromatic, tonal idiom and virtuoso passages are typical features of this composer's works and account, to some considerable degree, for his popularity among pianists and audiences.

One of the accomplishments of the Canadian League of Composers in the 1950s was the collaborative publication of *14 Piano Pieces by Canadian Composers* (Oakville: F. Harris, 1955), a selection of individual movements chosen with the intermediate-level student in mind. Unfortunately this collection remains the only anthology of Canadian music scores produced to date.

ORCHESTRAL MUSIC

While Canadian orchestral composition in this period shows a marked preference for the neoclassical paths of Milhaud, Hindemith, Bartók, and Stravinsky, some of the composers who immigrated to Canada following World War II, such as István Anhalt, Otto Joachim, and Udo Kasemets, favoured stylistic elements from the twelve-tone school. At the same time Canadian composers as a group seemed to be antipathetic to the particular brand of post-romantic style favoured in American musical circles in the 1950s. It is an interesting phenomenon that few Canadian composers received their training in the United States in the post-war period whereas almost all Canadian performers, musicologists, and music educators went there for advanced study.

Programmatic works

Canadian composers have never gone to extremes in utilizing national themes in their large-scale orchestral works. Fewer than 20 per cent of the works cited at the end of this chapter are nationalistic in the sense that they employ Canadian folk materials or are inspired by other aspects of Canadiana. Nevertheless, some of the nationalistic works are significant and continue to maintain a place in the repertoire of Canadian symphony orchestras.

Harry Freedman's *Tableau* (1952) and *Images* (1957–8) are two such works. Each was inspired by Canadian painting, a subject of recurring interest with Freedman, whose early creative work was in the graphic arts rather than music. The inspiration for *Tableau* was the memory of an Arctic painting which Freedman had seen in the Winnipeg School of Art during his student days. To create a sound image of this scene he makes use of an 'icy' string quality and austere melodic lines derived from a twelve-note row. Each of the three movements of *Images*, 'Blue Mountain,' 'Structure at Dusk,' and 'Landscape,' is based on paintings by Lawren Harris, Kazuo Nakamura, and Jean-Paul Riopelle respectively which Freedman had seen in the mid-1950s. Unfortunately, only the first of these paintings can be traced and even it is given a different name by Freedman. 'Blue Mountain' is in fact based on Lawren Harris's *Lake and Mountains* (1927–8) (Art Gallery of Ontario).[8] In both musical works, then, it is not surprising to find that the depiction is general rather than specific, although the opening of 'Blue Mountain,' with its six-bar crescendo from *ppp* to *fff* culminating in a snap-motive (the dramatic cloud over the mountains), would tend to indicate at least some degree of concrete representation of the visual in sound. The angular melodic lines, strong dissonances, and feeling of space generated by the music in 'Blue Mountain' also capture the sharp, craggy peaks and stark loneliness of the Harris painting (see example 4-3).[9]

A work with many similarities to Freedman's *Images* is *L'Horoscope* (1958) by Roger Matton, a suite based upon a ballet inspired by an Acadian folk legend. In its colourful orchestration this work is indebted to the early ballet suites of Stravinsky (*Firebird*, 1910; *Petrouchka*, 1911). The opening theme in the clarinets represents the child in the story and serves as the unifying motive throughout the work. The treatment by Matton also calls to mind the melodramatic side of Honegger's work, a feature that is not surprising since Matton was a student of Honegger's wife, Andrée Vaurabourg. In contrast to the Freedman score, the depiction in *L'Horoscope* is much more concrete; for example, in the section 'La Forge' percussion instruments which imitate a blacksmith's shop are featured prominently.

Another ballet from this period based upon a Canadian theme is Robert Fleming's *Shadow on the Prairie* (1955). Using a more down-to-earth story (the problems of the early settlers of the West) and a cinema-like musical style, this score is less ambitious in purely musical terms than the Freedman and Matton works. Other programmatic works on national themes include Kelsey Jones's *Miramichi Ballad* (1954) and Murray Adaskin's *Algonquin Symphony* (1958) and *Saskatchewan Legend* (1959). Each of these works uses actual folk songs from different parts of Canada, Jones's from the Miramichi section of New Brunswick and Adaskin's from Algonquin Park, Ontario, and the prairie province of Saskatchewan. Claude Champagne's *Paysanna* (1953) is a patriotic work written for the coronation of Queen Elizabeth II and includes recognizable quotations from *God Save the Queen, O Canada,* and *La Marseillaise.*

The last major orchestral work of Champagne's deserves special attention. It is his *Altitude* (1959), for full orchestra, mixed choir, and Ondes Martenot. Complementary to his *Symphonie gaspésienne* (1945), which is a pictorial description in sound of the landscape and people of a part of eastern Canada, *Altitude* is a *fresque sonore* inspired by the spectacle of the Rocky Mountains. Deeply religious in tone, the work uses the text of a Huron Indian prayer which symbolizes man's act of worship and a prayer by St Francis of Assisi which is, in effect, a hymn of praise for the blessings of nature. Champagne employs a 'schéma topographique' which attempts to show diagrammatically the relation between the musical score and the mountains, from the 'époque primitive' to the 'époque moderne.' A third part, 'méditation,' is inserted between the other two (see example 4-4). To symbolize the mountain peaks Champagne employs a very high inverted pedal played by the Ondes Martenot, one of the first electronic instruments. The Ondes was selected to perform this bit of musical geography because of its ability to manipulate glissandi and thereby translate the 'schema topographique' into sound. The *Ondes* also emits an eerie, otherworldly quality of sound which creates a particularly vivid impression, especially in the section marked 'La Désolation.' The choral sections are chant-like, with the orchestra providing a colourful and picturesque, even melodramatic, backdrop.

Another work with a specified programme, this one international in scope, is *Guernica* (1952) by Clermont Pépin. The work is based upon the fresco which Picasso painted at the request of the Spanish government-in-exile for the Paris Exposition of 1937. The fresco is a surrealistic expression of horror at the Fascist

LAWREN HARRIS   Canadian 1885–1970
Lake and Mountains, 1927–8
oil on canvas
51½" × 63¼"   130.8 × 160.7 cm
ART GALLERY OF ONTARIO, TORONTO
Gift from the Fund of the T. Eaton Co. Ltd. for Canadian Works of Art, 1948

EXAMPLE 4-3 Harry Freedman, *Images* (1957–8), 'Blue Mountain,' beginning; facsimile of the composer's manuscript

EXAMPLE 4-4   Claude Champagne, *Altitude* (1959), 'schema topographique'

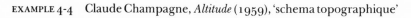

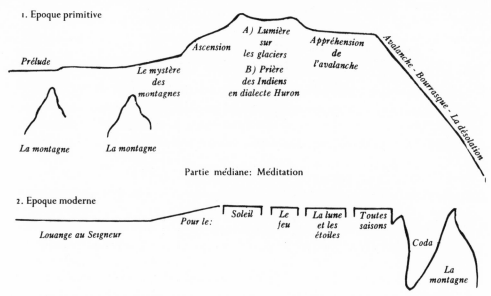

© Copyright 1961 BMI Canada Limited. Copyright assigned 1969 to Berandol Music Limited. Used by permission

bombing of the ancient centre of culture and democratic government in the Spanish province of Basque. The indiscriminate destruction of a cultural heritage and the murder of women and children became a symbol of Fascist brutality and man's inhumanity to man. Pépin viewed the mural first while he was a student in Paris (the fresco is now located in the Museum of Modern Art in New York), and his orchestral piece is the first in a series of Canadian works to present strong social or political commentary. In *Guernica* Pépin follows the example of the Soviet musical realist Shostakovich (e.g. *Symphony No. 7*, 'Leningrad,' 1941–2), using a clearly defined tonality and accompanying dissonance, foreboding rhythmic patterns (in the 'Marche funèbre' and 'Marche militaire'), and the trumpets of war. Unfortunately the musical means do not correspond to the surrealism of the Picasso mural and consequently Pépin's *Guernica* does not generate the same feeling of dramatic tragedy as does the original painting. Pépin's *Le Rite du soleil noir* (1955) is another symphonic poem, this one inspired by a work of the surrealist poet Antonin Artaud. As with *Guernica* Pépin selects a work in another art form as his point of departure but avoids using a parallel avant-garde style in his musical setting. *Le Rite* is middle-of-the-road in twentieth-century terms.

On the conservative side of the realm of programmatic orchestral music is Godfrey Ridout's *Music for a Young Prince* (1959), a concert overture commissioned by the CBC for the opening of the St Lawrence Seaway in 1959 by Queen

Elizabeth II and Prince Philip. Ridout's work consists of four movements evoking childhood and youth – 'Dreams,' 'From the Caboose,' 'The Cowboy and the Injun,' and 'Pageantry' – and the treatment is that of a well-crafted romantic work in the Elgar-Holst manner.

Abstract works

Significant as some of the programmatic works are, during this period Canadian composers more frequently showed a preference for neoclassical forms such as the symphony, serenade, concerto, suite, overture, and divertimento. It is surprising, therefore, that relatively few works are full symphonies (twenty minutes or more in length). Of the eight which use the title 'symphony,' only five are of this dimension. Many more composers were now capable of writing in the larger forms but chose not to do so, either because they preferred neoclassical conciseness or because they were not assured a performance outlet. Even with the establishment of the CBC Symphony, the Canadian composer of an extended work was not always guaranteed a first performance; second and third performances were even rarer. Canadian orchestras still tended to view their obligation to Canadian music as being fulfilled with the insertion of a ten-minute concert overture as an audience-settler at the beginning of a programme.

John Weinzweig's *Symphonic Ode* (1958) and Barbara Pentland's *Symphony for Ten Parts* (1957) are both short works. The Weinzweig work, commissioned by the Saskatoon Symphony, is in the composer's words, 'an extended movement of compressed symphonic proportions.'[10] In typical Weinzweig fashion the twelve-tone row is fragmented into motives which are then developed in a neoclassical manner. The row itself remains easily identifiable and, as in his other works, the musical organization is not hide-bound by strict serial procedures. In his preface to the score Weinzweig notes that the work has the structure of a rondo with variations, the rondo itself being the antithesis of Schönberg's idea of continuous variation.

Pentland's *Symphony for Ten Parts* also makes free use of the twelve-tone technique, but texturally it displays a strong influence of Webernesque pointillism. In the second movement the last forty-five measures are a retrograde of the first forty-five, further documenting Webern's influence on Pentland following her first exposure to Webern's music live at the Darmstadt festival in 1955. From this time on Pentland also became increasingly concerned with greater economy of means and more transparent textures while she was at the same time searching for new colour combinations. The dry humour of the second movement is characteristic of Pentland at every stage of her career.

Two of the works entitled 'symphony' are for strings alone: Jacques Hétu's *Symphonie pour cordes* (1959) and Robert Turner's *Symphony for Strings* (1960).

These works are similar in that they are romantic in expression and classical in construction. Each employs sonata and passacaglia forms and maintains a relation to a tonal centre though not in a functional sense. Both composers treat the strings in a conventional manner without attempting to extract from them new or unusual sonorities.

The other symphonies written in this period are quite varied in style. Samuel Dolin's *Symphony No. 2* (1957) is in the large-scale late-nineteenth-century tradition, coming closest to the symphonies of Shostakovich in the present century. Pépin's *Symphonie No. 2* (1957) is a gloomy but accessible work, ranging from the tonal and chromatic to the atonal; it employs classical forms (toccata, chorale, and fugue) and is tied together by insistent motor rhythms and ostinati. The overall effect calls to mind the style of Honegger, one of Pépin's teachers. Freedman's *Symphony No. 1* (1960) also follows the large-scale orchestral tradition. Classical in construction, with much evidence of orchestral colour and rhythmic vitality, the work shows the influence of Bartók. It was natural that Freedman, who was a professional player with the Toronto Symphony for almost a quarter of a century, should be so inclined to revel, as he does in this work, in a large orchestral sound.

By far the most complex and enigmatic large-scale Canadian orchestral work of this period is István Anhalt's *Symphony* (1954–8). According to composer-critic Marvin Duchow, the work 'must be accounted one of the very few substantial compositions of symphonic dimensions from the pen of a Canadian composer.'[11] Duchow, who reviewed a performance of the work at the International Conference of Composers in 1960, said that the remarkable thing about this symphony is the 'coalescence of its myriad thematic details into a sonorous unity of monumental proportions.'[12] The complexity of detail present from the outset in the work caused another reviewer, John Beckwith, to say that 'he [Anhalt] opens the door and ushers you into a room where a complex four-sided argument is in progress. Only later do you sense what it is about.'[13] The work is in a single movement divided into thirteen sections, which Beckwith has grouped into six parts in his analysis.[14] Acknowledging the influence of the post-Webern serial composers, Anhalt comments thus about this symphony:

> In composing the Symphony, I thought of the various combinations of pitches, rhythms, dynamics, instrumental ensembles, tempi, as coalescing into what one could call degrees on a 'density scale.' I attributed values on this scale to various combinations instinctively while composing this work. By this statement I do not want to imply, though, that I do not think it possible that such 'density scales' can be constructed objectively.[15]

Thematically the work makes free use of a twelve-tone series, emphasizing a four-note motive and an eight-note consequent which appear in various guises throughout. As he intimates above, Anhalt sees no purpose in a strict, mathematical serialization of tones but relies on a subtle form of rhythmic repetition to provide much of the unity in the work.

A number of abstract orchestral works in this period involve instrumental or vocal soloists. R. Murray Schafer's *Concerto for Harpsichord and Eight Wind Instruments* (1954), an early work by this composer, makes use of the baroque harpsichord in a twentieth-century neoclassical idiom. Two outer toccata-like movements act as a frame for a slow movement of free variations which is based on the chorale theme of the first movement. The style is 'quite French ... Milhaud, Honegger, etc., with perhaps a little early Stravinsky thrown in,'[16] according to the composer. Exhibiting some of the same neoclassical influences are John Beckwith's *Concerto-Fantasy* (1958–9) for piano and orchestra and Murray Adaskin's *Concerto for Bassoon and Orchestra* (1960).

More romantic in nature are Pierre Mercure's *Cantate pour une joie* (1955), Godfrey Ridout's *Cantiones mysticae* (1953), and Harry Somers's *Five Songs for Dark Voice* (1956), each of which features the solo voice with orchestra. The Mercure work, on seven verses by Gabriel Charpentier, is for soprano solo, SATB chorus, and orchestra. The chant-like treatment of the voice, the frequent ostinati in the instrumental parts, and the modal melodies and harmonies combine to produce an emotional yet unsentimental setting of the text. A certain Honegger-like melodramatic quality is also present. The first two lines of the final verse of the text sums up the spirit of optimism of the work:

le cri de joie est sorti de ma bouche
tout le monde danse sur les places[17]

In contrast to Mercure's *Cantate pour une joie* is Ridout's *Cantiones mysticae* for solo voice and orchestra, which was composed expressly for soprano Lois Marshall for the historic concert of Canadian works conducted by Leopold Stokowski at Carnegie Hall, New York, on Friday, 16 October 1953 (sponsored by BMI and BMI Canada Limited). Based on the *Holy Sonnets* (mostly after 1621) by John Donne, this work is stylistically conservative, combining as it does baroque-like textures and forms (strophic variations in the second movement) and Elgarian melodies, harmonies, and rhythms.

Somers's 'Dark Songs,' as the composer himself refers to them, are in a late romantic vein; they were written at a time when Somers was strongly influenced by Mahler, particularly his works for voice and orchestra. In reality a chamber symphony with obbligato voice, this work consists of five complete but concise movements in cyclical form. While the sharp, nervous rhythmic motives call to mind Somers's earlier *Passacaglia and Fugue* (1954) and the uneven ostinati show the influence of Stravinsky, the brooding, melancholic nature of the voice line is indebted to the late romantic, bittersweet style of Mahler. The pessimistic outcry of the text underlines the dilemma of modern man as he attempts to cope with the impersonality of the modern city, in this case Toronto. The text is by Michael E. Fram, with whom Somers had previously collaborated in the opera *The Fool* (1953). The first of the five poems contains the essence of the cycle:

> Now every grief is personal
> How can I walk in this city?
> Too many sightless eyes, too many hopeless hands,
> Too many and too many,
> Now every grief is personal.
> Too many avenues of pity,
> How can I walk in this city?

The final verse is one of resignation:

> How can I hold within me all that is?
> Some shape, some subtle touch will break me,
> Some joy explode me in a rain of stars
> To fall in ashes on this city.

> Now every grief is personal,
> Do not deny me, grant at last
> Encompassing compassion,
> To hold within me all that is,
> To care, past loving and past hate,
> That I may walk in your city.[18]

Symbolically, the musical texture of the work becomes leaner as the gloomy conclusion approaches with its plea for compassion.

A similar work in many ways is the *Wine of Peace* (1957) of John Weinzweig, although it is concerned with collective mankind rather than the individual person. This work is based upon texts of the seventeenth-century Spanish poet Pedro Calderón de la Barca ('Life is a Dream') and an anonymous Arabian poet ('City of Brass'). The work is dedicated to the United Nations, 'where the dreams of mankind for peace on earth can become a reality.'[19] The texts tell of the futility of man's quest for power and exhort him to 'taste the beautiful Wine of Peace, for tomorrow, the earth shall answer.' Weinzweig's setting is for soprano solo and orchestra. Udo Kasemets said of it: 'this deeply moving work comes possibly closest to summing up Weinzweig's various approaches to musical expression ... Through every bar of this composition shines John Weinzweig as we know him now: a profound thinker, a mature craftsman, a sensitive and warm man.'[20] Weinzweig again uses the twelve-tone row in a free manner, sometimes as a complete melodic line, sometimes broken up into motives. The row of the first movement implies triadic structures through its emphasis on thirds and fourths (perfect) and is, thus, appropriate to the the humanistic nature of the text. This humanistic quality is also underlined by the choice of the alto saxophone as an obbligato instrument to the voice, beginning in measure 8 with the second full statement of the row. In the second movement the tone row is similar in some respects (the first three intervals are the same), but here it emphasizes the descending minor second, giving a romantic 'sigh' quality to the motive. As with Somers's *Five Songs for Dark Voice* there is an obvious link with the works for voice and orchestra by Mahler. The general mood in the Weinzweig is, however, one of hope rather than resignation or dejection. Weinzweig's *Violin Concerto* (1951–4) is also romantic in expressiveness and classical in design, following the model of Berg's violin concerto (1935).

A stylistically more severe work is Pentland's *Concerto for Piano and String Orchestra* (1955–6). Composed soon after Pentland's visit to Darmstadt in 1955, the concerto predates the *Symphony for Ten Parts*, but, like it, it shows a strong influence of the post-Webern school. Webern's brevity and conciseness as well as his clarity of line appealed greatly to Pentland. In the notes for the record jacket of the RCI recording of the work Pentland states: 'my aim is always to write as much meaningful music using as few notes as possible. Every time I must copy a work I wish I had been more successful in this respect.'[21] Even though the economy of Webern influenced this work, the use of repeated fragments and pianistic figurations are features which are distinctly non-Webern in origin. Furthermore, although the composer tells us that 'the serial technique is employed as the cohesive means for the various permutations,'[22] the original form of the row is not obvious. As with Anhalt's *Symphony No. 1*, the listener is thrust immediately into the variational material without a clear presentation of the original. If Pentland's organizational methods are somewhat elusive, her vitality and humour are not. The latter are dominant characteristics of both the *Concerto for Piano* and the *Symphony for Ten Parts*.

Two other works of consequence for solo instrument and orchestra warrant discussion. They are *Concertante for Violin, Strings, and Percussion* (1955–7) by Otto Joachim and *Pièce concertante no. 1* (1957) for piano and orchestra by Jean Papineau-Couture. The Joachim work provides an interesting point of comparison with Pentland's *Concerto for Piano* in that it too uses the twelve-tone technique but in a much more straightforward manner. The complete row is stated linearly at the outset, followed by a chord containing all tones of the row and a slightly abbreviated restatement of the original. Measures 26–8 from the first movement (example 4-5) are typical of the strict manner in which Joachim used the twelve-tone technique in the 1950s. The original (o) form of the row is followed by the inversion (I) which is followed immediately by the retrograde inversion (RI). No other Canadian composer followed the dodecaphonic precepts more categorically. Combined with this structural organization in which the row material is

EXAMPLE 4-5   Otto Joachim, *Concertante for Violin, Strings, and Percussion* (1955–7), first movement, mm 26–8

readily identifiable, Joachim employs exotic, colouristic devices, no doubt derived from his lengthy stay of seventeen years in the Far East. The percussion includes high, intermediate, medium, and low gongs in the first movement and bongos and an African drum in the second, and last, movement. The solo violin often performs in concertante fashion over ostinato figures. The duo between the drums and the violin in the second movement proceeds gradually to a fever pitch upon which the work ends.

The *Pièce concertante no. 1* by Papineau-Couture illustrates another stylistic feature which became fashionable in Canada in the late 1950s as a result of the influence of the post-Webern group of composers. This feature, which has already been noted in Pentland's *Symphony for Ten Parts*, is the employment of canonic devices modelled after the music of Webern, the musicologist-composer

EXAMPLE 4-6   Jean Papineau-Couture, *Pièce concertante no. 1* (1957), section F
(in the composer's hand)

who began the renaissance of late-Gothic organizational techniques in the twentieth century. As indicated by the subtitle of the work, *Repliement*, meaning a
folding back, Papineau-Couture applied the retrograde principle to the entire
one-movement work so that the last half of the work is a note-for-note reversal of
the first half. While acknowledging another late-Gothic principle that the means
of organization should be hidden from view, Papineau-Couture judiciously
selected his melodic and rhythmic material so that it would 'remain recognizable in
both directions.'[23] Frequent reversible patterns of five sonorities are the natural
result (see example 4-6). It is interesting to note that this same principle of
reversibility may be found later in the work of Canadian painters, such as Yves
Gaucher, whose *Le Cercle de grande réserve* (1965) illustrates the same attention to
balance and symmetry.[24]

Many of the abstract orchestral works of the 1950s are of the non-symphony,
non-concerto variety, and most of them are fairly short (less than ten minutes in

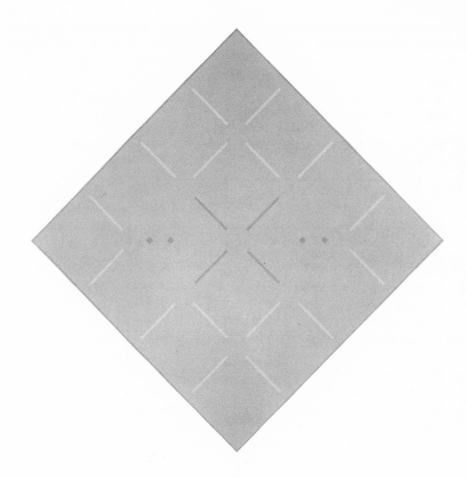

YVES GAUCHER   Canadian b. 1934
Le Cercle de Grande Réserve, 1965
acrylic on canvas
85″ diagonally, 60″ × 60″   215.9 cm, 152.4 × 152.4 cm
ART GALLERY OF ONTARIO, TORONTO
Gift from the McLean Foundation, 1966

length). Neoclassicism called for conciseness and clarity, and many of the abstract works follow these precepts: for example, Robert Turner's *Opening Night* (1955), Violet Archer's *Divertimento for Orchestra* (1957), Pierre Mercure's *Divertissement* (1957), André Prévost's *Scherzo* (1960), Murray Adaskin's *Serenade Concertante* (1954), and John Weinzweig's *Divertimento No. 3* (1959) for bassoon and string orchestra. Weinzweig's work also incorporates jazz-like elements into both the solo and orchestral parts.

Among the most frequently performed short, abstract works are Harry Somers's *Passacaglia and Fugue for Orchestra* (1954), *Fantasia for Orchestra* (1958), and *Lyric for Orchestra* (1960), each of which combines neoclassical structural features with a sense of rhythmic and dramatic urgency. *Passacaglia and Fugue* is typical of Somers's interest in baroque forms in the 1950s. The passacaglia theme, which is first stated by the cellos and basses and doubled by the bass clarinet and double bassoon, contains the first six notes of a twelve-tone row. The rhythmically static nature of the latter part of the theme contributes, however, to periodic interruptions in the momentum of the work, a feature to which Beckwith, as critic, called attention shortly after the piece was completed.[25] The *Fugue* employs a different row from the *Passacaglia* but maintains a stricter use of the twelve-tone technique. The use of agitated rhythmic figures and frequent repeated tones is typical of Somers and contributes to capturing what he refers to as 'the high-tensioned elements of our own time.'[26] Equally slow to gather momentum but more brilliant in its use of the orchestra is the *Fantasia* which was written four years later. Its rhapsodic style even approaches the melodramatic at times. *Lyric for Orchestra*, on the other hand, although it contains many of Somers's trademarks (rhapsodic solo passages, strongly rhythmic repeated notes), is more tightly knit than the other two works.

Triptyque (1959) by the late Pierre Mercure, which was composed for the Vancouver International Festival of 1959, follows very much the style of Ravel, who earlier in the century combined neoclassical clarity with orchestral brilliance. In a large ABA structure (two slow movements surround an allegro marcato section), it draws upon the same retrograde procedure found in Papineau-Couture's *Pièce concertante no. 1*. In the case of *Triptyque* the third movement is a retrograde of the first, so that, symbolically, the outer panels of the musical triptych are mirrors of each other.

The increase in musical composition in the 1950s was matched by a parallel increase in music education, especially at the secondary school level. A coming together of both these developments resulted in the recognition of the need for original compositions suitable for use in the schools. One of the first bodies to respond to this need was the Faculty of Music Alumni Association of the University of Toronto, which from 1955 to 1957 issued commissions to Canadian composers; these produced the *Little Suite for String Orchestra* (1955) by Harry Somers, *Fall Scene and Fair Dance* (1956) by John Beckwith, and *Three Songs to Music* (1957) by Healey Willan. Somers's work makes use of three Canadian folk songs, *Lukey's Boat, She's Like the Swallow,* and *Ah! Si mon moine voulait danser!* Beckwith's piece is for solo violin, clarinet, and string orchestra, and is simple and folk-like in style. Willan's work is a setting of three poems by Robert Herrick for SATB chorus and piano; it is typical of Willan in its use of faburden and antiphonal techniques. All three works were published by BMI Canada Limited. This annual commission was unfortunately discontinued and it was not until the Canadian Music Centre began the John Adaskin Project in 1962 that there was again a concerted effort to provide music for Canadian schools in a contemporary idiom and by Canadian composers.

CHAMBER MUSIC

One of the more obvious manifestations of neoclassicism in the years 1952–60 is the large quantity of chamber music written. A majority of these works are for the conventional string quartet, string or piano trio, duo sonata, and woodwind quintet, but a new trend towards unusual instrumental and vocal combinations is also apparent. Such combinations as voice, violin, and cello (Gabriel Charpentier, *Trois poèmes,* 1954); voice (without text), clarinet, and piano (Harry Freedman, *Two Vocalises,* 1954); and flute, oboe, and harpsichord (Kelsey Jones, *Sonata da Camera,* 1957; Oskar Morawetz, *Trio,* 1960) are cases in point. Many of these combinations are the result of composers writing on commission or for a particular occasion when only certain instruments or voices were available. The general approach of these works is neoclassical, emphasizing clarity of texture, contrapuntal techniques, and a return to the forms and sometimes the instruments of an earlier time.

Of the string quartets those by Jean Vallerand (1960), Clermont Pépin (No. 3, 1959), Otto Joachim (1956), Harry Somers (No. 3, 1959), and Barbara Pentland (No. 2, 1953) make use of the twelve-tone technique in one way or another. In this respect many Canadian composers seemed to be following the model of Stravinsky who gradually incorporated dodecaphonism into his works after 1952 and through his influence won for that particular 'ism' a degree of acceptance which it had not previously enjoyed. The most straightforward of the Canadian twelve-tone quartets is Joachim's; paradoxically it is also the work which has the most clearly defined tonal centre, achieved through a repeated return to a single tone in the opening statement. This technique of repetition of a single tone is used throughout the work and serves as an obvious unifying element. Most of the time the row is treated in a linear manner, with each voice carrying a different form of the row (original, inversion, retrograde, retrograde inversion) in whole or in part. The influence of Bartók is heard through the imaginative use of instrumental sonorities and a sense of dramatic urgency which permeates the quartet. Joachim was the violist in one of Canada's best and most active quartets of the 1950s, the Montreal String Quartet.

Pentland's *String Quartet No. 2* was written in memory of her brother, who was killed in a plane crash in Pakistan. The work is severe in style and quotes, in the viola part in the second movement, the Gregorian Introit *Requiem aeternam*. The five-movement work is tied together by the first five notes of a twelve-note row. During the 1950s this was one of the few Canadian works which received international recognition; it was selected for a first performance at the International Society for Contemporary Music World Festival at Stockholm, Sweden, in 1956.[27]

The quartets by Pepin (No. 3), Vallerand, and Somers (No. 3) have in common the fact that each was written upon commission, for the Saskatoon Summer Festival of Music, the Lapitsky Foundation of Montreal, and the Vancouver International Festival respectively. The Somers quartet is based upon themes from his first opera, *The Fool* (1953), and assumes much of the dramatic impact of that work. The opening melody in the cello is almost identical to the opening of the opera. The quartet, in one movement divided into several sections, frequently employs recitative passages reminiscent of opera. The dramatic use of silence is also a feature of this work as it is in the opera.

The Vallerand *Quatuor à cordes* has the subtitle *Variazioni sul tema a ricercar*, indicating that variations on a theme are to be searched for. The tone row, indeed, is elusive and never seems to appear in a clear statement. The listener and analyst is confronted by a series of variations without the original, a device favoured by post-Webern composers such as Boulez. The actual unifying elements are melodic and rhythmic motives, notably the rising melodic third.

Pépin's *Quatuor à cordes no. 3* consists of only an adagio and a fugue, with a return to the adagio at the end followed by a prestissimo coda. Thus the work has an overall ABA structure. Repeated-note figures form an important unifying element in this work (either one tone or short motives). The fugue has a *galant* feeling about it which is in contrast to the sombre adagio.

Two other quartets of the 1950s merit attention: the *String Quartet No. 1* (1953–5) of Glenn Gould and the *String Quartet No. 2* (1954) of Robert Turner. Gould's quartet is clearly an anachronism in that it is closest in style to early Schönberg (*Verklärte Nacht*). Late romantic in form and content, it stands alone as the major work by one of Canada's most talented and most controversial performing musicians. Turner's quartet, in contrast, is neoclassical in style, although it is not without romantic elements. Composed on a commission from McGill University for the Fiftieth Anniversary of the Conservatorium of Music in 1954, this quartet shows the influence of the classic-romantic US composers, such as Roy Harris, with whom Turner had studied a short while before he wrote the quartet.

As in the chamber music of the previous decade, the favoured medium in the 1950s was piano and a single instrument; after 1960 such works would diminish in quantity as neoclassicism waned. With the exception of István Anhalt's *Sonata for Violin and Piano* (1954), a work clearly indebted to Schönberg, the pieces for violin and piano are generally neoclassical (or neo-baroque) in structure and romantic in mood. Somers's two sonatas (1953 and 1955) are avowedly so, and those by

Archer, Jones, Morawetz, and Turner follow very much the same pattern. The tone row upon which the Anhalt work is based emphasizes the minor and major second (and their inversions, the major and minor seventh) and the major and minor third (and their inversions, the minor and major sixth), the former through octave displacement creating tension-filled disjunct melodies and the latter compensating with warm, romantic vertical sonorities. The almost constant motion and busy three-part texture also contribute to the quality of stream-of-conscious expressionism which is conveyed by this sonata.

Somers considered his *Sonata No. 1* (1953) and *Sonata No. 2* (1955), both for violin and piano, to have a closer affinity to the nineteenth than to the twentieth century. Built upon short germinal motives, they feature a combination of agitated repeated notes, long flowing lines, and fugal expositions. In keeping with Somers's concern in the 1950s with baroque forms, there is a walking-bass figure in the second movement of *Sonata No. 2*. Above all, Somers maintains an element of drama and unpredictability.

Similar to Somers in his use of the baroque walking-bass and ritornello techniques coupled with long, lyrical lines is Morawetz in his *Sonata No. 1* (1956) for violin and piano. In contrast to the Somers sonatas, however, the Morawetz work proceeds smoothly and directly without dramatic interjections. Violet Archer's *Sonata No. 1* (1956) and *Prelude and Allegro* (1954) exhibit certain neobaroque and neoclassical features such as the cantus-firmus technique, the walking bass, the gigue form, and the fugue. Archer follows the style of her teacher Hindemith to the extent of favouring endings on a final major chord. Kelsey Jones's *Introduction and Fugue* (1959) includes many of the same characteristics with more virtuoso results. Turner, in the second movement of his *Sonata for Violin and Piano* (1956), also employs a baroque-like repeated-bass pattern (i.e. ground bass), but at the same time he makes more of an attempt to exploit the unusual sound resources of the violin (e.g. sul ponticello, pizzicato, etc) as well as irregular rhythms.

A singular work for unaccompanied violin is the *Suite pour violon seul* (1956) by Jean Papineau-Couture. In three movements, it adopts the dry, staccato style typical of many neoclassical works. Also a virtuoso display piece, it becomes a parody of a baroque gigue in its last movement.

Pentland's *Duo* (1960) for viola and piano shows once again Webern's influence on the composer. Based upon a five-note row which eventually expands to include all twelve tones, this work is economical and texturally lean. Frequent repetition of tones or groups of tones contributes to its comprehensibility, as does the prominence of the minor-third interval in the row structure. Unusual sound effects are achieved in the second movement by stopping the string with the edge of the fingernail. The use of silence as an integral part of the sound concept as well as the humour in the last movement are significant features of Pentland's style.

The works for cello and piano by Archer, S.C. Eckhardt-Gramatté, and

Joachim are very much in contrast to each other. Archer's *Sonata for Cello and Piano* (1956) is romantic in mood and classical in construction; the Eckhardt-Gramatté *Duo concertante* (1959), on the other hand, is more dissonant and diffuse but equally romantic. Its second movement was inspired by a mobile of Alexander Calder, who is 'known throughout the world as the artist who made sculpture move.'[28] The pointillistic wanderings of the piano and the lack of bar-lines contribute to the free feeling which can be associated with the visual perception of a mobile. In the *Sonata for Cello and Piano* (1954) Joachim follows his pattern of using the twelve-tone row in a clear and undisguised manner, and in the cello part he employs only the complete and untransposed forms of the row (original, retrograde, inversion retrograde inversion) throughout the first movement. This work exhibits a considerable degree of wit and vitality through octave displacement and rhythmic interest. It, together with Pentland's *Duo*, illustrates that Canadian music of this period is not without humour.

Considering the growth in popularity of wind instruments by mid-century, there is a surprising lack of chamber music written for winds in Canada in the 1950s. However, two works, the *Quintet for Wind Instruments* (1957) by Udo Kasemets and the *Serenade for Woodwind Quintet* (1960) by Turner, are worthy of comment. Both works are somewhat out of character for these composers. Kasemets's *Quintet* is written in the neoclassical style of Stravinsky and Milhaud, complete with canonic devices at the beginning and parody technique in the middle section. Turner's *Serenade*, on the other hand, utilizes the twelve-tone technique, although in a free manner, a new departure for this composer. The row used is interesting for the way in which it outlines four triads (C minor, E major, B-flat major, and F-sharp minor), thus allowing for the retention of tertian and tonal implications within the twelve-tone system. The use of ritornello and parody techniques also calls to mind Stravinsky and the French neoclassicists. This work is an example of contemporary Canadian music which is emotional in content and listener-oriented, an aesthetic point of view to which Turner subscribes.[29]

Other chamber music works of the 1952–60 period involving woodwinds include Talivaldis Kenins's *Divertimento* (1960) for clarinet and piano, a neoclassical piece which is tightly knit around motives which favour the interval of the fourth, melodically and harmonically. Eldon Rathburn's *Conversation for Two Clarinets* (1956) is a frothy piece in two-voice counterpoint which was adapted from his film score *Honey Bees and Pollination* (National Film Board of Canada). Pépin's *Quatre monodies pour flûte seule* (1955) is more adventurous in the new types of flute sounds which it explores, but nevertheless it hearkens back to the baroque in its use of the dance forms *badinerie* and *gigue*.

Much more advanced in idiom is Serge Garant's *Asymétries no. 2* (1959) for clarinet and piano. Under the influence of Boulez, with whom he became acquainted while he was a student of Messiaen's in the early 1950s, Garant estab-

lishes a structure which 'rests on the use of asymmetrical rows of sounds, durations, attacks and dynamics.'[30] It is one of the few examples in Canadian music to
follow the precepts of total serialization of the post-Webern school.

More generally, however, Canadian composers in the 1950s experimented
with unusual sound combinations rather than with avant-garde organizational
techniques. Works along this line include Anhalt's *Comments* (1954) for contralto
voice and piano trio, which is based upon three short news clippings from the
Montreal *Star*; Alexander Brott's *Sept for Seven* (1954) which is a setting for
narrator and six instruments of five Canadian poems by different authors, somewhat reminiscent of Walton's *Façade*; Jean Coulthard's *The Devil's Fanfare* (1958), a
chamber ballet for three dancers, violin, and piano with the musicians performing
on stage behind a filmy curtain. The Baroque Trio of Montreal was directly
responsible for the composition of at least two works during this period,
Morawetz's *Trio* (1960) and Jones's *Sonata da camera* (1957); both are for the
baroque trio-sonata combination of flute, oboe, and harpsichord and both are
written in a neo-baroque style. Turner's *Variations and Toccata* (1959) for an
unusual combination of ten instruments (woodwind quintet plus string quintet)
shows this composer again using the twelve-tone technique with tonal implications.

In the 1950s Canadian composers were beginning to answer the call to
produce chamber music works, as well as orchestral works, for young performers.
One such example is Keith Bissell's *A Folk-Song Suite for Woodwinds* (1960), which
was written for the Scarborough Public School Woodwind Ensemble (Toronto).
The work is in a traditional vein and is quite approachable both technically and
musically. The scoring is for two flutes, two clarinets, and bass clarinet (or bassoon), thus avoiding the more difficult and rarer oboe and horn parts.

One of the most important innovations in Canadian music in the 1950s was
that of electronic music. Centring on the work of the late Hugh LeCaine at the
National Research Council in Ottawa from 1952, Canada assumed a leadership
role, largely through LeCaine's efforts, in the development of sophisticated electronic music hardware, such as the touch-sensitive organ keyboard and the serial
sound-structure generator. LeCaine's compositions are few but significant, the
best known from the 1950s being *Dripsody* (1955), a work created by tape manipulation of the sound of a single drop of water. Subtitled *An Etude for Variable
Speed Recorder*, *Dripsody* is an example of *musique concrète*, wherein the raw material
of the work is the sound of a drop of water recorded on a tape about half an inch
long. Through various splicing and re-recording techniques rhythmic patterns
were established with tones of frequencies from 45 cps to 8000 cps. Structurally
and texturally the piece is neoclassical in style. Le Caine also made an important
contribution by assisting in the establishment of one of the first electronic music
studios in a North American university at the University of Toronto in May 1959
(it was the first in Canada).

While the development of electronic music was taking place, a move which was greeted with unjustifiable fear and trepidation in many musical circles, paradoxically there was also a growth in new music for small, intimate instruments or groups of instruments associated with the rebirth of the performance of early music. Harry Somers's *Sonata for Guitar* (1959) is an example of a work which belies the notion that contemporary music is excessively technical and impersonal.

SONG

Considering the number of outstanding Canadian singers who emerged in the 1950s, such as Lois Marshall, Maureen Forrester, Jon Vickers, Teresa Stratas, Léopold Simoneau, Donald Bell, Pierrette Alarie, Claire Gagnier, Mary Morrison, Phyllis Mailing, and the late James Milligan, it is perhaps surprising that more solo songs were not written during this time. It seems that Canadian composers were more interested in instrumental sonorities alone or in a combination of voices with instruments. In fact, some of the more outstanding works of the period in any medium are for voices with instruments, such as John Weinzweig's *Wine of Peace*, Harry Somers's *Five Songs for Dark Voice*, Jean Papineau-Couture's *Psaume CL* (1954), and Claude Champagne's *Altitude*. Most of the singers mentioned above performed Canadian works from time to time, but two, Mary Morrison and Phyllis Mailing, built their considerable reputations in the 1960s and 1970s around their specialization in Canadian works.

A number of works for solo voice and piano (or a chamber grouping of a few instruments) are worthy of note. Somers's *Three Simple Songs* (1953) and *Conversation Piece* (1955) are unpretentious works, the former characterized by a free use of the twelve-tone technique and the latter by a pedal-tone G throughout. Each shows Somers's individuality and sensitivity to the unique character of a given text; the texts of both works are by Toronto poet Michael E. Fram. R. Murray Schafer's *Minnelieder* (1956) for soprano and woodwind quintet is an early work by this composer; it is based upon medieval German love poems. Although it begins with a twelve-tone statement, overall it is closer in style to the music of Carl Orff with its ostinato figures and modal patterns. The final song (of thirteen) shows the influence of plainsong and medieval secular song in its free-flowing, irregular rhythm; the simultaneous cross-relation (D−D-sharp) in the same song gives a touch of twentieth-century bite to the vertical sonorities. Udo Kasemets's *Three Miniatures* (1956) on poems by Percy Bysshe Shelley is neoclassical in its clarity of texture, simplicity of melody, and economy of material. Motives extracted from the twelve-tone row form the basis of the unifying structure through repetition. Similarly free in its use of the twelve-tone technique is Harry Freedman's *Two Vocalises* (1954); in this case the composer treats the voice as another instrument in counterpoint with the clarinet and piano. The second of the two vocalises emphasizes an asymmetrical rhythmic figure (3+3+2).

The most avant-garde vocal piece of the period is Serge Garant's *Caprices* (1953–4), a work very much in the post-Webern idiom. Based on four poems by Federico García Lorca, the Spanish poet of the people who was killed by the Fascists at the beginning of the Spanish Civil War, *Caprices*, according to the composer, does not try to create Spanish music but rather 'to recreate the poems musically: the gentle and coy "Guitare," the grave lyricism of "Cactus," the wild violence of "Agave," and the pointillist vision of "Croix." '[31] The melodic intervals of augmented and diminished octaves and augmented fourths, together with much octave displacement in both the voice and piano, depict the agonizing features of the text. Although this work is the first in which Garant uses the serial technique of the post-Webern school, one is impressed more by the expressive setting of the text than by the structural complexity.

Other works of the period which are more conservative include Pierre Mercure's *Dissidence* (1955) (three songs on poems by Charpentier which were subsequently expanded into *Cantate pour une joie*), André Prévost's *Musiques peintes* (1955), Violet Archer's *The Twenty-Third Psalm*, Lorne Betts's *Five Songs* (1952), Kelsey Jones's *To Music* (1957), Godfrey Ridout's *Cantiones mysticae* (1953), Jean Coulthard's *Spring Rhapsody* (1958), and Oskar Morawetz's *Mother, I Cannot Mind My Wheel* (1955) and *My True Love Hath My Heart* (1955). Less extended songs by Welford Russell, Kenneth Meek, Samuel Dolin, Marvin Duchow, and Maurice Dela are in a straightforward, post-romantic style.

CHORAL MUSIC

Choral music between 1952 and 1960 is characterized by a growing quantity of sacred music, both liturgical and non-liturgical, as well as an increased number of folk-song arrangements for various choral groupings. *Folk Songs of Canada* (1954) and *Chansons de Québec* (1957), both coedited by Edith Fowke and Richard Johnston, are among the best-known examples of the latter. The choral repertoire also contains a few works which are large in scope, often employ instruments along with the voices, and are either sacred or secular in nature.

One of the unaccompanied sacred works is Otto Joachim's *Psalm* (1960) which is based upon a text combining the Lord's Prayer and words by the eighteenth-century German poet, Friedrich Klopstock. The parts alternate and combine with sung and spoken declamation, the former sometimes following a strict twelve-tone series or chanting on a single tone. The affirmation of faith which is proclaimed in the text is reinforced by the pedal-tone E which appears at the beginning and end of the work.

Two of the choral works in this period were designed for liturgical use in the Roman Catholic church, the missae brevi by Gabriel Charpentier (1952) and Claude Champagne (1951). Charpentier's three-voice mass, written while the composer was studying with Nadia Boulanger, is clearly derivative of late-medieval and renaissance styles. Champagne's mass, on the other hand, is in a nineteenth-century harmonic idiom. Both works are in a note-against-note style without involved contrapuntal activity.

Other choral works include John Weinzweig's *Am Yisrael Chai* (1952), Harry Somers's *Where Do We Stand, O Lord?* (1955), and Godfrey Ridout's *Pange lingua* (1960). Weinzweig's work, the title of which means 'Israel lives,' was commissioned by the Canadian Jewish Congress for the 1953 Jewish Festival in Toronto; it is a cheerful but emotion-filled piece for mixed chorus and piano. It is characterized by strong march rhythms, homophonic chanting, and harmonic cross relations. Somers's work, on a text by Michael E. Fram, is in the form of a chorale passacaglia and fugue, calling to mind Somers's *Passacaglia and Fugue* for orchestra of the previous year, as well as his *Sonata No. 2 for Violin and Piano*. The text is despairing in tone, raising as it does basic questions about life and death in the post–atom-bomb era. Somers's characteristic repeated-note motive, which is present in the fugue subject, permits clarity of presentation of the insistent text but results in a static quality of the musical line. A return of the opening material at the end reveals the rounded form of the work. In contrast, Ridout's *Pange lingua* is not concerned with the dramatic issues of the twentieth century but rather with the mysteries of the Crucifixion and Resurrection of Our Lord as expressed by the medieval theologian St Thomas Aquinas. The musical idiom of this work is that of the late nineteenth-century English cathedral and shows kinship with the music of Healey Willan, one of Ridout's mentors and greatest admirers.

The most extended choral work of this period is *Psaume CL* (1954) by Jean Papineau-Couture, a full-scale cantata of twenty minutes' duration for soloists, chorus, wind ensemble, and organ. The six sections are tied together by a rising scale pattern which, although embellished in a variety of ways, is always identifiable, like a *cantus firmus*. Another unifying factor is the frequent use of the interval of the perfect fourth, both melodically and harmonically. The stark counterpoint, lean texture, frequent canonic treatment, and ground-bass and ostinato figures add up to a style which is reminiscent of Stravinsky's *Symphony of Psalms* (1930).

During this period Willan expanded his contribution to liturgical music with the publication of a junior choir book for the church year (*We Praise Thee*, vols I and II, 1953 and 1962) and a setting of the *Order of Holy Communion* (1955) for the Lutheran Church (Missouri Synod). One of his best-known non-liturgical sacred works, *O Lord, Our Governor* (1953), was performed as one of the homage anthems at the coronation of Queen Elizabeth II in Westminster Abbey on 2 June 1953. Based on various psalm verses, it is set for mixed chorus, orchestra, and organ and is appropriately festive in nature. In addition, the CBC commissioned Willan to compose the *Coronation Suite* (1952–3) for performance on the radio network on Coronation Day. This work consists of five movements, including an orchestral 'Prelude' and 'Intermezzo,' two unaccompanied motets ('Ring Out Ye Crystall

Spheres,' based on John Milton's *On The Morning of Christ's Nativity*, 1629, and 'Come Ready Lyre,' with words by Toronto clergyman, James Edward Ward), and the finale 'Come, Thou Beloved of Christ' for soli, chorus, and orchestra. The *Suite* as a whole combines Willan's various stylistic features, from the simplest plainchant-like melody to the jubilant polychoral writing for voices and instruments.

On the secular side Violet Archer's *Proud Horses* (1953) and Jean Coulthard's *More Lovely Grows the Earth* (1957), are each set for SATB chorus in a chromatic, tonal idiom. Kelsey Jones's *Songs of Experience* (1958) are settings of two of the twenty-seven poems from the 1794 collection of that name by William Blake. The music is mildly dissonant and follows the dramatic import of the words. Each song is in a rounded form. Willan's *Three Songs to Music* (1957) and Somers's *Two Songs for the Coming of Spring* (1957) are simple works suitable for use in the schools or by amateur choirs.

The number of arrangements of Canadian folk songs grew significantly in this period under the stimulation of an increasing national awareness of the folk heritage and the growth of music in the schools. Leslie Bell, Richard Johnston, Keith Bissell, Howard Cable, Godfrey Ridout, and Claude Champagne were some of the main contributors to this repertoire; they drew upon the collections of folklorists Marius Barbeau, Helen Creighton, Kenneth Peacock, Carmen Roy, and Luc Lacourcière.

ORGAN MUSIC

Organ music composed in the 1950s in Canada continued to be functional and oriented towards church services; it consisted mainly of preludes, voluntaries, and assorted short works. Public organ recitals were infrequent, and when they took place the works played were invariably selected from the masterpieces of the eighteenth and nineteenth centuries. It is significant that the revival of the so-called classic or mechanical-action organ, which took place in Germany as early as 1910 and in the United States in the 1930s and after World War II, did not get under way in Canada until the late 1950s and early 1960s. The major organ-builder in the country, Casavant Frères of St Hyacinthe, Québec, began to model its instruments after the tracker organs of the seventeenth and eighteenth centuries from 1958 onwards. At the same time the largest mechanical-action instrument in North America up to 1960, made by the von Beckerath firm of Germany, was installed in the Basilica of St Joseph's Oratory in Montreal in that year. The acceptance of this type of instrument in Canada coincided with a growing interest in the organ as a solo-recital instrument.

One of the few concert works of the period was composed by Raymond Daveluy who became organist of St Joseph's Oratory in 1960. His *Sonate en sol* (no.

3) (1959–60) is of symphonic proportions; even though its harmonic vocabulary is clearly that of the nineteenth century, the work is marked by clarity of texture and form. The first movement is in a sonata form with two contrasting subjects, the second consists of a sombre chaconne, and the third features a three-voiced fugue.

The other major work is Willan's *Passacaglia and Fugue No. 2 in E Minor* (1959), a piece very much in contrast to the Daveluy sonata. Willan's work maintains the heavy, thick style of its notable predecessor, the *Introduction, Passacaglia and Fugue* (1916) discussed in chapter 1. Intensely chromatic, the second *Passacaglia* is less extended and not so technically demanding as its predecessor.

The remaining organ works are clearly functional pieces. Composed in response to specific needs, they serve as preludes, offertories, and postludes (i.e. service music) for the church organist. In most cases the works are of limited technical difficulty. Willan's works from this category, such as *Thirty-six Short Preludes and Postludes on Well-known Hymn Tunes* (1960), are models of their type and are known and played internationally.

OPERA

As the previous decade (1941–51) marked the beginning of opera production on a sustained basis in Canada, the 1950s saw the beginning of the composition of opera for stage presentation. (Willan's earlier *Transit Through Fire*, 1942, and *Deirdre of the Sorrows*, 1945, were written as radio operas even though they were staged at a later date.) Since opera production was still in its infancy, it was natural that the first operas composed were of the chamber-opera type; that is, each was short in length (one act only), each employed a few soloists and no chorus (except for Betts's works which used a women's chorus), and each used a small orchestra or piano for accompaniment. The principal examples are Barbara Pentland's *The Lake* (1952; libretto by Dorothy Livesay), John Beckwith's *Night blooming Cereus* (1958; libretto by James Reaney), Lorne Betts's *Riders to the Sea* (1955; libretto adapted from J.M. Synge) and *The Woodcarver's Wife* (1960; libretto adapted from Marjorie Pickthall), Maurice Blackburn's *Une mesure de silence* (1953–4; libretto by Marthe Blackburn), Harry Somers's *The Fool* (1953; libretto by Michael E. Fram). With the exception of Betts's *Riders to the Sea*, which is based on the one-act play of that name by Irish playwright J.M. Synge, the libretti are by Canadian authors. The plots vary considerably, from Pentland's *The Lake*, which is concerned with relations between the white settlers and Okanagan Indians in British Columbia in 1873, to Beckwith's *Night Blooming Cereus*, which lays bare the foibles and vicissitudes of small-town life in southwestern Ontario. Somers's *The Fool* and Blackburn's *Une Mesure de silence* are international in theme and less tied to a particular time and place.

The Fool, to quote the composer, 'is about the tragedy which occurs when one is forced by events or circumstances to make decisions which will alienate or destroy that which one loves or is close to.'[32] Set in a medieval court, there are four characters; the King, the Queen, the Lady-in-Waiting, and the Fool. 'On one level they are one person, four different aspects of our inner world. On another level they represent four different aspects of our society. And on still another level they are as they are, four different people.'[33] The librettist Fram indicated that he was striving for a work which would have the 'simplicity and clarity of a Greek tragedy, and which would be, in somewhat the same way as Greek tragic myth, meaningful and absorbing upon several different levels to the modern Canadian audience.'[34] A critic commenting on the first performance of *The Fool* at a Canadian League of Composers' concert on 17 November 1956 took the libretto to task, saying that it was much too vague and complicated to serve as the basis for a good opera.[35] Similar criticisms were levelled at the libretto after the opera's revival at the 1975 Stratford Festival. Is it possible that the critics may be guilty of the same shortcoming which caused the Fool's tragedy – the need to place reason above all else? The King silences the Fool because times are grave and mirth and beauty have to give way to reason. The Fool, in contrast, speaks out against the strictures of the Protestant work ethic which so often stifle artistic life. In setting this enigmatic plot Somers drew on a variety of stylistic idioms, as he did later in *Louis Riel* (1967); each is related to a particular dramatic purpose. There are four levels of vocal setting (spoken words, dramatic sung recitation, sung line, and full sung line in the traditional sense). Furthermore, twelve-tone technique (twentieth century), tonal folk song (nineteenth century), chorale and motet style (eighteenth century), and ground-bass figures (seventeenth century) can all be found at different points in the score.

Une Mesure de silence by Maurice Blackburn, which received its first stage performance on the same programme as *The Fool*, is a *comédie* in the French tradition. The musical style, which is akin to Poulenc's, is predominantly lyrical in nature. Achieving classical balance and proportion throughout, the work is an 'entertaining piece of operatic *divertissement*' which, according to critical response at the time of the first performance, is what Canadian audiences were looking for in a Canadian opera.[36]

SELECTED WORKS

composer	title	score	recording
PIANO MUSIC			
Anhalt, István	*Fantasia* (1954)	Berandol, 1972	Col 32110045/46
Brott, Alexander	*Vignettes en caricature* (1952)		RCI 397

composer	title	score	recording
Coulthard, Jean	*Three Dances for Piano (1953–4)	No. 3 Harris, 1955	
	Twelve Preludes for Piano (1954–63)	Nos. 1, 2, 3 BMI Can, 1959	
	White Caps (1954)	BMI Can, 1953	
Dela, Maurice	La Vieille Capitale (1952)	BMI Can, 1953	
Eckhardt-Gramatté, S.C.	3 Klavierstücke (Suite VI) (1928–52)	CMC ms film 15/34	RCI 224; RCA CCS-1018
Garant, Serge	Asymétries No. 1 (1958)	CMC ms film 7/36	RCI ACM 2
	Pièce pour piano no. 1 (1953)	CMC ms film 7/35	RCI ACM 2
	Variations pour piano (1954)		RCI 135; RCI ACM 2
Glick, Srul Irving	Four Preludes (1958)	GVT, 1968	London CTLS 5107
Gratton, Hector	Crépuscule (1952)	BMI Can, 1956	RCI 132
Joachim, Otto	L'Eclosion (1954)	BMI Can, 1968	RCI 133
Karam, Frederick	Scherzo	BMI Can, 1953	
Kasemets, Udo	*Six Preludes for Piano (1952)	No. 2 Harris, 1955	
Kenins, Talivaldis	Concertino for Two Pianos Alone (1956)		Latvian CSRV 2258; Vogt L-2258
Lafortune, Lucien	Prélude	BMI Can, 1953	
Mather, Bruce	Like Snow (1960)	CMC ms film 11/17	CMC tape
	Smaragdin (1960)	CMC ms film 11/18	
Moisse, Séverin	Variations (sur un thème Huron, 1615)	BMI Can, 1955	
Morawetz, Oskar	Fantasy, Elegy and Toccata (1956)	Leeds, 1968	CBC SM 182
	Scherzino (1953)	Harris, 1955	RCI 397
Morel, François	Deux études de sonorité (1952–4)	BMI Can, 1966	RCI 251; CBC SM 182
Pentland, Barbara	Interlude (1955)	Waterloo, 1968	
	Three Piano Duets after Pictures by Paul Klee (1958)	CMC ms film 12/42	RCI 242
	Toccata (1958)	BMI Can, 1961	RCI 242; CBC SM 162
Pépin, Clermont	Trois pièces pour la légende dorée (1956)	Leeds, 1971	
Schafer, R. Murray	Polytonality (1952)	Berandol, 1974	

* In *14 Piano Pieces by Canadian Composers* (Oakville: F. Harris 1955)

composer	title	score	recording
Somers, Harry	*Piano Sonata No. 5* (1957)	Berandol, 1979	Mel SMLP 4023; CBC SM 162 (inc); RCI 450–52
Tremblay, Gilles	*Phases et réseaux* (1956–8)	Berandol, 1974	RCI 228; CBC SM 162 (inc)

ORCHESTRAL MUSIC

composer	title	score	recording
Adaskin, Murray	*Algonquin Symphony* (1958)	Ricordi, 1962	3rd movement Dom S1372; CAPAC-CAB tape 2
	Concerto for Bassoon and Orchestra (1960)	CMC ms film 1/10	CBC SM 143
	Saskatchewan Legend (1959)	Ricordi, 1961	
	Serenade Concertante (1954)	Ricordi, 1956	RCI 129; Col MS 6285; *Musican* rec. 8
Anhalt, István	*Symphony* (1954–8)	BMI Can, 1963	CMC tape
Archer, Violet	*Divertimento for Orchestra* (1957)	BMI Can, 1968	
Beckwith, John	*Concerto-Fantasy* (1958–9)	CMC ms film 7/4	CMC tape 146
	Fall Scene and Fair Dance (1956)	BMI Can, 1957	Lethbridge
	Music for Dancing (1948; orchestrated 1959)	BMI Can, 1961	CBC SM 47
Brott, Alexander	*Three Astral Visions* (1959)	Summit, 1973	RCI 188
Champagne, Claude	*Altitude* (1959)	BMI Can, 1961	RCI 179
	Paysanna (1953)	ms (NatLibOtt)	CBC SM 214
Coulthard, Jean	*A Prayer for Elizabeth* (1953)	BMI Can, 1961	CMC tape 245
Dela, Maurice	*Scherzo* (1952)	Berandol, 1974	CBC SM 132
Dolin, Samuel	*Symphony No. 2* (1957)	CMC ms film 21/33	CMC tape 61
Fleming, Robert	*Shadow on the Prairie* (1955)	CMC study score	RCI 129; *Musican* rec. 2
Freedman, Harry	*Images* (1957–8)	BMI Can, 1960	Col MS 6962; RCI ACM
	Symphony No. 1 (1960–1)	CMC ms film 6/3	
	Tableau (1952)	Ricordi, 1960	CMC tape 90
Healey, Derek	*Concerto for Organ, Strings and Timpani* (1960)	CMC ms	CBC SM 143
Hétu, Jacques	*Symphonie pour cordes*, Op. 2 (1959)	CMC ms film 17/1	RCI 293

composer	title	score	recording
Joachim, Otto	*Concertante for Violin, Strings and Percussion* (1955–7)	BMI Can, 1960	RCI 293
Jones, Kelsey	*Miramichi Ballad* (1954)	Boosey, 1972	RCI 291; CBC SM 163
	Suite for Flute and Strings (1954)	CMC ms film 10/3	RCI 191
Kasemets, Udo	*Concerto for Violin and Orchestra* (1957)	Berandol (rental)	CMC tape 470
McCauley, William A.	*Five Miniatures* (1958)	Leeds, 1968	Dom S-69006; Merc 50277
Matton, Roger	*L'Horoscope* (1958)	CMC study score	RCI 185
	Mouvement symphonique 1 (1960)	Ricordi, 1978	RCI 454
Mercure, Pierre	*Cantate pour une joie* (1955)	Ricordi, 1960	RCI 155
	Divertissement (1957)	Ricordi, 1970	RCI 154
	Triptyque (1959)	Ricordi, 1963	Col MS 6962
Morawetz, Oskar	*Overture to a Fairy Tale* (1956)	Boosey, 1959	CBC SM 308; *Musican* rec. 5; CAPAC-CAB tape 13
	Symphony No. 2 (1959)	CMC ms film 14/3	CBC SM 104
Morel, François	*Antiphonie* (1953)	BMI Can, 1960	RCI 180; Louisville LS 661
	Le Rituel de l'espace (1956–8)		RCI 213; RCA CCS-1007
	Rythmologue (1957–9; rev 1970)		RCI 298-301; McGill ST 77003
Papineau-Couture, Jean	*Pièce concertante no. 1* (1957)	BMI Can, 1961	Col MS 6285
	Prélude (1953)	CMC ms film 11/27	RCI ACM
	Pièce concertante no. 3 (1959)	CMC ms film 11/32	RCI 293; RCI ACM
Pentland, Barbara	*Concerto for Piano and String Orchestra* (1955–6)	CMC ms film 12/13	RCI 184
	Symphony for Ten Parts (1957)	BMI Can, 1961	RCI 215; RCA CCS-1009
Pépin, Clermont	*Guernica* (1952)	CMC study score	Audat 477-4001; RCI ACM; CAPAC-CAB tape 12
	Le Rite du soleil noir (1955)	CMC ms	RCI 155; RCI ACM
	Symphonie No. 2 (1957)	CMC ms	RCI 213; RCI ACM
Perrault, Michel	*Sea Gallows* (1958)	Bonart, n.d.	RCI 185
Prévost, André	*Scherzo* (1960)	CMC ms film 9/26	CMC large tape 12

composer	title	score	recording
Ridout, Godfrey	*Cantiones mysticae* (1953)	Harris, 1956	CMC
	Music for a Young Prince (1959)	CMC study score	CMC tape 78
Schafer, R. Murray	*Concerto for Harpsichord and Eight Wind Instruments* (1954)	CMC ms	RCI 193
Somers, Harry	*Five Songs for Dark Voice* (1956)	Berandol, 1972	RCI 286; RCA LSC 3172
	Passacaglia and Fugue for Orchestra (1954)	BMI Can, 1958	RCI 180; Louisville LS 661
	Fantasia for Orchestra (1958)	BMI Can, 1962	RCI 230; RCA LSC 2980
	Little Suite for String Orchestra (1955)	BMI Can, 1956	
	Lyric for Orchestra (1960)	BMI Can, 1963	CMC tape 98
Symonds, Norman	*Concerto Grosso for Jazz Quintet and Orchestra* (1957)		RCI 181
Turner, Robert	*Children's Overture* (1958)	CMC ms film 13/3	RCI 334; CBC SM 63
	Nocturne (1956–65)	Berandol, 1972	RCI 334; CBC SM 63
	Opening Night (1955)	BMI Can, 1960	RCI 179; CBC SM 163
	Symphony for Strings (1960)	CMC ms film 13/5	RCI 214; RCA CCS-1008
Weinzweig, John	*Divertimento No. 3* (1959)	Leeds, 1963	CBC SM 317
	Symphonic Ode (1958)	Leeds, 1962	Louisville
	Violin Concerto (1951–4)	CMC ms film 8/22	RCI ACM 1
	Wine of Peace (1957)	CMC study score	RCI ACM 1; Musican rec 3
Willan, Healey	*Elégie Heroique* (1960), concert band	Boosey, 1971	CMC tape 600

CHAMBER MUSIC

composer	title	score	recording
Adaskin, Murray	*Sonatine Baroque* (1952), solo violin	Ricordi, 1961	RCI 73
Anhalt, István	*Comments* (1954)	CMC ms film 15/3	
	Sonata (1954), violin and piano	CMC ms film 15/4	RCI 220; RCA CCS-1014
	Trio (1953), violin, cello, piano	CMC ms film 15/2	RCI 229; RCA CCS-1023

composer	title	score	recording
Archer, Violet	*Prelude and Allegro* (1954)	BMI Can, 1958	RCI 136
	Sonata No. 1 (1956), violin and piano	CMC ms film 16/15	RCI 196
	Sonata for Cello and Piano (1956)	CMC ms film 16/14	RCI 139
	Trio No. 2 (1956–7)	CMC ms film 16/13	RCI 241
Bissell, Keith	*A Folk-Song Suite for Woodwinds* (1960)	Boosey, 1963	
Brott, Alexander	*Sept for Seven* (1954)	CMC ms film 3/22	RCI 131
Buczynski, Walter	*Divertimento for Four Solo Instruments*, Op. 15 (1957)	CMC ms film 20/27	RCI 338; CBC SM 74
Charpentier, Gabriel	*Trois poèmes de St. Jean-de-la-Croix* (1954)	CMC ms	
Coulthard, Jean	*The Devil's Fanfare* (1958)	CMC ms film 5/11	
	Duo Sonata for Violin and Piano (1952)	BMI Can, 1963	
	String Quartet No. 2 (Threnody) (1953; rev 1969)	Berandol, 1975	RCI 386
Dolin, Samuel	*Sonata for Violin and Piano* (1960)	BMI Can, 1968	MelsMLP 4021
Eckhardt-Gramatté, S.C.	*Duo Concertante for Cello and Piano* (1959)	CMC ms film 15/28	RCI 224; RCA CCS-1018
Eggleston, Anne	*Piano Quartet* (1954–5)	Jaymar	CMC tape
Fleming, Robert	*A Two-Piece Suite* (1959), oboe, clarinet, and bassoon	Leeds, 1970	Dom s-69004; CAPAC-CAB tape 11
Freedman, Harry	*Two Vocalises* (1954)	CMC ms film 6/16	
Garant, Serge	*Asymétries No. 2* (1959)	CMC ms film 7/32	
Gould, Glenn	*String Quartet No. 1* (1953–5)	Barger & Barclay, 1956	RCI 142; Col MS 6178
Joachim, Otto	*String Quartet* (1956)	BMI Can, 1960	RCI 190
	Sonata for Cello and Piano (1954)	BMI Can, 1963	RCI 139; CBC SM 113
Jones, Kelsey	*Introduction and Fugue* (1959), violin and piano	CMC ms film 10/6	RCI 220; RCA CCS-1014
	Sonata da camera (1957)	Peters, 1972	RCI 192
Kasemets, Udo	*Quintet for Wind Instruments* (1957)	Berandol (rental)	RCI 218; RCA CCS-1012
Kenins, Talivaldis	*Divertimento* (1960)	Boosey, 1970	Dom s-69004
LeCaine, Hugh	*Dripsody* (1955)		Folkways FMS 33436

composer	title	score	recording
Mann, Leslie	*Five Improvisations*, Op. 10 (1954)	CMC ms film 25/17	RCI 215; RCA CCS-1009
Morawetz, Oskar	*Sonata No. 1* (1956), violin and piano	CMC ms film 14/9	RCI 194
	Trio (1960)	CMC ms film 14/11	RCI 219; RCA CCS-1013
Morel, François	*Cassation* (1954), woodwind septet	CMC ms	RCI 128
Papineau-Couture, Jean	*Suite pour violon seul* (1956)	Peer, 1966	RCI 222; RCI ACM RCA CCS-1016
	Quatuor à cordes no. 1 (1953)	CMC ms	RCI 363; RCI ACM
Pentland, Barbara	*Duo for Viola and Piano* (1960)	CMC ms film 12/21	RCI 223; RCA CCS-1017
	String Quartet No. 2 (1953)	CMC ms film 12/19	CMC tape
Pépin, Clermont	*Quatre monodies pour flûte seule* (1953)	Leeds, 1971	Dom s-69006; RCI ACM
	Quatuor à cordes no. 2 (1955–6)	CMC ms	*Musican* rec. 9; RCI ACM
	Quatuor à cordes no. 3 (1959)	CMC ms	Col MS 6364
Perrault, Michel	*Sextuor* (1955)	Bonart, n.d.	RCI 125
Rathburn, Eldon	*Conversation for Two Clarinets* (1956)	Huron, 1971	Dom s-69004
Rogers, William Keith	*Sonatina* (1952), viola and piano	BMI Can, 1954	RCI 223; RCA CCS-1017
Somers, Harry	*Sonata No. 1 for Violin and Piano* (1953)	BMI Can, 1968	RCI 221; RCA CCS-1015
	Sonata No. 2 for Violin and Piano (1955)	BMI Can, 1968	RCI 222; RCA CCS-1016
	Sonata for Guitar (1959)	Caveat, 1972	RCI 409
	String Quartet No. 3 (1959)	Marseg, 1977	CBC SM 45
Turner, Robert	*Serenade for Woodwind Quintet* (1960)	CMC ms film 13/13	CBC SM 139
	Sonata for Violin and Piano (1956)	CMC ms film 13/10	CBC RCI 194
	String Quartet No. 2 (1954)	BMI Can, 1963	CMC tape
	Variations and Toccata (1959)	CMC ms film 13/12	RCI 215; RCA CCS-1009
Vallerand, Jean	*Quatuor à cordes* (1960)	CMC ms film 6/22	RCI 141; Col MS 6364

S O N G (for voice and piano unless otherwise indicated)

Archer, Violet	*The Twenty-Third Psalm* (1952)	BMI Can, 1954	

composer	title	score	recording
Betts, Lorne	*Five Songs* (1952) [James Joyce]	CMC ms film 19/31	
Coulthard, Jean	*Spring Rhapsody* (1958) [Bliss Carman, W.H. Marshall, L.A. MacKay, D.C. Scott], voice and orchestra	Waterloo, 1977	RCI 203
Dela, Maurice	*La Lettre* [Henri Barbusse]	BMI Can, 1956	
Dolin, Samuel	*Chloris* [William Strode]	BMI Can, 1961	
Duchow, Marvin	*For a Rose's Sake* [anonymous medieval French]	BMI Can, 1956,	
Fleming, Robert	*Four Songs on Poems of John Coulter* (1946–54)		RCI 248
Freedman, Harry	*Two Vocalises* (1954), soprano, clarinet, and piano	CMC ms film 6/16	
Garant, Serge	*Caprices* (1953–4) [F. García Lorca]	CMC ms film 7/34	RCI 201; RCI ACM 2
	Et je prierai ta grâce (1952)	CMC ms	RCI ACM 2
Johnston, Richard	*Bruce County Ballad* [traditional]	BMI Can, 1954	
Jones, Kelsey	*To Music* (1957) [Robert Herrick]	CMC ms film 10/12	RCI 203
Kasemets, Udo	*Three Miniatures* (1956) [Percy Bysshe Shelley]	BMI Can, 1960	
Meek, Kenneth	*There Is No Rose of Such Virtue* [anonymous English]	BMI Can, 1957	
Mercure, Pierre	*Dissidence* (1955) [Gabriel Charpentier]	CMC ms film 10/22	RCI 201
Morawetz, Oskar	*Mother, I Cannot Mind my Wheel* (1955) [Walter Savage Landor]	Leeds, 1962	
	My True Love Hath My Heart (1955) [Sir Philip Sidney]	Leeds, 1962	
Prévost, André	*Musiques peintes* (1955) [Gatien Lapointe]	CMC ms film 9/41	
Ridout, Godfrey	*Cantiones mysticae* (1953) [John Donne], voice and piano or orchestra	Harris, 1956	
Russell, Welford	*My Lute, Awake* [Sir Thomas Wyatt]	BMI Can, 1955	RCI 333
Schafer, R. Murray	*Kinderlieder* (1958) [B. Brecht]	Berandol, 1975	CBC SM 141

composer	title	score	recording
	Minnelieder (1956) [medieval German], soprano and woodwind quintet	Berandol, 1970	RCI 218; RCI ACM; RCA CCS-1012
	Three Contemporaries (1956)	Berandol, 1976	
Somers, Harry	*Conversation Piece* (1955) [Michael E. Fram]	BMI Can, 1957	
	Three Simple Songs (1953) [Michael E. Fram]	CMC ms film 31/14	
Vallerand, Jean	*Quatre poèmes de Saint-Denys Garneau* (1954)	CMC ms film 6/24	RCI 393

CHORAL MUSIC

composer	title	score	recording
Archer, Violet	*Proud Horses* (1953) [A.M. Sampley]	CMC ms film 16/22	RCI 189
	Three French-Canadian Folk Songs (1953)	BMI Can, 1962	
Betts, Lorne	*The Souls of the Righteous* (1957)	Waterloo, 1960	
Champagne, Claude	*Missa brevis* (1951)	BMI Can, 1955	
Charpentier, Gabriel	*Messe I* (1952)	CMC ms	RCI 189
Coulthard, Jean	*More Lovely Grows the Earth* (1957) [Helena Coleman]	CMC ms film 5/28	RCI 189
Joachim, Otto	*Psalm* (1960)	BMI Can, 1961	RCI 206
Jones, Kelsey	*Songs of Experience* (1958) [William Blake]	CMC ms film 10/9	RCI 189
Papineau-Couture, Jean	*Psaume CL* (1954)	BMI Can, 1964	RCI 128; RCI ACM
Ridout, Godfrey	*Pange lingua* (1960)	Waterloo, 1960	CMC tape 278
Somers, Harry	*Two Songs for the Coming of Spring* (1957)	BMI Can, 1957	RCI 206
	Where Do We Stand, O Lord? (1955)	BMI Can, 1955	RCI 130
Turner, Robert	'Anyone Lived in a Pretty How Town' from *Two Choral Pieces* (1952)	CMC ms film 13/20	RCI 206
Weinzweig, John	*Am Yisrael Chai* (1952)	Leeds, 1964	CMC tape 274
Willan, Healey	*O Lord, Our Governor*	Novello, 1953	HMV ALP 1057
	Coronation Suite (1952–3)	BMI Can, 1953	

composer	title	score	recording
	Missa brevis XI (1953)	Gray, 1953	CBC SM 314
	Order of Holy Communion (Lutheran) (1955)	Concordia, 1955	
(arr)	*Sainte Marguerite* (1952)	Harris, 1952	
	Sun of Righteousness (1952)	BMI Can, 1952	
	Three Songs to Music (1957)	BMI Can, 1957	
	We Praise Thee, vols I and II	Concordia, 1953, 1962	

ORGAN MUSIC

Brown, Allanson G.Y.	*Improvisation on the Plainsong 'Urbs Beata'*	BMI Can, 1955	
Daveluy, Raymond	*Sonate en sol, no. 3* (1959–60)	CMC ms	RCI 225; RCA CCS-1019
France, William	*Oboe Tune* and *Gavotte*	BMI Can, 1953	SR-101568 (*Oboe Tune*)
George, Graham	*Elegy* (1958)	Gray, 1968	
	Two Preludes on 'The King's Majesty' (1959)	Gray, 1963	CMC tape
Karam, Frederick	*Divertimento*	BMI Can, 1959	
	Gigue	BMI Can, 1957	
Meek, Kenneth	*Three Preludes*	BMI Can, 1960	
Morel, François	*Prière* (1954)	BMI Can, 1965	
Ridout, Godfrey	*Three Preludes on Scottish Tunes* (1959)	GVT, 1960	
Turner, Robert	*Six Voluntaries* (1959)	BMI Can, 1968	RCI 226; RCA CCS-1020
Willan, Healey	*Epithalame* (1956)	BMI Can, 1957	
	Five Pieces for Organ (1957–8)	BMI Can, 1959	
	A Fugal Trilogy (1958)	Oxford, 1959	No. 2 Col ML 6198
	Interlude for a Festival, arranged from *Coronation Suite* (1953)	BMI Can, 1953	
	Passacaglia and Fugue No. 2 in E Minor (1959)	Peters, 1959	CBC SM 202
	Rondino, Elegy and Chaconne (1956)	Novello, 1957	
	Ten Hymn Preludes	Peters, 1956–8	
	36 Short Preludes and Postludes on Well-known Hymn Tunes	Peters, 1960	

composer	title	score	recording
OPERA			
Beckwith, John	*Night Blooming Cereus* (1953–8) [James Reaney]	CMC ms film 7/1	
Betts, Lorne	*Riders to the Sea* (1955) [J.M. Synge]	CMC ms film 19/1	
	The Woodcarver's Wife [Marjorie Pickthall]	CMC ms film 19/2	
Blackburn, Maurice	*Une Mesure de silence* (1953–4) [Marthe Blackburn]	CMC ms	
Pentland, Barbara	*The Lake* (1952) [Dorothy Livesay]	CMC ms film 12/1	
Somers, Harry	*The Fool* (1953) [Michael E. Fram]	CMC ms film 31/1	RCI 272

CHAPTER FIVE

The 1960s
The New Romanticism

I have no doubt ... [that] Canadian orchestral and chamber music will figure more and more prominently on international programmes and Canadian music [will] take its proper place in the international scheme of things.

    Alfred Frankenstein, in John Beckwith and Udo Kasemets, editors, *The Modern Composer and His World* (1961)

Several developments in the late 1950s and early 1960s had a salutary effect on Canadian music. The Canadian Music Centre, which opened in 1959, began its series of catalogues of Canadian music: the orchestral catalogue appeared in 1963 (supplements 1968, 1971; 2nd edition, 1976), followed by the catalogues of chamber music (1967; supplements 1973, 1976), keyboard music (1971; supplement 1976), choral music (1966; supplement 1970; 2nd edition, 1978), vocal music (1967; 3rd edition, 1976), and microfilms (1970). In addition, the CMC produced the *Canadian Contemporary Music Study Courses* which were in the form of taped and written analyses of works by Canadian composers. Unfortunately the project did not continue beyond the analyses of three works: Harry Somers's *Suite for Harp and Chamber Orchestra* (1949), Murray Adaskin's *Serenade Concertante* (1954), and Jean Papineau-Couture's *Pièce concertante no. 1* (1957). Under the leadership of John Adaskin the Canadian Music Centre began in 1962–3 to arrange for Canadian composers to visit schools and to write suitable works within the technical limitations imposed by the classroom and the student ensemble. Fifteen composers took part in the initial phase of this project which was limited geographically to the metropolitan Toronto area. In addition to promoting the performance of Canadian music, one of the essential principles of the project, which became known as the John Adaskin Project after the death of its founder in 1964, was that music education must include the creative aspects of music at all levels of study.

We have noted in chapter 4 that the International Conference of Composers, which took place at Stratford, Ontario, from 7 to 14 August 1960, under the joint auspices of the Canadian League of Composers and the Stratford Shakespearean Festival Foundation of Canada, established Canadian composers in the eyes of their colleagues in other countries. The conference took the form of a series of panel discussions, concerts, and social functions. Panel discussions were held on the following topics:

The Public and the Composer
The Training of a Composer
The Composer and his Métier: I Serialism
The Composer and his Métier: II Other Means
The Composer and the Performer
Copyright
Opera, Ballet, Theatre
Music by Synthetic Means
The Composer and his Métier: III Form
Résumé

There were five concerts – three orchestral, one of chamber music, and one of electronic music – in which Canadian works as well as others were performed.

A summary of the conference was published under the title *The Modern Composer and His World*, edited by John Beckwith and Udo Kasemets. It consists of a selection of the papers delivered at the panel sessions together with the discussions which followed. The book organizes the material into two categories, (1) 'The Composer in Today's World,' and (2) 'The Composer's Métier.' A conference summary is provided by the late Marvin Duchow of McGill University.

The conference itself reflected a great variety of tastes and approaches to musical composition. As the Swiss composer Heinrich Sutermeister says philosophically in his *Letter to a Young Aspiring Composer*: 'the way we decide to employ the world of tones to express our present experiences remains a personal matter.' Writing at a time when there was much division and controversy in musical circles regarding the place of twelve-tone, totally serial, electronic, aleatoric, and traditional music, Sutermeister adds: 'let us try to loosen the grip of short-sighted cliques and the power groups that rule the present music world in an unhealthy manner.'[1] Another paper on the training of composers, by the Cuban composer Aurelio de la Vega, asks for a new approach to the teaching of music, one which will not spend so much time on traditional harmony.[2] Gunther Schuller, an American composer and performer, makes a plea in 'Composer and Performer' for composers to write notes which it is possible to play.[3] In 'Serialism' the British composer Iain Hamilton pays tribute to the contributions of Schönberg's compositions and theoretical writings, and adds: 'it has been the responsibility of our century to restore to music some of its dignity after the subservience to the other arts which it had known during the latter half of the nineteenth century.'[4] Many other thought-provoking comments made during the conference were duly reported in *The Modern Composer and His World*. According to commentator Duchow, however, the speakers failed to come to grips with the problem of how to narrow the widening gap between the composer and his audience.[5]

The most significant outcome of the conference as far as the Canadian composer was concerned was the recognition which he received from his colleagues in other countries. As the headnote to this chapter indicates, the noted American critic Alfred Frankenstein, confessing that the only Canadian composer of whom he had previously heard was Healey Willan, felt that as a result of the conference Canadian orchestral and chamber music would become better known both in Canada and internationally. He added: 'It is obviously past high time for such a development.'[6]

An equally significant development in 1961 propelled Montreal into the front rank of developments in new music in Canada. The Semaine internationale de la musique actuelle, which was held in conjunction with the 1961 Montreal Festival, featured first performances in Canada of works by avant-garde composers Edgar Varèse, John Cage, Earle Brown, Morton Feldman, Mauricio Kagel, and Bruno Maderna. Only three Canadian works were presented at these concerts, Serge Garant's *Anerca* (1961; rev 1963) for voice and instrumental ensemble, Pierre Mercure's electronic ballet score *Incandescence* (1961), and István Anhalt's *Electronic Composition No. 3 'Birds and Bells'* (1960). The Semaine internationale was organized by the late Mercure and remains one of that composer's most important contributions to the promotion of new music in Canada.

Another high point in Canadian music in this decade resulted from the stimulation provided by the centennial celebrations of 1967. The number of new works (approximately 140) written at the request of the Centennial Commission, the CBC, and other bodies, as well as the greater number of performances of Canadian music, created a climate of activity unsurpassed before or since. The products of this activity warrant a chapter of their own; this chapter deals with works composed prior to centennial year in the period 1961–6.

PIANO MUSIC

After 1960 many Canadian composers abandoned neoclassicism and moved into avant-garde idioms for which the solo piano was not a suitable vehicle, and as a result the number of solo piano works declined. Nevertheless some works were written in a conservative style for solo piano, for example, Maurice Dela's *Deux impromptus* (1961), Jean Coulthard's *Aegean Sketches* (1961), Alain Gagnon's *Mirages* (1966) and *Sonate no. 3* (1966), and Talivaldis Kenins's *Sonata for Piano* (1961); and some piano music was written with a didactic purpose, for example,

Rhené Jaque's *Suite pour piano* (1961), Richard Johnston's *Second Suite* (1965), George Fiala's *Australian Suite* (1963), William K. Rogers's *Six Short Preludes on a Tone Row* (1963), and Ann Southam's *Three in Blue* (1965). Several works, such as Barbara Pentland's *Fantasy* (1962), Jacques Hétu's *Variations* (1964), Walter Buczynski's *Aria and Toccata* (1963), and Bruce Mather's *Fantasy* (1964), were dodecaphonic, and as such were no longer regarded as avant-garde. At the same time some composers experimented with avant-garde features which came into vogue in Europe in the late 1950s and adopted them in their works for piano. Serge Garant's *Pièce pour piano no. 2. (Cage d'oiseau)* (1962) with its unmeasured rhythmic sections and exploration of new sound possibilities and Udo Kasemets's graphic and aleatoric scores such as *Squares* (1962) and *The Fifth Root of Five* (1962–3) are examples of the latter.

Kenins's *Sonata for Piano* is a three-movement work in the classical-romantic tradition of Prokofief and Shostakovich. The first movement is in a rondo form, with sections ABACABA following a slow introduction in which the primary motive is stated. The introductory motive is retained in modified form in the body of the movement, its components being germinal to the main melodic and harmonic activity. The remaining two movements, which are linked together motivically, consist of a theme and variations and a rollicking rondo which abounds in pianistic figurations and running passages.

The twelve-tone works of Hétu and Pentland are very much in contrast, thus underlining the fact that twelve-tone writing is a technique and not a style. The Hétu *Variations* (1964) are very romantic in expressive content and employ many of the display elements of the nineteenth-century virtuoso. (This work was in fact written as the test piece for the national competition of the Jeunesses musicales in 1964.) It employs a symmetrical tone row, in which the last half is an almost exact inversion of the first half. As Glenn Gould points out, the arrangement of the notes in the row outlines two of a possible three diminished-seventh chords (C♯–E–G–B♭ and E♭–F♯–A–C). Gould observes that when these tones are sounded together, they 'produce that ubiquitous diminished seventh chord of hallowed nineteenth-century memory.'[8] The work consists of an introduction and four variations and makes use of various fugal techniques within the romantic display patterns.

Pentland's *Fantasy* (1962), on the other hand, also employs the twelve-tone technique in a free manner but in a much more austere and contemplative fashion. Sectional in construction, the work has some of the attributes of a renaissance fantasia in which melodic ideas are introduced, played with, and then discarded in favour of something new. Pentland maintains a subtle thread of unity through consistent use of certain melodic intervals featured in the row, particularly the perfect fourth, minor second, and major sixth. Rhythmic motives also play an important part in unifying the work, often in the uneven-ostinato fashion of Stravinsky.

One of the most interesting Canadian keyboard works of this period is

Garant's *Pièce pour piano no. 2*, which as *Cage d'oiseau* was originally a setting for soprano and piano of the poem of that name by Hector de Saint-Denys Garneau (see pp 134–5 below). *Pièce pour piano no. 2* is quite similar to the earlier *Cage d'oiseau*, since the soprano voice largely reinforces material found in the piano part. The piano version was realized soon after the composition of *Cage d'oiseau* at the request of dancer-choreographer Jeanne Renaud.

One of the leaders in aleatoric, chance, or indeterminate music in Canada was, and is, Udo Kasemets, a devoted admirer of John Cage. An early work of his in this vein is *Fifth Root of Five* (1962–3) which is for two pianists who also play five percussion instruments. To quote the composer, it is 'an essay in piano (and percussion) sonorities. Players can choose the sequence of the happenings and have much freedom in interpreting the information provided in the parts. Despite this apparent freedom the work is very rigidly organized, its form being derived from various operations with the number 5. Essentially [it uses] graphic notation, though use is made of many conventional symbols.'[9] The number of performance possibilities would seem to be limitless. In the foreword to another work, *Squares* (1962), Kasemets says: 'the purpose of this study (and it is primarily a study which can be used as a classroom exercise with composition students or as an étude for pianists) was to explore the various dimensions of sound and notation, their interrelationships and interchangeability.' Like Cage, Kasemets regards all sound as a potential source of music and each performance as a unique event.

In addition Kasemets says in his essay 'Eighteen Edicts on Education'[10] that 'the unhappiness of many people is caused by their inability to accept changes in the world.'[11] Kasemets feels strongly that non-linear (i.e. stream-of-consciousness) communication methods are superior, and his music after 1960 reflects this belief; according to him it is up to the reader/listener to arrange ideas into intelligible patterns. In his opinion James Joyce was the pioneer to follow and Buckminster Fuller, Samuel Becket, Marcel Duchamp, Marshall McLuhan, and John Cage are the modern-day prophets worth listening to. Kasemets's love of concrete poetry is yet another manifestation of this line of thinking. Kasemets observes, somewhat despondently, that 'the higher the steps on the educational ladder, the wider the separation of art from life.' In kindergarten 'life is art and art is life'; in elementary school 'life is life and art is art'; in high school 'life is anti-life and art is anti-art'; and in university 'life is anti-art and art is anti-life.' He concludes that our educational system is much to blame for man's inhumanity to man and suggests that 'what Western man needs more than anything else is elementary education in living.'[12] Furthermore, Kasemets believes in the need to break down interdisciplinary barriers and to use creative approaches based upon the new media and intermedia. 'To create is to learn. To learn is to create.'[13]

Otto Joachim, R. Murray Schafer, Micheline Coulombe Saint-Marcoux, John Beckwith, and many other Canadian composers besides Kasemets to some degree adopted these ideas and principles in their work since 1960.

ORCHESTRAL MUSIC

The variety of the orchestral music of this period precludes tidy categorization. Generally speaking, in adopting some of the avant-garde techniques of Pierre Boulez, Karlheinz Stockhausen, György Ligeti, and John Cage Canadian composers showed themselves to be moving away from the predominantly neoclassical styles of the 1940s and 1950s. Even so, as in the piano repertoire, many orchestral works in the 1960s continued to be written in neoclassical idioms and followed post-romantic tendencies. Many works were composed on commission and an increasing number were written for school or amateur use as a result of the stimulation of the Canadian Music Centre's John Adaskin Project.

That Canadian artists generally, and composers particularly, were slow to experiment with avant-garde techniques is usually attributed to an inborn conservatism and a national inferiority complex which causes us to frown upon experimentation. It is significant, however, that as national self-confidence grew in the 1960s, particularly as a result of the centennial celebrations in 1967, experimentation in the arts came to be tolerated if not completely accepted. One of the leading figures in breaking down the conservative element in the artistic world of French Canada over the previous two decades had been Paul-Emile Borduas (1905–60). His *Refus global* (1948), discussed in chapter 3, not only spoke out against the conservative political, social, and religious atmosphere which he felt was stifling French Canada, but his paintings served as beacons to a generation of young artists who wished to follow him in experimentation and abstract expression. In a similar way the Painters Eleven group, which was formed in Toronto in 1953, had championed abstract art and 'the expression of a long repressed desire on the part of eleven painters to disagree harmoniously in terms visually indigenous to this age,'[14] this at a time when abstract art was anything but popular.

Although in music certain 1950s works of Serge Garant and Gilles Tremblay used avant-garde techniques, there was no significant trend in this direction until the early 1960s. At this time composers such as Udo Kasemets, Otto Joachim, István Anhalt, Pierre Mercure, Clermont Pépin, R. Murray Schafer, and Harry Somers, in addition to Garant and Tremblay, began to employ aleatoric elements, graphic scores, prepared electronic tape, and unconventional placing of instruments and voices in the concert hall. The result was a body of literature which concentrated on new and interesting sounds considered for their own sake rather than merely as the raw material for development. At the same time music began to be seen as process rather than product, a concept obviously borrowed from the European and American avant garde and adopted whole-heartedly by Kasemets and others.

One of the earliest Canadian orchestral pieces to make use of some of these new techniques is Tremblay's *Cantique de durées* (1960), a work which divides the instruments into seven groups and thus creates a unique stereophonic effect.

EXAMPLE 5-1

Gilles Tremblay, *Cantique de durées* (1960),
instrumental plan:

    I percussion (metal, skin);

   II Ondes Martenot

  III percussion (glockenspiel, xylo-marimba,
       vibraphone, bells)

  IV strings;

   V piano

  VI percussion (wood block, Chinese blocks,
       maracas, gourd)

 VII winds (in two parts in body of hall)

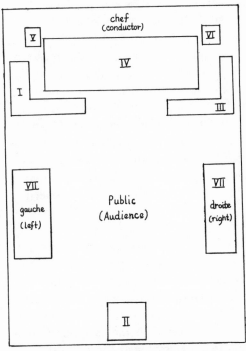

© Copyright 1972 Gilles Tremblay. Used by permission

Emphasizing percussion instruments and Ondes Martenot, the work is a poetic
'sound' piece featuring complicated rhythmic patterns, sustained blocks of tones,
and pointillistic interjections. The seven groups of instruments and their formation on stage is shown in example 5-1.

    Mercure's *Tetrachromie* (1963) is similar in its emphasis on percussion instru-
ments, but it omits the strings and Ondes Martenot and adds prepared electronic
tapes. As the title indicates, the work is concerned primarily with sound colour; the
four colours parallel the four ages of man and the seasons of the year – green for

springtime (birth), yellow for summer (youth), red for autumn (maturity), and white for winter (death). Electronic sounds are blended with conventional ones to such an extent that it is difficult to tell them apart. Conventional notation is employed but without definite rhythms; stopwatch indications maintain order. Commissioned by *Les Grandes Ballets canadiens* for the opening of the Place des arts in Montreal, the work weaves pointillistic interjections and polyphonic layers into a delicate network of tone colours.

Somers's *Stereophony* (1963) is also concerned with new sounds and new sound combinations. By a radical distribution of orchestral resources around the hall (even more so than in Tremblay's *Cantique de durées*), Somers attempts to achieve a maximum effect of circumference and height. The work was commissioned by the Toronto Symphony for performance in Massey Hall, the grandfather of Canadian concert-halls, which is shaped in the form of a horseshoe with two balconies. In the preface to the score Somers provides six different instrumental plans according to the different shapes of concert halls normally found.[15] Each instrumental grouping is mixed, both horizontally and vertically, with the lines joining the members of each family of instruments forming geometric shapes.[16] Precisely notated with much employment of antiphonal effects, the only aleatoric element in the work is the time-lag which results from the physical separation of the instrumental groups. The composer takes into account a lack of synchronization in his scoring. In addition to its unconventional groupings the work is lean in texture and possesses the series of crescendo-to-climax patterns characteristic of Somers. The repeated-tone opening in the trumpet serves as a unifying motive throughout, and pointillistic elements suggest an influence of the post-Webern school.

In another work of the early 1960s, *Five Concepts for Orchestra* (1961), Somers is more concerned with sound *per se* than with the neoclassical structures which were typical of him in the 1950s. The five movements, or concepts, are labelled 'planes of sound,' 'rhythm drums,' 'lines,' 'scherzando on ornaments,' and 'dynamics.'

Lignes et points (1964), a theme and eight variations for orchestra, was the last complete work written by Mercure before his untimely death in a motor accident. It is a work which stresses the relation between music and geometric shapes; each variation represents a different abstract shape – angles, oblique lines, spiral, point-counterpoint, curves, mixtures, spiral, right angles. An interesting phenomenon is the effect achieved by calling upon the orchestra to produce sounds like those of electronic music. As Mercure said: 'attacks of the notes ... reverberation, playing the tape backwards, filtering of harmonic structures, mixtures and durations, combinations of different elements and textures, slowing down and speeding up the tape, etc. – all this I have transferred to the symphony orchestra.'[17] Furthermore, not just the melodic shapes but also the amplitude of the sound is derived from geometric patterns (see example 5-2).

Yet another Canadian composer who moved gradually from post-roman-

EXAMPLE 5-2   Pierre Mercure, *Lignes et points* (1964), preface to score

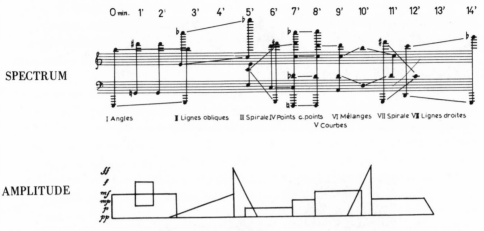

© Copyright 1970 Ricordi (Canada) Limited. Used by permission

ticism in the late 1940s, through neoclassicism to twelve-tone and serial procedures in the 1950s, and on to aleatoric music in the 1960s is Pépin. His *Monade* (1964) for string orchestra, like Mercure's *Lignes et points*, attempts to capture some of the sounds of electronic music through the individual use of the fourteen instruments of the ensemble – sometimes synchronized, sometimes not. Most of the traditional devices of string instruments are employed, such as glissandi, pizzicati, tremulandi, col legno, battute, and so on, sometimes in an aleatoric manner. The title *Monade* means, literally, the 'number one' or the 'ultimate unit of being';[18] the work fittingly begins and ends on a single tone. The piece exploits colouristic effects achieved through the sound-mass concept associated with György Ligeti and Krzysztof Penderecki.

Norma Beecroft's *Improvvisazioni concertanti* (1961) is another work which employs contemporary avant-garde techniques. It features the virtuoso solo flute set against sustaining strings and a colourful, pointillistic use of percussion in question-and-answer style with the flute. The texture is lean and Webernesque.

One of the most frequently performed orchestral works of this period is François Morel's *L'Etoile noire* (1962), a *tombeau* or dirge dedicated to the memory of Paul-Emile Borduas who died in self-exile in 1960. *L'Etoile noire* (1957) is the title of one of Borduas's last paintings. Morel's *tombeau* depicts the stark and sombre atmosphere and the thick textures of the painting as well as the gloom associated with the passing of a spiritual leader. The music is strongly dissonant.

Another work of dirge-like character is André Prévost's *Fantasmes* (1963), a 'mouvement symphonique pour grand orchestre.' This work, which expresses 'hallucinations, atmosphere of anguish, a world overthrown, an unending ten-

PAUL-EMILE BORDUAS   Canada, 1905–60
L'étoile noire, 1957
oil on canvas
gift of Gérard Lortie
960.1238
Coll. The Montreal Museum of Fine Arts

sion, in short, the fantastic despair of a nightmare,' was first performed 22 November 1963, the day of the assassination of President J.F. Kennedy, and it was dedicated to his memory: 'a victim of the world which I have described here in my music.'[19] The work has many of the characteristics of a nineteenth-century symphonic poem, including an ABA structure which follows the moods of anguish, hope, and, finally, resignation.

Many Canadian composers continued to write in neoclassical idioms in the 1960s even though neoclassicism was no longer the norm. Most of their works were composed on commission or with a particular performing group in mind, and many of these works featured a solo instrument with orchestra. For example, Alexander Brott's *Profundum praedictum* (1964) for double bass and string orchestra was commissioned by the Lapitsky Foundation of Montreal for the McGill Chamber Orchestra and bassist Gary Karr. In a sectional, variation form, this work treats the bass in a virtuoso manner, although it also exploits, in a rather grotesque way, its humorous characteristics: the last movement includes parodies of *God Save the Queen* and *Alouette!* Brott's *Triangle, Circle, and 4 Squares* (1963) for string orchestra possesses some of the same witty characteristics but is more tightly knit and concise.

The *Suite Lapitsky* (1965) by Jean Papineau-Couture, also commissioned by the Montreal foundation, features neoclassical elements, as does his *Concerto pour piano et orchestre* of the same year. Another work, John Weinzweig's *Concerto for Piano and Orchestra* (1965–6), infuses the twelve-tone technique with certain blues inflections while at the same time maintaining the leanness and transparency characteristic of neoclassicism. This piece features frequent dialogues between the piano and orchestra which towards the end take the form of pointillistic commentary by the piano against the backdrop of sustained strings. Jean Vallerand's *Cordes en mouvement* (1961) is an eclectic, middle-of-the-road piece which in its six movements draws upon elements as wide-ranging as medieval organum and twelve-tone writing. It also demonstrates different aspects of experimental string-writing.

The wind ensemble phenomenon, which originated and developed in the United States in the 1950s, spread to Canada in the 1960s. In a wind ensemble there is one instrument per part in contrast to the traditional concert band in which many instruments play a single part. The clarity and unique sound thus achieved (in effect, an orchestra without strings) is particularly suitable for works of a neoclassical nature. Canadian composers produced three works for wind ensemble during this period, two of which (Somers's *Symphony for Winds, Brass and Percussion*, 1961, and Weinzweig's *Divertimento no. 5*, 1961) were commissioned by an ensemble from the United States, the American Wind Symphony of Pittsburgh. The third work, *Sinfonietta* (1966) by Oskar Morawetz, has been recorded by the Eastman Wind Ensemble, the group which was largely responsible for the original development of the medium. The Somers work exhibits the composer's strong dramatic tendencies. Written for outdoor performance and a large and varied audience, it uses the twelve-tone system but emphasizes the open intervals and harmonic combinations which are close to diatonic harmony. As Somers indicated in a letter written to conductor Walter Boudreau of the American Wind Symphony on 1 April 1961, the unity of the work is achieved through its melodic and rhythmic motives. Ostinato figures are frequent. The long lines and extended crescendi which are Somers's trademarks from the time of his earliest orchestral works are also in evidence here and lend an element of tension and excitement to the work. Much lighter in texture and more akin to chamber music is the *Divertimento No. 5* by Weinzweig. This work adopts a modified concerto plan with three movements (fast, slow, fast) and with characteristic motivic play and much repetition. The format relies on dialogue, sometimes between two solo instruments and sometimes between solo and orchestra. With a classical sense of proportion, clarity of texture, and adherence to a mood of wit and humour, this is a true divertimento in the eighteenth-century sense of the term. Morawetz's *Sinfonietta* (1966) for winds and percussion is also written for the symphonic wind ensemble, but the harmonic and textual language is more akin to the nineteenth than to the twentieth century.

Similarly post-romantic in musical language is the *Concerto No. 1 for Piano and Orchestra* (1962) by Morawetz, which won a nation-wide competition sponsored by the Montreal Symphony Orchestra. Using a nineteenth-century harmonic vocabulary with many pianistic figurations and virtuoso passages, this work has enjoyed popular success. Roger Matton's *Concerto pour deux pianos et orchestre* (1964) likewise exudes the brilliance and virtuosity of the nineteenth-century concerto, but it adds diverse elements showing the influence of Stravinsky's large ballet scores, Honegger's motor rhythms, Debussy's sense of instrumental colour, and American jazz.

A significant body of orchestral literature resulted from the John Adaskin Project. In November 1963 week-long composer-in-the-classroom sessions involving fifteen composers and a number of teachers were held in several schools in the Toronto area. The sessions resulted in several works which were performed at a follow-up seminar in March 1965. In addition to fostering the composition of new works by the composers, the project gave focus to a virtually unexplored area in Canadian music education, that of the creation of original works by the students themselves. A subsequent conference in Toronto in November 1967 endorsed both these aims, and the Canadian Music Centre provided a catalogue of suitable instrumental works in 1968.[20] Since then a study of the significance of the project has been made,[21] and an updated guidelist of works for all performing media has been produced.[22]

Orchestral works by Murray Adaskin, Violet Archer, John Beckwith, Keith Bissell, Robert Fleming, Harry Freedman, Talivaldis Kenins, Clermont Pépin, Jean Papineau-Couture, R. Murray Schafer, and Harry Somers figure prominently in the 1968 catalogue. The majority are written in a moderately dissonant, neoclassical style, and technical difficulties are kept to a minimum. However, to date only a small percentage of the works have been published, and their widespread use has consequently been limited. One of the most imaginative and stylistically adventurous works which came out of the 1963 project, and also one of the most popular, is R. Murray Schafer's *Statement in Blue* (1964) (see example 5-3). Notated in a graphic score and following the heuristic approach of allowing the student to set and solve his own problems under guidance, the work provides an introduction to the technique of controlled improvisation. Such guidelines as 'imitate calm water – a pebble is thrown in – the water becomes calm again' or 'take the final three notes played by the previous soloist and improvise on them rhythmically' give the student performer the means to express his own individual imagination within a controlled, group situation. The work also introduces the student to the concept of art as process rather than fixed product – a concept which lent excitement to many artistic endeavours in the 1960s. In the absence of conventional notation Schafer gives detailed instructions in the prefatory notes to the score, the final one of which is that 'anything in this score may be omitted or changed if, in the opinion of the performers, it leads to an improvement.'

CHAMBER MUSIC

The chamber works of the early and mid-1960s show Canadian composers both writing for the conventional media of the string quartet (John Weinzweig, S.C. Eckhardt-Gramatté, Clermont Pépin), piano trio (Barbara Pentland), woodwind quintet (Harry Freedman, Jean Papineau-Couture, Weinzweig), and solo string and piano sonata (André Prévost, Papineau-Couture), and at the same time moving more and more to unusual combinations of instruments. In the latter category are Norma Beecroft's *Contrasts for Six Performers* (1962), for oboe, viola, xylophone, vibraphone, percussion, and harp; R. Murray Schafer's *Five Studies on Texts by Prudentius* (1962), for four flutes and soprano, and *Requiems for the Party-Girl* (1966), for soprano, flute, clarinet, horn, piano, harp, violin, viola, cello, and percussion; Harry Somers's *Twelve Miniatures* (1963–4), for soprano, recorder, viola da gamba, and harpsichord; Serge Garant's *Anerca* (1961; rev 1963), for soprano, flute, clarinet, bassoon, violin, viola, cello, harp, and percussion; Gilles Tremblay's *Kékoba* (1965; rev 1967) for percussion, Ondes Martenot, vocal trio; Sydney Hodkinson's *Interplay* (1966), for alto flute/piccolo, clarinet/alto saxophone, percussion, double bass; Otto Joachim's *Illumination I* (1965), for flute, guitar, piano, percussion I and II, and speaker; and Bruce Mather's *Orphée* (1963), for voice, piano, and percussion. Whereas the use of unique combinations of instruments tended to provoke a more avant-garde style, many of the conventional instrumentations also produced stylistically adventurous works.

The *String Quartet No. 3* (1962) by Weinzweig is a work of significant propor-

EXAMPLE 5-3   R. Murray Schafer, *Statement in Blue* (1964), beginning

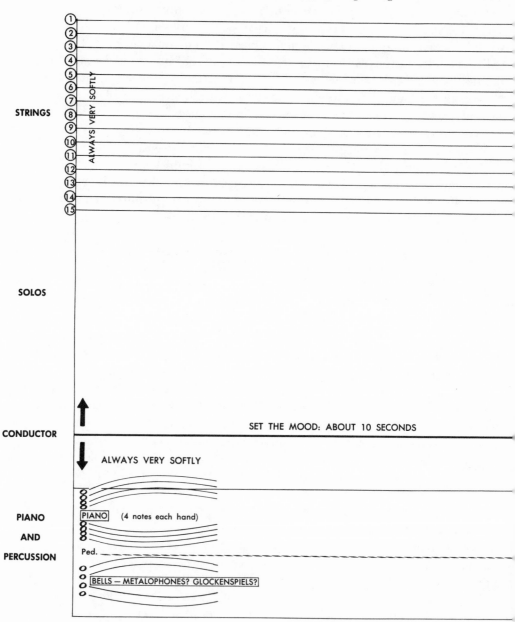

FADE TO NOTHING

Solo ① (Flute?)

Cool!

(Cue only if pianist reluctant)

PIANO   (different notes)

PIANO
R.H. only
different
notes

Ped. _ ⌡ Ped. _ _ _ _ _

tions. It is in five movements; the first, third, and fifth movements are adagio, framing the work and separating the fast second and fourth movements. The composer himself considers it a 'surrealistic work unlike his other compositions in that its creation was influenced by the free association literary methods of James Joyce,' which contribute to its 'shifting moods, fantastic images and considerable unrest and turmoil.'[23] The quartet is unified by the use of the same tone row throughout and employs the favourite Weinzweig device of breaking up the row into melodic motives and developing the fragmented parts in the classical manner. Rhythmic motives also play a large part in tying the work together. The row itself features the minor second (beginning of each four-note motive), which is a prominent interval throughout, both horizontally and vertically. The tension thus created is not resolved until a unison-octave c emerges at the conclusion of the work. The quartet possesses a unique combination of elements (constructive, emotive, colouristic). It is one of Weinzweig's more introspective and personal works, very much in contrast to the light, witty style of his series of divertimenti.

The style of Weinzweig's *Woodwind Quintet* (1963–4), however, is clearly derived from his divertimenti. It possesses the dry sparkle of neoclassicism coupled with allusions to 'cool' jazz. Harry Freedman's *Quintette for Winds* (1962) also shows a predilection for jazz, but it avoids the twelve-tone technique. Papineau-Couture's *Fantaisie pour quintette à vent* (1963) is neoclassical, like both Weinzweig's and Freedman's quintets.

Pentland's trios of this period (*Piano Trio*, 1963; *Trio con alea*, 1966) are severe and rhapsodic, features typical of this composer. To achieve a fantasy-like expression she incorporates in the *Trio con alea* improvisation or aleatoric 'zones.' In these sections the performers themselves become co-composers, following detailed instructions given before each of the nine zones. Pentland is typical of many composers in the 1960s in combining what were formerly considered to be the opposite poles of the stylistic spectrum – serialism and indeterminacy. The pointillism of her style, retained from the 1950s, blends easily with the improvisatory zones in works such as the *Trio con alea*.

At this time most young composers tended to avoid composing for the traditional media. One notable exception is André Prévost, who contributed two sonatas, one for violin and piano, the other for cello and piano. Eclectic in style, these works exhibit romantic lyricism, virtuoso writing for the instruments, twelve-tone technique, jazz elements, and the medieval folding-back principle. Prévost's tone rows are generally characterized by an emphasis on the semitone, and in his *Sonate pour violin et piano* (1960–1), where the serial technique is confined to the second and third movements, he employs a wedge-shaped, symmetrical row which, in development, is frequently fragmented, with the order of the tones altered. At the beginning of the third movement of the sonata there is an interesting use of the cumulative principle in lining out the material: through a process of several starts and stops the violin completes its first statement of the tone row only after fifty-six measures.

The *Trois caprices* (1962) for violin and piano of Papineau-Couture was written for the 1962 national competition of the Jeunesses musicales of Canada. As a test piece it was designed to challenge on technical and musical levels the performing ability of the contestants in a twentieth-century idiom. The work follows the lean, dry style of Stravinsky's neoclassicism, with ostinati of various types being an important feature of each caprice. True to its commission, the work is demanding from both technical and musical standpoints.

A few works of this period are unusual in their instrumentation but conservative in style. In this category are Murray Adaskin's *Rondino for Nine Instruments* (1961), S.C. Eckhardt-Gramatté's *Nonet* (1966), George Fiala's *Saxophone Quartet No. 2* (1961), Robert Turner's *Four Fragments* (1961), and John Weinzweig's *Clarinet Quartet* (1964–5). The Adaskin work is in a light, divertimento-like style, whereas Eckhardt-Gramatté's *Nonet* is thickly textured and excessively long. The *Quartet No. 2* for saxophones by Fiala is in a neoclassical style which alternates between imitative and homophonic sections, with strong tonal implications being effected by the prominence of the perfect fifth. Turner's *Four Fragments* for brass quintet and Weinzweig's *Clarinet Quartet* are both works suitable for school or amateur use, the latter having been written specifically for the John Adaskin Project. Turner's work, which was based upon the score written for a television documentary on Yosef Drenters, an Ontario sculptor, is in a simple folk-like idiom, whereas Weinzweig's work employs a swing manner within a twelve-tone framework as a subtle means of introducing high school students to an advanced musical style.

A number of Canadian composers, particularly the younger ones, seemed to be striking off in new directions, following the example of European and American composers such as Boulez, Stockhausen, Berio, Cage, and Varèse. The Stratford conference of 1960; the opening of electronic music studios at the University of Toronto, and later at McGill University and the University of British Columbia; the jet-age increase in musical exchange on all levels; the services provided by the Canadian Music Centre; the growth of university music departments – all contributed to greater activity and an added sense of confidence on the part of young Canadian composers, as well as a desire to move into new areas of musical creativity. Nowhere is this spirit of musical adventure more evident than in the realm of chamber music, where the requirements for performance were small and audiences were more willing to be challenged. Kasemets sums up this new attitude of the 1960s by saying that 'for the first time in history the Canadian composer feels a sense of belonging ... in a country which has spent much energy, and still does, a hundred years too late, trying to build a nineteenth-century tradition.'[24] In his preface to *Canavangard*, a series of published avant-garde works begun in 1967–8, Kasemets goes on to say that 'the realization that he too can be a part of the twentieth-century world has given the Canadian composer a new lease on life.'[25] For Kasemets this means not only that the Canadian composer deserves to be taken seriously, but that the composer himself has an obligation to move with the international avant garde. Kasemets himself had come to accept music as a process rather than a product, and accordingly his chamber music works, like his piano works, emphasize indeterminate and improvisatory aspects. 'I am a temporal man. My work is temporal. To me it has significance only at the moment of its doing.'[26] Like his mentor Cage, Kasemets believes that the performer is a co-composer rather than one who slavishly follows the minute instructions of the composer.

Many of Kasemets's works may be considered musical or theatrical games with the outcome unpredictable in each performance. 'If "to compose" means "to order musical materials, to give form to musical ideas", then *Trigon* is a composition.' This is Kasemets's opening statement in the foreword to the score of *Trigon* (1963). An intricately constructed graphic score which permits 1, 3, 9, or 27 performers to take part, the work is, in the composer's words, 'for only wholly dedicated musicians who do not mind spending considerable time and energy ... studying, preparing and rehearsing the score.' The performer in this work is also a composer; the main thing required of him is that, whatever he does, he must do it with ultimate conviction. There are four charts on the one-page score – Time Chart (centre); Sequence Chart (immediately above and below the Time Chart); Volume Chart (moveable sheet, to be superimposed on Time Chart); Event Chart (columns at left, right, top, and bottom of the score). These charts provide the means of co-ordinating the selected relationships between time, pitch, colour, and volume, 'designed to occur in an infinite number of constellations.'[27] This work may be realized as a simple, meditative work for one performer or as a brilliant, virtuoso showpiece for several, according to the composer.

Kasemets's *Timepiece* (1964), however, is a completely graphic score in which 'any one or more instruments or sound-producing media may be used.' The performer may begin with any one of the thirty-six events and proceed in any direction, providing he sounds all events once, and only once. Further instructions accompanying the one-page score give guidelines for the interpretation of the symbols for tempo, pitch, length, harmony, and so on. Less complicated than *Trigon*, *Timepiece* provides a framework within which the performer is asked to conjure up new sound patterns, not merely contenting himself with reproducing the product of someone else's imagination.

Other works by Kasemets include *Cascando* (1965), a 'phonographic stereosonophony' for one to 128 performers, which may be performed as either a straight piece or a listener-participation piece; *Contactics* (1966), which is a choreographic game in which each musician chooses a member of the audience and, using sounds according to a code, registers the person's position and movements in space in relation to his own position (the audience member must identify the musician who is 'performing' him); *Calceolaria* (1966), which is a time/space set of variations on a floral theme for any number of performers in any media; and *Variations [on Variations (on Variations)]* (1966), which is an illumination rather than an inter-

EXAMPLE 5-4   Serge Garant, *Anerca* (1961; rev 1963), beginning

(1)   S.D.C. = SIGNE DU CHEF
(2)   DURÉES + NUANCES   ad lib.   Les nuances + attaques doivent être brutalement
       opposées. Les durées doivent être de moyennes à
       courtes ; jamais longues. Petites notes ; rapides,
       arrêts : courts.

pretation of *Variations Done For Gerald Van de Wiele* by Charles Olson, itself a set of three variations on the last recorded poem of Arthur Rimbaud.

Another composer who has effected a revolutionary stylistic change in the direction of aleatoric or indeterminate music since the early 1960s is Otto Joachim. His *Illumination I* (1965) for flute, guitar, piano, percussion I and II, and speaker is a work without score in which a controller-conductor, unseen by the audience, operates the stand-lights of the performers during the performance. Each musician performs only when his score is illuminated, the speed and/or volume being dependent on the intensity of the lighting. The choice of fragments and their order is determined by the individual performer; specific pitch notations (twelve-tone) are given for pitched instruments. The speaker may select any text or texts in any one or more languages. The total result is indeterminate and each performance is, *ipso facto*, unique.

However, most Canadian composers rejected such radical manifestations of 'chance' and, following the models of some of the European avant garde, chose to combine the opposite poles of the stylistic spectrum, indeterminacy and serialism, within the same composition. One of the earliest examples of a Canadian work to intersperse aleatoric elements within a fully prescribed, serial work is *Anerca* (1961; rev 1963) by Serge Garant (see p 105 above). *Anerca*, based upon Inuit poems in an English translation by Edmund Carpenter, is for soprano and eight instrumentalists (see example 5-4). In the Inuit language *anerca* means, literally, 'the soul, the breath of life.' The text is filled with poetic images of the land and life in the frozen north. In his setting Garant employs twelve-tone writing combined with improvised rhythmic and melodic zones. Wide leaps are characteristic of the vocal as well as the instrumental parts, and minute attention is given to dynamics and experimental sound effects. The three-note motive ($C\sharp-C\natural-D$) is usually stated using octave displacement; its inversion comprises notes 4, 5, and 6 of the row with a motivic augmented fourth in between. Rhythmic patterns also contribute to the overall unity. Even though the frequently complicated polyphonic texture is difficult to rationalize in relation to the simplicity of the Inuit text, the work does reflect the poet's sense of awe and wonder before the vast northern landscape.

Gilles Tremblay's *Kékoba* (1965; rev 1967) is another example of a work of this period which combines chance and prescribed elements in an avant-garde idiom. The work employs a graphic score (for the most part), improvisation sections (both guided and free), and an instrumentation calling for Ondes Martenot, percussion, and three voices (the vocalists are also required to help out as percussionists at various points) (see example 5-5). It probes new sound dimensions in the manner of Stockhausen and a type of mysticism associated with Tremblay's mentor Messiaen. The centre of attention is the Ondes Martenot (an instrument which Tremblay himself learned to play when he was a student of the inventor, Maurice Martenot, in the 1950s), which is monophonic and capable of creating glissandi and intermediate pitches. A great variety of percussion instruments

EXAMPLE 5-5   Gilles Tremblay, *Kékoba* (1965; rev 1967), p 4 bis (in the composer's hand)

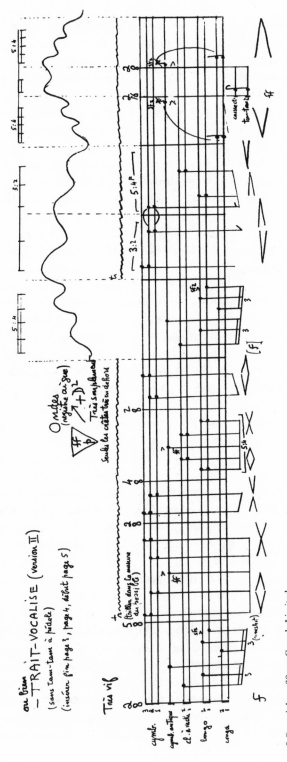

rounds out the instrumentation. The composer explains the title of the work thus: 'Each word is uttered according to its significance or "aura" which surrounds it. Thus *stella* (Latin for "star") sparkles and gleams in Latin, English, Russian, Bengali, Chinese, French, Arabic and Hebrew. It is from the latter that the title of the work is taken.'[28] The work includes two mobiles (one of which is polyphonic), which are controlled-improvisation devices which Tremblay has also favoured in many of his later works. Materials are constantly seen in new ways even though the basic components remain the same. There is a universal quality about the text of *Kékoba*, reflected in the instruments and voices, which comes not from East or West, nor from one country or another, but from mankind as a whole. In *Kékoba* there is no conductor but the ondist serves as the co-ordinator of the ensemble. The effect of this work on the listener begins with bewilderment and ends with fascination. He or she has to adapt to a new notion of time in which 'moments of action are followed by moments of contemplation.'[29] Such a concept, borrowed from Eastern cultures, became increasingly popular among Canadian composers during the late 1960s and into the 1970s.

Sydney Hodkinson's *Interplay* (1966) also employs indeterminacy as a device. Subtitled 'a histrionic controversy for four musicians,' this piece won first prize in the Jeunesses musicales's national Young Composers' Competition in 1967 and second prize in the International JMC competition of the same year. The score is prefaced with a quotation from Samuel Beckett's *Molloy. Malone Dies. The Unnameable* (1953), which indicates the stream-of-conscious nature of the work:

> Not to want to say, not to know what you want to say, not to be able to say what you think you want to say, and never to stop saying, or hardly ever, that is the thing to keep in mind.[30]

Interplay is an exploration of various aspects of sound with an emphasis on colouristic pointillism and new percussion sonorities. There are aleatoric sections which are tied together, as is the work as a whole, by motivic cells. At certain points the instrumentalists emit vocal sounds such as 'ssss,' 'ch,' and so on. The work is marked off not by bar lines but by time intervals.

A work which also explores the world of the subconscious is Schafer's *Requiems for the Party-Girl* (1966), which consists of the arias from *Patria II* (1966–72), itself only the second part of a work-in-progress. *Requiems* consists of a cycle of connected arias documenting the mental collapse and suicide of a young woman. The text is by the composer, with quotations in German and French from Franz Kafka and Albert Camus; it shows Schafer moving towards the utilization of subjects with a contemporary social and/or political message. The party-girl is the prototype of 'those strange harlequinesque creatures one meets occasionally at parties beneath whose furious demonstrations of gregariousness and *joie de vivre* one detects obscure signs of terror and alienation.'[31] The girl is resolved to commit

EXAMPLE 5-6   R. Murray Schafer, *Requiems for the Party-Girl* (1966), from
Patria II (1966–72), p 7

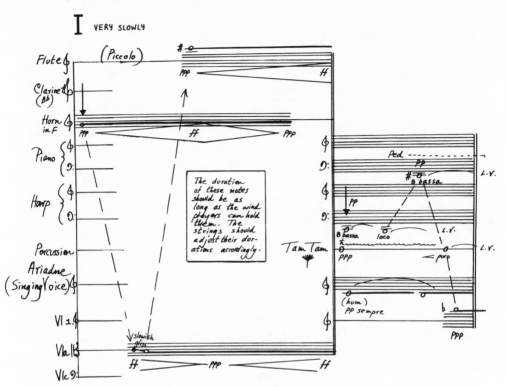

© Copyright 1978 Berandol Music Limited. Used by permission

suicide and knows that no one will prevent her. Schafer's score utilizes limited
improvisation and a half-sung, half-spoken vocal style. Above all it makes dramatic use of instrumental and vocal sonorities to create a realistic musical drama in
the tradition of Berg's *Wozzeck* (1922) (Schafer himself prefers the term 'theatre of
confluence' in reference to *Patria*). Schafer uses a wedge-shaped, symmetrical
tone row which moves in contrary motion by half step, thus underlining the
importance of the semitone as a unifying factor, and fragments the row to form
different melodic patterns. Much of the time note values are non-specific, with
bar-lines and cues holding the work together (see example 5-6). It is to Schafer's
credit that in this and other works he has been able to achieve the maximum
dramatic effect with the least complicated notational means. Increasing international respect has been accorded Schafer since the mid-1960s; *Requiems for the
Party-Girl* was awarded the Fromm Music Foundation Prize for 1968.

Schafer's *Five Studies on Texts by Prudentius* (1962), which predates the *Requiems*
by four years, is based upon an entirely different kind of text, Prudentius's *Tituli*

EXAMPLE 5-7   Bruce Mather, *Orphée* (1963), ending (in the composer's hand)

historarium (Scenes from History), which were originally written as commentaries to biblical scenes painted on the walls of medieval churches. Prudentius, a third-century Latin poet, was the first to present Christian doctrines in strict, classical literary forms. In his setting Schafer appropriately chooses the strictest musical form, that of the canon, and combines it with elements of chance. The work is scored for voice and four flutes, the latter either live or prerecorded. The scenes chosen by Schafer move from the story of Adam and Eve (no. 1), through Moses and the Law (no. 2), to the birth of Christ (no. 3), the Passion according to John (no. 4), and finally the revelation of John (no. 5). In the first part two of the entries follow the inverted form of the canonic subject while the remaining two follow that of the *dux*. Each voice proceeds at its own tempo, at first not seeking synchronization but gradually coming together at the end of the section. In the second song, which deals with Moses and the Law, the canonic structure is more complicated – a three-part rhythmic canon at the distance of one bar exists over a melodic canon at the unison distributed among two pairs of flutes performing in alternate corners of the concert hall. Schafer contributes to the element of chance or, more properly, the lack of exact synchronization through the placing of the singer on stage and the four flutes in four corners of the room. This use of unusual spacing of resources has been noted in other Canadian works of the period, namely Somers's *Stereophony* (1963), Mercure's *Tetrachromie* (1963) and *Lignes et points* (1964), and Tremblay's *Cantique de durées* (1960). Throughout the remainder of the *Five Studies* the canonic devices remain, some freer than others. The deft structural combination of the strict and the free, the imaginative choice of text, the dramatic vocal line, and the subtle sense of timbre in this his first work in an avant-garde idiom explain to a large degree why Schafer was to become one of the dominant figures in Canadian music in the 1960s and 1970s.

Two final works of unusual instrumentation are Mather's *Orphée* (1963) and Somers's *Twelve Miniatures* (1963–4). Both have in common with many of the works discussed above an exotic text, but both avoid the use of aleatoric or chance elements in their realization. The text of *Orphée* is taken from the *Album des vers anciens* (1891–3) of the French poet and philosopher Paul Valéry. The poem, a sonnet, tells of Orpheus, the famous musician of Greek mythology, who through the power of his singing and lyre-playing can move mountains and turn rocks into gold. The poem also hints at the romantic ideal which considers music supreme among the arts as a result of its ability to express the inexpressible. The work employs a twelve-tone idiom featuring the melodic intervals of the major, minor, and augmented second and the perfect fourth, with frequent octave displacements. Rhythm and texture also play a unifying role. The imaginative use of the piano (sometimes requiring four staves of notation) and percussion is an elaborate foil to the essentially simple vocal line. All of this score is precisely notated in contrast to many of the works discussed above. One senses that there is a struggle between matter, represented by the instruments, and music, represented by the human voice, with music emerging triumphant at the conclusion (see examle 5-7).

Twelve Miniatures by Somers reflects the conciseness and careful attention to detail of the haiku poems upon which the work is based. The haiku, a short, seventeen-syllable poem intended to express a single emotion, has been popular in Japan for the past seven hundred years. Because of its brevity it depends on the power of imaginative suggestion, as do Japanese ink sketches. This characteristic of economy and compactness obviously appealed to Somers, whose work is also tightly knit and brief. As Brian Cherney in his monograph on the composer indicates, Somers 'assigned an individual pitch cell to each part within a song' in order to 'suggest the idea of fixed scales prevalent in Eastern music.'[32] Each voice or instrumental part uses certain tones from the twelve, as well as individual rhythmic motives and dynamic patterns. There is very little trespassing of one part upon the material of the other. Within each part the order of the tones sometimes remains the same, sometimes varies slightly, but in all cases melodic and rhythmic unity are readily recognizable by the ear. This fragmentation of the tone row is particularly suitable for the depiction of the property of 'internal comparison' which is a characteristic of haiku.[33] Furthermore the delicate sounds of the voice, recorder, viola da gamba, and spinet suggest traditional Japanese musical sonorities.

Within these limitations there is much variety. 'Night Lightning' (no. 4) is only three short measures in length but passes dynamically from ff to pppp. 'The Portent' (no. 5) makes imaginatve use of quarter-tones within the compass of a semi-tone. In the final song, 'The River' (no. 12), Somers returns to melodic and rhythmic motives from the beginning of the set of songs but interchanges the tones of the recorder and spinet. *Twelve Miniatures* is a particularly successful example of a composer achieving 'maximum depth with the minimum means,' a goal which Somers had set for himself in this work.[34]

ELECTRONIC MUSIC

In the 1960s electronic music for the first time assumed a significant role in Canadian music. The pioneer efforts of Hugh LeCaine at the National Research Council in Ottawa in the 1950s were followed by the opening of electronic music studios at the University of Toronto in 1959, McGill University in 1963, and the University of British Columbia in 1964. These facilities encouraged many composers to acquaint themselves with the new hardware and techniques and to compose works for electronic instruments using either concrete or synthetic sounds or a combination of both. Some composers, however, rejected electronic music, feeling that existing instruments were sufficient for what they wanted to say. Some even went full circle by composing electronic-sounding pieces with the use of only conventional instruments.

A few interesting works resulted from the efforts of the small band of Canadian composers who, first, could gain access to an electronic music studio for long-enough periods to do serious work, and, secondly, were interested in doing so. The first instructor in electronic music at the University of Toronto, Myron Schaeffer, composed *Dance R4 ÷ 3* (1961), a work in neoclassical style using sine tones and ostinato figures. Robert Aitken's *Noësis* (1963), on the other hand, is a more varied work, including as it does white noise and various concrete sounds in addition to the purer sine tones. Pierre Mercure's *Incandescence* (1961) is a ballet score whose music is realized entirely by electronic and synthetic means. Commissioned by the Riopelle Dance Group of Montreal, this work is characterized by delicate, sustained tones.

The most extended electronic compositions written by a Canadian composer at this time are two works entitled *Electronic Composition No. 3* (1960) and *Electronic Composition No. 4* (1962) by István Anhalt. No. 3 was produced at the Electronic Music Laboratory of the NRC in Ottawa and No. 4 at both the NRC and the Columbia-Princeton Center in the United States. The sound material of No. 3 consists entirely of sine tones, sometimes in clusters of several hundreds. Many of the resultant sounds, which are all produced synthetically, are similar to the sounds of birds and bells. The complex texture typical of Anhalt's music is present here, although the uniformity of the sound source provides a readily apparent sense of unity. *Electronic Composition No. 4* is a more varied work because its material consists of sine-tone mixtures as well as filtered and modified white noise spectra. Conveying a stream-of-conscious diffuseness, this work nevertheless holds the attention of the listener through an interesting combination of sounds as well as the effective use of silence.

Anhalt has written no works exclusively for electronic means since *Electronic Composition No. 4*. After this time most Canadian composers, with a few exceptions such as Barry Truax, Gustav Ciamaga, and the members of the Canadian Electronic Ensemble (1971–), have regarded electronic music as just another sound source to be used in conjunction with conventional instruments or voices.

An early example of such a combining of traditional and electronic sounds may be found in Norma Beecroft's *From Dreams of Brass* (1964), a work which utilizes electronic music 'primarily as an extension of existing orchestral and vocal sounds.'[35] Udo Kasemets's *Variations [on Variations (on Variations)]* (1966), discussed above, also contains prepared tape material. R. Murray Schafer makes use of prepared tape in some of his works of this period, such as the television opera *Loving/Toi* (1963–5), the choral work *Gita* (1967), and the work for youth, *Threnody* (1966–7). In some works the prepared tapes consist of electronic modifications of vocal or instrumental sections of the same piece. Anhalt employs this technique in his *Cento* (1966) for live and prerecorded voices.

CHORAL MUSIC

Three general comments may be made regarding choral music of this period. One is that in the field of school music, under the stimulation of the John Adaskin Project, there was an expansion from the simple arrangements of Canadian folk songs which characterized the 1950s to more stylistically contemporary fare. Secondly, there was an increase in the number of extended works of the cantata type. Thirdly, church anthems in a conservative style continued to be written and published.

The John Adaskin Project produced a number of significant works in the choral field, notably Harry Freedman's *Three Vocalises* (1964) and Harry Somers's *The Wonder Song* (1964), both for unaccompanied mixed voices. Each work was commissioned by the Canadian Music Centre and grew out of the experiences of the composers in the classroom. Each has one or more didactic as well as musical purposes. Freedman says in his preface to the score for *Three Vocalises* that he wants to 'accustom young performers to new sounds and rhythms,' and by avoiding a text he wishes 'to place the emphasis on purely musical elements.'[36] The voices are treated very much like instruments and the writing is primarily linear. The three vocalises are 'Chorale,' 'Soliloquy,' and 'Chant.' Somers's *The Wonder Song* is more a rhythmic study with its 7/8 metre and basically two-part texture. The text by the composer himself is in a light-hearted vein, underlining Somers's sense of humour and conveying to the youthful singers the fact that choral singing in a modern idiom can be fun.

Other works designed to be sung by youth or amateur choirs with or without instrumental accompaniment include Jean Coulthard's *Signature of God* (1964), Keith Bissell's *Newfoundland* (1964), and Godfrey Ridout's *Four Sonnets* (1964), *When Age and Youth Unite* (1966), and *The Dance* (1960). *The Dance*, an extended part-song with orchestral accompaniment, is based on a translation by J.A. Symonds of *Carmina burana* CXXXVII, one of the medieval Latin secular songs composed and sung by errant students or young ecclesiastics. Ridout captures the youthful earthiness of the text, the opening lines of which are 'cast aside dull books and thought; / Sweet is folly, sweet is play.' Ridout's irregular rhythms follow the natural accentuation of the text. Mostly in a traditional, tonal framework, the work is in a note-against-note style which is typical of dance songs of almost any age.

The significant increase in the composition of sacred and secular cantatas was an important feature of Canadian music of the 1960s. Texts are based on sources as wide-ranging as the story of Jonah in the Old Testament to eye-witness accounts of the atomic bombing at Nagasaki on 9 August 1945. Many of the texts make a moral statement regarding life and society in the mid-twentieth century. John Beckwith's *Jonah* (1963) and Kelsey Jones's *Prophecy of Micah* (1963) each extract a moral from the Old Testament stories. *Jonah* emphasizes the importance of individual obedience to God's will and the power of forgiveness and tolerance, while the *Prophecy of Micah* exhorts all nations to cease making war and 'to do justly, love mercy, and to walk humbly with thy God.' Whereas *Jonah* contains a personal message about individual obedience, the story of Micah is imbued with present-day concerns that man as a social being is headed for self-destruction unless he abandons war. Beckwith's score draws on techniques and procedures from various periods to express the timelessness of the story of Jonah – Hebrew chant, sixteenth-century Latin words and Protestant hymn style, seventeenth-century cantata format, and twentieth-century twelve-tone technique (with tonal implications). The work ends with an unaccompanied chorale on a text by Canadian poet Jay Macpherson. In a much more melodramatic way Jones in *Prophecy of Micah* employs techniques closely allied with the style of the nineteenth century and post-romanticism in the present century. The text was adapted by Rosabelle Jones from the book of the Old Testament prophet Micah. The augmented intervals (second and fourth) as well as repeated rhythmic motives in the percussion serve as unifying factors.

Robert Turner's *The Third Day* (1962), an Easter cantata which may be performed in concert form or as incidental music for the Resurrection story, is a large-scale work commissioned by the CBC and based upon texts selected from medieval and renaissance sources by Peter Howarth. Like Beckwith's *Jonah*, Turner's work uses a twelve-tone row which has strong tonal implications. The intervals of the row include three major thirds and a rising half-step between the last two notes; much use is made of thirds and octaves in the choral writing.

A much more adventurous work from the stylistic point of view is Beecroft's *From Dreams of Brass*, a cantata dealing with the central core of Christian belief.

The text is by Jane Beecroft, the composer's sister, who was at the time of composition Sister M. Ignatia Beecroft, IBVM. The work is scored for male narrator, mixed chorus with soprano solo, orchestra (brass, strings, and percussion), and prepared tape and is an imaginative, if somewhat melodramatic, setting which combines Webernesque pointillism with electronic means. 'If you seek to own the earth in time and space, seek first the One by whom all things are given ... Love liberates and floods Man's soul with Light, revealing there the image of Himself ... by Light ordered into infinite design reordered Man moves by the Law Supreme. In all things, order.' Cast symbolically in three sections, the work uses three contrasting musical means – voices, instruments, and electronic tape. It is optimistic in tone, in contrast to most other works in this genre and to the general pattern of Canadian literature which has been interpreted as dwelling on the central theme of the unsuccessful struggle against life and nature.[37] The musical means employed by Beecroft are among the most avant-garde of any Canadian musical score to that date.

In the area of secular cantatas there are three works which merit attention and which represent a wide variety of textual material. Beckwith's *The Trumpets of Summer* (1964) deals with a Canadian view of Shakespeare at his quadracentennial; Freedman's *The Tokaido* (1963–4) is based upon Japanese verse; and R. Murray Schafer's *Threnody* (1966–7) is a strong anti-war statement.

Beckwith's work, on a text by Margaret Atwood, satirizes in a kindly but effective way the treatment of Shakespeare at the hands of our educational institutions and the Stratford Festival. Utilizing a variety of techniques derived from his radio collages of this same period, Beckwith makes a statement on 'how Shakespeare is reflected in modern Canadian life.'[38] The work is a period piece, its rather self-consciously satirical mood closely tied to a particular time and place. The most effective sections are the 'Prologue' and the 'Epilogue' which transcend these limitations.

Freedman's *The Tokaido* is also a theatrical piece which uses the twelve-tone technique, but here its similarity with Beckwith's work ends. The text is based upon Japanese haiku, tanka, and senryu poems, and the music reflects the pointillistic-impressionistic character of the haiku and the sombre quality of the tanka. Inspired by the woodblock prints of Hiroshige and Oliver Statler's *The Japanese Inn* (New York: Random House 1961), which is an account of Hiroshige's stay at one of the inns on the Tokaido (the way between Tokyo and Kyoto), the work is generally delicate and subdued. The poems, which are grouped according to season, are prefaced by an introduction and followed by an epilogue. The instrumental forces, for woodwind quintet, provide commentary on the poetry as well as a link between the sections of the work. Without using traditional Japanese musical devices the work attempts to capture the moods of Japanese poetry and prints.

In Schafer's *Threnody* a Japanese text totally unlike haiku poems forms the

EXAMPLE 5-8   R. Murray Schafer, *Threnody* (1966–7), p 25

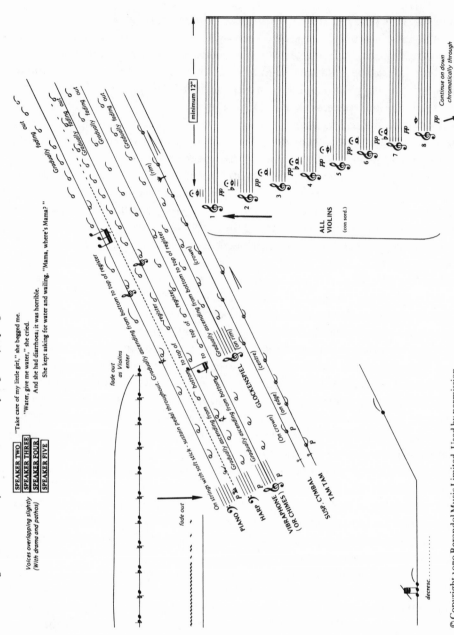

© Copyright 1970 Berandol Music Limited. Used by permission

basis of the work. As a grim reminder of the horrors of nuclear war Schafer uses for part of his text eye-witness accounts by children and young people of the atomic bombing of Nagasaki on 9 August 1945, combined with comments and telegrammes to and from the Potsdam Conference (July 1945) which followed the successful testing of the atomic bomb – the work is an uncomfortable one, to say the least. The tragedy of nuclear war is set off against the seeming indifference of the political leaders who control the destiny of the world. This is a work intended to be performed until such time, as the composer says, that its message will no longer be needed.[39] The score, which calls for choir, youth orchestra, five narrators, and prepared tape, is sometimes graphic, sometimes specifically notated in pitch and rhythm, and sometimes only generally so (see example 5-8). The fact that the work can be performed by a high-school orchestra and choir and still produce an overwhelming dramatic impact is testimony to the considerable skill of the composer.

SONG

With the ever-increasing national awareness of the 1960s one might expect that the songs written by Canadian composers would be settings of Canadian poetry, but the song texts in this period were infrequently Canadian. The reasons are both practical and artistic. The problem of copyright often prevented the Canadian composer from using Canadian poetic material freely; moreover, in the 1960s the composer often preferred to choose a subject remote in time and place. Bruce Mather's *Song of Blodeuwedd* (1961) and other works are based on mythological subjects seen through the eyes of English poet Robert Graves. Japanese haiku were a favourite source of texts (Alfred Kunz, *Love, Death and Fullmoonnights*, 1964; Udo Kasemets, *Haiku*, 1961; Harry Somers, *Twelve Miniatures*, 1963–4), as were Chinese lyrics (Barbara Pentland, *Three Sung Songs*, 1964), Eskimo texts (Harry Freedman, *Anerca*, 1966; Serge Garant, *Anerca*, 1961–3), and European poems of a much earlier time (Bernard Naylor, *The Nymph Complaining for the Death of Her Faun*, 1965; John Beckwith, *A Chaucer Suite*, 1962; Jean Coulthard, *Six Medieval Love Songs*, 1962; Godfrey Ridout, *The Ascension*, 1962). Only a few Canadian composers used contemporary Canadian texts (Walter Buczynski, *How Some Things Look*, 1966; Keith Bissell, *Two Songs of Farewell*, 1962–3; Serge Garant, *Cage d'oiseau*, 1962). Lorne Betts (*A Cycle of the Earth*, 1962) and Oskar Morawetz (*Four Songs*, 1966) used the poetry of Bliss Carman, an expatriate Canadian of an earlier generation. Only Harry Somers wrote his own texts for songs (*Evocations*, 1966), although R. Murray Schafer wrote the texts for larger vocal works (*Loving/Toi*, 1965; *Requiems for the Party-Girl*, 1966).

In the 1960s there continued to be a disappointing paucity of solo song in published form. Many of the songs required something other than piano accompaniment, and because of the added expense publishers were not convinced to increase their output of Canadian works.

The songs of Bissell, Coulthard, Naylor, and Morawetz remain stylistically conservative. The text of the first of Bissell's *Two Songs of Farewell* was composed by a Chinese guide who accompanied Claude Bissell, then president of the University of Toronto, during a visit to mainland China in 1962; it was written as Bissell was saying good-bye to the guide; later Bissell wrote the text of the second song in reply. Each poem is a touching testament to the personal bond which may grow in a relatively short time between persons of widely differing social and political persuasions. The musical settings utilize a nineteenth-century tonal style. Coulthard's *Six Medieval Love Songs* are also rooted in the musical style of the nineteenth century and make no attempt to draw on medieval devices, such as those found in Beckwith's *Chaucer Suite*. Naylor's *The Nymph Complaining*, on a text by Andrew Marvell, is in a style reminiscent of Gustav Holst. Morawetz's *Four Songs* are settings of poems by Bliss Carman dated 1895 to 1913, and are written in the musical style of approximately the same period.

Beckwith's *Chaucer Suite* for alto, tenor, and baritone voices (unaccompanied) varies from one to two to three parts in texture. Utilizing monodic passages, polyphonic techniques of the fourteenth century, and twentieth-century harmonies, the work is typical of this composer's eclecticism and his sensitivity to the historical context. Freedman's *Anerca* (1966) employs the same text as Garant's work of the same name but adds another verse and the original Inuit text. The setting is in a free twelve-tone idiom with repeated motives and conventionally notated melodies and rhythms. Wide melodic leaps of major sevenths and augmented octaves are typical. In general, it is more gentle and lyrical than Garant's setting, and thus more evocative of the mood of the text. Buczynski's *How Some Things Look* on a text by Jane Beecroft is a collection of thirteen short poems set in a witty style reminiscent of Webern.

Vocal works by Garant, Kasemets, and Somers are more avant garde in idiom. Garant's *Cage d'oiseau* (1962) – the later solo piano version *Pièce pour piano no. 2* (1962) was discussed on p 107 – explores the expressionistic depths of its text in the musical language of the avant garde. The poem *Cage d'oiseau* by Hector de Saint-Denys Garneau first appeared in *Regards et jeux dans l'espace* (1937) and speaks metaphorically, and, as it turned out, prophetically, of the poet's body as a bird-cage in which death resides (Saint-Denys Garneau died in 1943 at the age of 31 after a short and illness-ridden life).[40] Garant's setting represents a mutation of post-Webern elements (pointillistic and serial, with individual dynamic markings for many notes) and aleatoric or chance style (use of the forearm on the keyboard, free rhythm, use of silence, closing of the piano lid, slapping the wood of the piano with the knuckles or the palm of the hand). One must add that the sensitive and musical quality of Saint-Denys Garneau's poetry is such that it has been set by a

number of Canadian composers besides Garant, including Bruce Mather and
Jean Papineau-Couture.

Kasemets, like several other Canadian composers (Somers, Kunz, Freedman),
found inspiration in Japanese haiku, but Kasemets's *Haiku* (1961), for voice, flute,
cello, and piano, following the chance procedures he adopted in the 1960s,
provides the performer with situations in which he, the performer, must make
choices and thereby become a co-composer. Thus every performance of *Haiku* is
unique. Somers's *Evocations* also makes use of aleatoric elements and free-rhythm
and graph notation, but it adds another element which represents a growing trend,
that of seeking new sound possibilities for the human voice.[41] Composers had
been doing this with instruments for most of the century, but, except for certain
pioneer works such as Schönberg's *Pierrot Lunaire* (1912), the idea of extending
the sound potentialities of the human voice did not come into vogue until the
1960s. At this time sounds expressing the nuances of the words became pre-
eminent while organizational technique remained secondary. Somers's four songs
(with texts by the composer) are 'sound' pieces with the words themselves being
picturesque and onomatopoeic. There are strong associations with nature – 'loon,
night ... mist ... water ... stillness ... shattered ... shimmers ... spinning ... moon ...
womb ... tomb.' In song no. 3 Somers employs one of his trademarks, that of a
cumulative building up from a germinal motive, through a long crescendo, to a
climax. Although the work is notated precisely from the melodic standpoint while
remaining free rhythmically, it ends with a graphic notation in the piano part (see
example 5-9). Somewhat sardonically Somers adds as a postscript a specified
melodic figuration which he calls a 'suggestion for tired pianists.'

OPERA

The most noteworthy feature of Canadian opera in the 1960s was that original,
full-length stage productions were created for the first time. This coming of age
was heralded by a performance of the substantially revised version of Healey
Willan's *Deirdre*, which was originally written as a radio opera in three acts and first
broadcast on 20 April 1946 on the CBC. The revision (plus insertions), which
occupied Willan during much of 1962 and 1964–5, resulted in the first stage and
public performance on 2 April 1965 by the University of Toronto's Faculty of
Music Opera School. Willan regarded *Deirdre* as his finest work and did not
apologize for the obvious Wagnerian influence on the style. The *leitmotiv* principle
is used to represent persons or events and the harmonic vocabulary is clearly that
of Wagner's. However, the use of ostinati, parallelisms, and non-continuous
melodic phrases betray Willan's English origins.

Equally significant but at the opposite end of the stylistic spectrum is
R. Murray Schafer's *Loving/Toi* (1965) which was first produced as a bilingual

EXAMPLE 5-9   Harry Somers, *Evocations* (1966), song no. 3, ending,
in the composer's hand

© Copyright 1968 BMI Canada Limited. Copyright assigned 1969 to Berandol Music Limited. Used by permission

opera for television (Schafer prefers to call it an audiovisual poem rather than an
opera). Two important French-Canadian composers co-operated with Schafer in
this work: Gabriel Charpentier was responsible for the French part of the libretto
and Pierre Mercure for the actual television production. Schafer himself wrote the
English part of the text. *Loving* is a drama about love between the sexes. The work
consists of four parts, each of which may be performed separately: *The Geography
of Eros* (1964) for soprano, piano, harp, six percussion instruments, recorded
voices; *Vanity* (1965) for mezzo-soprano, harpsichord, harp, mandolin, Spanish
guitar (electric guitar, banjo), violin, cello, percussion, recorded voices; *Modesty*
(1965) for soprano, live string quintet, two taped quintets; *Air Ishtar* (1965) for
soprano, piano (celesta), six percussion instruments, string bass, recorded voices.
The total work consists of a mixture of prepared tape and live performance,
graphic and conventional notation, and three types of roles – sung, spoken, and

danced. The approach is surrealistic and non-linear; its stream-of-conscious and ambiguous nature is both erotic and thought-provoking as it explores the theme of love in all its aspects. According to the composer it 'has no plot in the usual meaning of the term, that is no situations arranged in a logical order proceeding from point A to point B. On the contrary, the scenes are interrelated regardless of time and space, without any specific chronology or topography.'[42] The singers are not individual characters but attitudes in the manner of a medieval allegory. Even though the musical language is that of the avant garde of the 1960s, the use of the love theme and the principle of the fusion of the arts suggest a strong philosophical kinship with the music dramas of Wagner. Indeed, from this point onward Schafer's romantic tendencies have become more and more apparent.

The remaining operas of the period are either designed for school use (Barnes, Kunz, Bissell) or are chamber operas (Vallerand, Sirulnikoff, McIntyre, McPeek). Most noteworthy of these is Le Magicien (1961) by Vallerand which is 'a light-hearted confection about an inept illusionist who brings two painted figures to life.'[43] These two, Harlequin and Columbine, indulge in mischief and eventually fall in love. The musical style is appropriately French neoclassical and emphasizes the parody technique (especially jazz 'blues').

The culmination of opera in the 1960s came in centennial year with the presentation of no less than five operas on national subjects, the most noteworthy being Louis Riel by Harry Somers. These will be discussed at the beginning of the next chapter.

BALLET

The 1960s also saw the creation of original scores for ballets for the first time in Canada. Harry Freedman's three-act ballet Rose Latulippe (1966) was actually the first full-length ballet to be written and produced in North America. It was commissioned by the Royal Winnipeg Ballet, a company which attained professional status in 1949. The story, set in Quebec in 1740, centres on a young girl who is high-strung and deeply religious. A Mardi Gras party which she is attending is interrupted by the appearance of 'the Stranger' who exercises power over Rose and attracts her away from her fiancé, Anselme. The girl loses her reason and runs away into the night where the Stranger and her friends find her in a deserted churchyard. After he revives her, the Stranger departs silently into the night. Freedman's style shows an affinity for the neoclassical ballets of Stravinsky and the nationalistic American ballets of Copland. Although he employs a twelve-tone row, he uses one which has strong tonal and folk-like implications; it is frequently broken up into motives. The work is sectional, has many repeated parts, and, typical of Freedman, makes colourful use of the instruments of the orchestra. It has a rhythmic sparkle and wit which accounts, in large measure, for its initial success. A prepared electronic tape is an integral component of the work.

EXAMPLE 5-10   Gerhard Wuensch, *Sonata brève*, Op. 26 (1963), end of third movement

A ballet which employs electronic tape exclusively is *Incandescence* (1961) by Pierre Mercure. This tasteful, imaginative, and poetic work (not a full-length ballet) points up the great loss which music in Canada suffered on the composer's premature death.

ORGAN MUSIC

Canadian organists, except for those holding teaching positions in schools of music, practise their craft in the conservative confines of the churches. Many of them carry on the nineteenth-century English tradition of composing functional music, usually for special occasions, for their instrument and choir. Few composers who are not themselves organists have composed organ music in Canada. The majority of works which have been written are either in a late-nineteenth-century chromatic idiom or in the neo-baroque style of Hindemith. Examples of works in a nineteenth-century idiom are Robert Fleming's *Three Pieces for Organ* (1962) and Healey Willan's *Andante, Fugue and Chorale* (1965). Examples of neo-baroque works are *Sonata* (1963) by Keith Bissell, *Three Fugues* (1964) by Graham George, and *Sonata brève* (1963) by Gerhard Wuensch. Wuensch's sonata, in three movements, features contrapuntal texture, tertian harmonies with added tones, ostinato figures, and traditional formal structures such as song form (ABA in the second movement) and toccata (third movement). Like Hindemith dissonances often have an ultimate resolution in a major triad; see example 5-10. Walter Buczynski's *Five Atmospheres* (1966) is rhapsodic in style, and explores new and unusual sound possibilities (i.e. 'atmospheres') of the organ. The work is stylistically more adventurous than most of its contemporaries.

Two organ works from the period make use of the twelve-tone technique, Alfred Kunz's *Three Excursions* (1964) and Otto Joachim's *Fantasia* (1961). The first movement of the Kunz score is based upon a twelve-tone passacaglia theme which is stated four times in the lowest voice, the featured intervals being the perfect fourth, fifth, and minor second. The two upper parts are freely derived from the theme. The middle movement, which consists of only eight measures, is an accumulation of semitone clusters proceeding from dynamic level 'ppp' to 'ffff' and ending with the 'flat of the hand covering as many keys as possible.'

Fantasia is one of the last works Joachim wrote in the twelve-tone idiom before he abandoned it in favour of chance or aleatoric procedures. As with its ancestors, the sixteenth- and seventeenth-century keyboard and instrumental fantasias, this work consists of several contrasting sections. Unity is achieved through Joachim's usual strict use of the tone row, plus rhythmic motives, particularly the snap rhythm (a sixteenth note followed by a dotted eighth). The row is less confined to horizontal movement than in Joachim's previous twelve-tone works and often crosses voices and appears in a vertical arrangement. The texture of the work is lean and transparent and the sonorities are strongly dissonant. As a tribute to Bach, the acknowledged master of the fantasia form and the composer whom Joachim admires above all others,[44] *Fantasia* quotes the B-A-C-H theme (B-flat, A, C, B-natural) towards the end.

SELECTED WORKS

composer	title	score	recording
PIANO MUSIC			
Archer, Violet	*Theme and Variations for Piano* (1963)	Waterloo, 1964	
Buczynski, Walter	*Amorphus* (1964)	CMC ms film 20/46	CBC SM 162
	Aria and Toccata (1963)	CMC ms film 20/43	CBC SM 162
Coulthard, Jean	*Aegean Sketches* (1961)	BMI Can, 1964	Mel SMLP 4031
Dela, Maurice	*Deux Impromptus* (1961)	BMI Can, 1964	
Fiala, George	*Australian Suite* (1963)	BMI Can, 1963	CCM-2 (inc)
Gagnon, Alain	*Mirages* (1966)	CMC ms film 22/24	RCI 252
	Sonate no. 3 (1966)		RCI 274; Select CC15.007
Garant, Serge	*Pièce pour piano no. 2 (Cage d'oiseau)* (1962)	Berandol, 1969	RCI 252; RCI ACM 2
Hétu, Jacques	*Petite suite pour piano,* Op. 7 (1962)	CMC ms film 17/11	RCI 252
	Sonate pour deux pianos (1962)	CMC ms film 17/12	RCI 227; RCA CCS-1021
	Variations (1964)	Berandol, 1970	CH SMS-2937; Col 32 110045; JMC 4; RCI 251
Jaque, Rhené	*Suite pour piano*	BMI Can, 1961	
	Deuxième suite pour piano	BMI Can, 1964	Mel SMLP-4031
Johnston, Richard	*Second Suite for Piano* (1965)	BMI Can, 1965	
Kasemets, Udo	*Fifth Root of Five* (1962–3), two pianos	Berandol, 1969	
	Squares (1962)	Berandol, 1969	
Kenins, Talivaldis	*Sonata for Piano* (1961)	Harris, 1964	CBC SM 301; RCI 366; Coronet 850 C-3763; UR4M-3764
Mather, Bruce	*Fantasy* (1964)	CMC ms film 11/20	CBC SM 48
Pentland, Barbara	*Fantasy for Piano* (1962)	BMI Can, 1966	RCI 242
	Shadows/Ombres (1964)	Waterloo, 1968	RCI 242

composer	title	score	recording
Pépin, Clermont	*Ronde villageoise* (1956–61), two pianos	CMC ms	RCI ACM
Rogers, William Keith	*Six Short Preludes on a Tone Row* (1963)	BMI Can, 1963	
Southam, Ann	*Three in Blue – Jazz Preludes* (1965)	BMI Can, 1966	CCM-2
	Four Bagatelles (1961)	Berandol, 1974	Mel SMLP 4031

ORCHESTRAL MUSIC

composer	title	score	recording
Archer, Violet	*Three Sketches for Orchestra* (1961)	BMI Can, 1966	CBC SM 119
Beckwith, John	*Concertino* (1963), horn and orchestra	Berandol, 1976	
Beecroft, Norma	*Improvvisazioni Concertanti* (1961)	Leeds, 1973	Audat 477-4001; CAPAC-CAB tape 12
Bissell, Keith	*Divertimento for Strings* (1964)	Kerby, 1972	
Brott, Alexander	*Profundum praedictum* (1964)	CMC ms film 3/18	RCA LSC 3128; CAPAC-CAB tape 7
	Triangle, Circle, and 4 Squares (1963)	CMC ms	RCI 216; RCA CCS-1010
Fleming, Robert	*'You Name It' – Suite* (1964), school string orchestra	GVT , 1965	CMC
Freedman, Harry	*Fantasy and Allegro* (1962)	CMC ms film 6/4	RCI 238; RCI ACM
	A Little Symphony (1966)	Leeds, 1974	
Glick, Srul Irving	*Sinfonia Concertante for String Orchestra* (1961)	Summit, 1973	RCA LSC 3128; CAPAC-CAB tape 9
Hodkinson, Sydney	*Caricatures* (1966)	Ricordi, 1969	
Kenins, Talivaldis	*Nocturne and Dance* (1963) (Youth Orchestra Series)	Boosey, 1969	CMC tape
Mather, Bruce	*Elegy* (1959), alto saxophone and strings	Waterloo, 1965 (piano and saxophone)	Golden Crest RE 7037
Matton, Roger	*Concerto pour deux pianos et orchestre* (1964)	CMC study score, 1964	RCI 442; Cap SW 6123; CRI 317; CAPAC-CAB tape 5

composer	title	score	recording
	Mouvement symphonique II (1962)	CMC study score, 1962	RCI 230; *Musican* Rec 9
Mercure, Pierre	*Lignes et points* (1964)	Ricordi, 1970	RCI 230; RCA LSC 2980
	Tetrachromie (1963)	CMC ms film 10/20	Col MS 6763
Morawetz, Oskar	*Concerto No. 1 for Piano* (1962)	CMC ms film 14/5; Leeds, 1966 (2-piano score)	RCI 213; Cap SW 6123; CAPAC-CAB tape 4
	Passacaglia (1964)	Leeds, 1967	CMC tape 467
	Sinfonietta for Winds and Percussion (1965)	Leeds, 1967	RCI 292
Morel, François	*L'Etoile noire* (1962)	BMI Can, 1964	Col MS-6962; Odyssey Y31993
Papineau-Couture, Jean	*Concerto pour piano et orchestre* (1965)	CMC ms film 11/34 (2-piano score)	RCI 235; RCI ACM
	Suite Lapitsky (1965)	CMC ms film 11/30	
Pépin, Clermont	*Monade for Strings* (1964)	CMC ms	RCA LSC 3128; CAPAC-CAB tape 1
	Three Miniatures for Strings (1963)	Oxford, 1966	
Prévost, André	*Fantasmes* (1963)	Berandol, 1970	RCI 230; RCA LSC 2980
	Pyknon (1966), violin and orchestra	Okra, 1970	CMC tape 626
Ridout, Godfrey	*Fall Fair* (1961)	GVT, 1966	Audat 477-4001; CAPAC-CAB tape 9
	Overture to 'Colas et Colinette' (1964)	GVT, 1971	Select SSC-24.160
Schafer, R. Murray	*Statement in Blue* (1964)	BMI Can, 1966	Mel SMLP 4017
	Canzoni for Prisoners (1962)	Berandol, 1977	
Somers, Harry	*Five Concepts for Orchestra* (1961)	BMI Can, 1964	CMC tape 147
	Movement for Orchestra (formerly *Abstract for Orchestra*) (1961–2)	Ricordi, 1964	CMC tape 141
	Picasso Suite (1964)	Ricordi, 1969	CBC SM 241
	Stereophony (1963)	Kerby, 1972	CMC tape 171
	Symphony for Winds, Brass, and Percussion (1961)	Peters, 1969	CBC SM 134

composer	title	score	recording
Surdin, Morris	*Concerto for Accordion and Strings* (1966)	CMC ms film 28/18	RCI 238
Symonds, Norman	*The Nameless Hour* (1966)	Leeds, 1971	CBC SM 104; Decca DL 75069; CAPAC-CAB tape 6; *Musican* rec 7
Tremblay, Gilles	*Cantique de durées* (1960)	CMC ms film 13/31	
Vallerand, Jean	*Cordes en mouvement* (1961)	CMC ms	RCI 216; RCA CCS-1010
Weinzweig, John	*Divertimento No. 5* (1961)	Leeds, 1969	RCI 292; RCI ACM 1
	Piano Concerto (1965–6)	CMC ms film 8/23	CBC SM 104

CHAMBER MUSIC

composer	title	score	recording
Adaskin, Murray	*Quiet Song* (1963), violin and piano	Leeds, 1964	
	Rondino for Nine Instruments (1961)	CMC ms film 1/16	RCI 215; RCA CCS-1009
	Divertimento No. 3 (1965), violin, horn, bassoon	CMC ms film 1/22	RCI 405
Archer, Violet	*Sonata* (1965), horn and piano	CMC ms film 16/19	RCI 412
Beecroft, Norma	*Contrasts for Six Performers* (1962)	CMC ms film 7/25	CMC tape 360
	Tre Pezzi Brevi (1960)	Universal, 1962	Dom s-69002; CAPAC-CAB tape 10
Cherney, Brian	*Interlude and Variations* (1965)	Jaymar, 1970	RCI 364
Eckhardt-Gramatté, S.C.	*Nonet* (1966)	CMC ms film 15/31	CMC tape 535
	String Quartet No. 3 (1962–4)	CMC ms film 15/29	
Fiala, George	*Quartet No. 2 for Saxophones* (1961)	Berandol, 1970	RCI 279
Fleming, Robert	*Three Dialogues* (1964), flute or oboe and piano	CMC ms	CBC SM 268
Freedman, Harry	*Quintette for Winds* (1962)	Kerby, 1972	RCI 208; RCI ACM; *Musican* rec. 6
	Variations for Flute, Oboe, and Harpsichord (1965)	CMC ms film 6/13	RCI 219; RCI ACM RCA CCS-1013
Gagnon, Alain	*Quatuor à cordes no. 2* (1965)	CMC ms	RCI 363

composer	title	score	recording
Garant, Serge	*Anerca* (1961; rev 1963)	BMI Can, 1967	RCI 217; RCA CCS-1011; RCI ACM 2
Glick, Srul Irving	*Suite Hebraïque* (1961), arranged for clarinet and piano (1963)	Boosey, 1968	Dom s-69004
Hétu, Jacques	*Quatre pièces pour flûte et piano* (1965)	Billaudot, 1969	Madrigal MAS-402
Hodkinson, Sydney	*Interplay* (1966)	CMC ms film 23/51	RCI 298-301
Joachim, Otto	*Illumination I* (1965)	BMI Can, 1968	CMC tape 390
Jones, Kelsey	*Rondo for Solo Flute* (1963)	Waterloo, 1972	RCI 219; RCA CCS-1013
Kasemets, Udo	*Calceolaria* (1966)	BMI Can, 1967	
	Cascando (1965)	Berandol, 1970	Marathon MS 2110
	Contactics (1966)	BMI Can, 1967	
	Timepiece (1964)	Berandol, 1969	
	Trigon (1963)	Berandol, 1969	
	Variations [on Variations (on Variations)] (1966)	BMI Can, 1967	
Keetbass, Dirk	*Three Miniatures for Solo Flute* (1963)	Jaymar, 1971	RCI 215; RCA CCS-1009
Kenins, Talivaldis	*Concertante for Flute and Piano* (1966)	Boosey, 1972	Dom s-69006; CAPAC-CAB tape 11
Mather, Bruce	*Orphée* (1963)	CMC ms film 11/15	RCI 217; RCA CCS-1011
Morawetz, Oskar	*Fantasy for Cello and Piano No. 1* (1962; rev 1970)	CMC ms	CBC SM 305
Morel, François	*Quintet for Brass* (1962)	CMC ms	CBC SM 216
	Etude en forme de toccate (1965)	BMI Can, 1968	
Papineau-Couture, Jean	*Fantaisie pour quintette à vent* (1963)	BMI Can, 1968	JMC C. 30
	Trois Caprices (1962), violin and piano	Peer, 1971	RCI 243; RCI ACM
Pentland, Barbara	*Piano Trio* (1963)	CMC ms film 12/23	RCI 242
	Trio con alea (1966), violin, viola, and cello	CMC ms film 12/25	CMC tape 467
Pépin, Clermont	*Quatuor à cordes no. 4* (1960) (*Hyperboles*)	CMC ms	

composer	title	score	recording
Prévost, André	*Sonate pour violoncelle et piano* (1962)	Ricordi, 1973	RCI 356
	Mouvement pour quintette de cuivres (1963)	Excello, 1967	
	Sonate pour violon et piano (1961)	BMI Can, 1968	Baroque JA-19002; CBC SM 172
	Triptyque (1966)	CMC ms	RCI 297
Saint-Marcoux, Micheline Coulombe	*Quatuor à cordes* (1966)	CMC ms	RCI 363
Schafer, R. Murray	*Five Studies on Texts by Prudentius* (1962)	BMI Can, 1965	CMC tape
	Requiems for the Party-Girl (1966), from *Patria II* (1966–72)	BMI Can, 1967; Berandol, rev 1978	RCI 298-301; RCI ACM; CRI SD 245; Mel SMLP 4026
Somers, Harry	'Etching – The Vollard Suite,' from *Picasso Suite* (1964), solo flute	Ricordi, 1969	CBC SM 114
	Theme for Variations (1964)	BMI Can, 1966	
	Twelve Miniatures (1963–4)	BMI Can, 1965	RCI 217; RCA CCS-1011
Southam, Ann	*Rhapsodic Interlude for Violin Alone* (1963)		Mel SMLP 4021
Tremblay, Gilles	*Kékoba* (1965; rev 1967)	BMI Can, 1968	RCI 240
Turner, Robert	*Four Fragments for Brass Quintet* (1961)	Peer, 1972	
Weinzweig, John	*Clarinet Quartet* (1964–5)	Leeds, 1970	Dom s-69004
	String Quartet No. 3 (1962)	CMC ms film 8/29	RCI 362; RCI ACM 1
	Woodwind Quintet (1963–4)	CMC ms film 8/30	RCI 218; RCA CCS-1012; *Musican* rec. 3

ELECTRONIC MUSIC

Aitken, Robert	*Noësis* (1963)		Folkways FMS 33436
Anhalt, István	*Electronic Composition No. 3* (1960)		Marathon MS 2111
	Electronic Composition No. 4 (1962)		Marathon MS 2111

composer	title	score	recording
Mercure, Pierre	*Incandescence* (1961)		CMC tape 393
Pedersen, Paul	*Themes from the Old Testament* (1966)		CAPAC QC-1273 (inc)
Schaeffer, Myron	*Dance R4 + 3* (1961)		Folkways FMS 33426

CHORAL MUSIC

Beckwith, John	**Jonah* (1963)	BMI Can, 1969	
	The Sharon Fragments (1966)	Waterloo, 1966	Cap ST 6258
	*The Trumpets of Summer (1964)	CMC ms film 7/7	RCI 340; Cap ST 6323
Beecroft, Norma	**From Dreams of Brass* (1963–4)	CMC ms film 7/27	RCI 214; RCA CCS-1008; CAPAC-CAB tape 8; *Musican* rec. 8
Bissell, Keith	**Newfoundland* (1964)	CMC ms film 19/50	
Coulthard, Jean	*Signature of God* (1964)	Berandol, 1970	RCI 226
	Auguries of Innocence (1965)	Berandol, 1969	RCI 226
Freedman, Harry	*Three Vocalises* (1964)	Leeds, 1965	
	*The Tokaido (1963–4)	CMC ms	RCI 341; CBC SM 142; Decca DL 75244; RCI ACM
Joachim, Otto	*Psalm* (1961)	BMI Can, 1961	RCI 206
Jones, Kelsey	**Prophecy of Micah* (1963)	CMC ms film 10/11	RCI 355
Mather, Bruce	*La Lune mince* (1965)	CMC ms film 11/9	RCI 299-301; *Musican* rec. 5
Ridout, Godfrey	**The Dance* (1960)	Novello, 1964	CMC tape 363
	Four Sonnets (1964)	GVT, 1964	
	When Age and Youth Unite (1966)	GVT, 1966	
Schafer, R. Murray	**Threnody* (1966–7)	Berandol, 1970	Mel SMLP 4017
Somers, Harry	*Gloria* (1962)	GVT, 1964	RCA LSC 3043
	God the Master of this Scene (1962)	GVT, 1964	Cap ST 6258
	The Wonder Song (1964)	BMI Can, 1964	CBC SM-19
Turner, Robert	*Prophetic Song* (1961)	Peer, 1971	
	*The Third Day (1962)	CMC ms film 13/19	CMC tape 322
Willan, Healey	*Anthem for the Centennial of Canadian Confederation* (1966)	BMI Can, 1966	Sim T 55562-3

* Cantata

composer	title	score	recording

SOLO SONG (for voice and piano unless otherwise indicated)

composer	title	score	recording
Beckwith, John	*A Chaucer Suite* (1962), alto, tenor, and baritone	CMC ms film 7/17	
	Four Songs from Ben Jonson's 'Volpone' (1961), voice and guitar	BMI Can, 1967	
Betts, Lorne	*A Cycle of the Earth* (1962; orchestrated 1967) [Bliss Carman]	CMC ms film 19/37	
Bissell, Keith	*Two Songs of Farewell* (1962–3) [Claude Bissell]	Waterloo, 1963	CBC SM 79
Buczynski, Walter	*How Some Things Look* (1966) [Jane Beecroft]	CMC ms film 20/36	
Coulthard, Jean	*Six Medieval Love Songs* (1962) [Latin, translated Helen Waddell]	CMC ms film 5/45	
Freedman, Harry	*Anerca* (1966) [Eskimo, translated Knud Rasmussen]	CMC ms film 6/19	CMC tape 454
Garant, Serge	*Cage d'oiseau* (1962) [Saint-Denys Garneau]	BMI Can, 1968	RCI ACM 2
Kasemets, Udo	*Five Songs for Children* (1964) [Laura E. Richards, William Allingham, Christina Rosetti]	BMI Can, 1964	
	Haiku (1961), voice, flute, cello, and piano	BMI Can, 1963	CMC large tape 15
Kunz, Alfred	*Love, Death and Fullmoon-nights* (1964), voice and instruments [haiku]	CMC ms film 24/28	
Mather, Bruce	*The Song of Blodeuwedd* (1961) voice and orchestra [Robert Graves]	CMC ms film 11/13	
Morawetz, Oskar	*Four Songs* (1966) [Bliss Carman]	CMC ms film 14/22	
Naylor, Bernard	*The Nymph Complaining for the Death of Her Faun* (1965), voice and instruments [Andrew Marvell]	CMC ms film 26/2	
Pentland, Barbara	*Three Sung Songs* (1964) [Chinese, translated C. Candlin]	CMC ms film 12/31	

composer	title	score	recording
Ridout, Godfrey	*The Ascension (Cantiones mysticae no. 2)* (1962), voice and orchestra	Harris, 1971	
Somers, Harry	*Evocations* (1966) [Harry Somers]	BMI Can, 1968	CBC SM 108

OPERA

Barnes, Milton	*Byron, the Wonderful Bandit* (1965) [Jack Oldfield and Helen Conway-Marmo]	CMC ms film 18/1	
Bissell, Keith	*His Majesty's Pie* (1966) [Keith Bissell]	Waterloo, 1966	
Kunz, Alfred	*The Watchful Gods* (1962) [Alfred Kunz]	CMC ms film 24/12	
McIntyre, Paul	*This Is Not True* (1966) [James Schevill]	CMC ms	
McPeek, Benjamin	*The Bargain* (1963) [Benjamin McPeek]	CMC ms film 25/54	
Schafer, R. Murray	*Loving/Toi* (1965) [R. Murray Schafer and Gabriel Charpentier]	Berandol, 1979	Mel SMLP 4035-6
Sirulnikoff, Jack	*This Evening* (1960) [Omar Shapli]	CMC ms film 28/2	
Vallerand, Jean	*Le Magicien* (1961) [Jean Vallerand]	CMC ms film 6/21	
Willan, Healey	*Deirdre* (1946; rev 1962–5) [John Coulter]	Berandol, 1972 (vocal score); Berandol Musicache (full score)	CMC tape 275

BALLET

Freedman, Harry	*Rose Latulippe* (1966)	CMC ms film 6/6	
Mercure, Pierre	*Incandescence* (1961)		CMC tape 393

ORGAN MUSIC

Bissell, Keith	*Sonata for Organ* (1963)	BMI Can, 1964	
	Trio Suite for Organ	Waterloo, 1963	
	Two Preludes for Organ	Waterloo, 1963	
Boivin, Maurice	*Deux pièces pour orgue*	BMI Can, 1964	

composer	title	score	recording
Buczynski, Walter	*Five Atmospheres for Organ* (1966)	CMC ms film 20/54	
Champagne, Claude	*Prière* (1963)	CMC ms	RCI 254
Clarke, F.R.C.	*Six Hymn-Tune Voluntaries* (1964)	Waterloo, 1964	
Ducharme, Guy	*Prélude pour un dimanche après la pentecôte*	BMI Can, 1962	
Fleming, Robert	*Three Pieces for Organ* (1962)	CMC ms film 4/28	
France, William	*Prelude on 'Morecambe'*	GVT, 1963	
George, Graham	*Three Fugues* (1964)	Berandol, 1970	CMC tape
	Suite on 'Grace Church, Gananoque' (1965)	Abingdon, 1972	
	Passacaglia on 'Lobe den Herren' (1963)	Gray, 1967	
Joachim, Otto	*Fantasia* (1961)	BMI Can, 1961	RCI 225; RCA CCS-1019
Kunz, Alfred	*Three Excursions for Organ* (1964)	CMC ms film 24/31	
Togni, Victor	*Five Liturgical Inventions* (1965)	World Library, 1966	
Willan, Healey	*Andante, Fugue and Chorale* (1965)	Peters, 1965	
	Fugue in E Minor (c 1960)	BMI Can, 1963	
Wuensch, Gerhard	*Sonata brève*, Op. 26 (1963)	Avant, 1966	

CHAPTER SIX

1967
Centennial Celebrations

But it is with human beings as with birds: the creative instinct has a great deal to do with the assertion of territorial rights.

Northrop Frye, *The Bush Garden: Essays on the Canadian Imagination* (1971)

The year 1967 marked the one-hundredth anniversary of the signing of the British North America Act which established the confederation of the Canadian colonies and provided the constitution under which modern-day Canada has emerged. Centennial celebrations brought forth a flurry of activity at both the local and the national levels, not the least of which were many musical presentations, new concert halls, and new works by Canadian composers. Some of the musical works focused on historical material (for example, Harry Somers's opera *Louis Riel*); some dealt with contemporary Canadian situations and problems (such as John Beckwith's *Place of Meeting* and István Anhalt's *Cento*). Many works were written on commission for a particular performer or group of performers (such as Otto Joachim's *Contrastes* for the Toronto Symphony and Clermont Pépin's *Quasars* for l'Orchestre symphonique de Montréal). For six months Expo 67 in Montreal served as the focal point for performances and commissions through its World Festival of Music and the Canadian Pavilion's Festival Katimavik, while the Centennial Commission's Festival Canada stimulated Canadian music throughout the country. For the first time Canadian composers had a relatively high profile, and a few even earned a significant proportion of their income through the various commissions they received.

Centennial year was a time for stock-taking and soul-searching as well as for celebration, and works in various musical genres reflected different ideas and concerns. The Canadian Music Centre, which played a vital role in bringing about this wave of musical creativity, compiled a comprehensive, but admittedly incomplete, list of 130 works which were composed in honour of Canada's one-hundredth birthday.[1] This list may be summarized as follows:

stage works (opera, ballet, puppet theatre)	16
radio opera	4
orchestral works	34
fanfares	4
chamber music (not including voice)	23
choral works	26
vocal works	14
keyboard works	7
film sound tracks	2

From this tabulation one can identify a strong preference for ensemble works (opera, orchestral, choral, and chamber) and a distinct lack of interest in solo keyboard music. This phenomenon is indicative of the social nature of most of the music written for the coming together of Canada's peoples during centennial year. One of the most significant musical outcomes of these celebrations was the impetus given to types of composition, particularly opera, which up to this time had been beyond the financial resources of Canadian performing groups.

OPERA

Harry Somers's *Louis Riel* (1967) stands as the most ambitious and most significant single work composed by a Canadian in connection with the centennial celebrations. It is a full-length, trilingual opera in three acts, with a cast of twenty-six soloists and a full orchestra augmented by special percussion instruments and prepared electronic tapes. Commissioned by the Canadian Opera Company, the production of *Louis Riel* was made possible by a grant from the Floyd S. Chalmers Foundation. It is not only a powerful national drama which focuses on the tragedy of a man caught in the web of French-English-Indian rivalry as well as the religious and social bigotry of the early settlements of the Canadian West, but it is also a story of human tragedy which transcends time and nation. As librettist Mavor Moore states: 'he [Riel] is an immensely colorful personification of some of the great liturgical themes of mankind. One is that of the idealist driven mad by continued betrayal by ruthless realists in whom he mistakenly trusts. Another is that of the thinker paralyzed by his thinking, the Hamlet syndrome. Another is that of the half-breed, the schizophrenic outsider who belongs to no people. Still another is that of the leader of a small nation standing in the way of "progress": is he hero or fool? And what of a mad-man unjustly hung?'[2] *Louis Riel* is filled with dramatic irony directed at the problems of the Canadian political and social arena, problems for which solutions have become no simpler with the passage of time.

Significantly *Louis Riel* is termed a music drama; the emphasis is consistently on the drama, with music serving as a vehicle rather than as an end in itself. As in R. Murray Schafer's *Requiems for the Party-Girl* (1966) one senses the influence of Berg's *Wozzeck*, another work in which an individual is caught in a web of circumstance beyond his control. Like Berg, Somers draws upon a variety of musical means, utilizing four different stylistic approaches – folk, atonal-abstract, diatonic, and various mixtures of the three.[3] Certain identifiable themes or motives recur, 'taking on different shapes according to the way events progress.'[4] At certain points Somers uses material to which a general audience can relate directly (e.g. the lullaby sung by Riel's wife Marguerite at the opening of Act III and the chorus 'We'll Hang Him Up the River' in the courtroom scene); at other points he chooses electronic tape when the drama calls for more surrealistic means (such as when Riel sees himself as the prophet David in the last scene of Act I and in the trial scene at the end where events have gone beyond Riel's power of comprehension). For the most part pitches and rhythms are specified, with some use being made of graphic notation (Act I, p 53 of score) and aleatoric writing (p 64 of score). The texture of the work is generally lean and melodies often revolve around one tone, with or without embellishments (see example 6-1). Harmonic intervals of the major seventh and minor ninth predominate in the atonal sections, with perfect fourths and fifths in the modal-diatonic parts. Another significant stylistic feature is the way in which Somers uses the cumulative principle, both within a phrase and over a complete act of the opera. A melody often results from what appears to be a series of false starts. Musical event is piled upon musical event in a long line until tension at the climax reaches the breaking-point, such as in the lament 'Kuyas' sung by Marguerite (Act III, Sc i). The dramatic power of the story, the depth of character depiction, the colour and variety of musical styles, all combine to produce a music drama which has justifiably enjoyed two revivals (1968, 1975) as well as a television presentation.[5]

The companion work created on commission for the Canadian Opera Company in 1967 was *The Luck of Ginger Coffey*, with music by Raymond Pannell and libretto by Ronald Hambleton, based upon the novel of the same name by Brian Moore. The musical style is reminiscent of Gian Carlo Menotti and Kurt Weill; the work has not enjoyed the revivals of its companion piece.

The other operas by Canadian composers which received premières in 1967 were all for radio, and each was commissioned by the CBC. They are Murray Adaskin's *Grant, Warden of the Plains*, Kelsey Jones's *Sam Slick*, and Robert Turner's *The Brideship*. Each of the operas is concerned with a Canadian theme, and in particular a theme connected with the settlement of the country in the nineteenth century. *Grant, Warden of the Plains*, with libretto by Mary Elizabeth Bayer, is based on incidents in the life of a Métis leader, Cuthbert Grant, in the Selkirk settlement in Manitoba around 1823. The musical idiom, designed for a general radio

EXAMPLE 6-1   Harry Somers, *Louis Riel* (1967), end of Act I (in the composer's hand)

audience, is a neoclassical, modal-diatonic style with inclusion of fiddle tunes and folk-like song elements. Motives are based upon perfect fourths and fifths and are obviously derived from folk sources.

Jones's *Sam Slick*, with a libretto by Rosabelle Jones which is based on Thomas Haliburton's *The Clockmaker* (1836), is also light and neoclassical in style, with the motivic augmented fourth providing dissonance and tension. The work, which follows the comic-opera tradition of using spoken dialogue, attempts to capture the spirit of wit and irreverence characteristic of the fictitious Sam Slick, the garrulous Yankee clockmaker who plied his trade in nineteenth-century Nova Scotia.

Turner's *The Brideship*, with a libretto by Vancouver writer George Woodcock, concerns itself with an episode in 1862 in which a hundred orphan girls were shipped to Victoria, BC, in order to provide wives for the miners who had arrived earlier and populate Vancouver Island. The musical style chosen by Turner is neoclassical, but leaner and more subdued than either Adaskin's or Jones's operas.

BALLET

The most significant ballet connected with the centennial celebrations was Harry Freedman's *Rose Latulippe* (1966) which, because it was completed earlier, has been discussed in chapter 5. Another ballet is *Heritage* by Srul Irving Glick, which was commissioned by the New Dance Group of Toronto. This modern-dance ballet is a saga of the Jew in Canada. Employing Jewish melodic and rhythmic figures in a romantic and theatrical manner, it is one of several works by Glick which illustrates his interest in the Jews in Canada.

ORCHESTRAL MUSIC

In keeping with the ideal of reaching as wide an audience as possible orchestral works by Alexander Brott, Maurice Dela, Srul Irving Glick, Morris Surdin, and Louis Applebaum are in a light style. The Brott *Centennial Colloquy*, written two years earlier in 1965, makes use of the parody technique, a favourite device of Brott's; the melody of *O Canada* forms the humorous subject for a fugue which follows the serious introduction. Dela's *Projection* (1966) and Glick's *Symphony No. 2* both employ jazz-like sections, while Surdin's *Concerto for Accordion and String Orchestra* and Applebaum's *Concertante* for small orchestra employ elements of the commercial style familiar to listeners though television and radio scores. On the other hand the *Symphony-Concerto* for piano and orchestra by S.C. Eckhardt-Gramatté, much like Healey Willan's *Deirdre*, is a reminder that nineteenth-century romanticism still had strong adherents among a few of Canada's composers in 1967. Motivic, tonal, and full of pianistic display, this work is, in the words of the composer, 'like life.'[6] Indeed, it represents well the life of its creator, an intense, excitable, and romantic personality.

Several 1967 works use the more contemporary styles current in the mid-1960s. One of the most avant-garde of them is *Contrastes* by Otto Joachim, which alternates between graphic and specified notation and aleatoric and serial use of the twelve-tone row, always emphasizing the element of contrast. The work, with its long dramatic line, conveys a feeling of direction not always found in sound-block pieces of the period. Although employing large-scale forces, it is a lucidly contructed work, as are Joachim's earlier works. One orchestral work, István Anhalt's *Symphony of Modules*, is so complex and technically demanding that it has yet to receive a first performance. Bruce Mather's *Orchestra Piece 1967* uses a dense polyphonic style as it exploits both colourful and subdued percussive sonorities which issue forth in pointillistic fashion over a cushion of sustained strings. The overall effect is complex and quasi-oriental in the manner of Messiaen. Clermont Pépin's *Quasars* (Symphony No. 3), also in a twelve-tone idiom, is thicker in texture, favours the instruments of the percussion family, and employs the Ondes Martenot in creating an atmosphere of 'almost stars,' the literal meaning of the title. Also featuring the Ondes is Micheline Coulombe Saint-Marcoux's *Modulaire*, a work which exploits unusual instrumental colours within a neoclassical structural framework. François Morel's *Prismes-Anamorphoses*, which is scored without strings (i.e. for wind ensemble), shows once again this composer's affinity for extra-musical visual connotations. *Prismes* refers to the 'filtering of colours through structure,' and *anamorphoses* to the reflection of form 'transformed as in geometry according to certain optical operations.'[7] This is a tone poem which does not use either 'themes or motives but textures or different tensions for contrast.'[8] The traditional ABCBA plus coda structure is retained and the work mixes specified and aleatoric elements. Jacques Hétu's *L'Apocalypse*, Op. 14, subtitled *Fresque symphonique d'après l'apocalypse de Saint-Jean*, is more conservative stylistically and retains a strong element of melodrama.

John Weinzweig's *Concerto for Harp and Chamber Orchestra* is a work in a single extended movement with six interconnected sections. Although it follows the trend of exploiting instrumental colours *per se*, it retains the lean texture and rhapsodic sections characteristic of its composer. The colouristic elements of the harp are explored in a dialogue between the solo instrument and the orchestra and result in a *Klangfarbenmelodie* typical of post-Webern pointillism (see example 6-2). Weinzweig, one of the Canadian composers most concerned with bridging the gap between the present-day composer and his audience without compromising the composer's message and style, provides a formal outline of the work in the introduction to the published score.

Harry Freedman's two 1967 works, *Armana* and *Tangents*, both employ the large orchestra in a traditional way; both use the twelve-tone technique freely, and both have titles which play on the imagination of the listener rather than provide a concrete meaning. *Armana* is an Inuit word which appealed to the composer for its sound alone. *Tangents* is a set of symphonic variations, presumably 'flying off' from the central point A, the first note of the tone row (see example 6-3). Both works are eclectic. *Armana* contains jazz, South-American elements, and French-Canadian fiddle tunes, as well as neoclassical ostinati. *Tangents* proceeds through a set of continuous variations and improvisations which result in a passacaglia-like structure. *Tangents* was commissioned by the National Youth Orchestra of Canada under a grant from the Centennial Commission, but the composer did not let that fact limit his style because, as he said, 'most of them [the players] are just about ready to become professionals.'[9]

CHAMBER MUSIC

A number of chamber music groups commissioned composers to write works for them under grants received from the federally-sponsored Centennial Commission. In the resulting pieces some of the composers continued in well-worn paths (e.g. Kelsey Jones, *Sonata da chiesa*; Jean Papineau-Couture, *Sextuor*; Jean Coul-

EXAMPLE 6-2   John Weinzweig, *Concerto for Harp and Chamber Orchestra* (1967), beginning

CONCERTO FOR HARP AND CHAMBER ORCHESTRA

JOHN WEINZWEIG (1967)

✱ PLAY DOUBLE STOPS „DIVISI" WHEN MULTIPLE STRINGS ARE EMPLOYED.

thard, *Ballade of the North*; Jacques Hétu, *Quintette*; S.C. Eckhardt-Gramatté, *Nonet* (1966) and *Piano Trio*, while others who had previously espoused neoclassicism began to move into the realm of chance music, to deal with music more as process than as fixed product. In the latter category is John Beckwith's *Circle, with Tangents*, which explores open form at the same time as it experiments with new instrumental sonorities. The work calls for harpsichord and thirteen solo strings, and, as is indicated in its detailed preface, employs distinguishing colour markings in the score to indicate cues (RED), cut-offs (BLUE), and co-ordinated parts (BROWN). These modifications of traditional notational practices are necessitated by the new freedom associated with controlled improvisation and open form. Although Beckwith had long been sympathetic to Cageian innovations (Kasemets's *Squares*, 1962, was dedicated to him and performed by him and the composer), he had, for the most part, continued to write in a neoclassical idiom (with the addition of twelve-tone writing in *Jonah*, 1963, and *Trumpets of Summer*, 1964). In *Circle, with Tangents* each instrument retains its own individuality by playing its own unique motive. Although the work shows Beckwith to be moving towards more impro-visational music, it retains some of the Beckwith trademarks from earlier periods, for example, dance-like rhythms, ostinati, and touches of humour.

Although Barbara Pentland had used controlled-improvisation techniques in *Trio con alea*, she chose not to do so in *Septet* (1967), perhaps because of the difficulties of using the organ, which has a dominant role in the work, in ensemble with the other instruments (horn, trumpet, trombone, violin, viola, and cello). However, Norma Beecroft, who had combined electronic tape with live perform-ance and spoken voice in *From Dreams of Brass*, does so again in *Two Went to Sleep*, for voice, flute, percussion, and prepared tape; the text is based on *Parasites of Heaven* (1964) by Leonard Cohen. In this work the sound elements are combined in a colourful manner, utilizing both pointillism and sound-block principles. The rhythm is unmetred and some parts are improvised; the score is marked off in seconds. A work which creates an interesting and amusing parody of the transition from the complete serialism of the late 1950s and early 1960s to the chance procedures and controlled improvisation of the mid-1960s is Sydney Hodkinson's *Dissolution of the Serial* or *Who Stole My Porridge*. What begins as an extremely serious serial work gradually dissolves into jazz, blues, and Dixie, and ends in a flurry of accelerated honky-tonk piano of the 1920s. This and later works cited in chapter 7 indicate that perhaps one of the greatest contributions of new music in the twentieth century may turn out to be the restoration of humour to music.

CHORAL MUSIC

It is not surprising that choral works formed a major part of Canada's centennial celebrations, since group singing is one of the accepted avenues for the outward expression of nationalistic feeling. The centennial works are varied, both in the texts used and in the musical styles in which they are set. A number of them employ texts by Canadian poets and explore contemporary Canadian social issues, while others pursue topics less tied to time and place. Some of the shorter works use the type of patriotic text that one would expect on a national anniversary (Louis Applebaum's *Chorale Canada*, Violet Archer's *Centennial Springtime*, God-

EXAMPLE 6-3   Harry Freedman, *Tangents* (1967), ending

frey Ridout's *When Age and Youth Unite,* and Healey Willan's *Anthem for the Centennial of Canadian Confederation.*

István Anhalt's futuristic *Cento,* written on commission for the University of British Columbia's Chamber Singers, is for voices without instruments; in this work Anhalt is a pioneer in exploring the sound potentialities of the human voice. After an exhaustive search for new sonorities *via* concrete or electronic means in the 1950s and 1960s Anhalt came to believe, like Luciano Berio and others, that the voice was an untapped source for new sound. In *Cento* some of the voices are prerecorded on tape and some are spoken live in a controlled-improvisation fashion. The text consists of a selection of ninety-nine words from parts of the poem *An Ecstasy* (1963) by Eldon Grier. The number of words is symbolic of Canada approaching its centennial, and, according to the composer, the poem is 'blunt, sober, tense, festive ... [it] sputter[s] with aggression in places, in others it convey[s] the feeling of ecstasy.'[10] The text begins and ends with an admonition for the future rather than a glorification of the past. Anhalt is not concerned with singing in the traditional sense but with a 'clearly articulated, and highly inflected, speech'[11] (see example 6-4). The final words have a double meaning, for music and society, as the singers proclaim, 'let us hear our voices again.' While the overall effect of the work is that of a mosaic of non-linear, verbal sounds, its message concerning the plight of the individual in the modern, mechanized world is clear.

John Beckwith's *Place of Meeting* is also concerned with the problems of human fulfilment in the modern world. However, this text by Dennis Lee castigates the modern city, with particular reference to the city of Toronto. The literal translation of 'Toronto,' from the Huron Indian, is 'place of meeting.' The work, which was commissioned by the Toronto Mendelssohn Choir, utilizes a stream-of-consciousness approach to various sounds of the city, from newspaper hawkers to TV commercials, complete with sarcastic and bitter references to the shortcomings of the technological society and to Toronto as a city of branch plants for multinational corporations ('made in New York ... Hong Kong ... Akron ... Düsseldorf'). Torontonians are portrayed as victims struggling for survival: 'Yonge St. flows to the kingdom of absence ... Canada is that country which does *not exist.*' Beckwith's score is an extended one (twenty-five minutes) and it employs large resources – large chorus, tenor solo, blues singer, guitar, narrator, orchestra, and two conductors. The work is in a free twelve-tone idiom, tied together by three-note motives and a small jazz ensemble which appears several times. Controlled improvisation is used extensively in the crowd scenes.

Not all of the extended choral works of 1967 are in an avant-garde idiom. Several follow the traditional twentieth-century post-romantic and neoclassical paths. Alexander Brott's *Centennial Cerebration* is based upon a bilingual text written by the composer himself and employs parodies of *O Canada* and *La Marseillaise.* Also stylistically conservative are Violet Archer's *Cantata sacra,* which is based on late-medieval dialogues, Jean Coulthard's *Pastorale Cantata* based on biblical psalms, Bernard Naylor's *Missa da camera*, and Keith Bissell's *Christmas in Canada*. André Prevost's *Terre des hommes*, composed for the opening of Expo 67's World Festival/Festival mondial, is a neo-romantic work which moves from despair to hope in its anti-war text by Michèle Lalonde. Its three movements are entitled 'Alienation,' 'Identification,' and 'Humanisation.' Three choirs, two narrators, large orchestra, and Ondes Martenot are used together with a minimum of counterpoint and a maximum of melodramatic effect.

Two smaller works, by Oskar Morawetz and Jean Papineau-Couture, were commissioned by the Festival Singers of Canada. Morawetz's *Two Contrasting Moods* is based on a text by the late-nineteenth-century Canadian poet Archibald Lampman; its chromatic, tonal style is very much in keeping with the nature of the text. Similarly Papineau-Couture's *Viole d'amour* employs a musical style suited to its text, which is taken from the more recent *Mémoire sans jour* (1960) by Rina Lasnier. Papineau-Couture uses a severe, dissonant, neoclassical style which is uncompromising in its demand on the singers. He does not employ avant-garde vocal techniques.

Two significant large choral works written in 1967 were not the result of centennial commissions. The first is Roger Matton's *Te Deum*, which was conceived for the inauguration of the Grand Théâtre de Québec but first performed in honour of the sixty-fifth anniversary of l'Orchestre symphonique de Québec. It combines the traditional Latin *Te Deum* ('We praise you, O God!') with a French text on the Creation written by Quebec poet Félix-Antoine Savard. The work shows the influence of both the dramatic qualities of Honegger's oratorios and the austere spiritualism of Stravinsky's *Symphony of Psalms* (1930). The vigorous, asymmetrical rhythmic ostinati, the brilliant orchestration, especially the colourful use of percussion, and the Debussy-like parallelisms all contribute to making this eclectic work a convincing example of its type.

R. Murray Schafer's *Gita*, which is outwardly far removed from things Canadian, is based on the original Sanskrit of the *Bhagavad Gita*, the scriptures which are to the Hindu what the New Testament is to the Christian. While the general theme of the *Gita* is the horrors of war, the excerpt which Schafer employs emphasizes the fact that man must be free from desires of the senses in order to achieve tranquillity. *Gita*, like *Threnody*, is for chorus, orchestra, and prepared tape; like *Threnody* it also employs a mixture of traditional and graphic notation as well as controlled improvisation. Most of Schafer's scores from this point on not only use graphic notation but also may be considered works of art in their own right, a feature which reflects Schafer's early training in the graphic arts as well as his growing tendency to view all art as one. Furthermore, he influenced a number of younger composers in this matter, and an increasing number of elaborate, graphic scores appeared in the late 1960s and early 1970s. In *Gita* Schafer is again successful in achieving a convincing dramatic effect while using the most direct and economic notational symbols. At the same time even though the appeal of

EXAMPLE 6-4   István Anhalt, *Cento* (1967), p 2

SECTION I_a

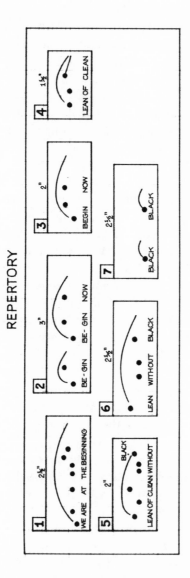

REPERTORY

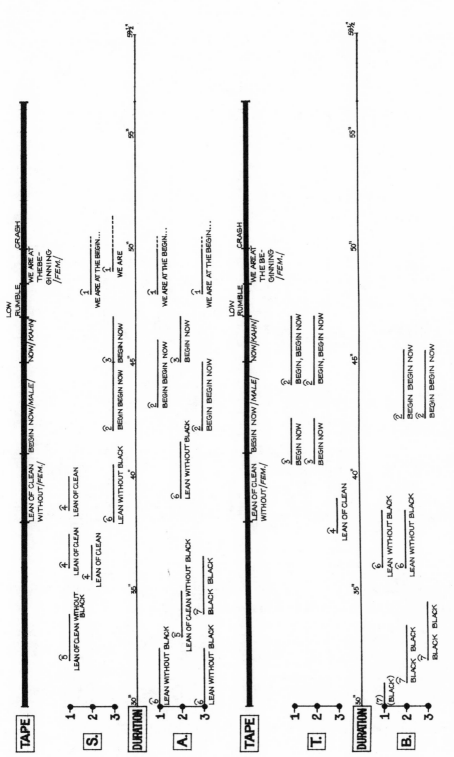

EXAMPLE 6-5 Robert Fleming, *The Confession Stone* (1967), beginning

Gita, like the *Bhagavad Gita* itself, is to the emotions rather than to the intellect, the composer achieves a lucidity of form and texture in the work. *Gita* was composed on a commission from the Fromm Music Foundation for the Tanglewood, Massachusetts, Festival in 1967.

SONG

Robert Fleming's *Confession Stone*, a cycle of eight songs written for and dedicated to contralto Maureen Forrester, is one of the few works written in centennial year for the traditional combination of voice and piano. Based on poems on the Virgin Mary by the American black poet Owen Dodson, the music captures the sincerity and personal nature of the text. The work is thoroughly romantic, occasionally sentimental. The style is close to that of early Vaughan Williams, with its many parallel fifths, sevenths, and ninths, frequent ostinati, and simple, folk-like melodies (see example 6-5). A vocal work with stylistic affinity to Fleming's *Confession Stone* is Murray Adaskin's *Of Man and the Universe*. The text by Alexander Pope is, like the text of Fleming's work, idealistic in outlook and dwells on the far-off, the romantic. Adaskin's setting is for voice, violin, and piano.

Many of the other vocal works written in centennial year employ texts which are closely connected with Canadian topics. Serge Garant's *Phrases I* uses part of a speech by Pierre Bourgault, at the time leader of the separatist Rassemblement pour l'indépendance nationale. Harry Somers's *Kuyas*, an excerpt from the opera *Louis Riel*, uses a simple but suggestive Cree Indian poem whose title means, literally, 'long ago'; it tells of hunting on the Canadian prairies. Bruce Mather's *Madrigal* is a setting of a poem by the French-Canadian mystic Hector de Saint-Denys Garneau.

Musically these works are very different. In Garant's work the voice is blended with the instrumental sounds. Ten sequences are played without interruption and may be performed in any order. *Phrases I* is typical of those 1960s works which combine serial and aleatoric elements (see example 6-6). The strong emphasis on percussion instruments and the many points of non-specified rhythms create a colourful work which is simultaneously free and controlled. It is interesting to note that the percussionist determines the direction of the pianist's part at certain places, rather than vice versa, one indication of the growing importance of the percussion instruments.[12]

With poetic licence Somers bases *Kuyas* on a west-coast Indian melody from the Nass River rather than on a perhaps more musically uninteresting Cree Indian song to match the text. The work, which is for voice, flute, and percussion, may be sung in any voice range but the composer instructs the singer always to inform the flutist to modulate accordingly. The melody tends to revolve around one note at a time; eleven different lengths of fermata are used, which the performer may

EXAMPLE 6-6   Serge Garant, *Phrases I* (1967), sequence L, p 5 (in the composer's hand)

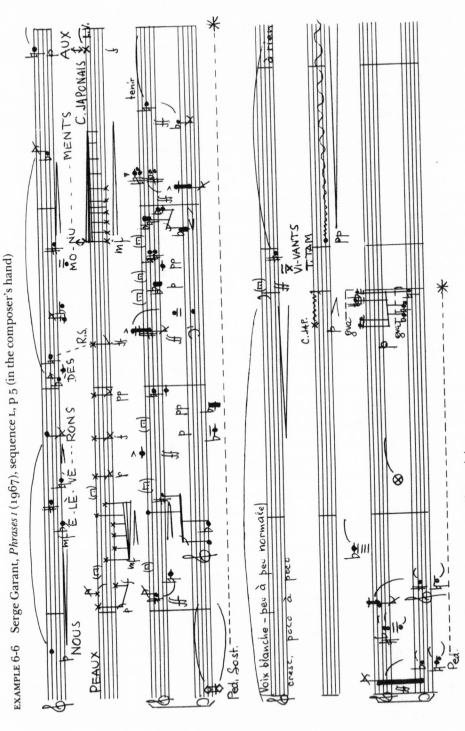

interpret freely or strictly as he wishes. The melodic intervals favoured are perfect fourths, fifths, and augmented fourths, and the line proceeds in a chant-like fashion, with much repetition and cumulative piling up of notes for dramatic effect.

Madrigal is the first in a series of five works by Mather which are based upon the work of Saint-Denys Garneau. His poetry, which is characterized by mysticism and great sensitivity, has frequently been used by composers following the cultural awakening in Quebec, a process which Saint-Denys Garneau had hoped for in the 1930s, but which came to pass only in the 1960s. Mather's setting reflects the delicate and imaginative text. The flute and voices act in *concertato* with the other instruments which periodically insert pointillistic bursts of sound between statements of the text. A Toronto-born Canadian who has become absorbed in the francophone world through his education, marriage, and professional activities, Mather represents, in this work and others, the best example of a bridge between the 'two solitudes' in Canadian music.

KEYBOARD MUSIC (PIANO AND ORGAN)

The nature of the piano did not lend itself to the national celebrations of centennial year. Furthermore, in Canada and elsewhere the piano was generally being used less as a solo instrument and more as only a part of an ensemble. One exception, however, is the *Suite Borealis* by Barbara Pentland. As the composer states, it is 'an imaginative journey across Canada as our forefathers might have experienced it – a brief *A Mare Usque ad Mare* panorama.'[13] This 'suite of the north,' as its title indicates, has five movements corresponding to the five sections of the country – 'Unknown Shores' (Maritimes), 'Settlements' (Quebec), 'Rapids' (Ontario), 'Wide Horizons' (Prairies), and 'Mountains' (British Columbia). The work is an expression of feelings, colours, and sensations rather than pictorial images of the different geographical regions of the country. In typical Pentland fashion it is characterized by a rhapsodic style made up of pointillistic, disjunct melodies, repeated rhythmic motives, constantly changing dynamics, and a texture which is basically contrapuntal but which exploits the full range of sound of the piano. A single twelve-note row ties each of the movements together.

Another exception is Walter Buczynski's *Sonata for Piano*, subtitled 'Dzięki' (i.e. 'thanksgiving'). It intersperses aleatoric sections with rhythmically specified ones and is unified by means of a six-note chromatic figure which is doubled at the major second below. The pointillism contributes to an effect of wit and humour, a feature typical of much of Buczynski's music.

Another work of interest, though not of significant musical substance, is a *potpourri* set of variations by eight composers, which is based on a Toronto opera-house waltz by Carl Zickoff, dated 1874. The piece is symptomatic of a general revival of interest in early Canadiana of all types, largely as a result of the centennial celebrations. The variations for two pianos, by Louis Applebaum, John Beckwith, Samuel Dolin, Frank Haworth, Talivaldis Kenins, Godfrey Ridout, Harry Somers, and Morris Surdin, were written for the opening of the new wing of the music division of the Toronto Public Library. In tongue-in-cheek fashion Somers named his contribution the *T.M.L. New Wing Variant Waltzer by Henri Été de Tor* and Beckwith called his the *Variation Piquant sur la Toronto Opera House Waltz.* Polytonality and parody associated with French neoclassicism are favoured by several of the composers in their settings.

The organ works written in 1967 are also few in number. Violet Archer's *Chorale Improvisation on 'O Worship the King,'* which was commissioned by Edmonton organist H. Hugh Bancroft for his recital at Expo 67, is a conservative piece which was obviously designed for a general audience. The opening interval of the hymn (a perfect fourth) is used as a prominent motive, both melodically and harmonically. Barrie Cabena's *Homage* is a set of musical portraits of ten of Canada's most distinguished organists, past and present. The movements include 'MacMillan's Majesty' (Sir Ernest MacMillan), 'Raymond's Rownde' (Raymond Daveluy), 'Willan's Whim' (Healey Willan), 'Gilbert's Grownde' (Kenneth Gilbert), and 'Hugh's Hornpipe' (Hugh McLean). The individual pieces attempt to highlight particular traits of personality or musical specialties among Cabena's colleagues in the profession.

ELECTRONIC AND FILM MUSIC

The focus for Centennial celebrations was Expo 67 in Montreal, and music and the other arts played an important part in that most successful of international exhibitions. Many of the exhibits used original film and prepared tape music to tell their various stories. As a result hundreds of thousands of Canadians and non-Canadians came into direct contact with Canadian electronic and film music. Many heard electronic music for the first time at these exhibits and readily accepted the new and unusual sounds in this context. Electronic music as the new functional art medium received wide exposure through Expo 67.[14]

One of the most popular exhibits was the National Film Board's Labyrinth in which the viewer was sent off into a symbolic maze of life – man's entry into the world, his energies and aspirations, his confidence and uncertainty, his suffering and his sacrifices, and finally the desolation of death and the promise of new birth. The composer of the score for this exhibit was Eldon Rathburn, a staff member of the NFB since 1947. The work uses conventional instruments to depict the surface features of life but electronic music to portray the world of the unknown, the labyrinth.

Other music composed for Expo 67, some of which uses electroacoustic sound in whole or in part, includes Otto Joachim's *Katimavik* (Canadian Pavilion), Gilles Tremblay's *Sonorisation du Pavillon du Québec,* Serge Garant's *L'Homme et les régions polaires* (Man and the Planet Pavilion), Maurice Blackburn's *Water* (Quebec Pavilion), and R. Murray Schafer's *Kaleidoscope* (Chemical Pavilion).

Original films, which were prominent at Expo 67, included *A Place to Stand*, which was produced by the Ontario government and featured a score by popular-music composers Dolores Claman and Richard Morris. In addition, both electronic and acoustic music was written for the Velleman puppet shows by William McCauley (*The Beauty and the Beast*), Norma Beecroft (*Undersea Fantasia*), and Robert Fleming (*Laurentian Parade; Why There Are No Frogs on the Queen Charlotte Islands*).

Through Expo 67 Canadian composers proved that they were able to communicate cogent and contemporary musical ideas to the public at large.[15]

SELECTED WORKS (composed in 1967 unless otherwise indicated)

composer	title	score	recording
STAGE WORKS			
Opera			
Adaskin, Murray	*Grant, Warden of the Plains* [Mary Elizabeth Bayer]	CMC ms film 1/7	CMC tape 479
Jones, Kelsey	*Sam Slick*	CMC ms film 10/1	CMC tape 489
Pannell, Raymond	*The Luck of Ginger Coffey*		
Somers, Harry	*Louis Riel*	CMC ms film 31/2	CMC tape 505 A, B, C
Turner, Robert	*The Brideship*	Peer (rental only)	CMC tape 504
Ballet			
Glick, Srul Irving	*Heritage*	CMC ms film 8/8	CMC tape 665
ORCHESTRAL WORKS			
Anhalt, István	*Symphony of Modules*	CMC ms	
Applebaum, Louis	*Concertante for Small Orchestra*	CMC ms film 2/4	CMC tape 599
Brott, Alexander	*Centennial Colloquy* (1965)	CMC ms film 3/14	CMC tape 384
	Paraphrase in Polyphony	CMC ms	RCI 235
Dela, Maurice	*Projection*	CMC ms film 21/13	CMC tape 541
Eckhardt-Gramatté, S.C.	*Symphony-Concerto for Piano and Orchestra*		RCI 328; RCA LSC 3175

For other works see 'Comprehensive Catalogue of New Canadian Music Written in Honour of Canada's Centennial Year, 1967,' *Musicanada*, 7 (December 1967).

composer	title	score	recording
Freedman, Harry	*Armana*	CMC ms film 6/8	CMC tape 515
	Tangents	Leeds, 1971	CBC SM 296; RCI ACM; Audat 477-4001; CAPAC-CAB tape 3; *Musican* rec. 4
Glick, Srul Irving	*Symphony No. 2*	CMC ms film 8/9	CMC tape 596
Hétu, Jacques	*Apocalypse*, Op. 14	CMC ms film 17/3	CMC tape 943
Joachim, Otto	*Contrastes*	Ricordi, 1968	CMC tape 588
Mather, Bruce	*Orchestra Piece 1967*	CMC ms film 11/3	CMC tape 501
Morel, François	*Prismes-Anamorphoses*		RCI 292
Pépin, Clermont	*Quasars (Symphonie no. 3)*	Leeds, 1976	RCI 387; RCI ACM; *Musican* rec. 12
Surdin, Morris	*Concerto for Accordion and String Orchestra*	CMC ms film 28/18	RCI 238
Saint-Marcoux, Micheline Coulombe	*Modulaire*	CMC ms	CMC tape 738
Weinzweig, John	*Concerto for Harp and Chamber Orchestra*	Leeds, 1969	CBC SM 55; RCI ACM 1

CHAMBER MUSIC

composer	title	score	recording
Beckwith, John	*Circle, with Tangents*	BMI Can, 1968	CMC tape 512
Beecroft, Norma	*Elegy* and *Two Went to Sleep* (1966–7)	CMC ms film 7/29	RCI 404; *Musican* no. 10
Coulthard, Jean	*Ballade of the North* (1965–6)	CMC ms film 5/18	
Eckhardt-Gramatté, S.C.	*Nonet* (1966)	CMC ms film 15/31	CMC tape 535
	Trio, violin, cello, and piano	CMC ms film 15/32	CMC tape 538
Garant, Serge	*Phrases I*	Berandol, 1969	RCI 240; RCI ACM 2
Hétu, Jacques	*Quintette pour instruments à vent*, Op. 13	CMC ms film 17/8	RCI 364
Hodkinson, Sydney	*The Dissolution of the Serial*		CRI SD 292
Jones, Kelsey	*Sonata da chiesa*	CMC ms	RCI 335; CBC SM 56; RCA LSC 3091
Morel, François	*Nuvattuq*, alto flute	CMC ms	RCI 409
Papineau-Couture, Jean	*Dialogues pour violon et piano*	Peer, 1973	
	Quatuor à cordes no. 2	CMC ms	RCI 362; RCI ACM
	Sextuor	CMC ms film 11/42	CMC tape 527

composer	title	score	recording
Pentland, Barbara	*Septet*	CMC ms film 12/26	CMC tape 544
Turner, Robert	*Diversities*, violin, bassoon, and piano	CMC ms film 13/16	RCI 239

CHORAL MUSIC

Anhalt, István	*Cento*	BMI Can, 1968	RCI 357
Applebaum, Louis	*Chorale 'Canada'*	CMC ms film 2/10	
	Song for the National Arts Centre [Earle Birney]	CMC ms film 2/5	
Archer, Violet	**Cantata sacra*	CMC ms film 16/44	CMC tape 458
	Centennial Springtime	CMC ms film 16/31	
Beckwith, John	**Place of Meeting*	CMC ms film 7/8	CMC tape 581
Bissell, Keith	*A Bluebird in March*	Waterloo, 1969	CMC tape 464
	*Christmas in Canada	CMC ms	
Brott, Alexander	*Centennial Cerebration*	CMC ms film 3/30	
Coulthard, Jean	**Pastorale Cantata*	CMC ms film 5/50	
Matton, Roger	**Te Deum*	CMC ms	RCI 290; Select SSC-24.188
Morawetz, Oskar	*Two Contrasting Moods* (1966)	CMC ms film 14/14	
Naylor, Bernard	*The Armour of Light*	Novello, 1967	
Papineau-Couture, Jean	*Viole d'amour* (1966)	CMC ms film 11/43	
Pépin, Clermont	*Pièces de circonstance*	CMC ms	
Prévost, André	**Terre des hommes*	CMC ms film 9/40	CMC tape 463
Ridout, Godfrey	*When Age and Youth Unite* (1966)	GVT, 1966	
Schafer, R. Murray	**Gita*	Universal (Can), 1977	CMC tape 566
Willan, Healey	*Anthem for the Centennial of Canadian Confederation* (1966)	BMI Can, 1967	

SOLO SONG (for voice and piano unless otherwise indicated)

Adaskin, Murray	*Of Man and the Universe*, voice, violin, and piano [Alexander Pope]	CMC ms film 1/23	CBC SM 277
Fleming, Robert	*The Confession Stone* [Owen Dodson]	Leeds, 1968	RCI 246
Garant, Serge	*Phrases I*, voice, piano, celeste, and percussion [Pierre Bourgault]	Berandol, 1969	RCI 240

* Cantata

composer	title	score	recording
Mather, Bruce	*Madrigal*, soprano, contralto, and instruments [Saint-Denys Garneau]	CMC ms film 11/16	
Ridout, Godfrey	*Folk Songs of Eastern Canada*, voice and orchestra	GVT, 1970 (voice and piano)	
Somers, Harry	*Kuyas*, voice, flute, and percussion [Cree Indian]	Berandol, 1971	CMC tape 508, 633

KEYBOARD MUSIC

composer	title	score	recording
Archer, Violet	*Chorale Improvisation on 'O Worship the King'*, organ	CMC ms film 16/52	ST-56722/23
Buczynski, Walter	*Sonata for Piano (Dzięki)*	CMC ms film 20/53	CBC SM 162
Cabena, Barrie	*Homage – Ten Portraits*, organ	Waterloo, 1967	CMC tape 577
Pentland, Barbara	*Suite Borealis* (1966), piano	CMC ms film 12/49	Mel SMLP 4031
Eight variations by different Toronto composers	*Variations on Opening a Music Library*, two pianos [based on a Toronto opera house waltz by Carl Zickoff, 1874]		
– Applebaum, Louis	– *Grande Valse à l'Envers*	CMC ms film 2/12	
– Beckwith, John	– *Variation Piquant sur la Toronto Opera House Waltz*	CMC ms film 7/20	
– Dolin, Samuel	– *Variations for Two Pianos*	CMC ms film 21/38	
– Haworth, Frank	– *Variation on the Toronto Opera House Waltz*	CMC ms film 23/47	
– Kenins, Talivaldis	– *Fugue on the Toronto Opera House Waltz*	CMC ms film 9/23	
– Ridout, Godfrey	– *Variation on a Canadian Theme* (?)	CMC ms film 15/41	
– Somers, Harry	– *The T.M.L. New Wing Variant Waltzer by Henri Eté de Tor*	CMC ms film 31/23	
– Surdin, Morris	– *Poco Giocoso Variation*	CMC ms film 28/22	

composer	title	score	recording
ELECTRONIC AND FILM MUSIC			
Blackburn, Maurice	film music for 'Water,' Quebec Pavilion		
Claman, Dolores, and Richard Morris	*A Place to Stand*, Ontario government film		
Delamont, Gordon	*Ontario Suite* (1965), film music for Ontario Pavilion	Kendor, 1967	1967
Garant, Serge	film music for *Man and the Polar Regions*, Man and the Planet Pavilion		
Joachim, Otto	*Katimavik*, electronic composition for Canadian Pavilion		
Rathburn, Eldon	film music for *Labyrinthe*		CAPAC-CAB tape 13 (inc)
Schafer, R. Murray	*Kaleidoscope*, multi-track electronic tape for Pavilion of Chemical Industries		
Tremblay, Gilles	24-track electronic music tape for Quebec Pavilion		

CHAPTER SEVEN

1968 to 1978
Recent Trends

The snows came early this year.
It is the beginning of a new ice age.
The wind howls at our ears as we dig for wood in the snow,
and I wonder
What this will do for music?
It'll toughen it up.
It'll reduce it to the lean shape, maybe even bare bones.
And its form will become clear as an icicle.
    From R. Murray Schafer, *Music in the Cold* (1977)

Since 1967 more music than ever before has been written by Canadian composers. The lists of holdings of the Canadian Music Centre, the main repository of scores and recordings, are witness to this fact.[1] Established composers continue to produce new works while a constantly growing group of young composers is also active.

Some interesting trends in the genres or types of compositions written in the post-centennial years can be identified. First, there has been a significant growth in the number of commissioned works, both in absolute terms and as a percentage of the whole. Of ninety orchestral works sampled for the period from 1968 to 1978, two-thirds were composed on commission. Furthermore, the Canada Council, which acts as a financial intermediary between the performing group and the composer (works are commissioned by an individual or performing group 'with a grant from the Canada Council'), has in the 1970s been responsible for the largest number of commissions. Other funding bodies include provincial arts councils (the Ontario Arts Council has been active in this regard) and various orchestral societies and performing groups. The CBC, formerly the primary commissioner of new works, now underwrites the cost of very few works. Although one cannot but rejoice at the encouragement of original orchestral music by commissions, there is reason to be concerned about the degree to which dependence on support from governmental and other granting agencies limits the freedom of the composer. Certainly the days of the romantic composer unshackled by practical considerations are over if they ever existed for the Canadian composer. Even R. Murray Schafer's rebellion against the time limit of ten minutes imposed on a work commissioned by the Toronto Symphony in 1970 had its limits; Schafer facetiously entitled the work *No Longer Than Ten Minutes* but then made it conform approximately to the prescribed time. There is always a delicate relationship between composer and commissioning body; one composer is said to have declared jokingly that his use of a large body of performers in a work sprang from his desire to see the commissioning group go bankrupt! The system works only if the composer finds a sympathetic performing group, or vice versa, and if both meet the approval of the Canada Council or some other granting body. The Canadian composer who expects to receive commissions today finds that he or she must develop a political *savoir-faire* not unlike that of the eighteenth-century musician who worked within the court-patronage system.

A second trend from 1968 to 1978 has been the increasing number of works composed for conventional chamber music ensembles, such as the string quartet, woodwind quintet, or brass quintet. Approximately 25 per cent of chamber music works fell within one of these categories; thus there has been a return to the proportions of the pre-1960 period when neoclassicism was in vogue. This phenomenon, however, seems today to be the result not so much of aesthetic or stylistic considerations but rather of the presence of permanently based ensembles who are commissioning new works. The Purcell String Quartet, which is quartet-in-residence at Simon Fraser University, has been particularly active in commissioning chamber works, and four of the most significant string quartets of the period were written for this group: Barbara Pentland, No. 3 (1969), R. Murray Schafer, No. 1 (1970), Harry Freedman, *Graphic II* (1972), and André Prévost, No. 2, 'Ad pacem' (1972). Similarly the Orford String Quartet commissioned John Beckwith's *Quartet* (1977), and the Brunswick String Quartet Clermont Pépin's *Quatuor à cordes no. 5* (1976).

For the same reason there has been a significant number of works for wind quintet written in the years 1968 to 1978. The Canadian Brass has exerted considerable influence by encouraging composers to write for it and by seeking out financial support (usually in the form of Canada Council or Ontario Arts Council grants) for the commissions. Such works as Walter Buczynski's *Olympics '76* (1976) and John Beckwith's *Taking a Stand* (1972) were written for the Canadian Brass.

An increase in the number of works for solo instrument without accompaniment (except electronic music in some cases) has also taken place (to about 15 per cent of the total). Here again the increase seems to be a result of the commission-ing policy of the Canada Council. Examples of such solo works include John Weinzweig's *Riffs* (1974) for flute, a commission initiated by flautist Robert Aitken.

In addition to the types of compositions and the circumstances under which they were written some interesting stylistic observations can be made about Cana-dian music since 1967. Generally speaking, the neo-romantic trend which began around 1960 has continued.[2] This is evident in the proliferation of music with an extramusical association of one kind or another, even in otherwise neoclassical genres such as the string quartet. Some of these works make a strong social or political statement. For instance, R. Murray Schafer's *North/White* (1973) for orchestra is an attack on the rape of the Canadian north by government and commercial interests in the name of progress. Srul Irving Glick's *i never saw another butterfly* (1968) for voice and piano is based upon actual statements by children who died in the concentration camp at Terezin, and John Weinzweig's *Dummiyah* (1969) for orchestra has the following inscription on its title page: 'Silence is the unspoken word / A shadow of something heard / Silence is the final sound of the Nazi holocaust.'[3] André Prévost's *Chorégraphie I* (1973) is a realistic depiction of the massacre of the Israeli athletes at the Olympic site in Munich in September 1972, and his *Quatuor à cordes no. 2 'Ad Pacem'* (1972) is a musical expression of his desire for world peace. Barbara Pentland's *News* (1970) for voice and orchestra is an unequivocally scornful statement of her reaction to the continual emphasis on bad and sensational news in the media, and *Foci* (1969) by István Anhalt, which is scored for an assortment of acoustic and electronic instruments, is a series of views on contemporary and past life and the inner events of the heart and mind. The text of Anhalt's work is taken from a variety of sources in an equally diverse array of languages; like a Mahler symphony, the work provides a sound picture of the world as the composer sees it.

Nationalism, an important feature of earlier romantic periods, has also been much in evidence in Canadian music after 1960, where there has been a growing trend to employ texts, subject material, or extramusical ideas from within the country, especially those related to Canada's native peoples. Harry Freedman's *Keewaydin* (1971) for ssa voices and prerecorded tape uses a text which is made up of Ontario place names taken from the Ojibwa language. Similarly, at the climax of his *Graphic II* (1972) for string quartet the players are required to shout out Ontario place names in Ojibwa, the names being chosen for their sound properties alone. Talivaldis Kenins's *Sawan-oong (The Spirit of the Wind)* (1973), a cantata for mixed chorus and orchestra, is based on an Ojibway-Cree Indian legend. Murray Adaskin's *Qalala and Nilaula of the North* (1969) is based on Inuit material, as is Derek Healey's *Arctic Images* (1971). Micheline Coulombe Saint-Marcoux's *Trakadie* (1970) grows out of its title, which is an Indian word for 'encounter on a stream,' and is realized as an encounter between prerecorded tape and percussion instruments. Similarly Saint-Marcoux's *Ishuma* (1974) for voice and mixed small ensemble, including Ondes Martenot, reflects the meaning of its title, which is the Inuit word for intelligence or the ability to think. Harry Freedman's *Klee Wyck* (1970) for orchestra is a tone poem inspired by the paintings of Emily Carr who was, in turn, much influenced by the Indians of the west coast. The title itself means 'the laughing one,' a pseudonym of the painter. And Norma Beecroft's *Three Impressions* (1973) for mixed chorus, piano, and/or percussion, on a text by Wayne Keon, utilizes modern Indian poetry. These and many other works display, on the part of the Canadian composer, increasing concern with those parts of the national mosaic which are far removed from his everyday experience.

Another manifestation of nationalism since 1967 has been the use of folk or historical themes as the basis of a work. While no single work has surpassed the dimensions of Harry Somers's music drama *Louis Riel* (1967), other significant works have appeared. John Beckwith, who has used Canadian themes as far back as his *Great Lakes Suite* (1949), does so again in his collage *The Journals of Susanna Moodie* (1973) (based on a cyclic poem by Margaret Atwood), in *Gas!* (1969) for twenty speaking voices on a 'found poem' assembled by the composer from various municipal and provincial traffic signs in south-central Ontario, and in *1838* (1970) on a text by Dennis Lee which satirizes the roles of the British, the Yankees, and the bishop in the William Lyon Mackenzie rebellion in Upper Canada in 1837. Another work using a historical theme is István Anhalt's cantata *La Tourangelle* (1975). Based on the dramatic story of Marie de l'Incarnation, who left her homeland and family in France for the pioneer task of establishing the Ursuline order in Quebec in 1639, *La Tourangelle* expresses the many psychological struggles of the prospective immigrant. It is not surprising that Anhalt, who left the relatively comfortable cultural surroundings of Budapest and Paris in the mid-1940s to take up the challenges of musical life in Canada, should identify with this story. What is surprising, however, is the mollification of Anhalt's musical style which this work represents.

Choral or solo-voice works utilizing Canadian folk-song material were characteristic of Canadian nationalism in the 1950s and early 1960s. Such works have dwindled since 1967, but there are some important exceptions: Harry Somers's *Five Songs of the Newfoundland Outports* (1968), Kelsey Jones's *Kishimaquac Suite* (1971), and Derek Healey's *Six Canadian Folk Songs* (1973). Somers's arrangements are quite intricate and use the original songs as a point of departure for a rhythmical and contrapuntal display which has caused at least one Newfoundlander to exclaim, 'we don't sing them like that!'[4]

Another tendency of romanticism, especially in the nineteenth century, was to seek out origins or first causes, and this Coulombe Saint-Marcoux attempts to do in *Alchera* (1973) for voice and instruments. The title of the work, which comes from an Australian tribal language, means 'a time for dreaming' or 'the time before matter was formed.'[5] Similarly Samuel Dolin's stage work *Drakkar* (1972) is based on the Vinland sagas which tell of the early Viking expeditions to the New World.

Historically romanticism has tended to explore exotic and unusual texts and ideas, particularly from the near and far East, and this is no less true of Canadian neo-romanticism in the 1960s and 1970s. Schafer has been particularly attracted to exoticism, as his orchestral triptych *Lustro* (1969–73), which was inspired by a trip to Turkey and Persia in 1969, indicates. *Divan i Shams i Tabriz* (1969; rev. 1970) and *Music for the Morning of the World* (1970–1), the first two parts, are based on texts by the thirteenth-century Mohammedan pantheistic mystic Jalal al-Dîn Rûmi. The third part of the triptych, *Beyond the Great Gate of Light* (1973), is based on writings of Rabindranath Tagore. Schafer's *East* (1972) for orchestra, his *In Search of Zoroaster* (1971) for large chorus and orchestra, and his *From the Tibetan Book of the Dead* ['Bardo Thödol'] (1968) for flute, clarinet, soprano solo, chorus, and tape are all instances of his interest in the exotic. To a lesser extent other composers have utilized materials and ideas from the East; for example, Brian Cherney's *Mobile IV* (1969) for soprano and chamber ensemble is based on a text by Tu Fu of the T'ang Dynasty; Jean Papineau-Couture's *Chanson de Rahit* (1972) for voice, clarinet, and piano is based on a text by the contemporary Chinese novelist Han Suyin; Alan Heard's *Voices* (1969) uses seven medieval Japanese poems in English translation; and Norma Beecroft's series of *Rasas I, II, III* (1968–74) are mood pieces inspired by the Hindu dance drama which enacts the legend of the deity Krishna and his consort Radha.

Using elements of nature as a point of departure for a work of art is another thoroughly romantic feature. One of the most noteworthy examples of the use of nature in recent Canadian music is Gilles Tremblay's *Fleuves* (1976) for orchestra. Another is Schafer's *String Quartet No. 2 'Waves'* (1976), a work which attempts to copy the asymmetrical wave patterns of the Atlantic and Pacific Oceans and transfer the wave motion to the rhythm and structure of the quartet. A concern with the musical depiction of visual colours and shapes has also characterized some recent works, such as Clermont Pépin's *Chroma* (1973) for full orchestra and *Prismes et cristaux* (1974) for string orchestra.

The predisposition of composers towards freedom of form, experimentation with new sound materials (electronic and acoustic), and unusual and evocative titles are additional manifestations of the neo-romantic spirit which has been an important part of Canadian music since 1960. A visual dimension has also been added to many composers' works through the presentation of slides, special lighting effects, or movement of the performers in the concert hall. In a few instances the sense of smell has been aroused through the use of incense, as in Otto Joachim's multi-media work *Mankind* (1972). A related trend has been for composers to make art works of their scores through elaborate graphic notation (Schafer has led the way in this regard).

At the extremes of freedom of form and sound experimentation lies the art-as-process (as opposed to art-as-product) school which, in Canada, continues to have Udo Kasemets as its most active musical exponent. In the 1970s Kasemets has become exclusively devoted to mixed-media and improvisatory presentations which date from his work at the Isaacs Gallery in Toronto (1965–9) and the Ontario College of Art (1970–   ). In November 1972 Kasemets organized a thirty-six-hour Cage-In at the Ontario College of Art to celebrate the sixtieth birthday of the avant-garde American composer John Cage with a marathon presentation of his music and readings. More recently Kasemets has produced what he terms a 'nature-sound-mix' entitled *Watearthundair: Music of the Tenth Moon of the Year of the Dragon* (1976) for the centennial celebration of the Ontario College of Art. Also his *KANADANAK* (1977) for readers, drummers, and audience is described as 'a celebration of our land and its people on the fourth day of the waxing phases of the first moon of the year of the serpent.'

An outgrowth of Cageian influences has resulted, in Canada and elsewhere, in a trend to deformalize concert manners with a view to minimizing the barriers between composers, performers, and audiences. Unorthodox spatial arrangements continue to be invented to create new sound experiences for the listener. Musical performances have even taken on the appearance of theatrical events; the performers are often asked to move about in the concert hall and utilize props of one kind or another. The score for Beckwith's *Taking A Stand* (1972), written for the Canadian Brass, includes a chart which indicates the procession of movements of each player throughout the work (moves are made at varying speeds as dictated by the music) (see example 7-1). Other works of this type include John Weinzweig's *Pieces of Five* (1976), Barbara Pentland's *Occasions* (1974), and Sydney Hodkinson's *Another ... Man's Poison* (1970).

The extension of sound resources by electronic means has continued to develop in Canadian music in the post-1967 period. More and more electronic-music laboratories have sprung up and the acquisition of various types of synthesizers has made the technical side of the composer's work much easier. A work by Otto Joachim entitled *5.9* (1971) is designed to show how quickly (30 minutes) an electronic work can be put together with a synthesizer in contrast to the older record-and-splice technique. Canadian composers have continued to develop the use of electronic means as an added instrument or choir, along with conventional instruments. Schafer, Saint-Marcoux, and Anhalt are among the most successful composers in this regard. A new feature of electronic music since 1967 has been the development of on-the-spot creation in contrast to advanced preparation in the tape studio. Joachim and Saint-Marcoux are leaders in this area. Paradoxically, as improvisation has reached out to include the electronic media, some composers have become increasingly ingenious in developing highly mathematical forms of organization in acoustic works – for example, Serge Garant in his *Offrande I, II* and *III* (1969–71).

EXAMPLE 7-1   John Beckwith, *Taking a Stand* (1972), preface

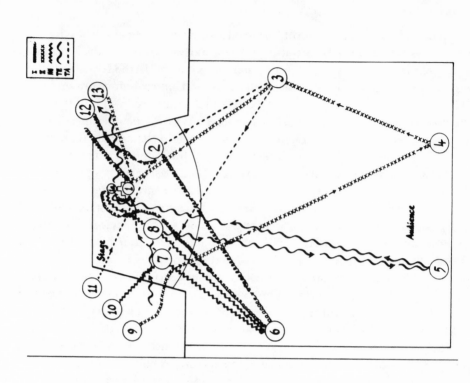

Premièred by the Canadian Brass at Stratford Festival, August 25, 1972.

Duration: about 15 mins.

I : 1st trumpet, playing trumpets in B flat and D
II : 2nd trumpet, playing trumpet in B flat and Flügelhorn
HN : Horn in F
TE : Trombone, playing also Euphonium.
TA : Tuba

Preparation:

I. Carry two trumpets plus two mutes (straight, cup) for B flat trumpet), begin with straight mute in B flat trumpet
II. Carry trumpet and Flügelhorn plus two trumpet mutes (straight, cup)
HN. Horn mute at **1a**
TE. Euphonium and two trombone mutes (straight, cup) at **5**
TA. Tuba mute at **3**

Positions:

Chart (right) shows processional movement of each player. Numbers indicate location of stands. Moves should be made with varying degrees of speed and slowness, and should appear motivated by the music.
Stand numbers correspond to circled numbers in the score. Stand **1a** should be played on a small raised platform with two or three steps leading up on each side. In the following short passages, the two participants should face each other and play "to" each other: I and II (C to E), TE and TA (E to F), I and TE (H to J).

Tempo and coordination:

Arrows in the score indicate cues (they are also given in the parts). MM marks affect only individual lines, not the ensemble. A stroke through a note-group suggests a rapid, irregular manner of playing.
Pauses and breaths are always flexible according to the context, and are marked with conventional pause-mark (sometimes in brackets), or comma, or hairline with comma.

Rehearsal procedure:

Suggested passages for separate rehearsal prior to full-ensemble rehearsal or walk-through
1 / Beginning to **B** without TE   5 / **F** to **H** without TA
2 / HN, TE, TA, **B** through **E**   6 / II and TE, **H** to **J**
3 / I and II, **B** through **E**   7 / J to **K**, I and TA, II and HN
4 / TE and TA, **E** to **F**   8 / L to end, HN and TA, I and II

Lighting:

It is recommended that, if possible, the piece begin and end in darkness. Lights on centre stage should fade up gradually during the first two lines of music in the score; they should fade to darkness again during the last two lines of music in the score.

Note:

The musical content has three sources — an original blues melody 52 bars long, heard at the start in the D trumpet, at the end in a different form in the horn, and elsewhere in the piece, various scale-formations derived from the same blues melody, and a changeable nine-note series, again related to the basic melody

In their search for new sounds some Canadian composers have continued to explore the potentialities of that most basic of sound sources, the human voice, and have used it in new and evocative ways. As noted earlier, the leader in this area has been Anhalt, who followed his *Cento* (1967) with a more extended work of larger scale, *Foci* (1969).[6] In *Foci* Anhalt extends the principle of word fragmentation to several languages and a variety of sources such as the New Testament, the Odyssey, Zohar, Ishtar, Voodoo, a dictionary of psychology, legal formulae, and so on. The overall effect is non-linear, but the message concerning the importance of the soul as the life principle is nevertheless clear. Other composers who have become similarly involved with vocal experimentation include Somers (*Voiceplay*, 1971, for solo voice), Saint-Marcoux (*Ishuma*, 1974, for voice and instruments), Denis Lorrain (*P-A*, 1970, for eight mixed voices), and Barry Truax (*Moon Dreams*, 1971, for vocal ensemble).

Lest the reader assume that most composers writing in the 1970s are avant garde, it should be noted that several of the older, and a few of the younger, composers continue to write in the neoclassical and post-romantic traditions. Such works as Oskar Morawetz's *Suite for Piano* (1968) and *Crucifixion* (1968) for unaccompanied mixed chorus, Violet Archer's *Concertino for Clarinet and Orchestra* (1971), Jean Coulthard's *Lyric Sonatina* (1969) for bassoon and piano, Adaskin's *Qalala and Nilaula of the North* (1969) for winds, strings, and percussion, Godfrey Ridout's *The Domage of the Wise* (1968) for SATB chorus, and Robert Turner's *Eidolons* (1972), subtitled *Twelve Images for Chamber Orchestra*, are written in more conservative idioms.

There is some indication that the stylistic pendulum may be swinging back towards the centre: composers such as John Weinzweig (*Pieces of Five*) and Jean Papineau-Couture (*Slano*, 1975) have recently returned to the writing of fully prescribed scores after having experimented with aleatoric and controlled-improvisation techniques in the 1960s and early 1970s. And others, such as Somers (*Music for Solo Violin*, 1973), Anhalt (*La Tourangelle*), Schafer (*String Quartet No. 2 'Waves,'* 1976), Alan Heard (*Sinfonia nello stile antico*, 1977, for orchestra), and Weinzweig (*Riffs*, 1974, for solo flute), have returned to the writing of music with clearly defined tonal centres in at least part of their works.

The last of the general features of post-1967 Canadian music, and one which is perhaps more significant than any other, is the increase in the number of works of a humorous nature. Whether this increase is the result of the greater self-confidence generated since the 1960s, or is a psychological release brought on by deleterious world events, or simply a desire for more communication between the composer and his audience is a matter of speculation. Quite often the humour is established through surprise quotations from familiar works (the device of quotation, humorous or not, is a favoured one in this period). For their contributions to Canadian humour alone, the following works are welcome additions to the literature: Gabriel Charpentier's *An English Lesson* (1968), which pokes fun at French-

English language difficulties; Schafer's *Son of Heldenleben* (1968), which satirizes the excesses of late-nineteenth-century German romanticism; Walter Buczynski's *Burlesque* (1970), which exposes the subconscious mind of the musician, whose teaching often interferes with the more desirable activities of practising and composing; Paul Pedersen's electronic work written just prior to Pierre Elliott Trudeau's wedding and entitled *For Margaret, Motherhood and Mendelssohn* (1971); Lothar Klein's *The Philosopher in the Kitchen* (1974), which juxtaposes the aesthetic and the biological in its 'gastronomical meditations for alto and orchestra'; Peter Paul Koprowski's *Quotations* (1978) for electronic tape, which shows the influence of the theatre of the absurd; Beckwith's *Taking A Stand* for five players, eight brass instruments, fourteen music stands, and one platform, which exploits the element of surprise associated with players moving about in the concert hall; Dolin's *Concerto for Piano and Orchestra* (1974) and Cherney's *Tangents I* (1975) for cello and prepared tape, both of which satirize the virtuoso performer; and Weinzweig's *Private Collection* (1971–5) for voice and piano, which parodies sixteenth-century love songs, operatic arias, and jazz 'scat' singers all in one work. However, the work which most captures this writer's imagination is Freedman's *The Explainer* (1976), a satire on contemporary music jargon and the music-appreciation lecturer. In a not-so-gentle fashion it lampoons the excesses and ambiguities of the new-music analyst and reminds the listener that the composer himself does, and indeed must, have the first and last word in the art of music.

Since 1967 there has been a great increase in the number of persons taking up the art of musical composition, not only because the number of full-time music students in Canadian universities has increased dramatically (in 1958 there were approximately 200 music majors studying at Canadian universities; by 1977 this number had swelled beyond 5000), but also because the creation of music itself has had greater appeal. In the 1950s and 1960s the areas of performance and music education attracted the largest number of students. While they still do so in the 1970s, more music students each year are specializing in the creation of music (composition) or the scholarly study of it (musicology). Before 1960 composers were generally trained either outside the university or outside Canada entirely, but this pattern has changed as more university schools and faculties of music have developed. Some of our younger composers (i.e. those born since 1940) are, in alphabetical order: Raynald Arseneault (b 1945); Kevin Austin (b 1948); Michael Baker (b 1942); Martin Bartlett (b 1939); Ginette Bellavance (b 1946); Richard Boucher (b 1946); Walter Boudreau (b 1947); Michel-Georges Brégent (b 1948); Lloyd Burritt (b 1940); Gordon Callon (b 1945); Brian Cherney (b 1942); Peter Clements (b 1940); Paul Crawford (b 1947); Victor Davies (b 1939); Marcelle Deschênes-Harvey (b 1939); Edward Dawson (b 1951); William Douglas (b 1944); John Fodi (b 1944); Clifford Ford (b 1947); Marc Fortier (b 1940); Steven Gellman (b 1948); Michel Gonneville (b 1950); Hugh Hartwell (b 1945); John Hawkins (b 1944); Alan Heard (b 1942); Richard Henninger (b 1944); Peter Huse (b 1938);

Peter Paul Koprowski (b 1947); Robert LePage (b 1951); Michel Longtin (b 1946); Denis Lorrain (b 1948); John Mills-Cockell (b 1943); David J. Nichols (b 1949); Nil Parent (b 1945); Jean-Claude Paquet (b 1950); Alex Pauk (b 1945); David Paul (b 1948); Allan Rae (b 1942); John Rea (b 1944); Myke Roy (b 1950); Donald Steven (b 1945); Jerome Summers (b 1944); Pierre Trochu (b 1953); Barry Truax (b 1947); and Claude Vivier (b 1948).

Like the United States, Canada may be said to be a country of immigrants. After World War II Canada benefited from the immigration of such composers as Oskar Morawetz, István Anhalt, Talivaldis Kenins, Richard Johnston, Otto Joachim, and Udo Kasemets. Since 1960 many more composers who were trained elsewhere have moved to Canada and continue to make a strong contribution to the creative musical life of the country; these include, in alphabetical order: Jack Behrens (b 1935, from USA to Simon Fraser University and the University of Western Ontario); Quenten Doolittle (b 1925, from USA to the University of Calgary); José Evangelista (b 1943, from Spain to Université de Montréal); Malcolm Forsyth (b 1936, from South Africa to the University of Alberta); Arsenio Girón (b 1932, from USA to the University of Western Ontario); Bengt Hambraeus (b 1928, from Sweden to McGill University); Derek Healey (b 1936, from England to the University of Guelph); Cortland Hultberg (b 1931, from USA to the University of British Columbia); Lothar Klein (b 1932, from USA to the University of Toronto); Rudolf Komorous (b 1931, from Czechoslovakia to the University of Victoria, BC); Michael R. Miller (b 1932, from USA to Mount Allison University); Robert Riseling (b 1937, from USA to the University of Western Ontario); Thomas Schudel (b 1937, from USA to the University of Regina); Ronald Tremain (b 1923, from New Zealand to Brock University); Elliot Weisgarber (b 1919, from USA to the University of British Columbia); Eugene Wilson (b 1937, from USA to the University of British Columbia); and Gerhard Wuensch (b 1925, from Austria and USA to the Universities of Toronto, Calgary, and Western Ontario). All these composers came to Canada to assume teaching positions in the university music schools which experienced an unprecedented growth in the 1960s and 1970s.

KEYBOARD MUSIC

The trend away from the piano as a solo vehicle, a trend which began around 1960, has continued to the present (1979). Nevertheless, while most Canadian composers prefer to incorporate the piano into chamber music ensembles, some composers have written interesting solo works which fall generally into one of three categories: experimental works which expand the sound resources of the piano as well as the structural elements of the music; neoclassical works in the style of the 1940s and 1950s; and didactic works designed to introduce contemporary idioms and performance techniques to the young player at an early stage in his or her development.

Of the experimental works John Weinzweig's *Impromptus* (1973) and Derek Healey's *Lieber Robert* (1974) use the retrospective-quotation technique which has found favour with many European and American composers in the late 1960s and early 1970s. The former consists of a series of short fragments, some from Weinzweig's own work and some from his memories of the past, which may be performed in any sequence (the composer has indicated a preference for the one he likes best). A certain amount of sound experimentation occurs with directions such as 'stamp pedal and floor simultaneously to cause strings to vibrate' (segment no. 4), 'fingers on music ledge' (segment no. 11), and 'slow, deliberate mimetic actions on keyboard surface only' (segment no. 20). Healey's work, on the other hand, combines live piano performance with prerecorded tape, while at the same time it uses many quotations from the works of Robert Schumann upon which the piece is based. Jean Papineau-Couture's *Complémentarité* (1971) also experiments with various new sound possibilities which can be derived from the piano (including a falling piano lid) and uses a combination of approximate and non-specified rhythmical values.

Barbara Pentland's *Vita brevis* (1973), Bruce Mather's *In memoriam Alexander Uninsky* (1974), and Jack Behrens's *Taos Portraits* (1976) all add a personal, extra-musical element but use the piano mostly in the traditional manner. *Vita brevis* is dedicated to 'J.H.', presumably the composer's husband, John Huberman, while *In memoriam* is in honour of a revered piano teacher of Mather's, and *Taos Portraits* is a series of musical sketches of the composer's associates at an artists' colony in Taos, New Mexico. Pentland's work is typically rhapsodic; the outer slow movements are separated by a fast centre movement which is itself characterized by dramatic bursts of four- to eight-note motives interrupted by silences. The work ends in a mood of resignation. Mather's work is linear and rhythmically complex; it is based on periodic and unidirectional phrases performed at ten different speeds. Behrens's piece uses the familiar-quotation technique interspersed with pointillistic and contemplative interjections.

More theatrical in nature are Walter Buczynski's *Zeroing In* (1971), *Zeroing In #5* (*'Dictionary of Mannerisms'*) (1972), and *Burlesque* (1970), each a one-performer piece for piano, voice, and prerecorded tape. Each provides an example of the humour found in many Canadian works of this period.

Noteworthy works for two pianos are John Hawkins's *Etudes for Two Pianos* (1974) and Bruce Mather's *Sonata for Two Pianos* (1970), each of which exploits the use of piano harmonics, sympathetic vibration of strings, and pointillistic textures. In addition to their contributions as composers, both Hawkins and Mather continue to play an important role as piano performers of new music.

Some of the older composers have continued to write in the neoclassical style of their earlier periods. Violet Archer's *Sonatina No. 3* (1973) follows, in each of its three movements, the tonal-modal harmony and two-part contrapuntal texture which are characteristic of her style. George Fiala's *Piano Music No. 1* (1976) is similarly neoclassical in its ostinati figures, modal harmonies, and lean, contrapuntal textures. However, Oskar Morawetz, whose early works such as the *Fantasy in D Minor* (1948) are clearly late-romantic in style, has moved towards the greater economy and leaner contrapuntal textures of neoclassicism in *Suite for Piano* (1968) and *Fantasy for Piano* (1973). At the same time romantic expressiveness remains one of the key features of these pieces. Another composer who follows the precepts of neoclassicism is Michael R. Miller, as can be seen in his *Fantasy Variations* (1971) for piano.

While many composers have chosen to ignore the piano as a vehicle for solo concert music, a significant number have composed teaching pieces or studies in an attempt to introduce contemporary music to the young. Such works as Brian Cherney's *Pieces for Young Pianists*, books I, II, III (1968), Barbara Pentland's *Music of Now*, books I, II, III (1969–70) (see example 7-2), Gerhard Wuensch's *Spectrum* (1969), thirty studies, Talivaldis Kenins's *Diversities* (1967), Jean Coulthard's *Music of Our Time* (1977), and the *Horizon Series*, books I, II, assembled by Waterloo Music Company Press, have been added to the earlier *12 × 12* (1951) by Harry Somers and *Twelve 12-tone Pieces* (1959) by Otto Joachim to form an important body of original material by Canadian composers for the beginning and intermediate player. Other composers who have contributed to this literature over the years are John Beckwith, George Fiala, Clermont Pépin, Derek Healey, Robert Fleming, Harry Freedman, Violet Archer, Ann Southam, and Udo Kasemets.

This development in the field of private studio teaching, which parallels the John Adaskin Project in school music, has been greatly enhanced by the addition of Canadian music to competitive festival and conservatory examination lists. One non-competitive festival, conducted by the Contemporary Showcase Association (renamed in 1979 Alliance for Canadian New Music Projects) has, in fact, specialized in this area by holding since 1970 a biennial festival which features only contemporary (and since 1976 only contemporary Canadian) music.[7] Besides solo-piano and organ classes the Contemporary Showcase festival includes all orchestral instruments, solo percussion, piano accordion, as well as chamber, orchestral, band, and choral ensembles. In addition, there is a category for student compositions with the stipulation that the composer must be under twenty-one years of age.

As noted throughout this book, Canadian organ music has generally been of the conservative, functional variety, music which an organist has composed for himself or his colleagues for use in a church service. Concert or recital pieces, such as Willan's *Introduction, Passacaglia and Fugue* (1916) and Joachim's *Fantasia* (1961), have been few and far between. An interesting feature of post-1967 music is that some of the younger composers have taken to writing concert pieces for organ and have expanded the sound dimensions of the instrument in doing so. Healey's *Summer 73/Ontario*, Op. 44, for organ and tape, Denis Lorrain's *Séquence* (1973), John Fodi's *Erro*, Op. 40 (1974), and Bruce Mather's *Music for Organ, Horn*

EXAMPLE 7-2

Barbara Pentland, *Music of Now* (1969–70), 'Duo (Pentatonic Canon),' Book 3, No. XIX

1. DUO (Pentatonic Canon)

Introducing $\frac{7}{4}$ meter by alternate $\frac{3}{4}$ and $\frac{4}{4}$ bars, which make it easier to read and to feel the rhythm.

This piece is "reversible" (see preface). When the R.H. is playing in the lower octave it should omit the final F in the cadence and hold the G.

and Gongs (1973) are cases in point. Other works which indicate a renewed interest in concert or extended organ music are Lorne Betts's *Improvisations on B-A-C-H* (1969) and *Lucis creator optime* (1976), Walter Buczynski's *Psalm for Organ* (1977), Clifford Ford's *Piece for Organ No. 2* (1973), Gerhard Wuensch's *Toccata nuptialis* (1976), and a series of sonatas for organ by Barrie Cabena. John Beckwith's *Upper Canadian Hymn Preludes* (1977) for organ and prepared tape blends his love of early musical Canadiana with certain Ivesian techniques and adds a touch of the 1970s with the addition of the electronic element.

A new category of keyboard music has come into being in this period through a series of works for the free-bass accordion, an instrument which has gained a degree of acceptance largely through the efforts of Joseph Macerollo, a Toronto-based performer and teacher. One of the most prolific composers of new music for the free-bass accordion is Gerhard Wuensch, as can be seen in his *Four Mini-Suites* (1968), *Sonata da camera* (1970), *Alberta Set* (1971), a series of twelve short tone paintings of Alberta, *Monologue* (1972), *Diversions* (1972), and *Deux sentiments* (1973). Each work uses a conservative, neoclassical style typical of Wuensch's other works. Other composers who have added to this repertoire are Samuel Dolin (*Sonata*, 1970; see example 7-3), Talivaldis Kenins (*Three Fugues*, 1973), and Morris Surdin (*Serious I–VIII*, 1969, and *Serious IX–XVI*, 1973). Dolin's *Sonata* shows the influence of electronic music by transferring to the medium of the acoustic accordion many of the effects of tape music.

ORCHESTRAL MUSIC

Orchestral music has continued along the paths established in the early 1960s, with the repertoire about evenly divided between works composed in a neo-classical idiom and those which experiment with new acoustic and organizational phenomena. Many of the works in both stylistic categories utilize extramusical elements, thus underlining the essentially romantic mood of the period. However, from the mid-1970s onwards one can note a tendency towards less experimentation, perhaps because a large percentage of the works were commissioned by orchestras whose players, conductors, and boards of directors are generally conservative in their tastes. There is also some indication that the composers themselves have grown weary of constant experimentation and are returning to more traditional means in their musical expression.

Most of the neoclassical works are by composers of the older and middle generations, with some exceptions. Murray Adaskin's *Nootka Ritual* (1974), *Qalala and Nilaula of the North* (1969), and *In Praise of 'Canadian Painting in the Thirties'* (1975) all employ the neoclassical idiom which Adakin has used since the late 1940s. As is obvious from the titles, each also has a nationalistic, extramusical element associated with it. A number of other works of the period likewise blend classical form and romantic content, for example, Milton Barnes's *Shebetim* (1974),

EXAMPLE 7-3 Samuel Dolin, *Sonata* (1970), beginning of first movement, 'Fantasy'

1. ⌐ *Bellows out,* V *bellows in.*
2. *Play these accents by forcing the bellows, producing a choked effect to the sustained cluster in the right hand.*
3. *At this point, the bellow direction is inwards. After the ♩ is played, push in the air button while sustaining the note. The bellow direction should then be changed on every sixteenth note. Keep the hand close to the keyboard and the fingers as close as possible to the keys. As continuous a sound as possible should be achieved.*

Norman Sherman's *Thesis for Orchestra* (1975), Alexander Brott's *Cupid's Quandary* (1975) and *The Young Prometheus* (1969), Jean Coulthard's *Canada Mosaic* (1974), George Fiala's *Montreal* (1968), Srul Irving Glick's *Lamentations: Sinfonia Concertante No. 2* (1972), Richard Johnston's *Portraits* (1972), Michael R. Miller's *Capriccio on the Seven Ages of Man* (1972), Ann Southam's *Waves* (1976), Elliot Weisgarber's *Autumnal Music* (1973), and Robert Turner's *Eidolons: Twelve Images for Chamber Orchestra* (1972).

Only a few works use the traditional title of symphony: Jacques Hétu, No. 3 (1971), Talivaldis Kenins, No. 4 (1972), Leslie Mann, No. 1 (1973), and Thomas Schudel, No. 1 (1971). Both Hétu's and Kenins's symphonies are for chamber orchestra, the former showing the influence of neoclassical counterpoint and the latter some experimentation with controlled improvisation and quarter-tones. The Schudel work is for a large orchestra and is motivic in its organization, whereas the Mann symphony is late-romantic in style. Three works come close to the symphony genre: *Symphonic Etudes (Symphony No. 3)* (1972) by Lothar Klein, *Symphonic Perspectives ('Kingsmere')* (1974) by Charles M. Wilson, and *Mouvement symphonique no. 3* (1974) by Roger Matton. Klein's and Matton's works show an indebtedness to Stravinsky, an important influence throughout both composers' careers. Wilson's piece has an extra-musical component in that it is based on a short story from *Noman* by Gwendolyn MacEwen. In this work the tension between the transplanted culture of Europe and the wild physical reality of the new world is translated into musical terms.

A number of works fall within the concerto genre. Robert Aitken's *Concerto for Twelve Solo Instruments and Orchestra* (1968) is in a traditional neoclassical style, a style from which Aitken was soon to depart in favour of experimental sound-mass and controlled-improvisation techniques. Other works showing one or more attributes of neoclassicism are Hétu's *Concerto pour piano* (1969) (see example 7-4) and *Fantaisie pour piano et orchestre* (1973), Klein's *Music for Violin and Orchestra* (1972), Lorne Betts's *Concerto for Violoncello, Piano and Orchestra* (1976), George Fiala's *Concerto for Violin and Orchestra* (1973) and *Sinfonietta Concertata* (1971) for free-bass accordion, harpsichord, and string orchestra, Kenins's *Concerto for Violin and Orchestra* (1974), Gerhard Wuensch's *Concerto for Piano and Chamber Orchestra* (1971), Turner's *Concerto for Two Pianos and Orchestra* (1971) and *Chamber concerto for Bassoon and Seventeen Instruments* (1973), Clermont Pépin's *Monade III* (1972) for violin and orchestra, Walter Buczynski's *Concerto for Violin, Violoncello and Orchestra* (1975), Alfred Kunz's *Concerto for Piano and Orchestra* (1975), Oskar Morawetz's *Improvisation for Cello and Orchestra* (1973), Godfrey Ridout's *Concerto Grosso* (1974) for violin, piano, and strings, and John Weinzweig's *Divertimento No. 4* (1968) for clarinet and orchestra. Some concerti or concerti grossi are more avant-garde in style than these works, as their use of prepared tape, aleatoric devices, quarter-tones, controlled improvisation, and theatrical staging indicates. Such works as Samuel Dolin's *Concerto for Piano and Orchestra* (1974), John Fodi's *Concerto for*

EXAMPLE 7-4   Jacques Hétu, *Concerto pour piano* (1969), beginning of third movement

Viola and Two Wind Ensembles (1972), Brian Cherney's *Chamber Concerto for Viola and Ten Players* (1974–5), Edward Dawson's *Concerto Grosso I* (1974), André Prévost's *Concerto pour violoncelle et orchestre* (1976), Norma Beecroft's *Improvvisazioni concertanti no. 3* (1973), and Weinzweig's *Divertimento No. 6* (1972) for alto saxophone and string orchestra employ some or all of these devices. Many of the works mentioned here, neoclassical and avant-garde both, were commissioned by a soloist who subsequently took part in the first performance.

A number of orchestral works which feature experimental techniques but without soloist have been written since 1967. Most contain an extra-musical association, several of which relate to Canadian topics. As with the concerti, elements of theatre are sometimes combined with the music so that the presentation of a work becomes not just a musical performance but also a theatrical event. New ways of presenting musical material, including the sound-mass principle associated with Ligeti and Penderecki, the group-composition or controlled-improvisation techniques of Stockhausen, and the music-as-process rather than music-as-product concepts of Boulez and Cage, may be found in the orchestral scores. These same works often expand the normal sound-producing sources through acoustic and electronic means. Some of the noteworthy avant-garde orchestral works include Micheline Coulombe Saint-Marcoux's *Hétéromorphie* (1970), Harry Freedman's *Graphic I* (1971) and *Tapestry* (1973), Serge Garant's *Offrande I* (1969) and *Offrande II* (1970), Hugh Hartwell's *Sonata for Orchestra* (1975), John Hawkins's *Variations for Orchestra* (1970), André Prévost's *Chorégraphie I* (... *Munich, septembre 1972* ...) (1973), *Chorégraphie III* (1976), and *Evanescence* (1970), John Weinzweig's *Dummiyah/Silence* (1969), Gilles Tremblay's *Fleuves* (1976), Derek Healey's *Arctic Images* (1971), Peter Clements's *Suite Grotesque* (1972), François Morel's *Radiance* (1971–2), Clermont Pépin's *Chroma* (1973) and *Prismes et cristaux* (1974), Barbara Pentland's *Res musica* (1975), and Robert Aitken's *Nekuia* (1971).

Undoubtedly the Canadian composer of avant-garde orchestral music who has attracted the widest attention since 1967, both in Canada and abroad, has been R. Murray Schafer. As a neo-romanticist Schafer represents in his works the epitome of the stylistic features which have dominated Canadian music since 1960. His *Son of Heldenleben* (1968), commissioned by the Orchestre symphonique de Montréal and only his second work for large orchestra (the first was *Canzoni for Prisoners*, 1962), is in content a semi-eulogistic and semi-satirical retrospective of late-nineteenth-century German romanticism. The quotations from the parent work of Richard Strauss have a surrealistic character which underline Schafer's love-hate relationship with his model. There can be no doubt, however, of the satirical nature of the programme notes attached to the score which contain 700 words of description – and all in one sentence!

As noted above, the Toronto Symphony offered Schafer a commission in 1970 but stipulated that the work be no longer than ten minutes in duration;

Schafer promptly incorporated this limitation into his title, *No Longer Than Ten Minutes*. Furthermore, Schafer imposed some conditions of his own: he insisted that the work be performed at the beginning of the concert or immediately following intermission; that the percussionist play long crescendi in response to applause (if any) at the end of the work (thus giving an open-ended dimension to the length); that a string quartet play a dominant seventh chord leading into the next piece; and finally that the work be performed only if all the composer's directions are followed.

Subsequent orchestral works by Schafer continue to exhibit extra-musical elements of one kind or another. *East* (1972), which was commissioned by the National Arts Centre Orchestra for its first European tour in 1973, is an instrumental meditation on a text from the Hindu *Isha-Upanishad* in English translation:

> The self is one. Unmoving it moves faster than the mind. The senses lag but self runs ahead. Unmoving it outruns pursuit. The self is everywhere, without body, without shape, whole, pure, wise, all-knowing, far-seeing, self-depending, all-transcending. Unmoving it moves far away, yet near, within all, outside all.[8]

The composer gives the following note of explanation as to how the text is translated into sound:

> The forty-eight words of the text are punctuated by forty-eight gongs, sounding approximately every ten seconds. Each letter in the text is given a pitch value depending on its frequency of occurrence in the text, and the note-patterns arising from the words form the harmonic and melodic material which the orchestra plays and occasionally sings.[9]

North/White (1973) is a work with a sociopolitical message, specifically a denunciation of the devastation of the Canadian north by governmental and commercial interests in the name of progress. Through the orchestra Schafer creates a realistic simulation of gurgling water and grinding machinery, and even includes a 'live' snowmobile to make his point. As in his earlier *Threnody* (1966), Schafer's message is unequivocal. *Train* (1976), for junior string orchestra and percussion with optional winds, was commissioned by the Contemporary Music Showcase Association and is a sequel to the composer's *Statement in Blue* (1964). Composed during a trip across the country and back again on the CPR in June 1976, the length of the work is scaled to the distance between Vancouver and Montreal. Each one thousand kilometres is represented by one minute of music, so that the work is four minutes and thirty-eight seconds in length. Each station-stop is punctuated by percussion, with night stations represented by bell instruments and day stations by drums.

Schafer's most ambitious works, in true romantic tradition, defy neat categorization. They are essentially multi-sectional stage works in progress. The first of these is *Loving/Toi* (1965), the second *Patria* (1966–78), and the third *Lustro* (1969–73). The first and third movements of the triptyque *Lustro* (Latin, 'light') feature the orchestra and thus may logically be discussed in this section.

Divan I Shams I Tabriz (1969, rev 1972), part 1 of *Lustro*, represents Schafer's strong interest in the mysticism of the Near East after his trip to Iran and Turkey in 1969. The work is scored for seven solo voices, full orchestra, and prepared tape, and is based on a lengthy mystical poem by the thirteenth-century Persian pantheistic poet Jalal al-Din Rumi. The theme of the poem is the gradual growing together of opposite elements – human and religious love. Schafer says that his piece is a personal statement without the sociopolitical overtones found in many of his works. He chooses to represent the disparate elements by placing his musical resources (including quadraphonic tape) throughout the concert hall; each group of thirteen quintets has its own leader who cues individual and ensemble attacks during the controlled-improvisation sections of the work. Each vocalist performs on a small percussion instrument as well. The audience is literally in the centre of the performance and thus engulfed by a highly romantic and emotionally charged work. Schafer confines his use of Persian elements to the text and certain techniques of form and does not attempt to introduce Persian rhythmic and melodic patterns into the score.

The second part of *Lustro*, *Music for the Morning of the World* (1970–1), is also based on a text by Rumi. It is scored for solo voice and four-track tape and is performed in total darkness (see example 7-5). The tape attempts to create a cruciform of sound at the beginning while the voice, in a series of meditative sections with ecstatic outbursts, underlines again the theme of love: 'before you die ... be drunken in love for love is all that exists.'[10] Part 3, *Beyond the Great Gate of Light* (1973), based on section LVI of *Gitanjali* by Rabindranath Tagore, combines the resources of parts 1 and 2. It begins with the same motive which ends the second part, and through motivic repetition, a long, slow crescendo, and pedal tones in the orchestra and tape moves towards the climactic resolution in peace. Schafer admits to having been moved by the death of a young boy during the composition of this movement. In general theme and intended effect *Lustro* is reminiscent of two great nineteenth-century romantic works, Wagner's *Tristan und Isolde* (1859) and *Mahler's Symphony No. 2 in C Minor 'The Resurrection'* (1894).

Third-stream music, a term coined by the American composer Gunther Schuller (*Symphonic Tribute to Duke Ellington*, 1955), was introduced to Canada by Norman Symonds through his *Concerto Grosso* (1957) for jazz quintet and symphony orchestra. In the 1960s third-stream music continued to make its presence felt on the Canadian music scene, largely through Symonds's efforts. His *Democratic Concerto* (1967) integrates the conventional orchestral and jazz ensemble (in this case a jazz quartet) by using jazz idioms in the orchestral parts and

EXAMPLE 7-5 R. Murray Schafer, *Music for the Morning of the World* (1970–1), pp 6–7 (in the composer's hand)

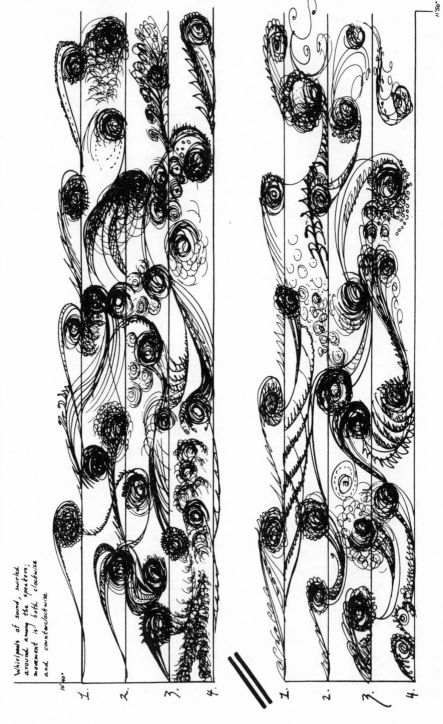

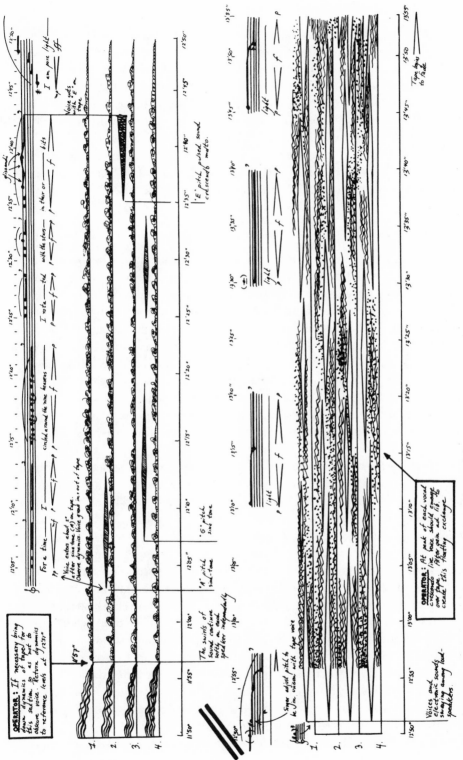

aleatoric sections when the jazz quartet is featured. More recently Lothar Klein has used jazz elements within neoclassical forms and textures, as in his *Trio Sonata* (1969) for clarinet, cello, piano or harpsichord, and jazz-set and in his *Design for Percussion and Orchestra* (1971). Works by younger composers such as Hugh Hartwell (*Soul Piece for 6 or 7 Players*, 1967; rev 1969) and Steven Gellman (*Odyssey*, 1971, for rock group, piano, and orchestra) also attempt to fuse the best from both worlds. *Images* (1977) by Donald Steven, a former rock performer, uses rock-music electronics in a colour-oriented, subdued, classical-contemporary style. In general, however, the combining of jazz or various types of popular music with classical music has been no more successful in Canada than elsewhere.

CHAMBER MUSIC

A glance at the repertoire points up the fact that chamber music has become the favourite medium of Canadian composers since 1967. The reasons for this are simple: chamber music combinations provide great flexibility, they are relatively economical, and they generally involve performers and audiences who are willing to be challenged. The balance between neoclassical and experimental chamber music works underlines this last point, for there are over twice as many works of an experimental nature as those which follow the more conservative path of neo-classicism. This situation is in contrast to the orchestral repertoire which is about evenly divided between the two stylistic categories. Paradoxically, since 1967 there has been a marked return to conventional chamber music combinations such as the string quartet, the woodwind quintet, and the brass quintet as a result of commissioning practices.

One of the most interesting phenomena of recent years has been the appearance on the Canadian concert scene of a number of mixed performing groups specializing in new music. The first of these is L'Ensemble de la société de musique contemporaine du Québec, which was established in 1966 under the direction of composer-conductor Serge Garant. Aided by provincial-government subsidies, the smcq and its ensemble very quickly made Montreal the leading centre of new music in Canada. Although they usually belong to the genres of chamber music, the works commissioned and performed by the smcq ensemble have required, from time to time, a substantial number of performers of diverse instrumentation. François Morel's *Iikkii* (1971) for eighteen solo instruments is one such example. The Société operates its own series of six to ten concerts of new music, Canadian and non-Canadian, every year. More modest in performance resources is the Lyric Arts Trio (Mary Morrison, soprano; Robert Aitken, flute; Marion Ross, piano) which serves as the basic performing unit of the New Music Concerts of Toronto (established in 1972). Although this association came into being six years after the smcq, it quickly rose to prominence not only nationally but internationally as well. Many of the leaders in the field of new music worldwide have been the guests of both the SMCQ and New Music Concerts. Frequently they appear as panelists or lecturers at preconcert sessions on the day of a concert featuring their work. During the 1977–8 season John Cage, Elliott Carter, and György Ligeti were presented by the New Music Concerts, and Olivier Messiaen and Krzysztof Penderecki were guests of the SMCQ in 1978–9. A frequent performing group at the New Music Concerts is Nexus, a percussion ensemble based in Toronto. Other new-music groups in Canada may be found in Halifax (inNOVAtions, 1972–), Winnipeg (Music Inter Alia, 1976–), Vancouver (Vancouver New Music Society, 1973– ; Days, Months and Years to Come, 1975–), Ottawa (Espace musique, 1979–), and Toronto (Array, 1972–). In these and other centres one is aware of a steady growth in audience interest in new music. These developments call to mind the loneliness and bitterness felt by Canadian composers in the early 1940s and voiced by John Weinzweig (see p 32 above). It would seem that Weinzweig's *complainte* was answered in the 1970s.

Not surprisingly many of the works showing neoclassical tendencies have originated with the middle and older generation of composers. Gerhard Wuensch's *Sonata for Soprano Saxophone and Piano* (1971), Kelsey Jones's *Quintet for Winds* (1968), Violet Archer's *Sonata for Clarinet and Piano* (1970), and Elliot Weisgarber's *Quartet* (1975) are cases in point. Similarly, Murray Adaskin's *Quintet for Woodwinds* (1974), Lorne Betts's *String Quartet No. 3* (1970), Robert Turner's *String Quartet No. 3* (1975), and Keith Bissell's *Suite for Bassoon, String Quartet and Percussion* (1977) follow paths previously established by these composers. Jean Coulthard's *Lyric Sonatina* (1969) for bassoon and piano is neoclassical in structure but nineteenth-century romantic in its lushness. S. Irving Glick's *Suite hébraique no. 3* (1975) for string quartet utilizes a *Gebrauchsmusik* style with Bartok-like rhythms. Of the Quebec-based composers, surprisingly few hold to the tenets of neoclassicism. George Fiala, a Ukrainian-born composer who has lived in Montreal since 1949, displays a neoclassical background in his *Sonata for Violin and Piano* (1969). Jacques Hétu's *Cycle* (1969) for piano, flute, clarinet, bass clarinet, bassoon, horn, two trumpets, and two trombones shows a mixture of lyrical and dramatic characteristics which are rooted in classical structures and serial-tonal organizations. A few younger composers have espoused neoclassicism at one time or another: Paul Crawford in *La Nuit étoilée* (1972) and *Quintet for Brass* (1975), Allan Rae in *Scarecrow* (1975), and John Hawkins in *Trio* (1975) for flute, xylophone, and cello.

The larger proportion of chamber music works, however, falls within what might be termed an experimental category. Unusual combinations of instruments and/or voices, novel ways of sounding the instruments or using the voice, use of prepared tape, employment of organizational techniques which feature various aleatoric devices, addition of a theatrical dimension – these comprise some of the ways in which composers have sought out new directions of expression. Like experimental orchestral pieces, some of these works include extramusical associations or fanciful titles. Gilles Tremblay's *Solstices* (1971) for flute (piccolo), clarinet, horn, contrabass, and percussion reflects the cycle of changing hours and seasons not only through its subtitle, *Les Jours et les saisons tournent*, but also through its mobile-type construction which allows it to begin at any one of several points according to the hour of the day and season of the year in which the performance takes place. 'Winter' features the horn, silence, and metallic sounds; 'Spring' the flute, melody, contrast, and general awakening; 'Summer' the clarinet, percussion, and insect sounds; and 'Winter' the double bass, storms, silences, and filtered sound. As Bruce Mather has pointed out, these are not 'gratuitous programmatic elements' but rather 'allusions to natural phenomena' à la Messiaen.[11] Mather is also quick to say that 'Tremblay's music never sounds like that of Messiaen,' the connection being more on a philosophical and aesthetic level.[12] Similarly emulating the spirit of religious mysticism found in Messiaen is Tremblay's *Oralléluiants* (1975) for soprano, flute, bass clarinet, horn, three contrabass, and two percussion which is based on the first Alleluia of the Pentecost Mass. The coming of the Holy Spirit (Pentecost) is portrayed with elaborate percussion, frequent use of mobiles, and complicated textures – all intended at the end of the work 'to have the impression of being on the threshold of the impossible, but in a relaxed manner.'[13]

Other chamber music works with prominent extra-musical elements and experimental means include R. Murray Schafer's *String Quartet No. 2 'Waves'* (1976), which is based on the asymmetrical patterns of the waves of the Atlantic and Pacific Oceans, not in a specific sense but in a general governing of the rhythm and structure of the piece. Schafer in this quartet attempts to capture the 'dynamic undulations of waves ... a liquid quality ... constantly flowing into everything else.'[14] Robert Aitken's *Kebyar* (1971) (the title means literally 'a sudden release of forces') combines elements of Eastern and Western music in a festive atmosphere; stylistically it represents a change from the structural concerns of Aitken's earlier works to free experimentation with instrumental and electro-acoustical sound colours. Aitken's *Shadows II 'Lalita'* (1972) also displays sound experimentation and an Eastern influence. Micheline Coulombe Saint-Marcoux's *Ishuma* (1974) for voice, violin, contrabass, trombone, three percussion, Hammond organ, Ondes Martenot, and synthesizer is based on a surrealistic work by Paul Chamberland entitled *Eclats de la pierre noire d'où rejaillit* (1966–9); *Ishuma* is the Inuit word for intelligence or the ability to think. The text deals with 'man's ability to transform reality by means of his own powers of concentration.'[15] One means by which the composer expresses stream-of-consciousness ideas is to use the live synthesizer rather than prerecorded tape; each performance is then unique and the piece is in a process of continual evolution. Serge Garant's series of three *Offrandes* (1969–71) and John Hawkins's *Remembrances* (1969) also use avant-garde techniques; furthermore, each makes reference to the musical past, through both direct musical quotation (particularly of the music of J.S. Bach) and symbolic suggestion; these works affirm that the Canadian composer, like his counterpart elsewhere, is ever mindful of his musical heritage. Another work with a prominent extra-musical element is André Prévost's *Quatuor à cordes no. 2 'Ad pacem'* (1972). It

EXAMPLE 7-6   André Prévost, *String Quartet No. 2 'Ad pacem'* (1972), score, p 27

displays the composer's preoccupation with the social and political tensions of modern life, tensions which are represented through the scoring of the instruments in inverse tessitura; that is, at the climax of the work the cello sounds the highest and the first violin the lowest (see example 7-6). The work ends on an optimistic note with the peaceful subsiding of tension.

It is interesting to note that French-Canadian composers tend to combine extramusical associations of a philosophical nature with experimental techniques. An example of such a work is Garant's *Chants d'amours* (1975), which is based on a varied series of love texts from King Solomon, Shakespeare, Petrarch, Saint Jean de la Croix, Sainte Thérèse d'Avile, and Ronsard to graffiti and *petites annonces* (i.e. short advertisements). The musical setting for soprano, contralto, baritone, and cello soli, three trumpets, two horns, three trombones, two harps, and percussion is characterized by disjunct melodies and complicated contrapuntal textures and rhythms. Other examples illustrating the same tendency, besides those by Tremblay, Saint-Marcoux, and Prévost mentioned above, are Claude Vivier's *Prolifération* (1968–9) and Clermont Pépin's *Monade IV* (1974) and *Monade VI* (1976). In contrast, English-Canadian composers tend to be less philosophical and more theatrical, calling upon experimental procedures to express their theatrical interests. Two examples are Otto Joachim's *Illumination II* (1969) and Harry Somers's *Improvisations* (1968), both aleatoric works in which the performers respond to various signals from the conductor or other stimuli.

CHORAL MUSIC

An interesting feature of post-1967 choral music is the continued development of the extended-voices idea. Composers often use words or word fragments to form

the basis of new and evocative sounds and textual formulations. In many cases
works evolve as designs in sound, with their meaning being transmitted in a
general way rather than through semantic constructions; thus they illustrate the
romantic ideal that music takes over where words leave off. The most ambitious
work in this regard is Harry Somers's twenty-five-minute *Kyrie* (1972) for SATB
soli, SATB chorus, flute, oboe, clarinet, cello, three trumpets, piano, and six percussion (see example 7-7). In this work Somers dissects all of the vowels and con-
sonants of 'Kyrie eleison' and 'Christe eleison' over an extended time period and
only at the end of the work do the words 'Kyrie eleison' appear in the text in the
normal way. Furthermore, Somers requires the singers to depart from traditional
vocal technique and provides them with detailed verbal and graphic instructions.
John Beckwith's *Gas!* (1969), for twenty speaking voices divided into two groups,
is similarly 'a vocal tone poem with widely varied colours and images and with
levels of "message" that are both on the surface and deep under it.'[16] The text is
what the composer refers to as a 'found poem' which he assembled from various
municipal and provincial traffic signs in south-central Ontario. Word fragments
and imitative sounds are used in counterpoint to spoken parts of the text.

In his *In Search of Zoroaster* (1971) R. Murray Schafer employs four choirs and
four conductors who come together for the first time during a given performance.
A theatrical work, it makes use of various devices such as humming, chanting,
percussive vocalizations, shouting, and so on, and purposefully avoids traditional
choral singing. Schafer states: 'for some time I have been aware of the necessity to
change the format of Western musical life in order to revive the true spirit of the
art ... to create an event of importance in social life, a celebration with sounds
transfiguring the human soul.'[17] Also in keeping with this ideal are two commissioned works for church choir by Schafer; the first, *Yeow and Pax* (1969) for
chorus, organ, and prepared tape, was written for the First Congregational
Church, Old Greenwich, Connecticut, and the second, *Psalm* (1972; rev 1976) for
chorus and percussion instruments (performed by the choir), was composed for
the Cathedral Church of the Redeemer, Calgary, Alberta. *Yeow and Pax* is based on
Isaiah 13:6–13 and 60:18–20, two texts from the Old Testament which move
from the extreme wrath of God ('Howl ye; for the day of the Lord is at hand; it
shall come as a destruction from the Almighty') to the promise of peace ('Violence
shall no more be heard in thy land ...; but the Lord shall be unto thee an
everlasting light, and the days of thy mourning shall be ended'). *Psalm*, on the
other hand, is based on the romantic Psalm 148 which exhorts all the forces of
nature to praise the Almighty; in his setting Schafer uses a variety of percussion
instruments played by the choir as well as a mixed graphic and conventionally
notated score.

André Prévost is another composer who is very much concerned with music as
a form of spiritual expression, although his means are more traditional than
Schafer's. For Prévost, 'every work of art has basically a religious impulse.'[18] Two

of his works from this period bring into focus this point of view: *Psaume 148* (1971) for chorus, four trumpets, four trombones, and organ and *Missa de profundis* (1973) for chorus and organ. The former is based on the same text as Schafer's *Psalm* but is given a more traditional treatment; the latter is based on Psalm 130 (Vulgate Psalm 129) – 'Out of the depths have I cried unto thee, O Lord' – and is a proclamation of hope for redemption. The antiphonal nature of the psalms is captured by Prévost in the musical texture, but, as in his instrumental works, there is little evidence of independent voice-writing or counterpoint.

Among other choral works which employ avant-garde techniques such as group improvisation and prepared electronic tape is Derek Healey's *Clouds* (1972). This work is based on the vowels of a Japanese haiku by Matsuo Basho '(Clouds pass from time to time giving men a rest from gazing at the moon'). The solo parts may be sung by a semi-chorus or played by instruments or relayed through an electronic reverberation unit; at many points the chorus sings only approximate pitches and its sounds may also be modified electronically during an actual performance. Experimentation with new sounds is also a concern of Jean Papineau-Couture in his *Paysage* (1968) for eight speakers, eight singers, and chamber ensemble. The work is based on a poem by Saint-Denys Garneau which concerns itself with the opposing forces of life (light) and death (shade), the former being represented by the singing voices and bursts of clear sound (triangle, cymbal) and the latter by speaking voices and low notes and dampened percussion. Ostinato figures, which are a feature of Papineau-Couture's music throughout his career, are much in evidence.

A significant number of younger composers have written choral works, many using avant-garde techniques. *Numbers in a Row* (1971) by David Paul is a singular work in that its text consists entirely of the numbers one to twelve, corresponding to the twelve-tone row. Fragmentation of the row, repetition of individual tones, spoken parts, kissing sounds, and finger-snapping all add up to a clever piece for mixed voices. Richard Grégoire's *Cantate* (1968) for twelve singers, organ, guitar, and percussion is built on a series of twelve tones which takes its proportions from the text itself. *Moon Dreams* (1971) by Barry Truax is a series of eight movements, on texts by e.e. cummings, which exploit text fragmentation and choral sounds *per se*. Denis Lorrain's *P-A* (1970) consists entirely of vowel and consonant sounds without any word formulations. In keeping with the predisposition of west-coast composers for the experimental, and sometimes the absurd, *Once Again – Pop* (1968) by Lloyd Burritt consists entirely of each member of a choral group blowing up a balloon until it goes pop!

Some composers have written works for youth chorus with the aim of exposing young people to new styles and techniques in choral singing. Harry Freedman's *Keewaydin* (1971) for ssa and optional prepared tape, on a text consisting of Ontario place names in the Ojibwa language, is one such example. Schafer's *Epitaph for Moonlight* (1968) for satb and optional bells, on the other hand, is based

EXAMPLE 7-7   Harry Somers, *Kyrie* (1972), beginning (in the composer's hand)

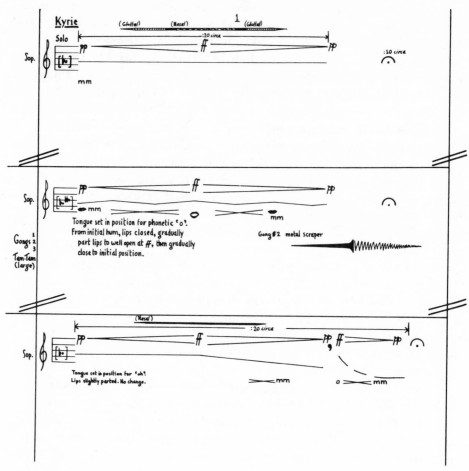

on a text made up entirely of onomatopoeic sounds concocted by a grade-seven class trying to invent a synonym for 'moonlight.' Such new words as 'nuyuyul, noorwahm, malooma, neshmoor, shiverglowa' were invented, and Schafer set the resultant text, using a graphic score. Schafer's *Miniwanka* or *The Moments of Water* (1971), similarly a pictorial piece for youth choir, describes the various states of water. The text is based on the words for water, rain, streams, fog, and ocean taken from various North-American Indian languages. Lothar Klein's *Orpheus* (1976), which is described by the composer as a 'lyrical essay for singers, instruments and dancers,'[19] was conceived for performance by college and university non-music majors or other amateur groups. The work utilizes texts from Virgil, Horace, Ovid, Boethius, the Greek Orphic hymns, and Poliziano's *Tale of Orpheus*

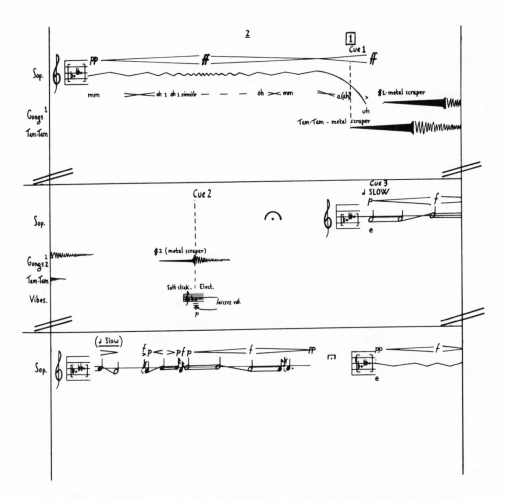

(1471) to depict the power of music and its significance in the daily lives of individuals: 'practice an art, a skill, a love until your final breath. Let it be your companion for life.'[20] The musical style of the work is akin to that of Carl Orff, with its narrow melodic ranges and frequent doubling of voice parts.

Choral works written in more traditional tonal-modal styles with fully pre-scribed, conventional notation comprise a significant number of the works written in this period. Those which are extended in length and call upon substantial instrumental as well as vocal resources include the following: Godfrey Ridout's *Cantiones mysticae No. III* (*The Dream of the Rood*) (1972), the text of which centers on a personal and mystical witness to Christ's Crucifixion; Jacques Hétu's *Les Djinns* (1975), which is based on the ode *Le Génie* (1820) by Victor Hugo; Milton Barnes's *Shir Hashirim* (1975), which is a setting of a section from the Song of Solomon; Keith Bissell's *Famous Men* (*In Praise of*) (1976), on a text from the Apocrypha;

Lorne Betts's *Margaritae sorori* (1975), on a text by the nineteenth-century English writer W.E. Henley; and Charles Wilson's *Song for St Cecilia's Day* (1976), on a text by W.H. Auden, which is one in a long line of tributes to the patron saint of music. Also noteworthy are the *Festival Te Deum* (1972) by F.R.C. Clarke; *Cantata festiva* (1974) by Michael R. Miller; and *Laus sapientiae* (1977) by Gerhard Wuensch, extended works composed, respectively, for the celebrations of the three-hundredth anniversay of the founding of Kingston, Ontario, the one-hundredth anniversary of the granting of the first diploma in music at Mount Allison University, and the centenary of the University of Western Ontario.

Some of the composers of experimental works have also written in more traditional idioms when the occasion or the commission has demanded it. Freedman's *The Flame Within* (1968), which was composed for Paul Almond's film *Act of the Heart*, uses a tonal idiom, as does his *Songs from Shakespeare* (1971–2). Also in a tonal style are Norma Beecroft's *The Living Flame of Love* (1968), Beckwith's *Three Blessings* (1968), John Hawkins's *Spring Song* (1974), and Clifford Ford's *Mass* (1976).

The choral arrangement of Canadian folk songs have continued to attract a limited number of Canadian composers. Some of the works arising from this interest include Somers's *Five Songs of the Newfoundland Outports* (1969) and *Trois chansons de la Nouvelle France*, Bissell's *Nous étions trois capitaines* (1968) and *Adieu de la mariée à ses parents* (1968), Robert Fleming's *Three Nova Scotia Folk Songs* (1972), Kelsey Jones's *Kishimaquac* (1971), and Derek Healey's *Six Canadian Folk Songs* (1973). Works which are based on Canadian-Indian texts or themes include Talivaldis Kenins's *Sawan-oong* (*The Spirit of the Wind*) (1973), Beecroft's *Three Impressions* (1973), and Beckwith's *The Sun Dance* (1968). Although it is not directly based on folk songs, Beckwith's *1838* (1970) utilizes a folk-like style in its satirical treatment of the William Lyon Mackenzie rebellion of 1837 in Upper Canada. The British, the Yankees, and the bishop all are subjected to the barbs of Dennis Lee's text and John Beckwith's music while Mackenzie emerges as the hero.

SONG

Since 1967 works for solo voice and piano have continued to diminish in proportion to those for voice and other instruments, a pattern already well established in the early 1960s. Most of the works for voice and piano are in a traditional style: for example, Keith Bissell's *Hymns of the Chinese Kings* (1968), Richard Johnston's *The Irish Book* (1971), George Fiala's *Four Russian Poems* (1968), Srul Irving Glick's *i never saw another butterfly* (1968) (see example 7-8), and Oskar Morawetz's *From the Diary of Anne Frank* (1970). The first three employ texts which are widely separated in time and place; the last two works are based on texts by Jewish children who experienced the Nazi holocaust in World War II. More experimental in nature are Harry Freedman's *Poems of Young People* (1968), a witty and satiric setting of poems

EXAMPLE 7-8   Srul Irving Glick, *i never saw another butterfly* (1968), ending

written by Toronto elementary and high-school students, and John Weinzweig's *Private Collection* (1975), a set of eight songs on varied texts by the composer. Weinzweig's work follows in substance and style his earlier *Trialogue* (1971) even to the point of including two songs from the earlier work. Theatrical effects, humour, non-semantic use of words and word-fragments, free ordering of the songs, and experimentation with new vocal sounds are stylistic features of both the *Poems of Young People* and *Private Collection*. Other works of interest for voice and piano include André Prévost's *Improvisation v* (1976), on a text by Lise Vézina-Prévost, and Jacques Hétu's *Les Clartés de la nuit* (1972), on poems by another Canadian poet, Emile Nelligan. Paul Crawford's *At Night on the High Seas* (1975) is exceptional because the younger generation of composers has usually tended to avoid the classic combination of voice and piano in favour of more exotic instrumental accompaniments. A work for two solo voices and piano, commissioned by the CBC for Lois Marshall and Maureen Forrester, is Kelsey Jones's *Songs of Winter* (1973), based on nineteenth-century Canadian poems adapted by Rosabelle Jones; it is written in the chromatic, tertian style typical of the composer.

Generally speaking, the works for solo voice and mixed instrumental ensemble are more avant-garde in style. These include Bruce Mather's five madrigals (1967–73), the first four of which are based on poems of Saint-Denys Garneau; they are expressionistic works which use a variety of instruments in the accompaniment and in which the instrumental colours and textures match the delicate poetry (see example 7-9). John Hawkins's *Waves* (1971), based on T.S. Eliot's *Four Quartets* (1943), is preoccupied with the cyclic recurrence of human and universal events in huge wave forms. The singer in this work also acts as the percussionist and is called upon to perform on a variety of instruments – maracas, chimes, glockenspiel, antique cymbals, small triangle, and small gong. Alan Heard's *Voices* (1969), which is set for mezzo-soprano, flute, cello, piano, and percussion, has long, disjunct phrases in the voice punctuated by instrumental interjections and dramatic silences, giving a sparse texture to these settings of English translations of medieval Japanese poetry. Norma Beecroft's *Rasas II* (1973) for flute (including bamboo flute), guitar (including fender-bass guitar), piano, electronic organ, harp, two percussion performers, and prepared tape draws upon a variety of texts to create a series of *rasas* or moods, traversing the time cycle from youth through maturity to old age. Like many of the works written in an avant-garde idiom Barbara Pentland's *News* (1970) and *Disasters of the Sun* (1976) carry with them a message; the former decries the prevalence of sensational news in the media, and the latter (through the text by Dorothy Livesay) the subjugation of women by society: 'if I'm a woman assure me I am human.' Both works make use of aleatoric zones, a feature of Pentland's music since her *Trio con alea* (1966). The element of humour is prominent in some of the avant-garde works, notably in Lothar Klein's *The Philosopher in the Kitchen* (1974) and Freedman's *Fragments of Alice* (1976).

EXAMPLE 7-9 Bruce Mather, *Madrigal II* (1968), beginning

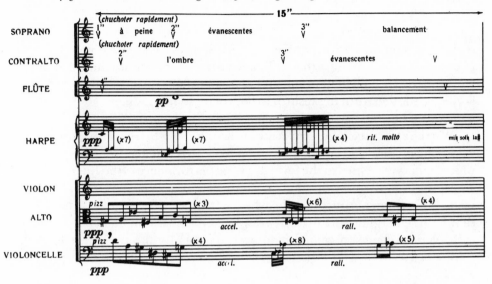

Canadian folk songs are the basis of some settings of songs in this period. Keith Bissell and John Beckwith have over the years been perspicacious in their use of Canadian folk songs, making arrangements of songs from the collections of Kenneth Peacock, Helen Creighton, and others. Recent examples are Beckwith's *Five Songs* (1969–70) and *Four Love Songs* (1969) and Bissell's *Six Maritime Folk*

Songs (1970), *Six Folk Songs from Eastern Canada* (1970), and *Ten Folk Songs of Canada* (1972).

Harry Somers's *Voiceplay* (1971) for singer-actor (male or female, any range) represents a continuation of two trends which Somers has followed since his *Evocations* (1966). These are the exploration of new vocal sounds through non-semantic word fragmentation and the expansion of musical performance to border on the theatre of the absurd. In both of these areas Somers admits to the influence of Ligeti's *Aventures* (1962) and *Nouvelles aventures* (1962–65) as well as Iris Warren's vocal technique for actors, which attempts to free the breath and voice from physical and emotional tensions. *Voiceplay* resulted from a lecture which Somers presented in the form of a vocal performance to the Inter-University Composers Symposium in Montreal in 1968. The purpose of his talk was to explain how he uses the voice in his compositions; by 'singing' his lecture he showed the emerging work to be (1) a display of the vocal range and possibilities of each soloist, (2) a musical composition, and (3) a work for theatre. The score itself consists of a set of cards. Two later works by Somers which follow similar precepts are *Zen, Yeats and Emily Dickinson* (1975) for female narrator, male narrator, soprano, flute, piano, and tape and the more modest *Love-In-Idleness* (1976) for soprano and piano.

The works of R. Murray Schafer for solo voice and instruments merit special attention. Throughout his career, from *Minnelieder* (1956) to *La Testa d'Adriane* (1978), Schafer has given a prominent place to the solo voice. This interest in the voice may be viewed as both the result of Schafer's first marriage to the Canadian mezzo-soprano Phyllis Mailing, and the fact that the solo voice is the most appropriate vehicle for expressing the romanticism which permeates his works. For instance, *Music for the Morning of the World*, the central part of the triptych *Lustro*, features the solo voice in its portrayal of the mystical fusing of religious and human love. *Adieu Robert Schumann* (1976) for contralto and orchestra is based on one of the greatest love stories of the nineteenth century; its text is taken from the diaries of Clara Schumann dating from her husband's first hallucinations, through his mental breakdown, to his ultimate death. Musical quotations from Schumann's works as well as signature motives identify the subject material. A quotation from one of Schumann's last songs, *Dein Angesicht* (Your Countenance), opens and closes the work. *La Testa d'Adriane* for voice and free-bass accordion, which is part 3 of Schafer's stage-work-in-progress, *Patria*, portrays through Adriane, who is in a state of suspension between this world and the next, the disappointments of earthly love. Schafer underlines the magical state by showing only the singer's head (by means of magician's mirrors), and setting off this illusion against the only other character, a circus barker who plays the accordion. The verbal text is spoken by the barker and is insignificant except to provide continuity and comic relief; the non-verbal text is much more important, proclaiming in a series of vocalizations by Adriane the various states of love. The fourth and final part of *Patria* to date, *Hymn to Night* (1976) for voice, orchestra, and prepared tape, is based on a text adapted from the eighteenth-century Christian mystic Novalis. Whereas part 2 of *Patria* (*Requiems for the Party-Girl*) is based on the theme of loneliness and alienation and part 3 (*La Testa d'Adriane*) on the theme of disappointment in love, part 4 (*Hymn to Night*) expresses a feeling of hope. It is interesting to note that in setting this theme Schafer returns in part to the neoclassical textures and motivic manipulation which were characteristic of his earliest vocal works, *Minnelieder* and *Kinderlieder* (1958).

OPERA

The success of Harry Somers's *Louis Riel* (1967), both in terms of popularity at the box-office and critical acclaim, initiated a burst of activity in opera after 1967. No fewer than twenty-five operas and theatre pieces (many of them in one act, some composed especially for television) were written by Canadian composers between 1967 and 1978. Surprisingly only a few are based on Canadian themes. One which is Canadian in theme is István Anhalt's *La Tourangelle*, which is labelled a dramatic cantata rather than an opera. It is a musical *tableau* on the life of one of the most noble figures in early Canadian history, Marie de l'Incarnation. According to the composer the work is concerned essentially with 'the search for order and meaning in life through the focus of religion – the search for God in other words.'[21] In seven sections set for five singers, sixteen instrumentalists, two tape machines, and Ondes Martenot, the work marks a turning away from the constant stylistic experimentation which was characteristic of so much music, including Anhalt's, in the 1960s and early 1970s. *La Tourangelle* returns to an earlier style, such as Honegger's *Jeanne d'Arc au bûcher* (1935), with its recognizable tonal centres, frequent ostinato figures, and dramatic recitations. The historical aspect of the piece is underlined by musical quotations from Palestrina's *Missa ad fugam* (section 6) and the Gregorian *Te Deum laudamus* (section 7). All in all, the work is in a much more approachable style than Anhalt's previous works, which had caused one of his colleagues to call him 'the heavy-weight among Canadian composers.'[22]

Another musical-dramatic work based on a Canadian theme is Charles Wilson's *Kamouraska* (1975), the libretto of which is an adaptation of the novel of the same name by Anne Hébert. This bilingual opera in three acts is one of five operas written by Wilson since 1972; like the others it follows a moderately dissonant style similar to that of Benjamin Britten's. Derek Healey's *Seabird Island* (1977) is based on a west-coast Indian legend; it too is in three acts. More tangentially related to Canadian themes is Samuel Dolin's *Drakkar* (1972), which is based on the Viking expeditions to the New World in the tenth century (the so-called Vinland sagas). The score calls for dancers, projected slides, and two synthesizers, as well as solo voices and chamber orchestra; a narrator carries the thread of the story. Stylistically one is reminded again of the eclecticism of Britten.

Operas based on historical or philosophic-historical themes, but non-Canadian, are Graham George's *King Theodore* (1973) and Charles Wilson's *Héloise and Abelard* (1972) and *The Summoning of Everyman* (1972). The style of George's work is indebted to Wagner and late nineteenth-century romanticism, whereas Wilson's two operas (a first for a Canadian composer to produce two operas in one year!) are consistent with his middle-of-the-road twentieth-century style.

In addition there are a few operas which are designed primarily for children, such as Clifford Ford's *Hypnos* (1972), John Rea's *The Prisoner's Play* (1973), and Charles Wilson's *The Selfish Giant* (1972). Some have humour or satire as the main thrust of the story: for example, Gabriel Charpentier's *An English Lesson* (1968) and *A Tea Symphony or the Perils of Clara* (1972), Walter Buczynski's *From the Buczynski Book of the Living* (1972), Violet Archer's *Sganarelle* (1973), Tibor Polgar's *The Troublemaker* (1968) and *The Glove* (1973), and Paul McIntyre's *The Little Red Hen* (1976). Stylistically these works represent a wide spectrum from the neoclassicism of Archer and Polgar, through the moderate dodecaphonism of McIntyre and Wilson, to the graphic scoring, controlled improvisation, and prepared-tape sections of Ford, Charpentier, and Buczynski. *An English Lesson*, described as an 'opera happening,'[23] infuses a great deal of humour and social commentary into its ten minutes. Commissioned by the Stratford Festival, it is a satirical play on French words which have been adopted into English, such as 'rendezvous,' 'savoir faire,' and so on. The work is performed by a teacher and four pupils, each of whose native language is English, with instrumental accompaniment of flute, English horn, French horn, two violins, two violas, two cellos, two pianos (harpsichord), and two vibraphones. As an example of bicultural humour in Canadian musical theatre it is without peer.

Two operas were written especially for television: Godfrey Ridout's *The Lost Child* (1976), a neoclassical work based upon the Christmas story; and Raymond Pannell's *Aberfan* (1977), a work of eclectic style with a libretto drawn from the tragic live-burial of 116 schoolchildren in the Welsh mining town of Aberfan on 21 October 1966. Aberfan was awarded the Salzburg prize for the best original television opera of 1977.

The musical-dramatic works which focus their attention upon one aspect or another of contemporary life, usually in a critical way, tend to employ experimental means in doing so. Otto Joachim's *Mankind* (1972) uses four readers (each an ordained cleric or authorized deputy of four of the major world religions), four synthesizers, organ, timpani, incense, and slides in exploring not only the common ground of various cultures but also the relationships between various forms of light and sound. Gabriel Charpentier, the composer of more than fifty scores for theatre, fully warrants his description of himself as a 'theatre musician.'[24] His *Orphée* (1969; rev 1972 as *Orpheus*) retells the Greek legend which espouses the power of music, using a chorus of singers and dancers, harp, percussion, piano, and Ondes Martenot as well as audience participation. Martin

Bartlett's *Five Directions* (1972), also a multimedia work, shows, in common with
some other Western works of art of the late 1960s and 1970s, the influence of the
Hindustan culture. Charles Wilson's *Psycho Red* (1977) probes the relationships
between a psychiatrist, his patient, and his wife in a drama of the human con-
sciousness which poses the ultimate question: 'who am I?' Although the musical
style is similar to that used in his previous works, Wilson here notates his score on
a time-grid, with note values shown by graphic rather than metric indicators. The
result is a greatly simplified score like Schafer's, but without the ornate embellishments of the latter. Udo Kasemets's *Watearthundair* (1976) and KANADANAK (1977)
purposely avoid conventional performance resources in presenting their social
message on the themes of conservation and the rights of native peoples. Harry
Somers's *Death of Enkidu* (1977) recounts an ancient Babylonian tale which mourns
the destruction of natural man by civilization. Many aspects of Somers's style in
this work are similar to the style of his *Louis Riel*, except for the length (*Death of
Enkidu* is in one act, although it is part 1 of a larger work entitled *Enkidu*) and the
instrumentation, which is of chamber music proportions. The companion piece at
the première of *Death of Enkidu* was Norman Symonds's *Lady in the Night* (1977), a
one-act, one-character opera which uses a jazz style reminiscent of the 1950s to
depict the amorous difficulties of a New York stripper.

Except for Charpentier, French-Canadian composers have not joined their
English-Canadian confrères in the writing of opera and theatre pieces. However,
they have been more active in the composition of film and ballet music.

ELECTRONIC MUSIC

Electronic music has been an integral part of new music in recent years. Following
the first development of the medium in Canada in the 1950s and 1960s and the
introduction of the voltage-controlled synthesizer around 1965, most composers
acquainted themselves with what it had to offer; some chose to use it, others did
not. Those who did used it as an added sound source and/or performer in their
works. Very few employed it to the exclusion of the traditional acoustic sounds of
voices and instruments. Surprisingly few young composers have concentrated on
electronic music. While most university music departments boast an electronic
music laboratory, the focal points of the medium have been the large centres, such
as Toronto (Canadian Electronic Ensemble), Montreal (Circuit international des
musiques électroacoustiques [CIME]), and Vancouver.

The advent of the synthesizer and the computer has had a marked effect on
electronic music in Canada, as elsewhere. For example, both Hugh LeCaine's
Mobile (*The Computer Laughed*) (1970) and Gustav Ciamaga's *Canon for Stravinsky*
(1972) make use of the new hardware. Ciamaga's work, a tribute to one of the
musical giants of the twentieth century for whom electronic music came too late,
incorporates the opening bars of Stravinsky's *Orpheus* (1947). Otto Joachim, who is

EXAMPLE 7-10   István Anhalt, *Foci* (1969), beginning (in the composer's hand)

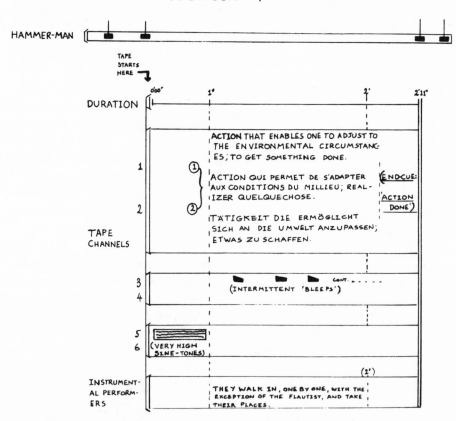

also a designer of electronic music equipment, points up the contrast between the old (i.e. pre-1965) and the new in electroacoustic composition. His 5.9 (1971) consists of approximately six minutes of music contrived by four channels of sound being superimposed during a total realization time of thirty minutes. In the early days of electronic music, when one had to rely on countless splicings and re-recordings, such a work would have taken many hours to produce. The synthesizer has thus greatly reduced the amount of time necessary for the realization of an electronic composition. Joachim himself emphasizes that, although the new hardware has made the mechanical side of the composition of electronic music considerably easier, the process of selection is just as difficult as before.

Representative examples of works by composers who use electronics in combination with one or more conventional instruments are István Anhalt's *Foci* (1969) for large orchestra (especially percussion), soprano, three two-channel tapes, and 'hammer-man' (see example 7-10), Paul Pedersen's *An Old Song of the Sun and the Moon and the Fear of Loneliness* (1973) and Gustav Ciamaga's *Solipsism While Dying* (1972) for soprano, flute, piano, and electronics, and John Beckwith's *Upper Canadian Hymn Preludes* (1977) for pipe organ and prepared tape. Whereas *Foci* is based on textual material which is both remote and introspective, the other works follow themes closer to home: Pedersen's work is based on an Inuit poem; Ciamaga's on Margaret Atwood's *Journals of Susanne Moodie* (1970); and Beckwith's on nineteenth-century Canadian hymn tunes.

The Canadian Electronic Ensemble (1971–), through its members David Jaeger, Larry Lake, James Montgomery, and David Grimes, has shown an inclination to combine electronic and conventional instruments as in Jaeger's *Fancye* (1973) for pipe organ, electronic tape, and visuals, Lake's *Face* (1976) for piano, four synthesizers, and four-channel tape, Montgomery's *Reconnaisance* (1975) for amplified string quartet, and Grimes's *Sotto Voce* (1976) for voice and prepared tape. Group improvisation using synthesizers is another technique followed by this ensemble, as it is also in the work of Montreal composer Micheline Coulombe Saint-Marcoux, a founding member of the Groupe international de musique électroacoustique de Paris (1969).

Other significant works which combine electronic and acoustic instruments vary from small-scale pieces such as Karl Kobylansky's *Thoughts* (1972) for chorus and tape and Robert Bauer's *Extensions II* (1975) for guitar and tape, through medium-sized works such as Barry Truax's *Trigon* (1974–5) for mezzo-soprano, alto flute, piano, and computer-synthesized tape, *She, a Solo* (1973) for mezzo-soprano and tape, and *Nautilus* (1976) for percussion and tape, to large-scale works such as István Anhalt's *La Tourangelle* and R. Murray Schafer's triptyque, *Lustro*. Some composers, particularly Michel Longtin and Ann Southam, have been concerned with the use of electronic music for films and other visual presentations such as dance. Vancouver-based composer Don Druick is also very much involved with mixed media, such as video, tape, dance, theatre, and film.

Recent works of 'pure' electronic music produced with or without the aid of computers have largely been the result of the efforts of the younger composers (i.e. those born around or after 1940). Some of the more interesting examples of their works include Peter Huse's *Space Play* (1969), which was inspired by the science-fiction notion that all sounds and physical space are materials for music; Michel Longtin's *Fedhibô* (1973), which is a realistic tone painting and hymn of praise 'to the Northern countries, to autumn and to love,' and his *Au nord du lac Supérieure* (1972), which was inspired by Lawren Harris's painting of the same name; Barry Truax's *Sonic Landscapes No. 3* (1975, rev 1977), which is a spatial environment with four computer-synthesized soundtracks (the work was awarded first prize in the computer music division of the fifth International Competition of Electroacoustic Music at Bourges, France, in the summer of 1977); and Saint-Marcoux's *Zones* (1972), a work in which different zones offer multiple views of the same sound object. A few works, such as Edward Dawson's *Concerto Grosso 1* (1974) and Martin Bartlett's *Lines from Chuang-Tau* (1973), give directions which allow for performance by either electronic or conventional instruments. Thus it seems that the two media are not that far apart after all.

POSTLUDE

I hope that three things have become apparent to the reader through these pages: that there is much more Canadian music in our present century than is generally believed; that this music encompasses the complete stylistic range of twentieth-century music; and that the quality of much of it is of a high calibre and deserves to be more widely known than is now the case.

The question of identifiable Canadian characteristics I shall leave open. Perhaps it is necessary for an outsider to identify these in any event, just as in language accents are recognized only by the outsider. During a visit to Canada for meetings of the International Music Council in 1975 the distinguished musician Yehudi Menuhin commented that he found Canadian music (and he heard a great deal of it during the course of the conference) to be particularly sensitive to the sounds of nature.[25] It would be nice to think that this is so and that down the road of history men and women will link Canadian music to nature in this way. However, it is the fervent wish of this author that Canadians and non-Canadians, musicians and non-musicians, will not wait for this day, or for other proclamations on the special characteristics of Canadian music, but that each will choose now to experience the excitement of coming to know and appreciate the musical literature of this time and place.

SELECTED WORKS

composer	title	score	recording

KEYBOARD MUSIC

Piano music

composer	title	score	recording
piano pieces by Adaskin, Archer, Applebaum, Beckwith, Cherney, Dolin, Eggleston, Elliott, Fiala, Fleming, Johnston, Turner, and Wuensch	*Horizons*, Books I, II	Waterloo, 1973	
Archer, Violet	*Sonatina No. 3* (1973)	CMC ms	
	Improvisations for Piano (1968)	CMC ms film 6/50	Mel SMLP 4031
Baker, Michael	*Sonata for Piano* (1975)	Harmuse, 1977	
Beckwith, John	*New Mobiles* (1971)	Waterloo, 1973	
Behrens, Jack	*Taos Portraits* (1976)	ms	
Buczynski, Walter	*Burlesque* (1970)	CMC ms	CMC tape 667
	Zeroing In (1971)	CMC ms	
	Zeroing In #5 (Dictionary of Mannerisms) (1972)	CMC ms	CGA 654369
Cherney, Brian	*Pieces for Young Pianists, I, II, III* (1968)	Jaymar, 1971–2	
	Six Miniatures (1968)	Jaymar, 1971	
Coulthard, Jean, Duke, D., and Hansen, J.	*Music of Our Time*	Waterloo, 1977	
Fiala, George	*Children's Suite* (1974)	Waterloo, 1976	
	Piano Music No. 1 (1976)	CMC ms	
Hambraeus, Bengt	*Carillon* (1972–4), two pianos		McGill ST 77002
Hawkins, John	*Etudes for Two Pianos* (1974)	CMC ms	
Kenins, Talivaldis	*Diversities* (1967)	Leeds, 1968	Nos 9, 12 Dom s-69002
	The Juggler. The Sad Clown (1969)	Boosey, 1969	Dom s-69002

composer	title	score	recording
Klein, Lothar	*Sonata* (1968)	Leeds, 1974	
Mather, Bruce	*In Memoriam Alexander Uninsky* (1974)	CMC ms	
	Sonata for Two Pianos (1970)	CMC ms	RCI 354; McGill ST 77002
Miller, Michael R.	*Fantasy Variations* (1971)	CMC ms	
Morawetz, Oskar	*Fantasy for Piano* (1973)	CMC ms	
	Suite for Piano (1968)	Leeds, 1971	CBC SM 187
Papineau-Couture, Jean	*Complémentarité* (1971)	CMC ms	RCI 384; RCI ACM
Pentland, Barbara	*Music of Now*, Books 1, 2, 3 (1969–70)	Waterloo, 1970	
	Vita brevis (1973)	CMC ms	
Saint-Marcoux, Micheline Coulombe	*Assemblages* (1969)	CMC ms	RCI 396
Surdin, Morris	*Fragmentations I, II, III* (1972)	S.E.L., 1974	
Tremblay, Gilles	*Traçantes* (1976)	Salabert, 1977	
Weinzweig, John	*Impromptus* (1973)	International, 1973	
Wuensch, Gerhard	*Spectrum*, Op. 41 (1969)	Leeds, 1971	

Organ music

Beckwith, John	*Upper Canadian Hymn Preludes* (1977), organ and tape	CMC ms	
Betts, Lorne	*Improvisations on B-A-C-H* (1969)	CMC ms	
	Lucis creator optime (1976)	CMC ms	
Buczynski, Walter	*Psalm for Organ* (1977)	CMC ms	
Cabena, Barrie	*Sonata da chiesa*	Jaymar, 1971	
	Sonata Festiva, Op. 42	Jaymar, 1971	
Fodi, John	*Erro* (1974), Op. 40	CMC ms	
Ford, Clifford	*Piece for Organ No. 2* (1973)	CMC ms	
Healey, Derek	*The Lost Traveller's Dream* (1970)	Jaymar, 1972	
	Summer 73/Ontario, Op. 44 (1973)	CMC ms	
Lorrain, Denis	*Séquence* (1973)	CMC ms	
Mather, Bruce	*Music for Organ, Horn and Gongs* (1973)	CMC ms	

composer	title	score	recording
Ridout, Godfrey	*Prelude* (from *Four Sonnets*) (1968), arr F.R.C. Clarke	GVT, 1968	
Wuensch, Gerhard	*Toccata nuptialis* (1976)	CMC ms	

Music for free-bass accordion

composer	title	score	recording
Dolin, Samuel	*Sonata* (1970)	Waterloo, 1972	RCI 385
Kenins, Talivaldis	*Three Fugues* (1971)	Waterloo, 1973	
Surdin, Morris	*Serious I–VIII* (1969)	Boosey, 1970	RCI 385 (inc)
	Serious IX–XVI (1973)	S.E.L., 1976	
Wuensch, Gerhard	*Alberta Set* (1971), Op. 55	Boosey, 1972	
	Four Mini-Suites, Op. 42 (1968)	Waterloo, 1970	RCI 385 (inc)
	Monologue (1972), Op. 60	CMC ms	
	Sonata da Camera (1970), Op. 48	Boosey, 1971	
	Diversions, Op. 64 (1972)	CMC ms	
	Deux sentiments, Op. 67 (1973)	CMC ms	

ORCHESTRAL MUSIC

composer	title	score	recording
Adaskin, Murray	*Diversion for Orchestra* (1969)	CMC ms	CBC SM 294
	Fanfare (1970)	CMC ms	CBC SM 163
	Qalala and Nilaula of the North (1969)	CMC ms	CMC tape 642–3
	Nootka Ritual (1974)	CMC ms	
	In Praise of Canadian Painting in the Thirties (1975)	CMC ms	
Aitken, Robert	*Concerto for 12 Solo Instruments and Orchestra* (1968)	Kerby, 1974	CMC tape 716
	Nekuia (1971)	CMC ms	CMC tape
	Spectra (1968)	Ricordi, 1973	CMC tape 715
Archer, Violet	*Concertino for Clarinet and Orchestra* (1971)	CMC ms	CMC tape 702
	Sinfonietta (1968)	CMC ms film 16/3	CBC SM 226
Barnes, Milton	*Shebetim* (1974), string orchestra	CMC ms	
Beecroft, Norma	*Improvissazioni concertanti II* (1971)	Leeds, 1974	RCA KRLI-0007; RCI 382; *Musican* rec. 9

composer	title	score	recording
	Improvissazioni concertanti III (1973)	CMC ms	
Betts, Lorne	*Concerto for Violoncello, Piano and Orchestra* (1976)	CMC ms	
Bissell, Keith	*Andante e Scherzo* (1971)	Kerby, 1972	
	Variations on a Canadian Folk Song (1972)	CMC ms	
Blair, Dean G.	*Concerto for Piano and Orchestra* (1977)	ms	Lethbridge
Brott, Alexander	*Mini-Minus* (1968)	Leeds, 1971	
	Cupid's Quandary (1975)	CMC ms	
	The Young Prometheus (1969)	CMC ms	RCI 310; Select CC 15-038
Buczynski, Walter	*Concerto for Violin, Violoncello and Orchestra* (1975)	CMC ms	
	Seven Miniatures for Orchestra (1970)	CMC ms	CBC SM 308
Cherney, Brian	*Chamber Concerto for Viola and Ten Players* (1975)	CMC ms	
Clements, Peter	*Suite Grotesque* (1972)	CMC ms	
Coulthard, Jean	*Canada Mosaic* (1974)	CMC ms	
Dawson, Ted	*Concerto Grosso I* (1974)	CMC ms	
Dolin, Samuel	*Concerto for Piano* (1974)	CMC ms	CMC tape
	Concerto Grosso (1970)	S.E.L., 1977	
Fiala, George	*Montreal*, Op. 8 (1968)	Berandol, 1969	RCI 291
	Concerto for Violin and Orchestra (1973)	CMC ms	
	Sinfonietta Concertata (1971)	CMC ms	RCI 385
Fleming, Robert	*Divertimento* (1970), organ, 2 oboes, and strings	ms	CBC SM 292
Fodi, John	*Concerto for Viola and Two Wind Ensembles* (1972)	CMC ms	
Forsyth, Malcolm	*Sagittarius* (1975), brass quintet and orchestra	CMC ms	CBC SM 328
Fortier, Marc	*Un doigt de la lune* (1968)	Jaymar, 1970	
Freedman, Harry	*Klee Wyck* (1970)	CMC ms	CMC tape 639
	Graphic I (1971)	CMC ms	
	Tapestry (1973)	CMC ms	
Garant, Serge	*Offrande I* (1969)	CMC ms	RCI 368; RCI ACM 2
	Offrande II (1970)	CMC ms	

composer	title	score	recording
Gellman, Steven	*Symphony in Two Movements* (1970–1)	Ricordi, 1972	CBC SM 295
	Odyssey (1971)	Ricordi, 1973	CMC tape 685
Glick, Srul Irving	*Gathering In* (1970), string orchestra	Summit, 1972	RCI 389
	Lamentations (Sinfonia Concertante No. 2) (1972)	CMC ms	
Hartwell, Hugh	*Sonata for Orchestra* (1975)	CMC ms	
Hawkins, John	*Variations for Orchestra* (1970)	CMC ms	2nd movement CMC tape 674
Healey, Derek	*Arctic Images* (1971)	Ricordi, 1977	CBC SM 265
	Primrose in Paradise (1975)	Presser	CBC SM 331
Heard, Alan	*Sinfonia nello stile antico* (1977)	CMC ms	
Hétu, Jacques	*Concerto pour piano*, Op. 15 (1969)	Berandol, 1976	CMC tape 762
	Symphonie no. 3, Op. 18 (1971)	CMC ms	RCI 436
	Fantaisie pour piano et orchestre, Op. 21 (1973)	ms	CMC tape 1032
Hodkinson, Sydney	*Fresco* (1968)	Jobert, 1971	
	Valence (1970)	ms	CRI SD 292
Johnston, Richard	*Portraits (Variations for Orchestra)* (1972)	CMC ms	
Kenins, Talivaldis	*Concerto for Violin and Orchestra* (1974)	CMC ms	CBC SM 293
	Symphony No. 4 (1972)	CMC ms	CBC SM 293
Klein, Lothar	*Music for Violin and Orchestra* (1972)	CMC ms	
	Symphonic Etudes (Symphony No. 3) (1972)	CMC ms	
Kunz, Alfred	*Concerto for Piano and Orchestra* (1975)	CMC ms	
McCauley, William	*Concerto Grosso* (1973)	Marseg, 1976	CBC SM 264
Mann, Leslie	*Symphony No. 1* (1973)	CMC ms	CBC SM 281
Mather, Bruce	*Music for Rouen* (1971)	CMC ms	CBC SM 331
	Music for Vancouver (1969)	CMC ms	CBC SM 143
Matton, Roger	*Mouvement symphonique no. 3* (1974)	CMC ms	
Miller, Michael R.	*Capriccio on the Seven Ages of Man* (1972)	CMC ms	

composer	title	score	recording
Morawetz, Oskar	*Memorial to Martin Luther King* (1968)	CMC film 14/7	RCI 212
	Improvisation for Cello and Orchestra (1973)	CMC ms	
Morel, François	*Iikkii (Froidure)* (1971)	Ricordi, 1974	RCI 367
	Radiance (1971–2)	Ricordi, 1974	RCI 367
Papineau-Couture, Jean	*Oscillations* (1969)	Berandol, 1975	CMC tape 583
Pentland, Barbara	*Res musica* (1975)	CMC ms	
Pépin, Clermont	*Chroma* (1973)	CMC ms	
	Monade III (1972), violin and orchestra	CMC ms	CMC tape
	Prismes et cristaux (1974)	CMC ms	CMC tape
Prévost, André	*Chorégraphie I (... Munich, sept. 1972...)* (1973)	CMC ms	CMC tape 907
	Chorégraphie III (1976)	CMC ms	
	Concerto pour violoncelle et orchestre (1976)	CMC ms	
	Evanescence (1970)	Ricordi, 1971	RCI 332; RCA VCCS 1640
Ridout, Godfrey	*Concerto Grosso* (1974)	CMC ms	CBC SM 289
Saint-Marcoux, Micheline Coulombe	*Hétéromorphie* (1970)	CMC ms	CMC tape 745
Schafer, R. Murray	*Cortège* (1978)	ms	
	East (1972)	Universal (Can), 1977	RCI 434; RCI ACM
	Lustro (1969–73)	Universal (Can), 1977	CMC tape 767
	No Longer Than Ten Minutes (1970; rev 1972)	Berandol, 1977	
	North/White (1973)	ms	
	Son of Heldenleben (1968)	Universal (Can), 1976	RCI 387; RCI ACM
	Train (1976)	Berandol, 1977	
Schudel, Thomas	*Symphony No. 1* (1971)	CMC ms	
Sherman, Norman	*Thesis for Orchestra* (1975)	CMC ms	CMC tape
Southam, Ann	*Waves* (1976)	CMC ms	
Tremblay, Gilles	*Fleuves* (1976)	Salabert, 1976	
Turner, Robert	*Chamber Concerto for Bassoon and 17 Instruments* (1973)	Waterloo, 1977	
	Eidolons: Twelve Images for Chamber Orchestra (1972)	CMC ms	CBC SM 265

composer	title	score	recording
	Variations on the Prairie Settler's Song (1974)	CMC ms	CBC SM 331
	Concerto for Two Pianos and Orchestra (1971)	CMC ms	
Wallace, William	*Ceremonies* (1974)	Berandol, 1977	
Weinzweig, John	*Divertimento No. 4* (1968)	CMC ms	CBC SM 134
	Divertimento No. 6 (1972)	CMC ms	
	Dummiyah (1969)	CMC ms	CMC tape
Weisgarber, Elliot	*Autumnal Music* (1973)	CMC ms	
Wilson, Charles M.	*Symphonic Perspectives* ('Kingsmere') (1974)	CMC ms	
Wuensch, Gerhard	*Concerto for Piano and Chamber Orchestra* (1971)	CMC ms	CMC tape

Third stream

composer	title	score	recording
Douglas, William	*Improvisations III* (1969)		RCI 358
Gellman, Steven	*Odyssey* (1971)	Ricordi, 1973	CMC tape 685
Hartwell, Hugh	*Soul Piece for 6 or 7 Players* (1967; rev 1969)	Berandol, 1969	
Klein, Lothar	*Trio Sonata* (1969)	Third Stream, 1970	
	Design for Percussion and Orchestra (1971)	Leeds (rental)	
Steven, Donald	*Images* (1977)	CMC ms	
Symonds, Norman	*Democratic Concerto* (1967)	CMC ms film 13/37	

CHAMBER MUSIC

composer	title	score	recording
Adaskin, Murray	*Quintet for Woodwinds* (1974)	CMC ms	
Aitken, Robert	*Kebyar* (1971)	Salabert, 1974	
	Icicle (1977), solo flute	Editions musicales	
	Shadows II, 'Lalita' (1973)	CMC ms	RCI 411
Archer, Violet	*Sonata for Alto Saxophone and Piano* (1972)	Berandol, 1974	RCI 412
	Sonata for Clarinet and Piano (1970)	Waterloo, 1973	RCI 412
Barnes, Milton	*Fantasy for Guitar* (1975)	McKee, 1978	
Beckwith, John	*Taking a Stand* (1972), brass quintet	Berandol, 1975	CMC tape 688
	Quartet (1977)	CMC ms	
Beecroft, Norma	*Rasas* (1968)	CMC ms	RCI 298-301; *Musican* rec. 11

composer	title	score	recording
	Rasas II (1972–3)	CMC ms	
	11 and 7 for 5 + (1975), brass quintet & tape		CBC SM 320
	Rasas III (1973–4)	CMC ms	
Betts, Lorne	*String Quartet No. 3* (1970)	CMC ms	
Bissell, Keith	*Overheard on a Saltmarsh,* soprano, flute, and piano	Kerby, 1972	
	How the Loon Got Its Necklace (1971), for narrator, string quintet, and percussion	CMC ms	RCI 388
	Suite for Bassoon, String Quartet and Percussion (1977)	CMC ms	
Buczynski, Walter	*Olympics '76* (1976), brass quintet	CMC ms	
Cherney, Brian	*Tangents I* (1975)	CMC ms	
	Mobile IV (1969)	Jaymar, 1970	
Coulthard, Jean	*Lyric Sonatina for Flute and Piano* (1971)	Waterloo, 1976	
	Lyric Sonatina for Bassoon and Piano (1969)	Waterloo, 1973	Mel SMLP 4032
	Threnody (String Quartet No. 2) (1953; rev 1969–74)	Berandol, 1975	RCI 386
Crawford, Paul	*La Nuit étoilée* (1972)	CMC ms	
	Quintet for Brass (1975)	CMC ms	
Dolin, Samuel	*Ricercar* (1974), solo guitar	S.E.L., 1977	Mel SMLP 4025
Douglas, William	*Improvisations III* (1969), clarinet and piano		RCI 358
Farrell, Dennis	*Suite catholique* (1973), double bass and organ		CBC SM 269
Fiala, George	*Sonata for Violin and Piano* (1969)	CMC ms	CMC tape 649
Freedman, Harry	*Graphic II* (1972), string quartet	CMC ms	RCI 394; RCI ACM
	Five Rings (1976), brass quintet	CMC ms	CBC SM 320
	Pan (1972), voice, flute, and and piano	CMC ms	RCI 404; RCI ACM
	Soliloquy (1970), flute and piano	Leeds, 1971	Dominion s-69006; CAPAC-CAB tape 10

composer	title	score	recording
	Tikki-Tikki-Tembo (1971), narrator and woodwind quintet	CMC ms	RCI 388; RCI ACM
	The Explainer (1976)	CMC ms	
	Encounter (1974), violin and piano	CMC ms	RCI ACM
	Toccata (1968), soprano voice and flute	Kerby, 1972	CBC SM 96
	Lines (1973; rev 1974), solo clarinet	CMC ms	RCI ACM
Garant, Serge	*Circuits II* (1972)		RCI 368; RCI ACM 2
	... chants d'amours (1975)	CMC ms	RCI ACM 2; RCI 422
	Jeu à quatre (1968), 16 players	CMC ms film 7/31	RCI 300; RCI ACM 2
	Offrande III (1971)	Salabert, 1973	RCI 367-370; RCI ACM 2
Gellman, Steven	*Mythos II* (1968), flute and string quartet	CMC ms	RCI 301
Girón, Arsenio	*Idols* (1974), cello and piano	ms	
Glick, S. Irving	*Suite hébraique no. 3* (1975)	CMC ms	
	Petite Suite (1969), solo flute	GVT, 1971	Dom s-69006
	Suite hébraique no. 2 (1969)	CMC ms	RCI 389
Hartwell, Hugh	*Septet* (1969)	Jaymar, 1971	
	Soul Piece for 6 or 7 Players (1967; rev 1969)	Berandol, 1969	
Hawkins, John	*Remembrances* (1969)	Jaymar, 1971	RCI 298-301
	Trio (1975), flute, xylophone, and cello	CMC ms	
Hétu, Jacques	*Cycle* (1969), Op. 16, solo piano and nine instruments	CMC ms	RCI 301
Hodkinson, Sydney	*Arc* (1969), soprano and four players	CMC ms	CBC SM 148
	Another ... man's poison (1970), brass quintet		
Joachim, Otto	*Illumination II* (1969)	Berandol, 1975	RCI 298
	Six Guitar Pieces (1971)	Preissler	RCI 392; Mel SMLP 4025
Jones, Kelsey	*Wind Quintet* (1968)	Peters, 1972	RCI 355
	Passacaglia and Fugue (1975), brass quintet	CMC ms	McGill ST 77004
Klein, Lothar	*Six Exchanges* (1972), alto saxophone	Tenuto, 1972	

composer	title	score	recording
	Eclogues (1972), guitar	Waterloo	
Komorous, Rudolf	*Rossi* (1974)	Universal (Can), 1975	CAPAC Portrait (inc)
Laufer, Edward	*Variations for Seven Instruments* (1967)	New Valley, 1972	
Lidov, David	*Fantasy for Bassoon and Piano* (1972)	CMC ms	Mel SMLP 4032
McCauley, William	*Five Miniatures for Brass Quintet* (1974)	Marseg, 1975	No. 4 Boot BMC-3003
Mather, Bruce	*Eine Kleine Bläsermusik* (1975)	CMC ms	SNE 501
Morel, François	*Me duele España* (1975), guitar	CMC ms	RCI 457
	Départs (1969)		RCI 367
	Iikkii (1971)	Ricordi, 1974	RCI 367
Papineau-Couture, Jean	*Chanson de Rahit* (1972)	CMC ms	CMC tape
	Le Débat du cœur et du corps de Villon (1977)	CMC ms	RCI ACM
	Slano (1975), string trio	CMC ms	
	J'aime les tierces mineures (1976), solo flute	Editions musicales	
Pentland, Barbara	*String Quartet No. 3* (1969)	CMC ms	RCI 353
	Occasions (1974), brass quintet	CMC ms	
	Interplay (1972), accordion and string quartet	CMC ms	Mel SMLP 4034
Pépin, Clermont	*Monade IV* (1974), violin and piano	CMC ms	
	Monade VI – Réseaux (1976), violin solo	CMC ms	
	Quatuor à cordes no. 5 (1976)	CMC ms	
Prévost, André	*Quatuor à cordes no. 2 'Ad pacem'* (1972)	CMC ms	RCI 394
Rodrigue, Nicole	*Deux atmosphères* (1974)		CAPAC Portrait (inc)
	Souffrière (1969), 2 flutes and 2 piccolos		CAPAC Portrait (inc)
Saint-Marcoux, Micheline Coulombe	*Genesis* (1975), woodwind quintet	Archambault, 1978	SNE 501
	Ishuma (1974), voice and instruments	CMC ms	RCI 422
	Trakadie (1970), percussion and tape		*Musican* rec. 13

composer	title	score	recording
Schafer, R. Murray	*Enchantress* (1971), soprano, flute, and eight cellos	Berandol,1978	
	Minimusic (1969), any combination of instruments or voices	Universal, 1971	
	String Quartet (1970)	Universal (Can), 1973	Mel SMLP 4026; Concert Hall SMS 2902; RCI 353; RCI ACM
	String Quartet No. 2 'Waves' (1976)	Berandol, 1978	RCI ACM
Somers, Harry	*Improvisation* (1968–9), narrator, singers, and instruments	Berandol	CMC tape 536
	Music for Solo Violin (1973)	Berandol, 1975	RCI 413
Steven, Donald	*Illusions* (1971), solo cello	Kerby, 1973	RCI 409
Symonds, Norman	*A Diversion* (1974), brass quintet	Kerby	CBC SM 320
Tittle, John Steven	*'It is all there all the time,'* double bass and harpsichord		CBC SM 269
Tremblay, Gilles	*Champs I* (1965; rev 1969), piano and percussion	Salabert, 1974	RCI 370
	Solstices (1971), flute, clarinet, horn, bass and percussion	CMC ms	RCI 298-301
	Souffles (Champs II) (1968), 13 players	Salabert, 1975	RCI 370
	Vers (Champs III) (1969), 12 players	Salabert, 1974	RCI 367-370
	Oralléluiants (1975)	CMC ms	CMC tape 896
Turner, Robert	*Fantasy and Festivity* (1970), solo harp	CMC ms	CBC SM 188
	String Quartet No. 3 (1975)	CMC ms	
Vivier, Claude	*Prolifération* (1968–9), Ondes Martenot, piano, and percussion	CMC ms	RCI 358
	Lettura di Dante (1974)		RCI 411
Weinzweig, John	*Pieces of Five* (1976), brass quintet	CMC ms	
	Riffs (1974), solo flute	International, 1974	CMC tape 883
Weisgarber, Elliot	*Quartet* (1975)	CMC ms	
Wilson, Charles M.	*5 × 4 × 3* (1970)	CMC ms	CBC SM 195

composer	title	score	recording
Wuensch, Gerhard	*Cameos*, Op. 46a (1969), flute and piano	Leeds, 1971	Dom s-69006
	Suite for Trumpet and Organ, Op. 40 (1970)	Avant, 1972	RCI 406
	Sonata for Soprano Saxophone and Piano (1971)	CMC ms	

CHORAL MUSIC

composer	title	score	recording
Archer, Violet	*Shout with Joy* (1976)	Waterloo, 1977	
Bancroft, H. Hugh	*Mass of Saint Thomas* (1974)	Waterloo, 1974	
Barnes, Milton	*Shir Hashirim* (Song of Songs) (1975)	CMC ms	
Beckwith, John	*Three Blessings* (1968)	Berandol, 1968	Cap ST-6323
	The Sun Dance (1968)	CMC ms	
	Gas! (1969)	Berandol, 1978	CMC tape 599
	1838 (1970)	Novello, 1970	
Beecroft, Norma	*The Living Flame of Love* (1968)	Waterloo, 1969	Poly ST 2917009; *Musican* no. 5
	Three Impressions (1973)	CMC ms	
Betts, Lorne	*Margaritae sorori* (1975)	CMC ms	
Bissell, Keith	*Famous Men* (*In Praise of*) (1976)	CMC ms	
(arr)	'Adieu de la mariée à ses parents' (1968)	GVT, 1968	
	Three Songs in Praise of Spring (1968)	Caveat, 1972	
(arr)	'Nous étions trois capitaines' (1968)	GVT, 1968	
Burritt, Lloyd	*Once Again – Pop!* (1968)		
Cabena, Barrie	*Psalm 150*, Op. 44	Huron, 1971	
	Three Motets, Op. 70 (1976)	GVT, 1978	
Clarke, F.R.C.	*Festival Te Deum* (1972)	CMC ms	
	Missa brevis	Waterloo, 1973	
Fleming, Robert	*Mass of Saint Thomas*	Waterloo, 1974	
	Three Nova Scotia Folk Songs (1971)	Waterloo, 1972	
	Mass (1976)	CMC ms	
Freedman, Harry	*The Flame Within* (1968)	Leeds, 1970	RCI 341; CBC SM 142; Decca DL-75244; RCI ACM
	Keewaydin (1971), SSA and optional tape	GVT, 1972	Poly ST 2917009

* Cantata

composer	title	score	recording
	Songs from Shakespeare (1972)	Composers Press, 1974	
Grégoire, Richard	**Cantate* (1968)		RCI 301
Hawkins, John	*Spring Song* (1974)	CMC ms	
Healey, Derek	*There Is One Body* (1972)	Chanteclair, 1975	
	Clouds (1972)	McKee, 1973	
	In Flanders Fields (1974)	Chanteclair, 1976	
(arr)	*Six Canadian Folk Songs* (1973)	Chanteclair, 1973	CBC SM 274
Hétu, Jacques	**Les Djinns*, Op. 22 (1975)	CMC ms	
Holman, Derek	*The Mass of Saint Thomas* (1974)	Waterloo, 1974	
	Weatherscapes (1973)	GVT, 1973	
Jones, Kelsey	*Kishimaquac* (1971)	CMC ms	
Kenins, Talivaldis	**Piae cantiones novae* (1968)	Waterloo, 1969	
	Psalm 150 (1970)	Waterloo, 1970	
	*Sawan-oong (The Spirit of the Wind) (1973)	CMC ms	
Klein, Lothar	**Orpheus* (1976)	CMC ms	
Kunz, Alfred	*Sketches of Waterloo County* (1974)	GVT, 1975	
Lorrain, Denis	*P-A* (1970)	CMC ms	
MacNutt, Walter	*Mass of St James*	Waterloo, 1974	
Miller, Michael R.	**Cantata festiva* (1974)	CMC ms	
Morawetz, Oskar	*Crucifixion* (1968)	Leeds, 1971	CMC tape 603
Naylor, Bernard	*Exultet mundus gaudio* (1969)	Roberton, 1972	
	Missa sine Credo (1969)	Roberton, 1973	
	Cantate Domino (1970)	Roberton, 1973	
Papineau-Couture, Jean	**Paysage* (1968)	CMC ms film 11/47	RCI 299; RCI ACM
Paul, David	*Numbers in a Row* (1971)	GVT, 1973	Poly ST2917009
Prévost, André	*Missa de profundis* (1973)	CMC ms	
	Psaume 148 (1971)	CMC ms	
Ridout, Godfrey	*The Domage of the Wise* (1968)	ms	CBC SM 86
	*Cantiones mysticae no. III (The Dream of the Rood) (1972)	CMC ms	
Schafer, R. Murray	*Epitaph for Moonlight* (1968)	Berandol, 1969	CBC SM 274; RCI ACM; Mel SMLP 4017

* Cantata

composer	title	score	recording
	From the Tibetan Book of the Dead (1968)	Universal, 1973	
	*In Search of Zoroaster (1971)	Berandol, 1976	
	Miniwanka, or The Moments of Water (1971)	Universal, 1973	RCI 434; RCI ACM
	Psalm (1972; rev 1976)	Berandol, 1976	RCI 434
	Yeow and Pax (1969)	Berandol (in preparation)	
Somers, Harry	*Five Songs of the Newfoundland Outports* (1969)	Chanteclair, 1969	RCI 339; CBC SM 105; RCA LSC 3154; CMC tape 833
	Trois chansons de la Nouvelle France	Chanteclair, 1977	
	*Kyrie (1970–2)	*Exile,* 1:3 (1973)	CMC tape 833
Truax, Barry	*Moon Dreams* (1971)		
Wilson, Charles	*Dona nobis pacem* (1970)	GVT, 1972	Poly ST2917009
	*Song for St Cecilia's Day (1976)	CMC ms	
Wuensch, Gerhard	*Laus sapientiae,* Op. 72 (1977)	CMC ms	

VOCAL MUSIC (for voice and piano unless otherwise indicated)

composer	title	score	recording
Beckwith, John	*Five Songs* (1970)	Waterloo, 1971	Select CC-15.073; CBC SM 77
(arr)	*Four Love Songs* (1969)	Berandol, 1970	CBC SM 111
Beecroft, Norma	*Rasas II* (1973), voice, instruments, and tape	CMC ms	
Bissell, Keith (arr)	*Ten Folk Songs of Canada*	Waterloo, 1972	CBC SM 168
	Hymns of the Chinese Kings	Waterloo, 1968	
(arr)	*Six Maritime Folk Songs,* Sets I and II	Berandol, 1970	CBC SM 168; RCI 419 (inc)
	Overheard on a Salt Marsh, voice, flute, and piano	Caveat, 1972	
	Six Folk Songs from Eastern Canada (1970)	Boosey, 1971	CBC SM 144
Brott, Alexander	*Songs of the Central Eskimos* (1972)		CBC SM 391
Crawford, Paul	*At Night on the High Seas* (1975)	CMC ms	

* Cantata

composer	title	score	recording
Fiala, George	*Four Russian Poems*, Op. 9 (1968)	Waterloo, 1973	
Freedman, Harry	*Poems of Young People* (1968)	CMC ms	Select CC-15.073; CBC SM 77; RCI ACM
	Fragments of Alice (1976), SAB soli and instruments	CMC ms	
	Toccata (1968), soprano and flute	Kerby, 1972	CBC SM 96; RCI ACM
Gagnon, Alain	*Que je t'accueille*, Op. 15 (1968), voice and instruments [Saint-Denys Garneau]	CMC ms	RCI 393
Glick, Srul Irving	*i never saw another butterfly* (1968)	Leeds, 1972	Select CC-15.073; CBC SM 77
Hawkins, John	*Waves* (1971)	CMC ms	RCI 300
Heard, Alan	*Voices* (1969), soprano and instruments	CMC ms	RCI 358
Hétu, Jacques	*Les Clartés de la nuit* (1972)	CMC ms	
Hodkinson, Sydney	*Arc* (1969), voice and instruments	CMC ms	CBC SM 148
Johnston, Richard	*The Irish Book* (1971)	Waterloo, 1971	
Jones, Kelsey	*Songs of Winter* (1973), SA and piano	CMC ms	
Klein, Lothar	*Philosopher in the Kitchen* (1974), voice and orchestra	CMC ms	CMC tape
Mather, Bruce	*Madrigal II* (1968), soprano, alto, and instruments	Jobert, 1970	RCI 300, 369; *Musican* no. 11
	Madrigal III (1971), alto voice, marimba, harp, piano	CMC ms	RCI 369
	Madrigal IV (1972), soprano, flute, piano	CMC ms	RCI 369; *Musican* no. 10
	Madrigal V (1973), soprano, alto and 19 instruments	CMC ms	
Morawetz, Oskar	*Father William* (1957; rev 1973, 1974)	CMC ms	RCI 391
	From the Diary of Anne Frank (1970)	Morawetz, 1973	CMC tape 623
Pedersen, Paul	*An Old Song of the Sun and the Moon and the Fear of Loneliness* (1973)	CMC ms	RCI 404

composer	title	score	recording
Pentland, Barbara	*Disasters in the Sun* (1976)	CMC ms	
	News (1970), voice and orchestra	CMC ms	CMC tape 713
Prévost, André	*Improvisation V* (1976)	CMC ms	
Saint-Marcoux, Micheline Coulombe	*Alchera* (1973), voice and instruments	CMC ms	
Schafer, R. Murray	*Adieu Robert Schumann* (1976), voice and orchestra	CMC ms	
	Enchantress (1971; rev 1972)	Berandol, 1978	
	Arcana (1972), voice and instruments	Universal (Can), 1977	RCI 434; RCI ACM
	From the Tibetan Book of the Dead (1968)	Universal, 1973	CMC tape 674
	Hymn to Night (1976)	CMC ms	
	La Testa d'Adriane (1978), voice and accordion	CMC ms	Mel SMLP 4034
Somers, Harry	*Love-In-Idleness* (1976)	CMC ms	
	Voiceplay (1971)	CMC ms	
	Zen, Yeats and Emily Dickinson (1975)	CMC ms	
Symonds, Norman	*Deep Ground, Long Waters* (1969)	Kerby, 1972	
Weinzweig, John	*Private Collection* (1971–5)	CMC ms	
	Trialogue (1971), voice, flute and piano	CMC ms	

OPERA AND MULTIMEDIA WORKS

composer	title	score	recording
Anhalt, István	*La Tourangelle* (1975)	CMC ms	CMC tape
Archer, Violet	*Sganarelle* (1973)	CMC ms	
Bartlett, Martin	*Five Directions* (1972)		
Beckwith, John	*The Shivaree* (1978) [James Reaney]	CMC ms	
Buczynski, Walter	*From the Buczynski Book of the Living* (1972)	CMC ms	
Charpentier, Gabriel	*An English Lesson* (1968)	CMC ms	CMC tape
	Orpheus (1969; rev 1972)		
	A Tea Symphony or The Perils of Clara (1972)	CMC ms	
Dolin, Samuel	*Drakkar* (1972)	CMC ms	

composer	title	score	recording
Ford, Clifford	*Hypnos* (1972)	CMC ms	
George, Graham	*King Theodore* (1973)	CMC ms	
Healey, Derek	*Seabird Island* (1977)		
Joachim, Otto	*Mankind* (1972)		
Kasemets, Udo	*KANADANAK* (1977)		
	Watearthundair (1976)		
McIntyre, Paul	*The Little Red Hen* (1976)	CMC ms	
Pannell, Raymond	*Aberfan* (1977)		
Polgar, Tibor	*The Glove* (1973)	CMC ms	
	The Troublemaker (1968)	CMC ms	
Rae, Allan	*Scarecrow* (1975)	CMC ms	
Rea, John	*The Prisoner's Play* (1973)	CMC ms	
Ridout, Godfrey	*The Lost Child* (1976)	CMC ms	
Schafer, R. Murray	*Patria I –*	Berandol, 1978	
	The Characteristics Man (1966–75)		
Somers, Harry	*Death of Enkidu* (1977)	CMC ms	
Symonds, Norman	*Lady in the Night* (1977)		
Wilson, Charles	*Héloise and Abelard* (1972)	CMC ms	
	The Selfish Giant (1972), children's opera	CMC ms	
	The Summoning of Everyman (1972)	CMC ms	
	Kamouraska (1975)	CMC ms	
	Psycho Red (1977)	CMC ms	

ELECTRONIC MUSIC

composer	title	score	recording
Anhalt, Istvan	*Foci* (1969)	Berandol, 1972	RCI 357
Bartlett, Martin	*Lines from Chuang-Tau* (1973)		
Bauer, Robert	*Extensions II* (1973) , guitar and tape		Mel SMLP 4028
Beckwith, John	*Upper Canadian Hymn Preludes* (1977), organ and tape	CMC ms	
Berg, Reinhard	*Gegenstimmung* (1972)		Mel SMLP 4027
Ciamaga, Gustav	*Canon for Stravinsky* (1972)		*Musican* no. 13
	Solipsism While Dying (1972)	ms	
	Invention No. 8 (1970)		*Musican* no. 13
Clements, Peter	*Poem* (1979), guitar and tape		
Dawson, Edward	*Concerto Grosso I* (1974)		
Druick, Don	*Cellophane Wrapper* (1970)		Mel SMLP 4027

composer	title	score	recording
Grimes, David	*Increscents* (1972), violin and tape		CAPAC Portrait (inc)
	Legend		CAPAC Portrait (inc)
	Sotto Voce (1976)		CAPAC Portrait (inc)
Hambraeus, Bengt	*Tornado* (1976)		McGill ST 76001
Huse, Peter	*Space Play* (1969)		RCI 373; Mel SMLP 4027
Jaeger, David	*Bwamerail* (1970)		*Musican* no. 13
	Fancye (1973), organ and tape		CAPAC Portrait (inc)
	Quanza Dueto (1976), 2 guitars and tape		CAPAC Portrait (inc)
Joachim, Otto	*5.9* (1971)		RCI 373
Kobylansky, Karl	*Thoughts* (1972), chorus and tape		
Komorous, Rudolf	*Anatomy of Melancholy* (1974)		CAPAC Portrait (inc)
Koprowski, Peter Paul	*Quotations* (1978)		
Lake, Larry	*Face* (1976), piano, synthesizer, and tape		CAPAC Portrait (inc)
	Sonata (1972)		CAPAC Portrait (inc)
LeCaine, Hugh	*Mobile* (1970)		RCI 373
Longtin, Michel	*Au nord du lac Supérieure* (1972)		
	Fedhibô (c 1972)		Mel SMLP 4027
	La mort du Pierrot (1971–2)		RCI 373
Montgomery, James	*Paris* (c 1976)		CAPAC Portrait (inc)
	Reconnaissance (1975), amplified string quartet		CAPAC Portrait (inc)
	Relations (1972), piano and tape		CAPAC Portrait (inc)
	White Fire (1974), amplified brass quintet		CAPAC Portrait (inc)
Paul, David	*Eruption* (1971)		RCI 373
Pedersen, Paul	*For Margaret, Motherhood and Mendelssohn* (1971)		RCI 373
	An Old Song of the Sun and the Moon and the Fear of Loneliness (1973)		RCI 404

composer	title	score	recording
Rea, John	*S.P.I. 51* (1969)		Marathon MS 2111
	-STER 1.3 (1969)		Marathon MS 2111
Saint-Marcoux, Micheline Coulombe	*Zones* (1972)		RCI 373
Southam, Ann	*Sky Sails* (1973)		MHIC
	Boat, River, Moon (1972)		Mel SMLP 4024
Truax, Barry	*Nautilus* (1976)		Mel SMLP 4033
	She, a Solo (1973)		Mel SMLP 4033
	Sonic Landscapes No. 3 (1975; rev 1977)		Mel SMLP 4033
	Trigon (1974–5)		Mel SMLP 4033

Group electronic works

composer	title	score	recording
Canadian Electronic Ensemble	*Arnold* (1977)		Music Gallery no. 8
(David Jaeger, David Grimes,	*Whale Oil* (1973)		Music Gallery no. 8
Larry Lake, James Montgomery	*Piano Quintet* (1976)		Music Gallery no. 8

Notes

CHAPTER ONE

1 W.O. Forsyth, 'Canadian Composers,' *Canadian Journal of Music*, 2 (June 1915)
2 Luigi von Kunits, 'Our Students,' *Canadian Journal of Music*, 2 (June 1915)
3 Harry C. Perrin, 'Music in Canada,' *University Magazine*, 10 (1911), 254ff
4 Pearl McCarthy, *Leo Smith, A Biographical Sketch*, vi
5 Helmut Kallmann, *A History of Music in Canada 1534–1914*, 24
6 Ibid, 208–14
7 Willi Apel, editor, *Harvard Dictionary of Music*, 2nd ed (Cambridge, Mass: Belknap Press of Harvard University Press 1969), 147–8
8 Kallmann, 200
9 Apel, 147
10 Augustus Bridle, 'Who Writes Our Music? A Survey of Canadian Composers,' *Maclean's Magazine*, 42 (15 December 1929), 20
11 Forsyth, 'Canadian Composers'
12 Augustus Bridle, 'Composers Among Us,' *Yearbook of the Arts in Canada 1929*, ed Bertram Brooker, 135
13 Kallmann, 244
14 Romain Gour, 'Alexis Contant, pianiste-compositeur,' *Qui?* 5 (décembre 1953), 25–40
15 Kallmann, 242
16 Romain Gour, 'Guillaume Couture, compositeur,' *Qui?* 3 (septembre 1951), 24
17 H.J. Morgan, *Canadian Men and Women of the Time*, 2nd ed (Toronto: W. Briggs 1912), 508
18 Gilles Bryant, 'The Music of Healey Willan,' *Musicanada*, March 1968, 5–7
19 Bridle, 'Who Writes Our Music?' 20
20 Kallmann, 255
21 For a complete study of Mathieu's life and works see Juliette Bourassa-Trépanier, 'Rodolphe Mathieu,' thèse de doctorat, Université Laval, 1972
22 Godfrey Ridout, 'Healey Willan,' *Canadian Music Journal*, 3 (Spring 1959), 9

CHAPTER TWO

1 Léo-Pol Morin, 'Pour une musique canadienne,' *Canadian Forum*, 8 (July 1928), 713–14
2 Rodolphe Mathieu, *Parlons musique*, 93
3 Ernest MacMillan, 'Problems of Music in Canada,' *Yearbook of the Arts in Canada 1936*, ed Bertram Brooker, 186
4 Willi Apel, *Harvard Dictionary of Music*, 2nd ed, 72
5 C. Marius Barbeau, 'French and Indian Motifs in our Music,' *Yearbook of the Arts in Canada 1929*, ed Bertram Brooker, 132
6 C. Marius Barbeau, 'Folk-Song,' *Music in Canada*, ed Ernest MacMillan, 34
7 John Weinzweig, 'The New Music,' *Canadian Review of Music and Art*, 1 (June 1942), 16
8 Ibid
9 Barbeau, 'Folk-Song,' 35–6
10 Whitehead admitted in a private conversation with the author (28/8/72) that he often sent off arrangments of folk songs to publishers without even playing them over at the piano, much to his regret later.
11 Giles Bryant, *Healey Willan Catalogue*, 41
12 Gilles Potvin, 'André Mathieu,' *Contemporary Canadian Composers*, ed Keith MacMillan and John Beckwith, 145–6
13 Andrée Desautels, 'The History of Canadian Composition 1610–1967,' *Aspects of Music in Canada*, ed Arnold Walter, 106
14 Bryant, *Healey Willan Catalogue*, 56

CHAPTER THREE

1 William S.A. Dale, 'Sculpture,' *The Arts in Canada*, ed Malcolm Ross, 41
2 Paul-Emile Borduas, 'Refus global,' reprinted in *La Revue socialiste*, Summer 1960, 57–65
3 Helmut Kallmann, *A History of Music in Canada 1534–1914*, 215. Also see *Canadian Journal of Music*, 2 (July 1915), 44
4 John Beckwith, 'Music,' in *The Culture of Contemporary Canada*, ed Julian Park, 149
5 Healey Willan, quoted in Beckwith, 'Music,' 144
6 Barbara Pentland, 'On Experiment in Music,' *Canadian Review of Music and Art*, 2 (August–September 1943), 25
7 Barbara Pentland, 'Canadian Music, 1950,' *Northern Review*, 3 (February–March 1950), 43–6
8 Jean Papineau-Couture, 'Que sera la musique canadienne,' *Amerique française*, 2 (October 1942), 24–6: 'Même si une musique proprement canadienne existait, il serait impossible d'expliquer ce qui la fait canadienne' (24).
9 Programme notes, RCI 251
10 Notes in the ms score, National Library of Canada, Ottawa
11 Both examples from Peter Mellen, *The Group of Seven* (Toronto: McClelland & Stewart 1970), 34, 141
12 Canadian Music Centre, *Canadian Music for Orchestra Catalogue*, 2nd edition (1976)
13 Harry Somers, *Suite for Harp and Chamber Orchestra*: 'Analysis,' 8

14 Ibid
15 Quoted in Tom Archer, 'Canadian Music in Wartime,' *Canadian Review of Music and Art*, 3 (June–July 1944), 33
16 A detailed discussion of the work is contained in Udo Kasemets, 'John Weinzweig,' *Canadian Music Journal*, 4 (Summer 1960), 4–18

CHAPTER FOUR

1 Helmut Kallmann, 'First Fifteen Years of the Canadian League of Composers,' *The Canadian Composer*, March 1966, 18
2 Ibid
3 Ibid
4 *Globe and Mail* (Toronto), 17 May 1951, 9
5 See John Beckwith, 'Canadian Recordings: A Discography,' *Canadian Library Association Bulletin*, 12 (April 1956)
6 Glenn Gould, programme notes, CBS ST 32 11 0046
7 John Beckwith, 'Composers in Toronto and Montreal,' *University of Toronto Quarterly*, 26 (October 1956), 47–69.
8 Art Gallery of Ontario, Toronto. There is a colour reproduction in Harris and Colgrove, eds *Lawren Harris* (Toronto: Macmillan, 1969), 75.
9 For further discussion see Lee Hepner, 'An Analytical Study of Selected Canadian Orchestral Compositions at Mid-Twentieth Century,' PH D dissertation, New York University, 1971.
10 John Weinzweig, *Symphonic Ode*, preface to score
11 Marvin Duchow, 'The International Conference of Composers at Stratford,' *Canadian Music Journal*, 5 (Autumn 1960), 9
12 Ibid
13 John Beckwith, 'Recent Orchestral Works by Champagne, Morel, and Anhalt,' *Canadian Music Journal*, 4 (Summer 1960), 47
14 Ibid
15 Quoted in ibid, 46
16 Programme notes, RCI 193
17 Text for Pierre Mercure's *Cantate pour une joie* by Gabriel Charpentier, verse 7. © Copyright 1955 by Editions Seghers, Paris; copyright assigned 1957 to G. Ricordi & Co. (Canada) Limited. Used by permission
18 Text for Harry Somers's *Five Songs for Dark Voice* by Michael E. Fram. Used by permission of the author
19 John Weinzweig, *Wine of Peace*, title-page notes
20 Udo Kasemets, 'John Weinzweig,' *Canadian Music Journal*, 4 (Summer 1960), 14–15
21 Programme notes, RCI 184
22 Ibid
23 Jean Papineau-Couture, 'Analysis of *Pièce Concertante no. 1 for Piano and Orchestra*: "*Repliement*"'
24 For a reproduction in colour see William Withrow, *Contemporary Canadian Painting* (Toronto: McClelland and Stewart, 1972), 173.

25 Beckwith, 'Composers,' 54

26 Programme notes, RCI 180

27 For further discussion of Pentland and this work in particular see Robert Turner, 'Barbara Pentland,' *Canadian Music Journal*, 2 (Summer 1958), 15–26. A list of works for 1938–58 is included.

28 H.H. Arnason, *Calder* (Princeton, NJ: Van Nostrand, 1966), 3

29 'Robert Turner: A Portrait,' *Musicanada*, May 1970, 11

30 *Canadian Chamber Music Catalogue* (Toronto: Canadian Music Centre, 1967), 135

31 Programme notes, RCI 201

32 Programme notes, RCI 272

33 Ibid

34 Quoted by George Falle, 'Canadian Opera,' *Canadian Forum*, 36 (December 1956), 206–7

35 John Kraglund, *Globe and Mail*, 19 November 1956; *Canadian Music Journal*, 1 (Winter 1957), 45

36 Falle, 'Canadian Opera,' 206

CHAPTER FIVE

1 John Beckwith and Udo Kasemets, eds, *The Modern Composer and His World*, 20

2 Ibid, 29

3 Ibid, 38

4 Ibid, 50

5 Ibid, 15–16

6 Ibid, 170

7 Clermont Pépin, 'Montréal: la semaine internationale de musique actuelle,' *Canadian Music Journal*, 6 (Autumn 1961), 29–31

8 Glenn Gould, programme notes, CBS 32 11 0045

9 Udo Kasemets, ed, *Canavangard: Music of the Nineteen Sixties and After*, 62

10 *Source*, 4 (July 1968), 37–43

11 Ibid, 41

12 Ibid, 43

13 Ibid, 42

14 Robert Ayre, 'Painting,' *The Arts in Canada*, ed Malcolm Ross, 41

15 The instrumental plan for Massey Hall is shown in Brian Cherney, *Harry Somers*, 96.

16 Ibid, 97

17 Programme notes, RCA LSC 2980 (RCI 230)

18 *The Concise Oxford Dictionary of Current English*, 6th ed (Oxford: Clarendon, 1976), s.v. 'monad'

19 André Prévost, *Fantasmes*, composer's note in score

20 Canadian Music Centre, *John Adaskin Project: Towards New Music in Education* (Toronto 1968)

21 Colleen Orr, 'The John Adaskin Project: A History and Evaluation,' M MUS thesis, University of Western Ontario, 1977

22 Patricia Martin Shand, *Canadian Music: A Selective Guidelist for Teachers*

23 John Weinzweig, *String Quartet No. 3* (1962), preface to ms score

24 Kasemets, *Canavangard*, 109

25 Ibid

26 'Udo Kasemets: A Portrait,' *Musicanada*, September 1969, 9

27 Udo Kasemets, *Trigon*, forward

28 Programme notes by Jacques Thériault, RCI 240

29 Andrée Desautels, 'The History of Canadian Composition, 1610–1967,' *Aspects of Music in Canada*, ed Arnold Walter, 132

30 Samuel Beckett, *Molloy. Malone Dies. The Unnameable* (London 1953)

31 Programme notes, RCI 299

32 Brian Cherney, *Harry Somers*, 111

33 Harold Stewart, *A Net of Fireflies* (Tokyo: Tuttle, 1960), 21

34 Programme notes, RCI 217

35 Programme notes, RCI 214

36 Harry Freedman, *Three Vocalises*, preface to score

37 Margaret Atwood, *Survival* (Toronto: Anansi 1972), 32ff

38 Programme notes, Cap St 6323

39 R. Murray Schafer, '*Threnody*: A Religious Piece for Our Time,' *Music: The AGO-RCCO Magazine*, 4:3 (May 1970), 35

40 Jacques Brault and Benoit Lacroix, eds, *Saint-Denys Garneau: Œuvres* (Montreal: Les Presses de l'Université de Montréal 1971), 33–4. For an English translation see John Glassco, editor, *The Poetry of French Canada in Translation* (Toronto: Oxford University Press 1970), 105.

41 See István Anhalt, 'The Making of *Cento*,' *Canada Music Book*, 1 (Spring–Summer 1970), 81–9; see also R. Murray Schafer, *When Words Sing*.

42 R. Murray Schafer, quoted by Desautels, 'Canadian Composition,' 138

43 Jean Vallerand, *Le Magicien*, note in ms score

44 'Otto Joachim, A Portrait,' *Musicanada*, June 1969, 11

CHAPTER SIX

1 'Comprehensive Catalogue of new Canadian Music Written in Honour of Canada's Centennial Year, 1967,' *Musicanada*, December 1967, 3–15

2 Mavor Moore, 'Louis Riel: The Theme is Timeless,' *Opera Canada*, September 1967, 44

3 Harry Somers, 'Louis Riel: The Score,' *Opera Canada*, September 1967, 46

4 Ibid

5 See R. Murray Schafer, *The Public of the Music Theatre. Somers' 'Louis Riel': A Case Study*

6 Programme notes, RCA LSC 3175 and RCI 328

7 Programme notes, RCI 292

8 Ibid

9 Harry Freedman, *Tangents*, composer's note in preface to score

10 István Anhalt, 'The Making of *Cento*,,' *Canada Music Book*, 1 (1970), 81

11 Ibid

12 Programme notes, RCI 240

13 Barbara Pentland, *Suite Borealis*, composer's note in ms score

14 See Francean Campbell, '*Expo* Sights and Sounds,' *Montreal Star*, 17 June 1967
15 See 'The Sound of Canadian Music at *Expo*,' *Canadian Composer*, July–August 1967, 8

CHAPTER SEVEN

1 See Canadian Music Centre catalogues; and see also *Musicanada* 11 supplemental listings (from November 1976).
2 George A. Proctor, 'Neo-classicism and Neo-romanticism in Canadian Music,' *Studies in Music from the University of Western Ontario* (London, Ont 1976); and 'Recent Trends in Canadian Music,' *Studies in Music from the University of Western Ontario* (London, Ont 1978).
3 John Weinzweig, *Dummiyah*, title page of ms score
4 Personal conversation with the author, November 1969
5 Micheline Coulombe Saint-Marcoux, *Alchera*, note on ms score
6 István Anhalt, 'The Making of *Cento*,' *The Canada Music Book*, 1 (Spring–Summer 1970), 81–9; István Anhalt, 'About *Foci*,' *Artscanada* (April–May 1971), 154–5; István Anhalt, 'Composing With Speech,' in *Proceedings of the Seventh International Congress of Phonetic Sciences* (Montreal 1971; repr The Hague: Mouton 1972)
7 Rachel Cavalho, 'Canadian Piano Music for Teaching,' *Musicanada*, June–July 1968, 5ff; and Ralph Elsaesser, 'Canadian Piano Music for Teaching,' *Musicanada*, August–September 1968, 10ff; see also the syllabi of *Contemporary Showcase*, 1972, 1974, 1976, and 1979, available from the Canadian Music Centre, Toronto.
8 R. Murray Schafer, *East*, preface to score
9 Ibid
10 R. Murray Schafer, *Music for the Morning of the World*, 10–11
11 Bruce Mather, 'Gilles Tremblay,' in Keith MacMillan and John Beckwith, editors, *Contemporary Canadian Composers*, 221
12 Ibid
13 Gilles Tremblay, *Oralléluiants*, preface to ms score
14 R. Murray Schafer, *String Quartet No. 2 'Waves*,' preface to score
15 Micheline Coulombe Saint-Marcoux, *Ishuma*, preface to ms score
16 John Beckwith, *Gas!*, preface to score
17 R. Murray Schafer, *In Search of Zoroaster*, preface to score
18 Quoted in Lyse Richer-Lortie, 'André Prévost,' *Contemporary Canadian Composers*, 188
19 Lothar Klein, *Orpheus*, preface to ms score
20 Ibid
21 István Anhalt, *La Tourangelle*, preface to ms score
22 Udo Kasemets, 'István Anhalt,' *Contemporary Canadian Composers*, 8
23 France Malouin-Gélinas, 'Gabriel Charpentier,' *Contemporary Canadian Composers*, 47
24 Ibid, 46
25 *Globe and Mail* (Toronto), 7 October 1975

Appendix

A Chronological Table of Canadian History, Music, and Other Arts 1900 to 1979

The following abbreviations are used in this table: M music; A other arts; H political or social history.

1900	M	*The Canadian Music Trades Journal* (until 1932)
	A	Art Museum of Toronto
		Rodolphe Girard (1879–1956). *Florence.* Psychological novel
1901	A	Ralph Connor (1860–1937). *The Man from Glengarry.* Novel
1903	M	Société symphonique de Québec (derived from Septuor Haydn), J. Vézina, conductor. Becomes L'Orchestre symphonique de Québec
1904	A	Bliss Carman (1861–1929). *Sappho: One hundred lyrics.* Poetry
		Pamphile Lemay (1837–1918). *Les Gouttelettes.* Poetry
		Sarah Jeanette Duncan (1862–1922). *The Imperialist.* Novel
1905	H	Alberta and Saskatchewan become separate provinces and join Confederation
	M	Alexis Contant (1858–1918). *Caïn.* First Canadian oratorio
		Alphonse Lavallée-Smith founds the Conservatoire national de musique in Montreal
	A	Duncan Campbell Scott (1862–1947). *New World Lyrics and Ballads.* Poetry
1906	H	First airplane flight in Canada
	M	*Musical Canada* begins publication (until 1933)
		First Toronto Symphony orchestra established (until 1918)
1907		Toronto String Quartet formed
1908	M	First competitive music festival in North America held in Edmonton
	A	Lucy Maud Montgomery (1874–1942). *Anne of Green Gables.* Novel
1910	M	Dubois String Quartet (Montreal)
	A	Stephen Leacock (1869–1944). *Literary Lapses.* Humorous sketches
1911	M	Marius Barbeau (1883–1969) begins collecting west-coast Indian songs for the National Museum, Ottawa
	A	Emily Carr (1871–1945) exhibits at *Salon d'automne,* Paris
		Pauline Johnson (1861–1913). *Legends of Vancouver.* Short stories

1912   A   Stephen Leacock. *Sunshine Sketches of a Little Town.* Novel

1913   M   Healey Willan (1880–1968) arrives to teach at the Toronto Conservatory of Music

          A   Algonquin Park school of painters groups around Tom Thomson (1877–1917)

              David Milne (1882–1953) exhibits at Armory Show in New York

              National Gallery Act

1914   H   World War I

          M   Guillaume Couture (1851–1915). *Jean le Précurseur,* oratorio. First performed in 1923

              Canadian Journal of Music (until 1919)

1915   M   Marius Barbeau begins collecting French-Canadian folk songs

1916   M   Healey Willan. *Introduction, Passacaglia and Fugue*

          A   Louis Hémon (1880–1913). *Maria Chapdelaine.* Publication posthumous. Novel

1917   A   John Daniel Logan (1869–1929). *Aesthetic Criticism in Canada*

1918   H   Enfranchisement of women

1919   H   Canada elected an independent member of the League of Nations

              Winnipeg General Strike

              First radio broadcast in Canada (Montreal)

          A   *The Canadian Bookman* (now *The Canadian Author and Bookman*)

              Formation of the Group of Seven – A.Y. Jackson, Arthur Lismer, J.E.H. MacDonald, Frederick Varley, Lawren Harris, Franklin Carmichael, Franz Johnston. First exhibition 1920

1920   A   *The Canadian Forum*

              Little Theatre movement

1921   A   Canadian Authors' Association

1922   A   Marjorie Pickthall (1883–1922). *The Wood Carver's Wife.* Verse drama

1923   H   US radio broadcasting begins on frequencies heard in Canada

          M   Toronto Symphony Orchestra (later Toronto Symphony), Luigi von Kunits, conductor

          A   E.J. Pratt (1882–1964). *Newfoundland Verse.* Poetry

1924   M   Hart House String Quartet (until 1945)

          A   Group of Seven achieves international recognition at Wembley Exhibition

1925   M   Canadian Performing Rights Society (CPRS)

          A   Frederick Philip Grove (1872–1948). *Settlers of the Marsh.* Novel

1927   M   First CPR-National Museum *Festival of Folk Art and Music,* Quebec City

              Ernest MacMillan (1893–1973). *Two Sketches for String Quartet*

              Claude Champagne (1891–1965). *Suite canadienne*

          A   Bertram Brooker (1888–1955) holds first exhibition of abstract art in Canada at the Arts and Letters Club, Toronto

              Frederick Philip Grove. *A Search for America.* Novel

              Mazo de la Roche (1885–1961). *Jalna.* Novel

1928   M   Second CPR-National Museum *Festival of Folk Art and Music,* Quebec City

              Helen Creighton (1899–) begins collecting Nova Scotian folk songs

              Ernest MacMillan. *Six bergerettes du bas Canada*

	A	Morley Callaghan (1903–). *Strange Fugitive.* Novel
		Sculptors' Society of Canada
1929	H	Stock market crash
	A	*Yearbook of the Arts in Canada,* edited by Bertram Brooker
1930	A	Camille Roy (1870–1943). *Histoire de la littérature canadienne*
1931	H	Statute of Westminster
	M	Ernest MacMillan becomes conductor of the Toronto Symphony Orchestra (until 1956)
	A	Vancouver Art Gallery
		University of Toronto Quarterly
1933	M	Vancouver Symphony
		Banff School of Fine Arts
	A	Claude-Henri Grignon (1894–). *Un Homme et son péché.* Novel
		Group of Seven replaced by Canadian Group of Painters. Lawren Harris begins to paint abstract art
		National (later Dominion) Drama Festival
1934	M	Les Concerts symphoniques de Montréal. Became Montreal Symphony Orchestra in 1954
	A	*La Relève* (until 1948). Edited by Hector de Saint-Denys Garneau, et al
		Morley Callaghan. *Such is My Beloved.* Novel
1935	M	Ernest MacMillan knighted by George V for service to music
	A	E.J. Pratt. *The Titanic.* Poetry
		Frederick Niven (1878–1944). *The Flying Years.* Novel
1936	H	Canadian Broadcasting Corporation created by act of Parliament
	M	Healey Willan. Symphony No. 1
		Ontario Registered Music Teachers' Association
	A	*The Canadian Poetry Magazine*
		Fritz Brandtner (1896–) paints abstract art
1938	A	Ringuet (né Philippe Panneton) (1895–1960). *Trente arpents.* Novel
1939	H	World War II
	M	John Weinzweig (1913–). *Suite for Piano No. 1.* First use of twelve-tone technique by a Canadian composer
	A	Contemporary Art Society (Montreal) (Paul-Emile Borduas, John Lyman, Goodridge Roberts, et al)
		Elford Cox (1914–), sculptor, experiments with abstract forms
		National Film Board
1940	M	BMI Canada
		Young Artists' Series in western Canada
	A	E.J. Pratt. *Brébeuf and His Brethren.* Epic poetry
		Alfred Pellan (1906–) returns to Canada from Paris and brings influence of surrealism with him
1941	A	Hugh MacLennan (1907–). *Barometer Rising.* Novel
		Sinclair Ross (1908–). *As For Me and My House.* Novel
1942	A	*Canadian Art (Arts Canada* after 1966)
		Canadian Review of Music and Art (to 1948)
		Anne Hébert (1916–). *Les Songes en équilibre.* Poetry

		Earle Birney (1904–). *David and Other Poems*
		Rex Desmarchais (1908–). *La Chesnaie.* Social novel
1943	H	Atomic energy project at Chalk River
	A	A.J.M. Smith (1902–). *A Book of Canadian Poetry.* Critical anthology
1944	M	Canadian Music Council
1945	H	Canada joins the United Nations
	M	Claude Champagne. *Symphonie gaspésienne*
	A	Hugh MacLennan. *Two Solitudes.* Novel
		Northern Review (until 1956)
1946	A	First show of *Les Automatistes* (Paul-Emile Borduas and disciples)
1947	H	Canadian Citizenship Act
	M	Composers, Authors, and Publishers Association of Canada (CAPAC) established from CPRS (1925)
	A	Paul Hiebert (1892–). *Sarah Binks.* Satirical novel
1948	A	*Prisme d'yeux*, manifesto issued by Alfred Pellan, Jacques de Tonnancour, Goodridge Roberts, Albert Dumouchel, et al
		Refus global, manifesto issued by Paul-Emile Borduas, Jean-Paul Riopelle, et al
		James Houston returns from Hudson's Bay with Eskimo carvings; the federal government takes over marketing of Eskimo carvings
1949	H	Newfoundland joins Confederation
	A	Earle Birney. *Turvey.* Novel
1950	A	Robertson Davies (1913–). *At My Heart's Core.* Drama
		Robert Elie (1915–). *La Fin des songes* (*Farewell My Dreams*). Novel
1951	M	Canadian League of Composers
	A	*Report on the Royal Commission on National Development in the Arts, Letters and Sciences,* 1949–51. Vincent Massey, chairman
		A.M. Klein (1909–1972). *The Second Scroll.* Novel
1952	H	Vincent Massey becomes first Canadian Governor-General
		CBC Television
	M	CBC Symphony Orchestra (until 1964)
	A	Painters Eleven (Toronto)
1953	A	Stratford Shakespearean Festival
1954	H	Canada a member of the International Control Commission in Indo-China. Beginning of role as an international peace-maker
	A	Ethel Wilson (1888–). *Swamp Angel.* Novel
		Venice Biennale. Works by Borduas, Riopelle, Binning. First Canadian abstract painters in an international exhibition
1956	M	*Canadian Music Journal* (until 1962)
	A	*Vie des arts*
		Tamarack Review
1957	A	Canada Council
		Jay Macpherson (1931–). *The Boatman.* Poetry
		Northrop Frye (1912–). *The Anatomy of Criticism*
1958	M	Musique de notre temps, formed in Montreal by François Morel, Serge Garant, Otto Joachim, Jeanne Landry

	A	*The Arts in Canada*, edited by Malcolm Ross
		Alden Nowlan (1933–). *The Rose and the Puritan.* Poetry
		James Reaney (1926–). *A Suit of Nettles.* Poetry
1959	M	Canadian Music Centre (Toronto)
		Electronic music studio, Faculty of Music, University of Toronto
		Canadian Opera Company (Toronto)
		Canadian Music Educators' Association
	A	Eric Nicol (1919–). *An Uninhibited History of Canada.* Humour
		Guy Robert (1933–). *Brousailles givrées.* Poetry
		Mordecai Richler (1931–). *The Apprenticeship of Duddy Kravitz.* Novel
1960	H	Beginning of the 'Quiet Revolution' in Quebec
	M	International Conference of Composers, Stratford
		National Youth Orchestra
		Vancouver Opera Association
	A	*La Relève*, an association of young Montreal artists opposed to existing political and artistic establishments
1962	A	First outdoor exhibit of sculpture by the National Gallery
		Marshall McLuhan (1911–). *The Gutenberg Galaxy.* Criticism
	M	John Adaskin Project of the Canadian Music Centre
1963	M	Electronic music studio, McGill University
1964	M	Canadian Association of University Schools of Music
		Electronic music studio, University of British Columbia
	A	'Canadian Painting 1939–63,' an exhibit at the Tate Gallery, London
		Musée d'art contemporain, Montreal
		Margaret Laurence (1926–). *The Stone Angel.* Novel
1966	M	La Société de musique contemporaine du Québec (Montréal). Serge Garant, music director
		Healey Willan. *Deirdre.* First Canadian opera produced by the Canadian Opera Company
		Harry Freedman. *Rose Latulippe.* First full-length ballet by a Canadian composer
1967	H	Centennial Year. Expo 67 in Montreal
	M	Centennial Commission commissions many new Canadian works
		Harry Somers. *Louis Riel*
1970	A	Pierre Berton (1920–). *The National Dream.* Popular history
1971	A	Theatre Canada
1972	M	New Music Concerts (Toronto). Robert Aitken, music director
		Array (Toronto)
		inNOVAtions (Halifax)
1973	M	Vancouver New Music Society
1974	M	*Dictionary of Contemporary Music*, edited by John Vinton (New York: Dutton, 1974). First full treatment of Canadian composers in an international reference work
1975	M	*Contemporary Canadian Composers*, edited by Keith MacMillan and John Beckwith
		Days, Months and Years to Come (Vancouver)

1976 M Music Inter Alia (Winnipeg)

1977 M *Compositeurs canadiens contemporains,* edited by Louise Laplante

    Alberta Composers' Association

    MUSICANADA: A Presentation of Canadian Contemporary Music in Paris and London sponsored by the Department of External Affairs and the Canada Council

1979 M First Annual Electronic Music Festival (Toronto)

Selective Bibliography

Capital letters identify subject entries.

Adaskin, Harry. 'Symposium of Canadian Contemporary Music, Vancouver, March 12–15, 1950, *Saturday Night*, 65 (11 April 1950), 23–4
Adaskin, Murray. 'Analysis of *Serenade Concertante*.' Toronto: Canadian Music Centre, 1961
ADASKIN, MURRAY
– 'List of Works,' *Musicanada*, May 1967
Anhalt, István. 'The Making of *Cento*,' *Canada Music Book*, 1 (Spring–Summer 1970), 81–9
– 'About *Foci*,' *Artscanada*, April–May 1971, 154–5
– 'Composing with Speech,' in *Proceedings of the Seventh International Congress of Phonetic Sciences*. Montreal 1971; repr The Hague: Mouton 1972
ANHALT, ISTVÁN
– 'List of Works,' *Musicanada*, November 1968
Archer, Thomas. 'Canadian Music in Wartime,' *Canadian Review of Music and Art*, 3 (June–July 1944), 32–5; 3 (August–September 1944), 25–8
– 'Claude Champagne,' *Canadian Music Journal*, 2 (Winter 1958), 3–10
ARCHER, VIOLET
– 'Condensed List of Works,' *Musicanada*, August–September 1968
– Crandell, Ev. 'Violet Archer,' *Music Scene*, May–June 1968, 7

Bail-Milot, Louise. 'Claude Champagne: son œuvre et ses procédés de composition.' Mémoire de maîtrise, Université de Paris 1972
Ball, Suzanne. 'Murray Schafer: Composer, Teacher, and Author,' *Music Scene*, May–June 1970, 7–8
Barbeau, C. Marius. 'French and Indian Motifs in our Music,' in Bertram Brooker, ed, *Yearbook of the Arts in Canada (1929)*. Toronto: Macmillan 1929
– 'Folk-Song,' in Sir Ernest MacMillan, ed, *Music in Canada*. Toronto: University of Toronto Press 1955

Barbeau, C. Marius, and Edward Sapir. *Folk Songs of French Canada.* New Haven: Yale
  University Press 1925
A Basic Bibliography of Musical Canadiana, comp F.A. Hall, S.L. Hall, D.B. Minorgan,
  K. Minorgan, N. Turbide. Toronto: University of Toronto Faculty of Music 1970
Beaudet, Jean-Marie. 'Composition,' in Sir Ernest MacMillan, ed, *Music in Canada.* Toron-
  to: University of Toronto Press 1955
Beckwith, John. 'Canadian Recordings, a Discography,' *Canadian Library Association
  Bulletin,* 12 (April 1956), 182–3
– 'Composers in Toronto and Montreal,' *University of Toronto Quarterly,* 26 (October 1956),
  47–69
– 'Music,' in Julian Park, ed, *The Culture of Contemporary Canada.* Ithaca: Cornell University
  Press 1957
– 'Music,' in Malcolm Ross, ed., *The Arts in Canada.* Toronto: Macmillan 1958. 44–51
– 'Notes on Some New Music Heard on CBC Radio,' *Canadian Music Journal,* 4:2 (Winter
  1960), 37
– 'Jean Papineau-Couture,' *Canadian Music Journal,* 3 (Winter 1959), 4–20
– 'Recent Orchestral Works by Champagne, Morel, Anhalt,' *Canadian Music Journal,* 4:4
  (Summer 1960)
– 'The Performing Arts,' *Canadian Annual Review for 1960.* Toronto: University of Toronto
  Press 1961. 328–36
– 'Music,' *Canadian Annual Review for 1961.* Toronto: University of Toronto Press 1962.
  396–407
– and R.M. Schafer. 'Music,' *Canadian Annual Review for 1962.* Toronto: University of
  Toronto Press 1963. 400–14
– 'Music,' *Canadian Annual Review for 1963.* Toronto: University of Toronto Press 1964.
  514–24
– 'Notes on *Jonah* by the Composer,' *Alphabet,* No. 8 (June 1964), 14–18.
– 'Notes on Criticism,' *Music Scene,* September–October 1967, 4
– 'About Canadian Music: the P.R. Failure,' *Musicanada,* July–August 1969
– 'Kasemets – Torrents of Reaction,' *Music Scene,* January–February 1970, 4–5
– 'What Every U.S. Musician Should Know About Contemporary Canadian Music,'
  Musicanada, May 1970
– 'Students Hear Their Own Music,' *University of Toronto Graduate,* Summer 1970, 61–4,
  97–9
– 'Canada,' In John Vinton, ed, *Dictionary of Contemporary Music.* New York: Dutton 1974
– 'A Festival of Canadian Music,' *Musicanada: A Presentation of Canadian Contemporary Music.*
  Ottawa: Department of External Affairs and the Canada Council 1977
Beckwith, John, and Udo Kasemets, eds. *The Modern Composer and His World.* Toronto:
  University of Toronto Press 1961
Beckwith, John, and Keith MacMillan. *See* MacMillan, Keith
BECKWITH, JOHN
– 'List of Works,' *Musicanada,* November 1967
BEECROFT, NORMA
– 'A Conversation with Norma Beecroft: The New World of Electronic Music,' *Canadian
  Composer,* October 1967, 34
– 'List of Works,' *Musicanada,* May 1969

– Winters, Ken. 'A Composer Who Doesn't Wear Music Like a Straightjacket,' *Canadian Composer*, November 1971, 4

BETTS, LORNE
– 'List of Works,' *Musicanada*, April 1970
Bird, C. Laughton. 'Composer in the School – Supervisor's Role,' *Musicanada*, May 1969, 5–6, 12, 16
Bissell, Keith 'Canadian Composer and the Public,' *Performing Arts in Canada*, 1 (1961), 58–9
Boese, H. 'Canadian Music – Will it Develop a National Style?' *Diapason*, June 1958, 8
Boothroyd, David A. 'Pentland, Freedman and Prévost: Three Canadian String Quartets, 1968 to 1972.' M.A. thesis, University of Western Ontario 1979
Borduas, Paul-Emile. 'Refus global' (1948), reprinted in *La revue socialiste*, Summer 1960, 57–65

BORDUAS, PAUL-ÉMILE
– Ethier-Blais, Jean. 'Paul-Emile Borduas,' in *Canada's Past and Present: A Dialogue*. Toronto: University of Toronto Press 1965
Bourassa-Trépanier, Juliette. 'Rodolphe Mathieu.' Thèse de doctorat, Université Laval 1972
– 'A Forgotten Composer,' *Canadian Composer*, April 1973, 30
Bradley, Ian L. *A Selected Bibliography of Musical Canadiana*. 2nd ed Agincourt, Ont: GLC 1976
– *Twentieth Century Canadian Composers*. Agincourt, Ont: GLC 1977

BRANSCOMBE, GENA
– Britten, Clarence. 'Gena Branscombe,' *Canadian Journal of Music*, 1:2 (June 1914), 25
– Hale, Katherine. 'Gena Branscombe Tenney, Song Composer,' *Canadian Courier*, *14* (4 October 1913), 19
– Hodgins, J. Herbert. 'Canadian Composer Has Two Selves – One for Her Music; One for Her Home,' *Maclean's*, 1 June 1925
Brass, Virginia. 'Music Is Big Business,' *Canadian Business*, 26 (April 1953), 22–4, 128
Brassard, François J. 'Une date pour la musique canadienne,' *Revue de l'université Laval*, 5 (avril 1951), 738–46
Bridle, Augustus. 'Is Canada Musical?' *Canadian Courier*, 14 (25 October 1913), 5–8
– 'Forty Years and Now; Canadian music from 1876 to 1916,' *Canadian Courier*, 21 (9 December 1916), 12–13, 24
– 'Two pères de musique' [Torrington and Couture], in *Sons of Canada*. Toronto 1916, 261–8
– 'Composers Among Us,' in Bertram Brooker, ed, *Yearbook of the Arts in Canada, 1929*. Toronto: Macmillan 1929
– 'Who Writes our Music? A Survey of Canadian Composers,' *Maclean's Magazine*, 42 (15 December 1929), 20, 30, 32
Britten, Clarence. 'Gena Branscombe,' *Canadian Journal of Music*, 1:2 (June 1914), 25
Brooker, Bertram. 'Art and Society,' in Bertram Brooker, ed, *Yearbook of the Arts in Canada* (1936). Toronto: Macmillan 1936

BROTT, ALEXANDER
– 'List of Works,' *Musicanada*, March 1969

Brown, Thomas. 'Healey Willan,' *Music Scene*, November–December 1967
Bryant, Giles. 'The Music of Healey Willan,' *Musicanada*, March 1968, 5–7
– ed. *Healey Willan Catalogue*. Ottawa: National Library of Canada 1972
Butler, E. Gregory. 'The Piano Sonatas of Harry Somers.' D.M.A. dissertation, University of Rochester, 1974

Campbell, Francean. 'Expo Sight and Sounds,' *Montreal Star*, 17 June 1967, 2
Campbell-Yukl, Joylin. 'Healey Willan: the Independent Organ Works.' PH.D. thesis, University of Missouri 1976
Canada. National Library. Music Division. Bio-bibliographical files contain information on Canadian music and musicians
Canada. National Museum of Man / Musée national de l'homme. *An Introduction to the Canadian Centre for Folk Culture Studies / Presentation du centre canadien d'études sur la culture traditionelle*. Ottawa 1973
Canada. *Report of the Royal Commission on National Development in the Arts, Letters and Sciences, 1949–51*. Ottawa: King's Printer 1951
The Canada Music Book /Les Cahiers canadiens de musique. Montreal: Canadian Music Council 1970–6
Le Canada musical. Revue mensuelle fondé et dirigée par C.O. Lamontagne. Montreal 1917–24 and 1930
'Canada on Records; Some Recording of works by Canadian Composers.' *Musicanada*, January–February 1970, 15. Supplement, October 1972
Canadian Broadcasting Corporation. *CBC Broadcast Recordings* (SM Series). Toronto: CBC 1973
– *The Canadian Collection/La Collection canadienne*. Toronto: CBC Merchandizing 1975; 1977; 1979–80
– *Catalogue of Canadian Composers*, ed Helmut Kallmann. Rev and enlarged ed. Toronto 1952; repr St Clair Shores, Mich: Scholarly Press 1972
– *Radio Canada International Transcriptions Catalogue/Catalogue des transcriptions de radio Canada international*. Montreal 1946–
– *Thirty-four Biographies of Canadian Composers/Trente-quatre biographies de compositeurs canadiennes*, ed V.I. Rajewsky. Montreal: CBC International Service 1964; repr St Clair Shores, Mich: Scholarly Press 1972
'Canadian Composers,' *Canadian Review of Music and Art*, 1 (February 1942), 17
'Canadian Composers and Their Centennial Commissions,' *Canadian Composer*, July–August 1967, 36
'Canadian Compositions,' *Canadian Review of Music and Art*, 1 (March 1942), 14
'Canadian Music Abroad,' *External Affairs*, 2 (August 1950), 296–8
Canadian Federation of Music Teachers' Associations. *A List of Canadian Music*. Toronto: Oxford University Press 1946
Canadian League of Composers. *Catalogue of Orchestral Music*. Toronto 1957
Canadian Music Centre. *Canadian Compositions for Band*. Toronto, n.d.
– *Canadian Music Featuring Saxophone*. Toronto 1972
– 'Canadian Music for Education,' *Music Across Canada*, May 1963, 10–12
– *Canadian Vocal Music/Musique vocale canadienne*. 3rd edition. Toronto 1976
– *Catalogue of Canadian Choral Music*. 3rd edition. Toronto 1978

- *Catalogue of Canadian Keyboard Music.* Toronto 1971. Supplement, August 1976
- *Catalogue of Canadian Music for Orchestra/Catalogue de musique canadienne pour orchestre.* 2nd edition. Toronto 1976
- *Catalogue of Canadian Music Suitable for Community Orchestras,* comp Jan Matejcek. Toronto 1971
- *Catalogue of Chamber Music/Catalogue de musique de chambre.* Toronto 1967. Supplement 1976
- *Catalogue of Microfilms of Unpublished Canadian Music.* Toronto 1970
- *Comprehensive Catalogue of New Canadian Music Written in Honour of Canada's Centennial Year.* Toronto 1967. Special issue of *Musicanada,* December 1967
- *John Adaskin Project. Report.* 'Toward New Music in Education.' Toronto, November 1968
Canadian Music Council. *Contemporary Music and Audiences.* Report of the Annual Meeting and Conference. Montreal 1969
Canadian Music Library Association. *A Bio-bibliographical Finding List of Canadian Musicians and Those Who have Contributed to Music in Canada,* ed Melva J. Dwyer. Ottawa: Canadian Library Association 1961
- *Musical Canadiana: a Subject Index.* Ottawa: Canadian Library Association 1967
Cavalho, Rachel. 'Canadian Piano Music for Teaching,' *Musicanada,* June–July 1968, 5–7, 12–13
Cavanagh, Beverley. 'Annotated Bibliography: Eskimo Music,' *Ethnomusicology,* 16 (1972), 479–87
CHAMPAGNE, CLAUDE
- Archer, Thomas. 'Claude Champagne,' *Canadian Music Journal,* 2 (Winter 1958), 3–10
- Bail-Milot, Louise. 'Claude Champagne: son œuvre et ses procédés de composition.' Mémoire de maîtrise, Université de Paris 1972
- Colpoys, Andrew. 'Claude Champagne, *Canadian Review of Music and Art,* 5 (December–January 1947), 14–15
- Duchow, Marvin. 'Inventory List of the Compositions of Claude Champagne,' *Journal of the Canadian Association of University Schools of Music,* 2:2 (Fall 1972), 67–82
- Duchow, Marvin. 'A Selective List of Correspondents Drawn from the Personal Documents of Claude Champagne,' *Journal of the Canadian Association of University Schools of Music,* 3:1 (Autumn 1973), 71–9
- Morin, Léo-Pol. 'Claude Champagne,' in *Musique.* Montreal: Beauchemin 1944
- Pilote, Gilles. 'L'enseignement du solfège ... Claude Champagne et ses contributions.' M.A. thesis, McGill University 1970
- Provost, Marie-Paule. 'Claude Champagne, l'un des nôtres.' Mémoire de licence, Université de Montréal 1970
- Walsh, Anne, Sister. 'The Life and Works of Claude Adonai Champagne.' PH.D. dissertation, Catholic University 1972
Chapman, Norman B. 'Piano Music by Canadian Composers after 1940.' PH.D. dissertation, Case Western Reserve University 1973
Charlesworth, Hector Willoughby. *Candid Chronicles.* Toronto: Macmillan 1925. Musical reminiscences, 315–28
Charpentier, Gabriel. *Musique canadienne à la télévision 1954–1963.* Montreal: Réseau français de télévision de Radio-Canada 1963
Cherney, Brian. *Harry Somers.* Toronto: University of Toronto Press 1975

Cluderay, L. 'Jean Coulthard,' *Music Scene*, March–April 1968, 5

CONTANT, ALEXIS

– Sandwell, B.K. 'Biographical Sketches: A. Contant,' *Musical Redbook of Montreal*, 1907, 99

Contemporary Showcase Association. Graded Syllabi. Non-competitive festival of contemporary, especially Canadian, music. Toronto 1972; 1974; 1976; 1979

COULTHARD, JEAN

– Cluderay, Lawrence. 'Jean Coulthard,' *Music Scene*, March–April 1968, 5

– Duke, David. 'Interim Catalogue of the Works of Jean Coulthard.' Toronto: Canadian Music Centre 1972

– Rowley, Vivian. 'The Solo Piano Music of Canadian Composer Jean Coulthard.' D.M.A. dissertation, Boston University 1973

Crandell, Ev. 'Violet Archer,' *Music Scene*, May–June 1968, 7

Creative Canada: A Biographical Dictionary of Twentieth-Century Creative and Performing Artists. Toronto: University of Toronto Press. Vol I 1971; Vol II 1972

Cross, Lowell M. *A Bibliography of Electronic Music.* Toronto: University of Toronto Press 1967

Delamont, Gordon. 'Jazz Composition: A Minority Report,' *Music Across Canada*, June 1963

Denis, Clotilde. 'Cérébralisme et lyrisme dans l'œuvre de Jean Papineau-Couture.' Mémoire de licence, Université de Montréal 1972

Dictionnaire biographique des musiciens canadiens, ed Sœurs de St Anne. Lachine, Québec 1922, 1935

'Down from Canada,' *Newsweek*, 42 (26 October 1953), 70. Report on Stokowski concert of Canadian music, 16 October 1953

Downes, Olin. Review of concert of Canadian music, Carnegie Hall, New York, 16 October 1953. *New York Times*, 17 October 1953

Duchow, Marvin. 'The International Conference of Composers at Stratford,' *Canadian Music Journal*, 5 (Autumn 1960), 4–16

– 'Claude Champagne,' *Music Scene*, September–October 1968, 7

– 'Inventory List of the Compositions of Claude Champagne,' *Journal of the Canadian Association of University Schools of Music*, 2:2 (Fall 1972), 67–82

– 'A Selective List of Correspondents Drawn from the Personal Documents of Claude Champagne,' *Journal of the Canadian Association of University Schools of Music*, 3:1 (Autumn 1973), 71–9

Duguay, Raoul L.Y. *Musiques du Kébèk.* Montréal: Editions du jour 1971

Duke, David. 'Interim Catalogue of the Works of Jean Coulthard.' Toronto: Canadian Music Centre 1972

– 'Neo-Classical Composition Procedures in Selected Works of Harry Somers, 1949–59.' M.A. thesis, University of North Carolina 1973

Duncan, Chester. 'A Note on John Beckwith,' *Northern Review*, 3 (1949–50), 47

– New Canadian Music,' *Northern Review*, 4 (August–September 1951), 13–16; and 4 (February–March 1951), 18–21.

Eastman, Sheila Jane. 'Barbara Pentland: A Biography.' M.A. thesis, University of British Columbia 1974

ECKHARDT-GRAMATTÉ, S.C.
- 'List of Works,' *Musicanada*, October 1969
- Matejcek, J. 'Winnipeg Composer S.C. Eckhardt-Gramatté Dies in Stuttgart Accident,' *Canadian Composer*, January 1975, 34

EDUCATION
- Bird, C. Laughton. 'Composer in the School–The Supervisor's Role,' *Musicanada*, May 1969, 5–6, 12, 16
- Canadian Federation of Music Teachers' Associations. *A List of Canadian Music.* Toronto 1946
- Canadian Music Centre. *John Adaskin Project: Towards New Music in Education.* Toronto, November 1968
- Cavalho, Rachel. 'Candian Piano Music for Teaching,' *Musicanada*, June–July, 1968, 5–7, 12–13.
- Contemporary Showcase Association. Graded syllabi. Toronto 1972; 1974; 1976; 1979
- Elsaesser, Ralph. 'Canadian Piano Music for Teaching.' *Musicanada*, August–September 1968, 10–11, 13, 16
- Shand, Patricia M. *Canadian Music: A Selective Guidelist for Teachers.* Toronto: Canadian Music Centre 1978
Elsaesser, Ralph. 'Canadian Piano Music for Teaching,' *Musicanada*, August–September 1968, 10–11, 13, 16
Encyclopedia of Music in Canada/Encyclopédie de la musique au Canada, ed H. Kallmann, Gilles Potvin, Kenneth Winters. Toronto: University of Toronto Press, forthcoming

Ferguson, Danise. 'The Major Cello Works of Talivaldis Kenins.' M.MUS. document, University of Western Ontario, 1975

FOLK MUSIC AND ETHNOMUSICOLOGY
- Canada. National Museum of Man. *An Introduction to the Canadian Centre for Folk Culture Studies*, ed Carmen Roy. Ottawa 1973
- Cavanagh, Beverley Anne. 'Annotated Bibliography: Eskimo Music,' *Ethnomusicology*, 16 (1972), 479–87
- Fowke, Edith, ed. 'A Reference List on Canadian Folk Music,' revised. *Canadian Folk Music Journal*, 6 (1978), 41–56
- Gillis, Frank, and A.P. Merriam, comps. *Ethnomusicology and Folk Music: An International Bibliography of Dissertations and Theses.* Middletown, Conn: Wesleyan University Press 1966
- Guédon, Marie-Françoise. 'Canadian Indian Ethnomusicology: Selected Bibliography and Discography,' *Ethnomusicology*, 16 (1972), 465–78
- Katz, Israel J. 'Marius Barbeau 1883–1969,' *Ethnomusicology*, 14 (1970), 129–42
- Klymasz, Robert B. *Bibliography of Ukrainian Folklore in Canada, 1902–1964.* Ottawa: National Museum of Canada 1969
- Lacourcière, Luc, and Félix-Antoine Savard. *Le Folklore acadien.* Toronto: Canadiana House, n.d. Reprinted from *National Museum of Canada Bulletin*, No. 126 (1952), 99–104
- Laforte, Conrad. *Le Catalogue de la chanson folklorique française.* Rev ed. Québec: Les Presses de l'université Laval 1977
- Mount Allison University. R.P. Bell Library. *Catalogue of Canadian Folk Music*, comp. E. Magee and M. Fancy; preface by G.A. Proctor. Sackville, NB 1974

Forsyth, Wesley Octavius. 'Clarence Lucas,' *Canadian Journal of Music*, 1 (May 1914), 4
– 'Canadian Composers,' *Canadian Journal of Music*, 2 (June 1915)
Fowke, Edith, ed. 'A Reference List on Canadian Folk Music,' revised. *Canadian Folk Music Journal*, 6 (1978), 41–56
FREEDMAN, HARRY
– 'List of Works,' *Musicanada*, January 1968
Frye, Northrop. *The Bush Garden: Essays on the Canadian Imagination*. Toronto: Anansi 1971

Gagnon, Ernest. *Chansons populaires du Canada*. Quebec: Bureau du foyer canadien 1865; repr Montreal: Beauchemin 1947
GARANT, SERGE
– McLean, Eric. 'Serge Garant: The Fascination of the Unknown,' *Music Scene*, January–February 1968, 8
Gibbon, John Murray. *Canadian Mosaic*. Toronto: McClelland and Stewart 1938
Gillis, Frank, and Alan P. Merriam, comp. *Ethnomusicology and Folk Music: An International Bibliography of Dissertations and Theses*. Middletown, Conn: Wesleyan University Press 1966
Gillmor, Alan. 'Contemporary Music in Canada,' *Contact*, 11 (Summer 1975), 3–13; and 12 (Autumn 1975), 15–24
Gingras, Claude. *Musiciennes de chez nous*. Montréal: Editions de l'ecole Vincent d'Indy 1955
GOULD, GLENN
– Skelton, Robert A. 'Weinzweig, Gould, Schafer: Three Canadian String Quartets.' D.M.A. document, University of Indiana 1976
Gour, Romain. 'Guillaume Couture, compositeur,' *Qui?* 3 (septembre 1951)
– 'Alexis Contant, pianiste-compositeur,' *Qui?* 5 (décembre 1953), 25–40
Grenier, Albert. 'Sonate pour deux pianos de Bruce Mather.' Mémoire de licence, Université de Montréal 1971
Guédon, Marie-Françoise. 'Canadian-Indian Ethnomusicology: Selected Bibliography and Discography,' *Ethnomusicology*, 16 (1972), 465–78

Hale, Katherine. 'Gena Branscombe Tenney, Song Composer,' *Canadian Courier*, 16 (4 October 1913), 19
Hamilton, Henry Cooke. 'Augustus Stephen Vogt, 1861–1926,' *Musical Canada*, 9 (June 1928)
– 'Dr. Healey Willan,' *Musical Canada*, 9 (December 1928), 3
– 'Dr. Albert Ham,' *Musical Canada*, 10 (April 1929)
– 'Wesley Octavius Forsyth,' *Musical Canada*, 10 (June 1929), 3, 8
– 'Dr. Frederick Herbert Torrington,' *Musical Canada*, 10 (September 1929)
Hepner, Lee, A. 'An Analytical Study of Selected Canadian Orchestral Compositions at the Mid-Twentieth Century.' PH.D. dissertation, School of Education, New York University 1971
Hines, Malcolm. 'An Analysis of John Weinzweig's Divertimento No. 6 for Saxophone and String Orchestra.' M.MUS. document, University of Western Ontario 1975
Hodgins, J. Herbert. 'Canadian Composer Has Two Selves – One for Her music; One for Her House,' *Maclean's*, 1 June 1925

Houlé, Léopold. 'Nos compositeurs de musique,' in Royal Society of Canada, *Proceedings and Transactions*, 3rd series, 40, section 1 (1946), 51–9

Howson, Jean Lochead. 'Canada has Music – and Music Problems,' in Canadian Association for Adult Education, *Food for Thought*, 9 (May 1949), 6–12, 16

Jarman, Lynne, ed. *Canadian Music: A Selected Checklist 1950–73/La Musique canadienne: une liste sélective.* Toronto: University of Toronto Press 1976

JAZZ, CANADIAN
– 'A Conversation with Norm Symonds,' *Canadian Composer*, December 1967, 16
– 'Duke Ellington Records Canadian Jazz Compositions,' *Canadian Composer*, September 1967, 10
– 'The Duke Plays Canadian Works on Latest Jazz L.P. Release,' *Canadian Composer*, September 1968, 12
– Godard, Peter, 'Will Pop Music Swamp the Classics,' *Canadian Composer*, May 1971, 12
– 'Jazz Composing in Canada,' *Canadian Composer*, December 1965, 26. Interview with Ron Collier
– 'Jazz in Concert,' *Music Across Canada*, February 1963, 18–21
– McNamara, Helen. 'Canada's Jazz Scene,' *Canadian Composer*, February 1972, 18
– McNamara, Helen. 'Jazz in Toronto,' *Music Scene*, November–December 1969
– 'Memories of Music in Toronto in the 30's,' *Canadian Composer*, December 1971, 12
– 'Review of Works by Collier, Delamont and Symonds,' *Canadian Composer*, January 1969, 40
– Symonds, Norm. 'Big Lonely,' *Canadian Composer*, February 1971, 22
– Symonds, Norm. 'Third Stream Music,' *Canadian Composer*, February 1969, 4
– 'Variety of Jazz Featured at *Expo*,' *Canadian Composer*, July–August 1967, 18
– Yorke, Ritchie. 'Canadian Pop Groups,' *Music Scene*, July–August 1969

Juchereau-Duchesnay, Alice. 'Musique au Canada,' *Culture*, 8 (mars 1947), 23–6

Kallmann, Helmut. *Catalogue of Canadian Composers.* Rev ed. Toronto: CBC 1952; repr St Clair Shores, Mich: Scholarly Press 1972
– 'A Century of Musical Periodicals in Canada,' *Canadian Music Journal*, 1:1, 2 (Autumn 1956; Winter 1957)
– 'Kanada,' *Die Musik in Geschichte und Gegenwart.* BD VII. Kassel: Bärenreiter Verlag 1958
– *A History of Music in Canada, 1534–1914.* Toronto: University of Toronto Press 1960
– *Canadian-built 19th Century Musical Instruments: A checklist.* 2nd ed, rev. Edmonton: Edmonton Public Library 1966
– 'First Fifteen Years of the Canadian League of Composers,' *Canadian Composer*, March 1966, 18
– 'Canada,' in Willi Apel, *Harvard Dictionary of Music*, 2nd and rev ed. Cambridge, Mass: Harvard/Belknap Press 1969
– 'Composers in a New Land – Musical Composition in Canada from 1867,' *Musicanada*, June 1969
– 'Music Composition,' *Canadian Annual Review for 1968*. Toronto: University of Toronto Press 1969. 473–6
– 'Bibliographie,' in *Aspects de la musique au Canada*. Montreal: Centre de psychologie et pedagogie 1970

– 'Music,' *Canadian Annual Review for 1969.* Toronto: University of Toronto Press 1970.
445–9
– 'Musical Composition,' in John E. Robbins, ed, *Encyclopedia Canadiana.* Toronto 1970
– 'Music,' *Canadian Annual Review for 1970.* Toronto: University of Toronto Press 1971.
552–64
Kasemets, Udo. 'John Weinzweig,' *Canadian Music Journal,* 4:4; (Summer 1960)
– , ed. *Canavangard: The Music of the 1960's and After.* Toronto: BMI Canada 1968
– 'Eighteen Edicts on Education,' *Source* (1968), 38ff
KASEMETS, UDO
– Beckwith, John. 'Kasemets – Torrents of Reaction,' *Music Scene,* January–February 1970,
4–5
Katz, Israel J. 'Marius Barbeau, 1883–1969,' *Ethnomusicology* (1970), 129–42
Keillor, Elaine. 'A Bibliography of Items on Music in Canada.' Toronto: University of
Toronto Faculty of Music Library, n.d. Items from *Canadian Journal of Music* (1914–16),
Conservatory Quarterly Review (1918–35), *The Etude* (1885–1937), *The Globe* (1936),
Musical Canada (1909–29)
Kendergi, M. 'La Société de musique contemporaine du Québec,' *Vie musicale,* 5/6 (1967),
20–5
KENINS, TALIVALDIS
– Ferguson, Danise. 'The Major Cello Works of Talivaldis Kenins.' M.MUS. document,
University of Western Ontario, 1975
Klymasz, Robert B. *Bibliography of Ukrainian Folklore in Canada, 1902–1964.* Anthropology
Paper, no. 21. Ottawa: National Museum of Canada 1969
Krehm, William. 'Our Composers' New Attack,' *Saturday Night,* 67 (22 March 1952), 19
Kunits, Luigi von. 'Our Critics,' *Canadian Journal of Music,* May 1915

Lagacé, B. 'François Morel, musicien canadien,' *Liberté 60,* 7 (January–February 1960)
Lapierre, Eugène. *La Musique au sanctuaire.* Montreal: Levesque 1932
– *Calixa Lavallée.* First published 1933. 2nd ed. Montreal: Les publications de la société
historique de Montréal, 1966
– *Pourquoi la musique.* Montreal: Levesque, 1933
– 'Un style canadien de musique.' First published 1939. Hull: Leclerc 1942
– 'Le Mouvement musical dans le Québec et son orientation,' *Culture,* 9 (December 1948),
361–70
Laplante, Louise, ed. *Compositeurs canadiens contemporains.* Montreal: Université du Québec
1977
Lasalle-Leduc, Annette. *La Vie musicale au Canada français.* Quebec: Ministre des affaires
culturelles 1964
Laurendeau, Arthur. 'Compositeurs canadiens: Rodolphe Mathieu, *Esquisse,' Le Canada
musical,* 19 May 1917, 4
– 'Musiciens d'autrefois: Guillaume Couture,' *L'Action nationale,* 36 (September 1950),
19–34; 36 (October 1950), 110–26
LeVasseur, Nazaire. 'Musique et musiciens à Québec – souvenirs d'un amateur.' *La
Musique,* 1919–22
Lister, W. Warwick. 'The Contemporary Sonata for Violin and Piano by Canadian Compos-
ers.' D.M.A. dissertation, Boston University 1970

Littler William. 'John Weinzweig: The CBC's Birthday Concert,' *Canadian Composer*, March 1973, 24
- 'A History of Canadian Music on Thirteen Records,' *Canadian Composer*, February 1975, 24–8
Logan, John Daniel. 'Canadian Creative Composers,' *The Canadian Magazine*, 41 (September 1913), 486–94
- 'Musical Composition in Canada,' *The Year Book of Canadian Art, 1913*. Toronto: Dent 1913
- 'Musical Currents in Canada,' *The Canadian Magazine*, 43 (July 1914), 270–7
- *Aesthetic Criticism in Canada. Its Aims, Methods and Status*. Toronto 1917

McCarthy, Pearl. 'TSO Proves Canadians Rank High as Composers,' *Globe and Mail* (Toronto), 28 January 1948
- *Leo Smith, A Biographical Sketch*. Toronto: University of Toronto Press 1956
McInnes, Campbell. 'Music in Canada,' in Bertram Brooker, ed, *Yearbook of the Arts in Canada, 1929*. Toronto: Macmillan 1929
MacKelcan, Fred R. 'Our Musical Future,' *Queen's Quarterly*, 44 (Spring 1937), 81–5
McLean, Eric. 'Serge Garant: The Fascination of the Unknown,' *Music Scene*, January–February 1968, 8
MacMillan, Cyrus J. 'The Folk Songs of Canada.' PH.D. dissertation, Harvard University 1909
MacMillan, Sir Ernest C. 'Problems of Music in Canada,' in Bertram Brooker, ed, *Yearbook of the Arts in Canada, 1936*. Toronto: Macmillan 1936
- 'Canadian Musical Life,' *Canadian Geographical Journal*, 19 (December 1939), 330–9
- ed. *Music in Canada*. Toronto: University of Toronto Press 1955
- 'Some Problems of the Canadian Composer,' *Dalhousie Review*, 36 (Summer 1956), 130–43
MACMILLAN, SIR ERNEST C.
- Sir Ernest MacMillan, 1893–1973.' *Canadian Composer*, July 1973
MacMillan, Jean Ross, comp. 'Music in Canada: A Short Bibliography,' *Ontario Library Review*, 24 (November 1940), 386, 396
MacMillan, Keith. 'Music,' in *Canadian Annual Review for 1964*. Toronto: University of Toronto Press 1965
- 'Of Garbage and Modern Music,' *Canadian Music Educator*, 6:2 (January–February 1965), 44–9
- 'New Canadian Operas,' *Opera Canada*, February 1965, 24
- 'Canadian Notes for *Notes*,' *Music Library Association Notes*, 23:2 (1966), 241–7; and *Notes*, 24:2 (1967)
- 'Music,' in *Canadian Annual Review for 1965*. Toronto: University of Toronto Press 1966
- 'Music,' in *Canadian Annual Review for 1966*. Toronto: University of Toronto Press 1967
- 'Music Teaching and the Living Music of Today,' *Musicanada*, 5 (October 1967), 5–6
- , ed. 'Towards New Music in Education,' John Adaskin Project *Report*. Toronto: Canadian Music Centre 1967
- 'Music,' in *Canadian Annual Review for 1967* Toronto: University of Toronto Press 1968
- 'Fixing Up the Musical Public Relations Failure,' *Canadian Composer*, September 1972, 34

– , and John Beckwith, eds. *Contemporary Canadian Composers*. Toronto: Oxford University Press 1975

McNamara, Helen. 'Canada's Jazz Scene,' *Canadian Composer*, February 1972, 18

MacNiven, Elina. 'Louis Riel,' *Opera Canada*, September 1967, 42

MacTavish, Newton. *The Fine Arts in Canada*. Toronto: Macmillan 1925

Marwick, William E. 'The Sacred Choral Music of Healey Willan.' ED.D. dissertation, Michigan State University 1970

Mason, Lawrence. Ten articles discussing the works of Canadian composers. *The Globe* (Toronto), Saturday issues, 30 May–31 October 1936

Massey Report. See Canada. *Report of the Royal Commission on National Development in the Arts, Letters and Sciences*

Matejcek, Jan. 'Winnipeg Composer S.C. Eckhardt-Gramatté Dies in Stuttgart Accident,' *Canadian Composer*, January 1975, 34

Mather, Bruce. 'La Société de musique contemporaine de Québec,' *Musicanada*, May 1968 and December 1969

– 'Notes sur "Requiems for the Party-Girl",' *Canada Music Book*, 1 (Spring–Summer 1970), 91–7

MATHER, BRUCE

– Grenier, Albert. 'Sonate pour deux pianos de Bruce Mather.' Mémoire de licence, Université de Montreal 1971

Mathieu, Rodolphe. *Parlons musique*. Montreal: Levesque, 1932

MATHIEU, RODOLPHE

– Bourassa-Trépanier, J. 'A Forgotten Composer,' *Canadian Composer*, April 1973, 30

– Bourassa-Trépanier, Juliette. 'Rodolphe Mathieu.' Thèse de doctorat, Université Laval 1972

May, Lucille. 'Music and Composers of Canada,' *Ontario Library Review*, 33 (August 1949), 264–70

Mazzoleni, Ettore. 'Music and the Massey Report. Do Handicaps Outweigh Hopes?' *Saturday Night*, 66 (17 July 1951), 12, 26

– 'Music in Canada,' *Queen's Quarterly*, 60 (Winter 1954), 485–95

Mercer, Ruby. 'Healey Willan,' *Opera Canada*, May 1968, 16

Mills, Isabelle M. 'Canadian Music: A Listening Program for Intermediate Grades.' ED.D. dissertation, Columbia University 1971. Ann Arbor: University Microfilms 72–17 218

Moogk, Edward. *Roll Back the Years*. Ottawa: National Library of Canada 1975. Canadian recordings to 1930

Moore, Mavor, 'Why Louis Riel,' *Opera Canada*, May 1966, 9

MOREL, FRANÇOIS

– Lagacé, B. 'François Morel, musicien canadien,' *Liberté 60*, 7 (January–February 1960)

Morin, Léo-Pol. 'Pour une musique canadienne,' *Canadian Forum*, 8 (July 1928), 713–14

– 'Musique canadienne,' *La Revue musicale*, 10 (décembre 1929)

– *Papiers de musique*. Montréal: Librairie d'action canadienne-française 1930

– *Musique*. Montreal: Beauchemin 1944

Mount Allison University. R.P. Bell Library. *Canadian Music Scores and Recordings: A Classified Catalogue*, ed G. Creelman, E. Cooke, G. King. Publication in Music No. 3. Sackville, NB 1976

– R.P.Bell Library. *Catalogue of Canadian Folk Music,* ed E. Magee and M. Fancy. Publication in Music no. 1. Sackville, NB 1974
– R.P. Bell Library. *Sources in Canadian Music: a Bibliography of Bibliographies,* ed G.A. Proctor. 2nd ed. Publication in Music no. 4. Sackville, NB 1979
Musical Canada: A Monthly Review and Magazine. Toronto 1906–28; Waterloo 1928–33
La Musique, 1919–24

Napier, Ronald. *A Guide to Canada's Composers.* 2nd ed. Willowdale, Ont: Avondale Press, 1976

Olnick, Harvey. 'Harry Somers,' *Canadian Music Journal,* 3:4 (Summer 1959); and 4:1 (Autumn 1959)
Orr, Colleen. 'The John Adaskin Project: A History and Evaluation.' M.MUS. thesis, University of Western Ontario 1977
Owen, Stephanie O. 'The Piano Concerto in Canada Since 1955.' PH.D. dissertation, Washington University 1969

Papineau-Couture, Jean. 'Que sera la musique canadienne?', *Amérique française,* 2 (October 1942), 24–6
– 'Canadian Compositions at Hartford,' *Canadian Music Journal,* 4:2 (Winter 1960), 35–7
– 'Analysis of *Piece Concertante No. 1 for Piano and String Orchestra (Repliement).'* Toronto: Canadian Music Centre 1961
PAPINEAU-COUTURE, JEAN
– Beckwith, John. 'Jean Papineau-Couture,' *Canadian Music Journal,* 3 (Winter 1959), 4–20
– Denis, Clotilde. 'Cérébralisme et lyrisme dans l'œuvre de Jean Papineau-Couture.' Mémoire de licence, Université de Montréal 1972
– Poulin, Roch. 'L'œuvre vocale de Jean Papineau-Couture.' Mémoire de licence, Université de Montréal 1961
– Rivard, Y. 'Jean Papineau-Couture's Return to Tone Colour,' *Music Scene,* July–August 1970
Peaker, Charles, ed *Organ Music of Canada,* vols I and II. Toronto: BMI Canada 1959; repr Toronto: Berandol 1969
Pentland, Barbara. 'On Experiment in Music,' *Canadian Review of Music and Art,* 2 (August–September 1943), 25ff
– 'Canadian Music, 1950,' *Northern Review,* 3 (February–March 1950), 43–6
PENTLAND, BARBARA
– Eastman, Sheila Jane. 'Barbara Pentland: A Biography.' M.A. thesis, University of British Columbia 1974
– Turner, Robert. 'Barbara Pentland,' *Canadian Music Journal,* 2:4 (Summer 1958)
Pépin, Clermont. 'Concert de musique canadienne organisé par la ligue canadienne de compositeurs,' *La Vie des arts,* 1956, 29
PERIODICALS
– *Canada Music Book/Les Cahiers canadiens de musique.* Montreal 1970–6
– Canadian Association of University Schools of Music. *Journal.* Vancouver and Ottawa 1971–

– *The Canadian Composer/Le Compositeur canadien.* Toronto 1965–
– Canadian Music Educators' Association. *Canadian Music Educator.* 1959–
– *Canadian Music Journal.* Sackville and Toronto 1956–62
– Federation of Music Teachers' Association (founded 1935). *Canadian Music Teacher,* 1947–
– *Culture vivante.* 1966–75
– *Musicanada.* Toronto: Canadian Music Centre 1967–70; Ottawa: Canadian Music Council 1976–
– *The Music Scene/La Scène musicale.* Don Mills: BMI Canada 1967–
– *Opera Canada.* Toronto 1963–
– *Performing Arts in Canada.* Toronto 1961–
– *Vie musicale.* 1965–71
Pilote, Gilles. 'L'enseignement du solfège ... Claude Champagne et ses contributions.' M.A. thesis, McGill University 1970
Potter, Keith, and John Shepherd. 'Interview with Murray Schafer,' *Contact,* 13 (Spring 1976), 3–10
Potvin, Gilles. 'Seven Leading Composers Look at the Music of Today and Its Public,' *Music Scene,* September–October 1967, 5
– '180 Years of Canadian Music,' *Music Scene,* November–December, 1968, 5–6
Poulin, Roch. 'L'œuvre vocale de Jean Papineau-Couture.' Mémoire de licence, Université de Montréal 1961
Proctor, George A. 'Preface,' to *Catalogue of Canadian Folk Music.* Sackville, NB: Mount Allison University 1974
– 'Foreword,' to *Canadian Music Scores and Recordings: A Classified Catalogue.* Sackville, NB: Mount Allison University 1976
– 'Neoclassicism and Neoromanticism in Canadian Music,' *Studies in Music from the University of Western Onario.* No. 1. London 1976
– 'Recent Trends in Canadian Music,' *Studies in Music from the University of Western Ontario.* No. 3. London 1978
– *Sources in Canadian Music: A bibliography of bibliographies.* 2nd ed. Sackville, NB: Mount Allison University 1979
– 'Music in Education: Canada,' in *Grove's Dictionary of Music and Musicians.* 6th ed. London: Macmillan 1980
– 'Canada,' in *Oxford Companion to Music.* 11th ed. London: Oxford University Press, in process
Provost, Marie-Paule. 'Claude Champagne, l'un des nôtres.' Mémoire de licence, Université de Montréal 1970

Richer-Lortie, Lyse. 'Muscadet [Muscadøc] ou le traitement électronique de la documentation concernant la musique au Canada,' *Canada Music Book/Les cahiers canadiens de musique,* 8 (Spring/Summer 1974), 27–35
Ridout, Godfrey. 'Editorial,' *Canadian Review of Music and Art,* 1 (December 1942)
– 'Canadian Composing,' *Here and Now,* 1 (December 1947), 78–80
– 'Healey Willan,' *Canadian Music Journal,* 3:3 (Spring 1959), 4–14
Rivard, Y. 'Jean Papineau-Couture's Return to Tone Colour,' *Music Scene,* July–August 1970

Robertson, C.B. 'Artists all!' *Canadian Magazine of Politics, Science, Art and Literature*, 73 (January 1930), 6, 46

Ross, Malcolm, ed. *The Arts in Canada.* Toronto: Macmillan 1958

Rousseau, Marcelle. 'The Rise of Music in Canada.' M.A. thesis, Columbia University 1951

Rowley, Vivian. 'The Solo Piano Music of the Canadian Composer Jean Coulthard.' D.M.A. dissertation, Boston University 1973

Roy, Leo. 'Quebec Composers,' *Musical Canada*, 11 (November 1930), 8–9

Ryder, Dorothy E. *Canadian Reference Sources. A Selective Guide.* Ottawa: Canadian Library Association 1973

Sainte-Anne, Soeurs de. *Dictionnaire biographique des musiciens canadiens.* 2nd ed. Lachine, Que: Mont-Sainte-Anne 1935

SAINT-MARCOUX, MICHELINE COULOMBE

– 'An Avant-Garde Composer's Insights Into Her Career,' *The Canadian Composer*, March 1974, 28

Saminsky, Lazare. 'Canadian Youth,' *Modern Music*, 19:1 (November–December 1941), 21–5

Sandwell, B.K. 'Biographical Sketches: A. Contant,' *Musical Redbook of Montreal*, 1907, 99

Schafer, R. Murray. 'Two Musicians in Fiction,' *Canadian Music Journal*, 4:3 (Spring 1960), 23–34

– 'Limits of Nationalism in Canadian Music,' *Tamarack Review*, 18 (1961), 71–8

– *The Composer in the Classroom.* Toronto: BMI Canada 1965

– *Ear Cleaning.* Don Mills, Ont: BMI Canada 1967

– 'Future for Music in Canada,' in Royal Society of Canada, *Proceedings and Transactions*, 4th series, 5 (1967), 37–43

– 'The Future for Music in Canada: A Searching Look Forward,' *Musicanada*, July 1967, 7, 10–13

– 'A Basic Course,' *Source*, 5 (1968)

– 'Music and Education,' *Music Scene*, January–February 1968, 5

– *The New Soundscape: A Handbook for the Modern Music Teacher.* Don Mills, Ont: BMI Canada 1969

– *When Words Sing.* Scarborough, Ont: Berandol 1970

– *The Public of the Music Theatre: Louis Riel – a Case Study.* Vienna: Universal 1972

– *The Book of Noise.* Wellington, New Zealand: Price Milburn 1973

– *E.T.A. Hoffmann and The Birth of Romantic Music.* Toronto: University of Toronto Press 1976

– *Music in the Cold.* Toronto: Coach House Press 1977

SCHAFER, R. MURRAY

– Ball, Suzanne. 'Murray Schafer: Composer, Teacher, and Author,' *Music Scene*, May–June 1970, 7–8

– Mather, Bruce. 'Notes sur "Requiems for the Party-Girl",' *Canada Music Book*, 1 (Spring–Summer 1970), 91–7

– Potter, Keith, and John Shepherd. 'Interview with Murray Schafer,' *Contact*, 13 (Spring 1976), 3–10

– Skelton, Robert A. 'Weinzweig, Gould, Schafer: Three Canadian String Quartets.' D.M.A. document, University of Indiana 1976

Shand, Patricia M. *Canadian Music: A Selective Guidelist for Teachers.* Toronto: Canadian
    Music Centre 1978
Shea, Albert, ed. *Culture in Canada: A Study of the Findings of the Royal Commission on National
    Developments in the Arts, Letters and Sciences* (1949–51). Toronto: Core 1952
Skelton, Robert A. 'Weinzweig, Gould, Schafer: Three Canadian String Quartets.' D.M.A.
    document, University of Indiana 1976
Smith, Frances. 'An Analysis of Selected Works by Harry Somers.' M.MUS. thesis, University
    of Western Ontario 1973
Smith, Leo. 'A Survey of Music in Canada,' in *British Association for the Advancement of Science
    Handbook of Canada.* Toronto: University of Toronto Press 1924. 90–4
– 'Competition Reveals Outstanding Musical Talent,' *Canadian Review of Music and Art,* 2
    (October–November 1943)
SMITH, LEO
– McCarthy, Pearl. *Leo Smith, A Biographical Sketch.* Toronto: University of Toronto Press
    1956
Smitherman, Mary. 'Canadian Composers,' *Ontario Library Review,* 15 (August 1930), 3–6
Somers, Harry. 'Analysis of *Suite for Harp and Chamber Orchestra.*' Toronto: Canadian Music
    Centre 1961
– 'Louis Riel: The Score.' *Opera Canada,* 8 (September 1967), 46
– 'Composer in the School. A Composer's View,' *Musicanada,* May 1969, 7–9, 13–16
SOMERS, HARRY
– Butler, E. Gregory. 'The Piano Sonatas of Harry Somers.' D.M.A. dissertation, University
    of Rochester 1974.
– Cherney, Brian. *Harry Somers.* Toronto: University of Toronto Press 1975
– Duke, David G. 'Neo-Classical Composition Procedures in Selected Works of Harry
    Somers, 1949–59.' M.A. thesis, University of North Carolina 1973
– Moore, Mavor. 'Why Louis Riel?', *Opera Canada,* May 1966, 9
– Olnick, Harvey J. 'Harry Somers,' *Canadian Music Journal,* 3:4 (Summer 1959); and 4:1
    (Autumn 1959)
– Smith, Frances. 'An Analysis of Selected Works by Harry Somers.' M.MUS. thesis, Uni-
    versity of Western Ontario 1973
Such, Peter. *Soundprints: Contemporary Composers.* Toronto: Clarke, Irwin 1972

Tanghe, Raymond. *Bibliography of Canadian Bibliographies/Bibliographie des bibliographies
    canadiennes.* Toronto: University of Toronto Press 1960. 2nd ed, ed Douglas Lochhead.
    Toronto 1972
Telschow, Frederick H. 'The Sacred Music of Healey Willan.' D.M.A. dissertation, Univer-
    sity of Rochester 1970
Theriault, J. 'Gilles Tremblay,' *Music Scene,* March–April 1970, 6–7
THESES Masters' and doctoral theses on Canadian music, musical activities, ethno-music,
    and music education are listed in:
– *A Basic Bibliography of Musical Canadiana.* Toronto: University of Toronto Faculty of
    Music 1970
– Bradley, Ian L. *A Selected Bibliography of Musical Canadiana.* 2nd ed. Agincourt, Ont: GLC
    1976

- Proctor, George A. *Sources in Canadian Music: A Bibliography of Bibliographies.* Sackville, NB: Mount Allison University 1975
Thistle, Lauretta. 'Music North of the Border,' *Saturday Review of Literature*, 35 (7 June 1952), 35–6

TREMBLAY, GILLES
- Theriault, J. 'Gilles Tremblay.' *Music Scene*, March–April 1970, 6–7
Turner, Robert. 'Barbara Pentland,' *Canadian Music Journal*, 2:4 (Summer 1958)

Vallerand, J. 'Regards sur la musique au Québec,' *Musical America*, 83 (September 1963), 18
Vinton, John, ed. *Dictionary of Contemporary Music.* New York: Dutton, 1974. Includes entries for thirty-four Canadian composers and article on 'Canada'

Walsh, Anne, Sister. 'The Life and Works of Claude Adonai Champagne.' PH.D. dissertation, Catholic University 1972
Walter, Arnold. 'What is Modern Music?', *Canadian Review of Music and Art*, 1:4 (May 1942), 7–8
- 'Music a Means to Unify Mankind,' *Canadian Review of Music and Art*, 3 (April–May 1944), 19–20
- 'Canadian Composition,' Music Teachers' National Association *Proceedings*, 1946
Winters, Ken. 'A Composer Who Doesn't Wear Music like a Straightjacket' [a profile of Norma Beecroft], *Canadian Composer*, November 1971, 4
Webb, Douglas John. 'Serial Techniques in John Jacob Weinzweig's Five Divertimentos and Three Concertos.' PH.D. dissertation, University of Rochester 1973
Weinzweig, John, 'The New Music,' *Canadian Review of Music and Art*, 1:5 (June 1942), 5

WEINZWEIG, JOHN
- Hines, Malcolm. 'An Analysis of John Weinzweig's *Divertimento No. 6 for Saxophone and String Orchestra.'* M.MUS. document, University of Western Ontario 1975
- Kasemets, Udo. 'John Weinzweig,' *Canadian Music Journal*, 4:4 (Summer 1960)
- Skelton, Robert A. 'Weinzweig, Gould, Schafer: Three Canadian String Quartets.' D.M.A. document, University of Indiana 1976
- Webb, Douglas J. 'Serial Techniques in John Jacob Weinzweig's Five Divertimentos and Three Concertos.' PH.D. dissertation, University of Rochester 1973
Willan, Healey. 'The Chromatic Element in Music,' *Conservatory Quarterly Review*, August 1919

WILLAN, HEALEY
- Brown, Thomas. 'Healey Willan,' *Music Scene*, November–December 1967, 8
- Bryant, Giles, ed. *Healey Willan Catalogue.* Ottawa: National Library of Canada 1972
- Bryant, Giles. 'The Music of Healey Willan,' *Musicanada*, March 1968, 5–7
- Campbell-Yukl, Joylin. 'Healey Willan: The Independent Organ Works.' PH.D. thesis, University of Missouri 1976
- Marwick, William E. 'The Sacred Choral Music of Healey Willan.' ED.D. dissertation, Michigan State University 1970
- Mercer, Ruby. 'Healey Willan.' *Opera Canada*, May 1968, 16
- Telschow, Frederick H. 'The Sacred Music of Healey Willan.' D.M.A. dissertation, University of Rochester 1970

Williamson, Nancy J. 'Canadian Music and Composers since 1949,' *Ontario Library Review*, 37 (May 1954), 118–22

Wilson, Milton. 'Canadian Music,' *Canadian Forum*, 30 (July 1950), 87–8; (August 1950), 113–14

Wood, Christopher. 'A Year of Canadian Music,' *Canadian Bookman*, 21 (June 1939), 13–16

– 'Healey Willan,' *Canadian Review of Music and Art*, 4 (October–November 1945), 11–12

– 'Memories of Music in Toronto in the Thirties,' *Canadian Composer*, December 1971, 12

The Yearbook of the Arts in Canada, 1928–29, ed Bertram Brooker. Toronto: Macmillan 1929

Yearbook of the Arts in Canada (1936), ed Bertram Brooker. Toronto: Macmillan 1936

Yearbook of Canadian Art, 1913. Toronto: Dent 1913

Yorke, Ritchie. *Axes, Chops and Hot Licks: The Canadian Rock Music Scene*. Edmonton: Hurtig 1971

Index

Note: Date(s) of Canadian composers are given in parentheses following the name. For biographical data on other Canadian artists see *Creative Canada* (1971–2).

This book

was designed by

ANTJE LINGNER

and was printed by

University of

Toronto

Press